THE FBI

THE FBI

a history

rhodri jeffreys-jones

yale university press / new haven and london

Published with assistance from the Louis Stern Memorial Fund.

Designed by Mary Valencia
Set in Minion type by The Composing Room of Michigan, Inc.
Printed in the United States of America by Vail-Ballou Press, Binghamton, New York.

Library of Congress Cataloging-in-Publication Data
Jeffreys-Jones, Rhodri.
The FBI : a history / Rhodri Jeffreys-Jones.
    p.   cm.
Includes bibliographical references and index.
ISBN 978-0-300-11914-5 (alk. paper)
1. United States. Federal Bureau of Investigation—History.　I. Title.
HV8144.F43J45　2007
363.250973—dc22

               2007014617

A catalog record for this book is available from the British Library.

A Caravan book. For more information, visit www.caravanbooks.org.

CONTENTS

PREFACE

This book stems from my long-standing interest in the American past, including especially the development of U.S. secret intelligence but also ranging more broadly from black and labor history through the rise of feminism. It is a background that has a bearing on my approach to the history of the FBI. Like most historians who have perused the FBI's case files, I have been impressed by their richness as a source, and I draw on them periodically in the following pages. But their seductive, vortex-like quality also impressed me. For this reason, I have tried to produce a work from a standpoint that is liberated from the bureau's filing system; in other words, it is the story of the FBI set in the context of broader historical currents.

As will be apparent from occasional comparisons made in the text, this is also a European's history of the FBI. Since the end of World War II, Europe has wobbled at varying speeds toward a federalist future. What could the European Union learn from the United States, I wondered, in the realms of policing, security arrangements, and anti-terrorism? To advance this inquiry, I proposed a "History of the FBI Project," embracing not only this book but also work on the idea of a European FBI, to be published separately elsewhere. Conversely, Americans addressing the problems of FBI reform have drawn lessons from the European experience, with results on which I comment from my own perspective.

The British Academy awarded a research grant to prime the History of the FBI Project. Subsequently, I received a research leave award from the Arts and Humanities Research Council, and a Leverhulme Research Fellowship. The Gerald R. Ford Foundation supplemented this generosity, as did the Carnegie Trust for the Universities of Scotland, and the School of History and Classics and the Moray Fund at my university. The University of Edinburgh additionally granted me extra leave following my stint as head of history. For all this financial and leave support, I am most grateful.

Looking over the e-mail and paper correspondence files relating to my research, I feel humbled by the way so many librarians and archivists give generous support to individual scholars. The same applies to those who organize invitations to speak at conferences or institutions, in this case ranging from the Organization of American Historians to the Edinburgh Theatre Workshop. To give just one example, in spite of the remoteness of her field from the history of the FBI, Sonya O. Rose of the University of Michigan set up a lively faculty and graduate seminar for me to address. I learned a great deal (though doubtless not enough) from these exposures to critical scrutiny, and extend my thanks to all those involved.

Douglas M. Charles was my co-applicant for the British Academy grant that primed the project. He then served as my research assistant, but his help went far beyond the remunerated hours. He has been a constant source of information and ideas, and a discerning critic. My deepest thanks go to him.

It gives me great pleasure, also, to express my gratitude to the following individuals who helped by offering advice or critiquing drafts of the book, or both: Allida M. Black, Robert W. Cherny, Francis D. Cogliano, John Dumbrell, Gary Durkin, Owen Dudley Edwards, Sidney S. Fine, John F. Fox, Jr., Alex Goodall, Michael Goodman, Susan-Mary Grant, Michael Heale, Arthur S. Hulnick, Loch K. Johnson, Robert Mason, Gail Williams O'Brien, Kathryn S. Olmsted, Susan Rosenfeld, Athan Theoharis, Christopher Waldrep, Thomas C. Wales, Hugh Wilford, Neil A. Wynn, and the anonymous reader for the publisher.

My agent Sydelle Kramer has been discriminating in her judgments and as supportive as ever. I acknowledge her help, and would like also to express my appreciation of the efforts of my editor at Yale University Press, Chris Rogers, and of his colleague Phil King, who together guided the project home.

At a time of family vicissitudes, my wife, Mary, has once again put up with the authorial absences and moods with which she has become all too familiar. To her, my thanks and everlasting love.

1

race and the character of the fbi

Although the Federal Bureau of Investigation is part of the U.S. Department of Justice, it has long been observed that it is an unjust organization. In the year 2003, people of Hispanic, African American, Asian, and Native American descent made up 33 percent of the United States population of 290 million. But members of those groups accounted for only 16.5 percent of the 11,633 special agents of the FBI.

The bureau's prejudice ran deeper than that of the nation at large. To take the indicative case of one ethnic group, African Americans made up 9.7 percent of the House of Representatives. This was a shortfall in that they formed 13.3 percent of the population. But the FBI was in a different league. Blacks composed just 5.5 percent of its special agent force.

Against this background, in recent years a concern has emerged that racial imbalance in the bureau endangered not just the welfare of minorities and the American system of justice, but also national security. That the imbalance persisted in defiance of the concern confirms the power of the dominant theme in the FBI's history, race.

The object here is not to plunge American readers into despair, however, or to supply Europeans with an opportunity to gloat. Police forces, it seems, have always had a checkered record. The Athenian police in the fifth and fourth centuries B.C. spied on aristocrats who were plotting to overthrow democracy, using house slaves of diverse races to do the job, and yet preventing those slaves from escaping or organizing their own rebellions. In the late twentieth century, the charge of "institutional racism" in the British police led to reforms that failed to silence the critics. Meanwhile, most of Britain's partners in the European Union were not even attempting to reform their police forces' hiring practices. In 2005, Europol, sometimes referred to as a European FBI, had among its police officers no nonwhite or Muslim employees.

These comparisons do not mean that Americans can be complacent about the FBI. The bureau needs to satisfy exceptionally high expectations because of the nature of its work in a country with worldwide responsibilities, and because it has long been regarded as the global leader among national criminal detection agencies. But its record of tolerance in comparison with its international peers does suggest the need for a fresh look at its history and provenance.

Today, we take it for granted that there should be a federal force to combat federal crimes. According to the *Christian Science Monitor*, by 2001 there were 3,300 federal crimes for the FBI to investigate. But the idea of Feds combating federal crimes is a relatively modern one. Before the 1870s, federal crime detection services in the United States barely existed.

The reasons for federal deficiencies in the area of law enforcement before the Civil War are not difficult to divine. For a long time America was a frontier society whose pioneers ran in advance of the institutions they had left behind. The Europeans who peopled America came from old worlds that had yet to develop the apparatus of the modern state. The Jeffersonian states' rights tradition strengthened the sentiment against Hamiltonian national institutions. Even when railroads snaked their way across state lines and businesses consolidated across huge areas, preindustrial, essentially local attitudes endured. Southern states would not agree on a uniform gauge for rail tracks. From 1836 until 1913, the United States lacked a central bank.

The secession of the Confederate States and the Union victory in the Civil War began to change all that. It weakened both the states' rights principle and the South's position of defending white supremacy. During hostilities, and for a period during the Reconstruction that followed the war, southern states were not fully represented on Capitol Hill. In the absence of southern opposition to creeping federalism, Congress enacted the Homestead Act and laws to permit the completion of transcontinental railroads. The resultant opening of the West further weakened the position of the former slave states. And it was the rump Congress that supported executive plans to establish federal detection and policing.

Even before the Civil War, government organizations occasionally used detectives. In February 1860, for example, a "special agent of the United

States Mail Department" investigated mail thefts, and his inquiries led to the apprehension of a fifteen-year-old boy. In the plaintive voice of a newspaper in Sandusky, Ohio, the teenager was the sole support to his widowed mother, and "much liked." Then, in the final flurry of the Civil War, President Abraham Lincoln established the United States Secret Service to prevent counterfeiting. Formed as a division of the Treasury Department, the service's responsibilities grew to include preventing tax evasion by moonshiners, and as a result of investigating these activities it began to develop professional skills in crime detection.

In July 1870, however, Congress broadened the scope for federal investigation through its creation of the Department of Justice. In the following year, a congressional appropriations bill for the first time authorized the attorney general to spend money on the unrestricted "detection and prosecution" of federal crimes. Consequently the Justice Department borrowed some detectives from the Secret Service for a special assignment. Such was the importance of the assignment that 1871 must surely rank alongside the commonly accepted year of 1908 as a significant founding date for the FBI.[1]

The assignment was to penetrate the Ku Klux Klan and help smash it. White terrorists, the Klansmen were bent on restoring the newly freed African American to a form of virtual slavery. In their effort to assert the superiority of white civilization, they whipped, shot, tortured, and hanged men, women, and children. The U.S. Army tried to restore order in the South, but the terrorists had a good intelligence system. When soldiers arrived, they would fade into the woods, or run off to different states or to Canada, only to return and to terrorize once again.

Unable to track down their enemy, army officers requested civilian detective help, and the Justice Department provided it. African American informants who knew the local terrain and people helped the Justice detectives as they began to operate in the troubled areas of the South. Panic soon began to set in, and Klansmen began to inform on their fellow terrorists in exchange for leniency. Prosecutions of Klansmen peaked in 1872, and locally based U.S. attorneys and army officers began to think the Klan had been annihilated.

That perception was premature. When the former Confederate states returned fully to the body politic, their congressmen blocked further appropriations to Justice Department detectives, and outrages against black citizens could therefore no longer be investigated. Intimidation returned in different guises, notably lynching. Nevertheless, an expectation had been created, and those fearful of white hate crimes would never again let go of the thread of hope, thin though it may have been at times, that the federal government would act as their guardian.

If it seems contentious to say that 1871 was a significant originating year for the FBI, it must be recalled that for decades there was an effective conspiracy to blot out and reinvent memories of Reconstruction. In an influential display of amnesia, early-twentieth-century historians portrayed Reconstruction as corrupt and overly punitive of the noble white South, with black Americans acting as easily duped pawns of unscrupulous northerners who sent in oppressive federal troops. The most prominent among these historians, William A. Dunning, asserted in 1907 that some members of the Ku Klux Klan had been "respectable."

In popular depiction, the Klan assumed a heroic role as the chivalrous defender of southern autonomy, virtue, and white womanhood. It appeared thus in D. W. Griffith's film *Birth of a Nation* (1915), in the wake of which the Klan revived as a national organization. Hostile reactions to the movie were a reminder that millions of Americans were still prepared to struggle against injustice, but they frightened future directors into ignoring the South, its violence, and those who struggled to stop it. Myopic Hollywood churned out, in the words of one shotgun-blasted civil rights worker, "Westerns instead of Southerns." Historians of the Secret Service tended to ignore what may have been the most valiant episode in its history, the fight against the Klan in the 1870s, and chroniclers of the FBI have afforded little importance to the bureau's share in Reconstruction memories. They have yet to catch up with those who, since the 1940s, have offered a corrective to the southern white version of Reconstruction history.[2]

In unwittingly denying the vital first chapter in its history, even the finest historians have distorted the story of the bureau. One consequence of the conspiracy of silence regarding its origins is that the FBI has remained relatively uninteresting to the mainstream historian. Just as secret intelligence has been a missing dimension of diplomatic history, so the FBI's contribution to domestic history has been underappreciated.

Once its underlying character has been more carefully examined, the FBI's history can offer supplementary insights into several aspects of American history, politics, and society. The bureau's role in the history of American federalism and anti-federalism has always been instructive, and was occasionally vital. American anti-communism is better understood in light of the bureau's liberal provenance. FBI history has made its distinctive contribution to the lexicon of disputes between liberals and conservatives. U.S. achievements and shortcomings in the areas of "homeland security" and anti-terrorism cannot be properly appreciated until one understands that the bureau came into being for those purposes, and has a tenacious tradition. A collapse in public faith in the bureau contributed substantially to the mid-1970s crisis in American democracy. Justice Department detectives whose rationales stretch back to the nineteenth century have developed public applications for privately developed information technologies with serious implications for personal privacy. The bureau's involvement in racial matters has long been recognized, but, even here, there has been a less than full appreciation of its impact, especially its positive impact.

A downturn in federal law enforcement activities in the last quarter of the nineteenth century contributed to memory loss about the 1870s. The Justice Department did continue to engage detectives, and by the 1880s it had adopted the Secret Service practice of calling them "special agents," a nineteenth-century habit that survived in the FBI after it had died out in other agencies. But these detectives operated on a reduced scale. The restored southern states retained their hostility to Justice's engagement of Secret Service operatives. The department's occasional resort to Pinkerton private detectives was even more unpopular, and had to be discontinued. It was not until the twentieth century that federal detection of domestic crimes regained its former prominence.[3]

In 1908, President Theodore Roosevelt decided that the Justice Department should have its own force of detectives, instead of having continually to borrow special agents from the Treasury Department. At first, hiring was done on an individual basis, and then in 1909 the new bureaucracy was formalized under the name Bureau of Investigation.

Roosevelt's decision to regularize the Justice Department force came against the background of a thoroughgoing and successful investigation, by special agents, of corruption in business and in Congress. At the end of a half century of rapid and largely unregulated industrialization, some businessmen had become Robber Barons who expected regular favors from the "Millionaire Congress" of the day. Roosevelt had been determined to stamp out capitalistic excesses that threatened to bring capitalism itself into disrepute. When his initiative is considered in tandem with special agents' previous work to protect African American rights, it is clear that the FBI has reason to be proud of its origins.

The year 1908 is still a significant founding date for the bureau, then, even if it does need to be paired with 1871. While it was the end of a proud beginning, however, it also marked the start of a time when the bureau slipped out of character.

The bureau soon began to display the racial biases for which it later became notorious. These prejudices became prominent following the passage in 1910 of the Mann Act, making interstate trade in prostitution a federal crime. The official title of the law, the White Slave Traffic Act, told its own story. Exploiting its provisions, the bureau began hounding the black boxing champion Jack Johnson. As the writer Damon Runyon observed, Johnson had never "stinted himself in the matter of indulgence," but the black fighter's real offense was not wild living as such—it was his thrashing of white boxers and sleeping with white women. The bureau pursued the African American champ partly out of its own prejudice and partly because, in the words of Johnson's biographer Geoffrey Ward, its leaders "felt that the public would never be satisfied until Jack Johnson was behind bars." The opinion of voters was important to an agency that was already eyeing the readiness of Congress to make appropriations.

Johnson fled the country to avoid jail, but he later returned and ended up behind bars anyway. To African Americans, his persecution sent a signal—one that became louder as the bureau stepped up its investigations of black citizens while apparently treading water in cases of racial harassment. Hearing in 1919 that the Justice Department was planning an inquiry into radicalism among African Americans, the celebrated intellectual W. E. B. Du Bois acidly observed: "We black folk have for some years been trying to get the United States Department of Justice to look into several matters that touch us." In the previous year, U.S. military intelligence had withheld a commission from Du Bois, evidently on account of his race. Prejudicial hiring soon came to characterize the bureau, too. Henceforth it would be judged by three criteria in racial matters: its efficacy against white terrorism, the degree to which its agents covertly harassed nonwhite minorities, and the diversity of its hiring practices.

When Du Bois made his remark, the Red Scare was raging in America. This prompts the observation that while race may be the dominant theme in the history of the FBI, it is by no means the only significant thread. The bureau had a wider list of mission deviations. In 1919 and subsequently, it threatened the civil liberties of white as well as black citizens. Its dubious surveillance practices did not apply just to the oppressed, but extended also to the powerful. Individuals who came under scrutiny included, for example, senators who opposed U.S. entry into World War II. The bureau discriminated against citizens for reasons that varied from gender to lifestyle, from sexual orientation to politics. There were periodic challenges to these out-of-character transgressions, but comprehensive recovery did not begin until the 1970s, and even then it was only partial.[4]

To depict the FBI as having been out of character with itself and with America for much of its existence is to accept as a premise a positive view of U.S. history. In more pessimistic style, it could be argued that the Feds as established in the 1870s were out of character, as Reconstruction was an anomalous period in American history. Continuing in this vein, the contention would be that, by the second decade of the twentieth century, America had reverted to its true conservative, fearful, nativist, xenophobic character, and that the FBI simply fell into line. It rather depends how you define the American character—is it about justice, fairness, and democracy, or not? Mindful of the fact that other nations have worse records of bigotry, the assumption in this book is that the United States is, characteristically, devoted to just and democratic values, and that an agency that flouts them is, therefore, out of character.

To say that the FBI slipped out of character may seem to invite the charge of originalism, that is, the habit of looking back to the bureau's 1871–1908 "prehistory" as a golden age, any deviation from which ranks as decline. Certainly, originalism is a sin to be avoided, and it must be remembered that enlightenment in one area, race, did not in the 1870s spread to other areas, like gender, where today a greater degree of equality is expected. However, for all its retrospectively identifiable shortcomings, the 1870s would appear to be a more inspiring decade of federal policing than other decades, like the 1930s or 1950s, that have been upheld for a variety of partisan reasons. Every generation has the power to choose its memories, and the obligation to justify them.

The reasons for the bureau's slippage out of character so soon after 1908 will mostly be familiar to students of the era. The post-Reconstruction redistribution of power ushered in decades of Afrophobic reaction, and the bureau's racially skewed enforcement of the Mann Act was just one chapter in the history of Jim Crow. Even had it been so minded, and that is an open question, Congress was in no position to apply the brake. Early attempts at congressional oversight of the bureau lacked credibility because they looked like partisan revenge against the Rooseveltian special agents who had investigated Congress. Executive vigor in the Progressive–World War I era meant a relative decline of the legislative branch. The growth of the federal government encompassed bureau expansion, ensuring that any abuses that might occur would be on a grander scale.

Contemporary events facilitated the bureau's character slippage. World War I and the Bolshevik revolution in Russia infused life into U.S. counterespionage, and opened new pastures for the practice of injustice. In the wake of war and revolution, a spurt of nativism extended from the Red Scare of 1919 to the ethnically biased immigration restriction laws of 1924, and encouraged the bureau in its dubious target selection.

Personalities played a role in the slippage. Enter J. Edgar Hoover, who joined the Department of Justice in 1917 and directed the bureau from 1924 until his death in 1972. Contrary to widespread belief, Hoover neither invented FBI racism nor banned black agents from employment, but he did personify southern conservatism on racial matters. During his tenure, Hoover and the bureau incurred the hatred of a wide spectrum of liberals; after his death, officials within the bureau joined in the tendency to blame its ills on his leadership, building on the image that the long-serving director had himself cultivated, that Hoover *was* the FBI. As the historian David Garrow points out, commentators have tended to attribute almost every FBI transgression to the malign influence of J. Edgar Hoover.[5]

That Hoover was a significant personality is beyond dispute. Partly because of historians' prejudices, however, and partly because of the efficacy of Hoover's propaganda machine, his prominence has led to the neglect of other personalities. Influential leaders preceded him, and indeed he languished in their shadow in the 1920s. In the many years since his death, a succession of FBI directors has helped to reshape the bureau, and they have each played a prominent public role.

Hoover's predecessors have all but vanished in unmerited obscurity, and they invite closer attention than they have hitherto received. Hiram C. Whitley, the Secret Service chief who orchestrated the Justice Department's assault on the Klan in 1871, needs to be rescued from an altogether contrived oblivion. John E. Wilkie, inventor of the "Indian rope trick" and gifted spymaster, was another important founder of the FBI. It was he who set up President Roosevelt's force of investigators, yet he has all but faded from view.

Wilkie's departure from the scene in 1908 and Roosevelt's retirement the following year marked a decline in the quality of federal police leadership. Yet Hoover was also preceded by still another prominent figure. William J. Burns led the postwar bureau and was the first of its chiefs to be called "director." He was a leader whose personality in the 1920s dwarfed that of his young successor. Burns was a brilliant investigator, but one who imported from the world of private detective work an array of malpractices. Against this immediate background, Hoover emerges less as an architect of FBI slippage than as an efficient consolidator.

Personalities in a quite different category have also played a vital role in shaping the destiny of the FBI and its contribution to American justice, namely those occupying the office of U.S. attorney general. Though hitherto relatively invisible to FBI historians, he (and in one case she) sat at the head of the table. One of the most influential was Amos T. Akerman, appointed by President Ulysses S. Grant in 1870, one week before the newly formed Department of Justice began to function. Akerman's was the iron political will behind Whitley's work leading to the destruction of the Klan. Yet he has been the victim, in the words of one historian, of "the conspiracy of historical silence that came down on Reconstruction integrationists." The historical profession's muteness obscured, then, not just the first stage in the FBI's history, but also the pioneering contribution of the office of the attorney general.[6]

Subsequent attorneys general varied in the attention they gave the FBI and its antecedents, but some of them had a major impact. A selective roll call of pre–World War II attorneys general illustrates their instrumentality in FBI affairs. If President Theodore Roosevelt was the big hitter behind Wilkie's emerging force of detectives, it was Charles J. Bonaparte, the attorney general who dreamed up the E Pluribus Unum label for blended whiskey, who applied his wit and determination to the defense of the embryonic bureau. In the Red Scare, Attorney General A. Mitchell Palmer pushed hard for the suppression of American dissent, using the bureau for that purpose ultimately to the dismay of J. Edgar Hoover, who was in charge of its radical division.

Three attorneys general during the interwar years turned their attention to reform. Harlan Fiske Stone, briefly at the head of Justice in 1924–25, replaced Burns with Hoover and decreed that the bureau should henceforth eschew political work and investigate only crimes. This was not what Hoover wanted to hear, but Stone's strictures had enduring influence.

Homer S. Cummings, attorney general from 1933 to 1939, is remembered as the official who helped Hoover turn the bureau into an efficient, non-venal organization, and to knock the American mobster off his glamorous pedestal, replacing him with the FBI's "G-man." But he also made a further, less heralded contribution. Hoover was trying to reshape perceptions of FBI history, and to give it a new character. Through the writings of Courtney Ryley Cooper and, later, Don Whitehead, the director sponsored a view of the FBI's past that had no room for antecedents; they portrayed the bureau's history as virtually synonymous with the efforts of Hoover himself, beginning in the early 1920s, flowering heroically with the early 1930s war on crime, and making no mention of black Americans. But Cummings remembered a forgotten man. In his book *Federal Justice* (1937), he gave an account of Akerman's war on the Klan. Though the account had little impact at the time, it preserved the vital thread of memory running back to Reconstruction days, and to the original character of federal law enforcement.[7]

What Cummings remembered about Justice's anti-Klan work would yield promising fruits. Frank Murphy succeeded Cummings and, like Stone, remained in the job for only a brief span. But shortly after his appointment at the start of 1939, the Justice Department established a civil rights unit. Hoover, whatever his racial views, was already opposed to terrorism, and had helped to quell a Klan resurgence in the 1920s. Now, a Justice Department unit that would pursue cases of lynching and other assaults on black citizens' rights would supplement his efforts. While it may be true that the civil rights revolution of the 1950s and 1960s promoted reform of the FBI, it can also be argued that the Justice-FBI assault on southern white terrorism from 1939 on reduced the culture of intimidation in the region, and gave civil rights workers the confidence to press for change. If the FBI had slipped out of character after 1908 there was, by the end of the 1930s, a glimmer of redemption.[8]

Of course, by 1939, the Feds had other things on their minds. With the approach of World War II, the FBI established itself as the leading U.S. civilian counterespionage agency. Already famous for its G-men, it began to produce a new kind of American hero. Leon G. Turrou was living testimony to the survival of cosmopolitanism in the FBI even in xenophobic times. Born in Poland and multilingual, he helped to foil the Rumrich spy ring, thus outwitting Germany's renowned secret intelligence service, the Abwehr. The bureau's image-boosting successes continued, and not only in the United States. From June 1940, President Franklin D. Roosevelt entrusted the FBI with anti-Nazi operations in Latin America. Hoover claimed successes in Chile and elsewhere, and, in distinctly non-nativist mode, began to think in terms of a global FBI.

But the director had by 1945 overreached himself politically. He had alienated his rivals in other wartime agencies, and his very successes made him a feared personality. And he would ultimately be frustrated by another factor directly related to the FBI's original justice mission, and to the degree that the bureau had departed from it. This was the public perception that the FBI engaged in racially prejudiced and cavalier practices reminiscent of those in Nazi Germany. The genocidal atrocities of the German political police were fresh in people's minds when, at the end of the war, the *Chicago Tribune* rounded on Hoover and accused him of trying to set up a "super Gestapo." This line of attack eventually brought dire consequences for the development of U.S. domestic security.

In reality, the relatively modest scale of FBI operations discredits the idea that it was the apparatus of an oppressive police state. At the end of the war, the United States had a population of some 140 million, and the FBI had 4,370 special agents—or one for every 32,037 citizens. Compare this with Hitler's Germany, where there was one Gestapo agent for every 2,000 citizens; or with postwar East Germany, whose communist secret police, the Stasi, had an agent for every 175 persons. Stalin's Soviet Union also had a well-merited reputation for blanket surveillance—one KGB officer per 5,830 people. Even in times of national peril, the FBI has never begun to approach such figures.[9]

The mud stuck, however, and the persuasiveness of the American Gestapo charge had a number of effects. Having been the creation of progressives in the 1870s and under the two Roosevelts, the FBI was becoming repellent to liberals. In the Red Scare of the 1950s, some liberals continued to perceive the bureau as a saner, more professional anti-communist vehicle than the more populist McCarthyite committees. But, gradually, the FBI became more attractive to the Right, and ultimately it became the darling of the neoconservatives. Politically weakened by early erosions of liberal support during the presidency of Harry Truman, the FBI lost its Latin American empire. Crucially, the National Security Act of 1947 forbade it from operating abroad, setting up a rival agency for that purpose, the CIA. This established the basis for the FBI-CIA rivalry that so undermined American national security.

Wilmoore Kendall, an authority on John Locke who had recently served in the fledgling CIA, offered a critique of the reasoning behind the new national security arrangement. Referring to the then-accepted offshore perimeter of national sovereignty, the philosopher complained of the "three-mile limit" mentality whereby the FBI was not permitted to operate beyond territorial waters, while the CIA was banned from domestic operations. Essentially, domestic intelligence did not talk to foreign intelligence, and this undermined the coordination of estimates of the threats that America faced.[10]

Notionally, Kendall was incorrect, as the director of the CIA wore another hat, that of director of central intelligence, with authority over the entire intelligence community, including the FBI. In practice, though, FBI-CIA rivalry became legendary, fulfilling at least some of Kendall's gloomy predictions. Hoover was bitterly resentful of the CIA, refused to hand over his Latin American spy network to the new agency, and peevishly reneged on his obligation to conduct security checks on potential CIA recruits.

Yet the problem was not just personal, but systemic. Neither Hoover's death in 1972 nor subsequent threats to American security brought about institutional contrition. The FBI-CIA feud continued to undermine national security and was a significant contributing factor in the disaster that befell on September 11, 2001. Each agency squirreled away information it thought might be useful, instead of sharing it with the other. America paid a high price for the FBI's departure from its intended character, for the resultant Gestapo fears of the 1940s, and for their institutional aftermath.

In the 1950s and 1960s, the FBI struggled to keep pace with the rest of America. At a time when the nation's mores were changing, Hoover indulged his voyeurism and leaked information about the gay or heterosexual activities of those he chose to victimize. As others had in 1919, he aimed to fuel an anti-communist scare for as long as it was to the bureau's advantage, but this time he exceeded the bounds of political prudence, and America would be less forgiving. Meanwhile, although there was universal support for its crime-fighting activities, the bureau proved ineffective in combating the Mafia. This failure provides a further illustration of how attorneys general could retard as well as promote the effectiveness of the FBI: Robert Kennedy cajoled the FBI to do better against the Mob, but his action in hiring a Chicago gangster to assassinate President Fidel Castro of Cuba set the worst kind of example.

Finally, and notoriously, the FBI harassed the now powerful civil rights movement. Agents set out to discredit its charismatic leader, Martin Luther King, circulating stories about his sexual promiscuity in an era when white public figures escaped scrutiny of their private lives. Grown men in the State Department wept as support for America receded in the United Nations, an American dream that went sour for the United States once darker-hued people formed independent nations, joined the organization, and took a close look at American society. What these observers saw was not the quiet work of the Justice Department's civil rights lawyers, but a lily-white FBI and the congressional rejection of anti-lynching bills. In vain did Hoover launch a counterpoint action with the new political climate in mind, ruthlessly using sexual smears to demoralize "White Hate" racists. Too little, too late, and improper, the maneuver did not save the FBI from its enemies.

The reforms of the 1970s came for a number of reasons. Hoover's death in 1972 meant it no longer required an act of bravery to speak out against him. The Vietnam War divided the nation, and weakened faith in the national executive and its institutions. The Watergate scandal of 1973–74 stimulated further distrust of the White House, and President Richard Nixon was forced to resign. It later emerged that W. Mark Felt, the number-two man in the bureau following Hoover's death, had leaked details of Nixon's transgressions to reporters from the *Washington Post*, contributing to the climate of opinion that put his own agency under the microscope. With the White House in disarray and the CIA engulfed in scandals of its own, it became open season for government critics in the press. The media churned out stories of FBI maltreatment of King, antiwar protesters, and a host of others. Spurred on by partisanship and ambition as well as by ideals, members of both houses of Congress joined the fray. With so many predators circling, the FBI had to change in order to survive.

Congress initiated some of the era's reforms. The Freedom of Information Act, for example, was a wide-ranging law that happened to open up some of the darker closets in FBI history. At the same time, significant change also came from the Republican administration of Nixon's successor, President Gerald R. Ford.

The executive's motivation was partly tactical. If the White House did not initiate reform on its own terms, it would have congressional reform thrust upon it. But Attorney General Edward H. Levi (1975–77) brought conviction to the process. He aimed to remove the reality as well as the appearance of FBI political malpractice. He split off the bureau's law enforcement function into a separate entity that would have to observe the highest standards of due process with regard to wiretaps and other surveillance practices. Levi realized the need for a more accommodating approach in the case of the bureau's national security function. Those working on counterespionage or counterterrorist cases would need to be more concerned with information and anticipation than with arrests and the furnishing of proof in court cases. Here, the procedural rules would be more flexible. But Levi was still determined that the comparatively free rein would apply only to genuine security cases, and not to the detriment of the rights of ordinary citizens.

The Levi reforms provoked long-term debate. Athan Theoharis, a chronicler of the FBI's record on civil liberties, argued that the bureau's obsession with political investigation had undermined national security, both in the Hoover era and in the case of 9/11. From that perspective, the Levi reforms improved not just American justice but also American security, a point that Katherine Sibley argued explicitly. But other historians, such as Richard Gid Powers, believe that Levi's reforms went too far, sacrificing the needs of security because of hypersensitivity on the issue of liberty. Some FBI veterans insisted that the Levi reforms had made the bureau "risk averse." Special agents afraid of being disciplined over possible civil liberties violations had not made the preemptive arrests that might have saved America from 9/11. From still another perspective, however, one could argue that neither the congressional nor the Levi reforms went far enough in achieving diversity. In that it remained white, male, and homophobic, the bureau continued to be ill equipped to serve either justice or security.[11]

Under President Jimmy Carter and then in the 1980s and 1990s, the FBI gradually began to accept the need for diversity. But this by no means heralded a universal swing to liberalism. Ronald Reagan loosened restrictions on the intelligence community, and the FBI engaged in political surveillance once again. Notably, it operated against Central Americans whom the Republican administration regarded as dangerously leftist. Simultaneously, however, the Reaganites and their Soviet counterparts set in motion the processes that led to the crumbling of European communism. This removed one of the main justifications for the irregular practices of the FBI, if not for the bureau itself. For President Reagan had helped end what some people had come to regard as the main reason for the FBI's existence, the Cold War.

The years from Reagan through George H. W. Bush and Bill Clinton were in some ways a time of hope and optimism. In this era, the FBI finally triumphed against the Mafia, a considerable contribution to America's image as a just and law-abiding nation. In the process, and indicating a potential breakdown of the three-mile-limit syndrome, the bureau reached overseas—FBI director Louis Freeh (1993–2001) visited Sicily to declare that, even in Corleone, the days of the gunman were numbered. Attacks on the Mafia had in the past been portrayed as examples of prejudice against people of southern European origin, but now they had become part of an American-Italian initiative.

Another indication of cosmopolitanism was the FBI's reform of its hiring practices. Aware of the need for diversity, Director William Webster

(1978–87) kept a tally card in his pocket indicating how many female and black agents the bureau had engaged. Attorney General Janet Reno (1993–2001) lifted the FBI ban on hiring gays.

But there were signs of continuing intolerance. Freeh refused to accept the authority of the first female U.S. attorney general, Reno, and developed into a loose cannon at the head of the FBI. Perhaps partly as a reaction to the new wave of immigrants arriving in America (yielding 28.4 million foreign-born in 2000, only one in six of them of European origin), there was a return to xenophobia in the country.[12] The FBI was not immune to the trend. It harassed Wen Ho Lee, a Chinese American scientist who was suspected of espionage but against whom no proof could be found. While its hiring practices were partly liberalized, the reform did not go far enough to satisfy minorities, or to suggest the FBI had fully lived up to its original promise as the dispenser of American justice.

The Al Qaeda attack in September 2001 triggered a flood of recriminations about America's unpreparedness. Of all the agencies that came under scrutiny, the FBI took the heaviest fire. Its lack of analytical capability and its risk aversion were two of the factors singled out. As this suggests, bureau critics were now as likely to belong to what the intelligence historian Richard Aldrich called the cost-benefit school as to the more familiar band of civil libertarians.[13]

The attack on the FBI was in some ways convenient for the government of George W. Bush, as it deflected attention from possible shortcomings in the White House's response to the terrorist threat. But the administration nevertheless decided neither to degrade the FBI nor to take away some of its vital functions and place them, as certain commentators demanded, in a new agency along the lines of the British internal security service, MI5.

Instead, reorganization and strengthening of the existing assets took place. Attorney General John Ashcroft (2001–5) took the lead in removing some of the regulations that restrained the FBI. Required to change its culture to make it a frontline agency in the fight against terror, the bureau developed a greater analytical capability. The FBI received a budget increase.

In dwelling on the incapacity of the FBI to anticipate a surprise attack, the bureau's critics tended to overlook the fact that surprise is nonsystemic. You cannot, by analyzing and remedying past oversights, prevent the next surprise attack, which will be, by definition, different. The Al Qaeda menace was, furthermore, no more than the threat of the day. Given the much higher casualties that can and do result from automobile accidents, gun crime, influenza, earthquakes, floods, and the spread of nuclear weapons, it is evident that the emphasis on terrorism was a political choice and one of limited lifespan, as was the decision to reshape and reinvigorate the FBI.

Nevertheless, the critics did identify weaknesses that had a significance above and beyond the bureau's capacity to preempt surprise attacks. One of these was its poor capacity in languages. The FBI had been unable to translate intercepted messages in Arabic that might have given a warning of the impending 9/11 attack. Both the translation deficiency and the related ethnic imbalance in its hiring practices came in for extensive scrutiny and condemnation.

The time had arrived for white, Christian, monoglotal Americans to ask themselves some hard questions. The damage was not limited to what had stemmed from one surprise attack. In spite of moves toward a greater cosmopolitanism, the modern bureau remained ethnically biased, a poor advertisement for American justice, and thus a recruiting sergeant for America's enemies.

In Reconstruction, Justice Department detectives held high the beacon of liberty. Then the bureau lost its character. Then came liberals' distrust, and the divide-to-weaken policy of 1947. Then came the reforms of process and hiring in the 1970s and after, confirming the FBI as the world's leading government detective agency. Then came the renewed xenophobia, and the penalty for it, vulnerability.

2

.

secret reconstruction: 1871–1905

Hiram C. Whitley told his detectives to "ascertain as far as possible the aims and objectives of the different secret sects of the South, known under one general head as the Ku Klux Klan." Once they had ascertained the facts, they were to report to him.[1]

Whitley pointed out that there would be no need for embroidery, as the facts would speak for themselves. Here are a few details of the account he gave the Justice Department of the work done by one detective G. Bauer. On a certain day, Bauer attended a Klan meeting in Dobson's store, on the Yorkville–King's Mountain highway in York County, South Carolina. He plied the Klansmen with drink. They then told him who killed a black man who had declared his intention to vote. Bauer further learned of a Klan scheme to stop murdering people—temporarily, at least—with the aim of deceiving Congress at a time when it was investigating Klan atrocities.

In a further report from Cleveland, Tennessee, Bauer told the story of a break-in at the local prison. After a fierce fight, a crippled black boy was snatched from his cell, and a rope was put around his waist and a bag over his head. Thereupon he was taken outside and hanged. Bauer obtained evidence of the identity of the executioner, whose mask had slipped during the struggle.

Whitley's matter-of-fact tone pervaded the rest of his lengthy narrative. On 22 August 1871, he recorded, an illiterate nineteen-year-old, William Washington Wicker, put his mark on a statement sworn before a United States commissioner in North Carolina. Just before Christmas 1870, Wicker had gone out riding with the Klan. Near Jonesboro, they threatened Jessie McIver, a black man. Then they called on his white relatives. At Dan

McIver's place, the two daughters played the piano and danced with the men. The Klansmen went on to Wesley McIver's, "showed ourselves," and ate cake, then to Dan McIntire's, again removing their disguises. The daughters of the McIntire house arose from bed and the Klan patrol enjoyed further piano music.

In the spring of 1871, Wicker and his musical colleagues had visited Sallie Gilmer's place. They lashed her. They also whipped Mary Godfrey and Stump Gilmer. In this raid, the Ku Kluxers opened fire on three black persons who ran from the house, killing one of them. Planning a further sortie, Wicker went to Mark McIver's to collect disguises. J. G. Hester and other confederates accompanied him. Whitley quoted Wicker's deposition on what happened next: "That same evening Hester made himself known to me as a U.S. detective and arrested me and R. N. Bryan, Jessie Bryan, John Gaster, Mark McIver, William J. Bryan and took us to Raleigh."

Twenty-one-year-old Susan J. Ferguson of Chatham County, North Carolina, similarly added her cross to a sworn deposition. Her father had been a conscript in the Confederate Army. But he and his family had been Union sympathizers, and this was probably why they attracted the attention of the Klan. One night, Klansmen burst into Susan's bedroom and dragged her outside to witness the flogging of her five brothers, all children. Fighting to rescue her brother John, she knocked the conical hat from the head of an assailant and recognized him as Dick Taylor. When she told him she would seek prosecution, he put a cocked pistol to her head. She refused to repent.

Three weeks later, the Klan returned to finish the business, or so they thought. They lashed Susan mercilessly. They forced her to witness her invalid mother being stripped naked and flogged. Susan testified nonetheless. Acting on Susan Ferguson's deposition, agent Hester secured arrest warrants for Taylor and four confederates whom she had also identified. He was hopeful that the local U.S. deputy marshal would serve them.

Evidence of such crimes flowed in from all over the South. J. J. O'Toole reported from Jasper, Florida, on a common type of beating. A gang of white men in disguise seized Edward Thompson and his wife and took them into a wood. Thomson's offense had been "that he was too good a black man." He was told to strip. Because he was slow in doing so, the leader of the gang, a former captain in the Confederate Army, broke the stock of his rifle over his head. The victim was then subjected to a fatal beating with "warrants," or leather belts: "He ceased to scream long before the band desisted from beating him."

A white bystander who had been forced to watch the event with a pistol held to his head was now ready to testify. Whitley related this and numerous other incidents in his routine reports. He or another official identified excerpts from the reports for the instruction of Congress, with the names of the secret agents removed. They were still in the field, and their cover had to be maintained.[2]

Hiram Whitley assembled his narratives in order to inform Congress. They drew, however, on operational intelligence, for Whitley directed America's first federal anti-terrorist intelligence program. He helped the army and federal attorneys destroy the power base of the Ku Klux Klan.

A consideration of Whitley's background reveals why he was well equipped to undertake that radical task. But this is no dewy-eyed exercise. Whitley's principles, insofar as they existed, were conservative. To those who knew him, Whitley must have been a striking character. His admirers reported he was six feet ten inches tall. They waxed eloquent in their allusions to his youthful prowess and strength, and believed his claim to have walked five hundred miles in seven days, and to have taken only a similar length of time to row seven hundred miles down the Red River from Loggy Bayou to New Orleans. Victorian hyperbole perhaps, but he was certainly a man of vigor. After leaving federal employment in 1874, he settled in Emporia, Kansas, where he ran a farm, built the Hotel Whitley, established the first street railway, and constructed an opera house. He remained a dynamic personality in fraternal and charitable organizations into his ninth decade.

Whitley had no special sympathy for the rights of African Americans. He had worked as a slave catcher, returning thirteen fugitive slaves to their masters in Missouri. He opposed the abolitionist movement. Before joining the Union cause, he drilled with a Confederate unit in New Orleans. He did not favor the enfranchisement of the freedmen.

His loyalties were dictated by ambition and pragmatism. In 1862, Union forces under the command of General Benjamin F. Butler overran New Orleans. Whitley cultivated the general, and enlisted under his command in the Seventh Louisiana infantry regiment. When Butler was dismissed from his post for over-harsh military rule, Whitley survived and continued to perform special services both in New Orleans and behind enemy lines. These special services included the elimination of outlaws. Whitley shot dead three men in Baton Rouge and New Orleans.[3]

Equipped with strong military references, Whitley found work after the war as a detective with the Internal Revenue Bureau. Formed in 1862 to raise money for the war, in peacetime the bureau had turned its attention from now-unpopular income tax collection to other sources of revenue, such as liquor and tobacco taxes. Whitley's job was to chase down moonshiners. He raided thirty-six stills in Virginia. There was an even heavier concentration of "blockaders," illegal distillers who ran the blockade of the revenue men, in the Blue Ridge areas of eastern Tennessee and the western regions of the Carolinas. These were to be strongholds of the Ku Klux Klan, with often the same men involved in the two activities. Whitley was already acquainted, then, with the nature of his future target.

In May 1869, Whitley succeeded William P. Wood as head of the Treasury Department's United States Secret Service. This agency, too, had been a wartime measure. Just a few hours before his assassination, President Lincoln had agreed to establish the Secret Service as a means of combating counterfeiting, then a serious threat to the financial stability of the Union. What the *New York Times* called "queer money" continued to be a problem in peacetime, and occupied much of Whitley's time. But in 1867, Congress had broadened the Secret Service's responsibilities to include a spectrum of anti-government fraud that ranged from mail robberies to illegal voting schemes and smuggling, all of which Whitley tried to combat, too.

In order to be closer to the criminals he was then pursuing, Whitley moved the Secret Service's headquarters from Washington to 63 Bleecker Street, New York City. He introduced a number of administrative reforms that prefigured the later practices of the FBI. He cleansed the operative arm of the agency of those he regarded as unsavory characters. His ideal agent was a man of military and middle-class background. Twenty-seven percent of his employees were informers, often with questionable associations, but the theory was that his elite officers would direct this lower mass. These men of probity made up 12 percent of the service. Whitley developed associations with local law enforcers, establishing the system whereby a relatively small federal agency would assist and supplement the work of local police, rather than growing into a major bureaucratic entity. He introduced a filing system to record the identities of forgers, incorporating personal details, aliases, criminal specialties, and, in an up-to-the-minute technological advance, photographs of the subject and his associates. Thus were established the antecedents of those modern phenomena, the mug shot and federal police data files on individual citizens.[4]

The administratively gifted gunslinger certainly needed these improved systems. A serious challenge lay ahead: the restoration of order in the South and, regardless of Whitley's views on the matter, the enforcement of civil rights for African Americans.

Lincoln's Emancipation Proclamation of 1863 and the Thirteenth

Amendment two years later had abolished slavery. The Fourteenth Amendment had in principle given black people the constitutional right to equal protection of the laws, and the Fifteenth Amendment enshrined the right to vote regardless of race, color, or previous condition of servitude. But many white southerners were unready for such change, their attitudes having been hardened by a war that had laid waste their homeland, killed 260,000 Confederate soldiers, and ended in bitter defeat. These white southerners fought ruthlessly against the ascendancy of the reforming Republican Party.

In 1866, in Pulaski, Tennessee, a group of men had formed the Ku Klux Klan. Similar initiatives followed in other former Confederate states. The names varied. Whitley's men reported on the Constitutional Union Guards, the Union and Young Men's Democracy, the White Brotherhood, the Knights of the White Camelia, and the Order of the Invisible Empire. But the detectives reported also that the rituals of all these groups were similar, and their goal was the same, the repression of black Americans through terror. Those known collectively as the Klansmen launched a campaign of violence against blacks and whites who tried to implement the new order. Operating at night and disguised in intimidating costumes, Ku Kluxers burned, beat, and murdered their way across the South. In Louisiana, a Knights of the White Camelia mob killed as many as two hundred black plantation workers on a single day in 1868; violence forced the Republican Party to abandon its presidential campaign in both Louisiana and Georgia.[5]

Congress responded. In May 1870, it passed the first of three Enforcement Acts. The aim was to stop the Klan's violent intimidations and disruption of a fair electoral process. Actions of this kind could now be prosecuted as conspiracies to prevent the operation of an act of Congress. The sentences imposed could only be light, an unsatisfactory arrangement considering the heinous nature of some of the crimes in question. But in the middle of the nineteenth century, the still-Jeffersonian nation had only a limited number of federal criminal statutes. Prosecution for murder and other serious offenses had to be under state law, and had to go through local courts, whose local juries were either unwilling to convict or too frightened to do so. Conspiracy convictions were the best that could be hoped for. A year or two in prison would be at least some kind of punishment for the wrongdoers and protection for the community, and the threat of arrest was a deterrent, especially as many of those wanted or detained by the federal authorities understandably if wrongly assumed that they would receive more serious sentences for their serious crimes.

The Department of Justice was formed in the following month and placed under the direction of the attorney general. The office of attorney general had been a cabinet-level post since 1790, but it was not until the creation of the Justice Department that the nation's chief law enforcement officer had an organization to back up his work. An appropriations statute defined the duty that lay behind the administrative innovation. In what is still the mission statement for the FBI, it charged the attorney general with "the detection and prosecution of crimes against the United States."[6]

President Grant selected a new attorney general, Amos T. Akerman, to meet the challenge. The appointee to the newly powerful post had a dual heritage. A native of New Hampshire, he had been educated at the Phillips Exeter Academy and at Dartmouth College, but had then moved to Georgia, where he studied and practiced law, and came to think of himself as a southerner. When General William T. Sherman threatened Georgia with his Union army, Akerman volunteered for the home guard. He got married, and the next day he set off to fight the Yankees.

Like Whitley, Akerman changed sides to work for the triumphant Union after the Civil War, becoming the only former Confederate to serve in a Reconstruction cabinet. There, however, the similarity ended. Akerman had been an antebellum advocate of black suffrage in Georgia. He was strongly committed to the defense of the new rights enjoyed by black citizens. In the course of the Justice Department's war on the Klan, Whitley displayed a distant detachment, orchestrating matters from New York. In a very different style, Akerman worked from Washington, in those days a southern city in all but name, and made personal forays into the difficult areas of the South to oversee enforcement. On one visit to South Carolina, he spent two weeks poring over evidence of Klan atrocities. Although Whitley was a tough and competent detective, it was Akerman who supplied the principled determination behind the efforts to crush the Klan. He is the first instance of an attorney general who set the agenda for federal law enforcement.[7]

In February 1871, a second Enforcement Act provided for federal supervision of voter registration. Two months later Ben Butler, by now out of the army and a Massachusetts congressman, secured passage of the third Enforcement Act. This targeted conspiracy and terrorism, provided for the suspension of habeas corpus, and became known as the Ku Klux Klan Act. In the meantime the U.S. Army, which still occupied recalcitrant areas of the South, was charged with the apprehension of terrorists. In May, President Grant sent sixteen additional companies of troops to what was by then the most troubled state, South Carolina.

Units from the Seventh U.S. Cavalry arrived in Yorkville, York County, a prime center of supremacist brutality where forty Klansmen had recently lynched a black militiaman, James Rainey. The cavalrymen's commander was Major Lewis W. Merrill. This officer regarded himself as an apolitical soldier, and was critical of abuses by Republicans as well as Democrats. But he had fought against marauding Confederate cavalry units in the Civil War, and knew what to expect when he took on the nightriders, many of whom had fought in gray or were commanded by former Confederate officers.

Merrill converted an old sugar house into a temporary jail ready to accommodate captured Klansmen, and took on an assistant, Louis F. Post, to record stenographically the anticipated confessions. For this work, Post received a Secret Service "honorarium" of fifty dollars. The major operated in a climate conducive to success. The new legislation's provision whereby those apprehended could be prosecuted in U.S. courts was a significant widening of federal powers. Furthermore, Congress was mindful of the need to justify its actions, and decided to root out evidence of Klan outrages and make it known to the public. In June–July, its joint committee to investigate Klan atrocities dispatched a three-man subcommittee to South Carolina, which was the reason for the Klan's intentions to call a pause in the killing.[8]

However, the Reconstructionists had a problem. The government had the upper hand in terms of armed force, and it had the apparatus to secure arrests and convictions, but first it had to catch the Klansmen and secure evidence against them. Colonel Harry Brown explained to a United States marshal the difficulties that arose when the military tried to serve arrest warrants on Ku Kluxers: "Whenever the troops advance, they run to the woods, or mountains, and as there are numerous parties, both blacks as well as whites ready to communicate information of the presence of troops, they have in consequence always been successful in making their escape." The military and the federal prosecutors complained that they were up against a wall of silence. In his first report, sent to Akerman on 29 September 1871, Whitley noted that, in the wake of the visit by the special congressional committee, the word was out that the South would be riddled with government spies and that all strangers had to be watched.

The cultural historian Andrew Hook has suggested that this conspiracy of resistance was connected with the Scottish provenance of some of the Klansmen, and he is not the only scholar to have suggested that the Celts imported their allegedly superviolent ways to the American South. The word "Klan" itself might be thought to derive from the Scottish word "clan," with its romantic associations of kin banding together to fight outside oppression. Some family names in the Klan-affected areas of North Carolina (McIver, McIntyre, Bryan) do suggest a Scottish or Scotch-Irish connection.

But in reality the ethnic composition of the Carolinas was too diverse to sustain a strict construction of the Scottish conspiracy theory. Southern communities shielded Ku Kluxers for different reasons. They were bound together by the memory of defeat, and by a determination to recover their autonomy. The joint congressional report identified a further factor, attributing the tight-lipped solidarity of the Klan counties of South Carolina to the local moonshining tradition. It might be added that Klansmen operated as secretly as possible for the same reason as any murderer, an aversion to the gallows.

The suspension of habeas corpus in a nine-county area of South Carolina on 17 November 1871 allowed Major Merrill to fill his improvised jail, and Louis Post busied himself taking evidence. But the army did not achieve these results alone. It relied on civilian intelligence. Colonel Brown recognized the need. He recommended, and it had become a standard request in troubled areas of the South, that two or more spies be sent in to remedy the intelligence deficit, and that they should be unencumbered by the presence of troops. These federal agents would receive local help. He could "mention some reliable negroes who will render excellent assistance."[9]

Attorney General Akerman had recognized the need for espionage from the outset, and had already recruited a detective force. In fact, the time would have been ripe, in 1871, for the formation within the Justice Department of an independent federal bureau of investigation. The political climate was favorable, as a majority in Congress wanted to help the freedmen. The Civil War had for the time being discredited states' rights, and a new, if short-lived, license for federal government existed that would have been compatible with the development of a national police force. Yet thirty-seven years were to elapse before Justice established its own bureau. In 1871, as the historian Everette Swinney remarked, "the Justice Department gave no thought to establishing a detective force of its own."[10]

This is not really surprising. Akerman faced an immediate crisis. In this circumstance, he lacked the time to set up a new organization. His other options were limited. Resort to the private sector was not yet considered a serious option. Events in Mississippi suggested that cooperation with the authorities in the southern states, even when Republican-controlled, would not yield results. Upon Mississippi's readmission to the Union, its governor

James L. Alcorn had early in 1870 established a Secret Service consisting of seven men, two of whom were black. But it fell victim to partisan attacks in the press and to budget cuts, and failed to halt the murderous activities of Klan terrorists. As for more conventional local police, they could not be used because in the former Confederate states they were, as Whitley put it, "governed by the popular prejudice." Military espionage would have been too obtrusive. Against the background of this catalog of deficiencies, the attractions of the Treasury Department's Secret Service were evident. It had a ready-made bureaucracy, and experience in undercover work.[11]

On 28 June 1871, Akerman wrote to "Colonel" Whitley (Whitley was still a major in his 1916 pension claim, but like Merrill and so many other veterans of the war was known as Colonel). He referred to Whitley's "experience in the detective system" and said he interpreted the will of Congress to be that similar expertise should be applied to the pursuit of those who resisted the enforcement laws. Whitley was to investigate crimes and produce the names of witnesses. The joint congressional "Committee on Outrages" might give further guidance as to his task, but Whitley was to use his own initiative. Whitley's unit received a modest initial appropriation of twenty thousand dollars, but the following year the Justice appropriation for enforcement rose to a million dollars.[12]

Whitley deployed a force of secret agents in the South. Their names appear in Whitley's confidential reports and are genuine, as can be deduced from the effort made not to reveal them in more public hearings and reports. But Whitley went to considerable lengths to disguise the true identities of his men. They set themselves up as businessmen seeking to relocate, liquor merchants based in large southern cities, peddlers, or farmhands in search of work. Whitley in some cases arranged for them to be arrested on charges of Klan atrocities, lest their immunity from apprehension aroused suspicion. All this secrecy was not just for operational reasons but also for fear of retribution. Informers are always a despised breed, especially when they are seen as traitors to their own cause, and it does seem likely that Whitley's agents were southerners or, at least, like Whitley himself, men who had spent time in the South, as it would not have been easy for a Yankee to adopt the speech and cultural patterns of the inhabitants of the former Confederate states and pass himself off as a Ku Kluxer. After the "Restoration," many who had fought for justice for African Americans had to relocate to escape punishment. The diaspora purged local memories, and this is one of several reasons why a significant story has remained untold.[13]

An elite corps of itinerant detectives took responsibility for enemy penetration. In his first composite report to Akerman based on their letters, Whitley mentioned by name six officers and three assistant officers. Bauer had a broad territory, operating not just in the troubled state of South Carolina but also in Tennessee and Alabama, where Michael Hayes served as his assistant and where two further officers were based. J. J. O'Toole, who had taken the deposition regarding the fatal beating of Edward Thompson, was based in Florida, and J. G. Hester with his two assistants in North Carolina. Whitley's relocation to New York had distanced him from these agents, but their letters did reach him within four days, and there was local coordination between his detectives and other parties to the enforcement process: the military, U.S. marshals, and U.S. district attorneys.[14]

The military presence in the South was unwelcome, yet the majority of southern white folk hated the Klan even more. As the aforementioned case of Susan Ferguson confirms, even in the face of the direst intimidation there were individuals in the white community who were prepared to help the federal detectives to accumulate evidence. Additionally, there were two other types of local informant who proved useful to Whitley's men.

Little imagination is required to understand why black Americans were willing to help with enforcement. John Page, an assistant detective in the Secret Service, told the story of his fellow Mississippian, a black man called Williams. A white man visited Williams at his home in Bethlehem, Marshall County, claiming to be a "State Detective" who sought information on the Klan. Williams offered to cooperate. However, the man was an impostor, and he told the local Klansmen that Williams was about to inform on them. The terrorists then visited Williams and meted out punishment not detailed in Page's report. Remarkably, the African American was still prepared to help Page, though he said this was only because of the security afforded by the proximity of federal troops.

Freedmen could help the federal authorities in humble, but no doubt effective, ways. Contributing to a 1930s oral history project to record the memories of former slaves, Brawley Gilmore of Union, South Carolina, recalled the days when the Klan would "come along at night a riding de niggers like goats" and lining them up on the banisters of Turk Creek bridge for target practice. A local "darkey blacksmith," John Good, shoed the horses used by the Klan, but he marked the shoes with a bent nail so that the federal authorities could track the nightriders. The Klan found out, and killed him.

In other cases, federal officials in the South employed black citizens not as informers but as investigators. In 1878, for example, the U.S. district attorney for South Carolina pressed the attorney general for permission to pay fifty dollars to a "shrewd colored detective" to investigate an alleged case of arson.[15]

The second category of local informer was the Klansman seeking clemency from federal prosecutors. Such an informer was known in local parlance as a "puker." His motivation may be at least partly understood in terms of lower-class reactions to upper-class diaspora.

Klansmen with the means to do so fled their military pursuers. In a letter to Akerman dated 13 November 1871, Major Merrill referred to the problem that men wanted for serious crimes in South Carolina had fled to Arkansas, Mississippi, Maryland, Virginia, Pennsylvania, Georgia, and, in the case of one murder suspect, Canada. They could be pursued with federal warrants and an extradition order, but would first need to be found.

In the course of one of his visits to South Carolina, Akerman had asked Merrill whether the Post Office could help locate these fugitives more precisely. Merrill thought it would be useful if trustworthy route agents could supply intelligence derived from the postmarks on letters addressed to selected individuals. But, as things turned out, this potential harbinger of modern privacy infringement was not needed. Those who could not afford to travel saw themselves as having been abandoned by their more affluent leaders, and did not want to take the rap. In exchange for promises of more lenient treatment, they began to inform, and once word got out that this was happening, a significant number of Klansmen rushed to cooperate with the authorities lest, if left behind, leniency would not be forthcoming.[16]

To attempt an assessment of the efficacy of the Justice Department's undercover work is to dip a toe into the bloodied waters of Reconstruction historiography. Some scholars have suggested that the enforcement effort, detective work included, was underresourced and lacking in commitment. W. E. B. Du Bois famously remarked of the Reconstruction years: "The slave went free; stood a brief moment in the sun; then moved back again toward slavery." His judgment that the brevity of enforcement resulted in the failure of Reconstruction ideals challenged the once widespread view among historians that, as the Klan threat was evanescent, enforcement rapidly became an unnecessary oppression of the white South. In several books, William A. Dunning argued that blacks had proved themselves unable to handle the responsibilities of voting and governing, and he condemned Reconstruction as overly harsh and corrupt. His interpretation dominated the historical consensus well into the twentieth century, and this outlook came to be known as the Dunning school. Acknowledging his debt to Dunning's *Essays on the Civil War and Reconstruction* (1897), the early-twentieth-century historian James Ford Rhodes characterized the Enforcement Acts as "against natural laws" and an instrument of "tyranny." He conceded that the Klan had been guilty of crimes but stated that "after 1872 the outrages of the Ku-Klux-Klan proper, for the most part, ceased." He amplified Dunning's research with a table of arrests and convictions of Klansmen to show there was a decline from a peak in 1872 to a negligible number by the end of the decade: proof, to Rhodes, that the problem was over.[17]

Officials in the 1870s would have concurred in the view that Klan violence declined in the short term. Crucially, however, they regarded this not as a spontaneous development, but as the consequence of federal enforcement. Consistent with this view, they attributed a later resurgence of violence with the retreat of federal authority.

In his September 1871 report to Akerman, Whitley predicted that a policy of arrests would produce a snowball effect, with those apprehended supplying evidence for further arrests. This would lead to the "crushing of the Ku Klux organization." Just under a year later, he indicated that he had achieved this goal. Public opinion had turned against the Klan, and a recent attempt to revive it in North Carolina had failed. While the "strong arm of the Government" was still needed, he was now concentrating anew on alternative work, fraud cases, and the renewed destruction of illicit whiskey stills.[18]

The numbers of arrests and convictions attained in these years confirm that the government detectives achieved a pinnacle in performance against the Klan and then changed their focus (Table 1). The composite figures on Klan arrests cited by Rhodes derived from annual reports sent in by U.S. attorneys for each of the southern districts. While the quality and character of these attorneys varied, some of them were formidable in their determination. Such a man was the U.S. attorney for the District of South Carolina, Major David T. Corbin. Badly wounded in the war while leading a unit of Vermont troops, he had languished in the Confederates' Libby Prison in Richmond, Virginia, and later took charge of the Freedmen's Bureau in Charleston. Elected to the state senate, he served briefly as its president.[19]

Corbin's figures for South Carolina and his accompanying testimony show that the Klan did not reform of its own accord, but was forced into submission. In 1871, there were 112 prosecutions under the Enforcement Act leading to 54 convictions, a success rate for the federal authorities of 48 percent. This compared with 40 prosecutions and 12 convictions under the heading "Internal Revenue," a success rate of 30 percent. In the following

Table 1. Enforcement Act and Internal Revenue Prosecutions in South Carolina, 1871–73

	Enforcement Act				Internal Revenue				USA
	Prosecutions pending	Prosecutions	Convictions	Conviction rate as % of prosecutions	Prosecutions pending	Prosecutions	Convictions	Conviction rate as % of prosecutions	Convictions
1870									32
1871	278	112	54	48	21	40	12	30	128
1872	1,207	96	86	90	47	132	96	73	456
1873	617	554	14	3	73	88	43	49	469
1873	617		14						102
1874	40		0						18
1875									3
1876									38
1877									0
1878									40
1879									1
1880									

Note: Data from Rhodes are italicized. All data are affected by a six-month reporting shift starting in 1873. For the years 1870 to 1872, the figures are for a year ending 31 December, but thereafter for a year ending 30 June.

Sources: Rhodes, *History of the United States*, 6:318; Returns for the Annual Report of the Attorney General, District of South Carolina, for 1871, 1872, and 1873, enclosed with Corbin to attorney general, 6 January 1872, 24 December 1872, and 15 October 1873, all in National Archives 2: RG60: General Records of the Department of Justice, Letters Received from South Carolina, 1871–84, M 947.

year there was a dramatic change of emphasis and fortune. The Justice Department received a million dollars for enforcement, and overspent that by $300,000. The 1872 figures show 96 prosecutions under the Enforcement Act with 86 convicted, a rate of 90 percent. Internal Revenue figures also boomed, but to a smaller extent: 132 prosecutions and 96 convictions, yielding 73 percent. The number of Klan prosecutions pending, however, had risen from 278 to 1,207.[20]

In 1873, there was a reversion to the earlier pattern. The number of prosecutions under the Enforcement Act was higher, but in only 14 of these 554 cases were the accused convicted, meaning federal successes were a mere 3 percent. Meantime, there was a success rate of 49 percent for the 88 Internal Revenue cases. Thus the shift away from enforcement convictions was both absolute and relative, and invites explanation. The redemptionist assertion that the Klan spontaneously declined is implausible. The nightriders did not did not grow angels' wings and fly away. Du Bois's observation that the will to enforce crumbled was true, but not the whole story. A further reason had to do with resources. The courts, whose funds were finite in spite of the emergency appropriation, were under strain. Prosecutions could be initiated, but not carried through indefinitely.

Yet the threat of prosecution affected the psychological climate, even if convictions did not always follow. Consistent with this, the final reason for the decline in the conviction rate is the success of federal enforcement policy, especially in the short term. In November 1872, Corbin claimed that "the Ku Klux Klan as an organization is substantially broken up." Some Klan remnants clung together, but he knew of few plans for renewed activity, and for the most part, Klansmen were "trembling lest they may any day find themselves marching off to jail." The long arm of federal justice even extended abroad. In one case, Justice agents and local supporters kidnapped Dr. J. Rufus Bratton in Canada. Bratton had led the sixty nightriders who had murdered Jim Williams, a South Carolina black militiaman.[21]

Another high-profile arrest occurred in December 1873, when Corbin was at last able to detain Major William T. Avery. This elusive figure was held to have been responsible for several brutal killings, including the murder of the black militiaman Rainey that had first drawn the Seventh Cavalry to Yorkville. Yet Avery was locally upheld as an exemplar of southern "honor." The reverence sprang from a reported incident when Avery's child fell sick and Corbin released him from detention to visit the invalid. When his little boy died, Avery, as good as his word, surrendered himself to the federal authorities despite being under the impression that he would be executed for his part in Klan murders. This exhibition of good faith seems to have caused a lapse of concentration on the part of the authorities, and Avery was allowed to vanish in the middle of his trial, reappearing only when President Grant pardoned him as part of a general amnesty. Like Bratton, he had had to spend some time in hiding, a fugitive from justice.[22]

Reporting this incident, Corbin said that in the ten months up to March 1874 there had been only three arrests on Ku Klux charges, and that in the April term of the circuit court he intended to discontinue most of the indictments against Klansmen. Two years later, he repeated the view that, following the deployment of detectives in the early 1870s, "withering prosecutions and punishments annihilated the Klan."[23]

There can be little doubt about the short-term success of the federal campaign against the Klan. Even a skeptical *New York Times* conceded in April 1872 that there had been "strict enforcement" in "some areas of the South," and a "general" decrease in terrorism. However, this was under the headline "KuKlux Waiting for the Ascendancy of the Democrats." Drawing on Whitley's research, the *Times* asserted that the Klan "is not extinct, but is only waiting for the coming of a more favorable time." By the time Corbin wrote his 1876 report, he had become less sanguine about the longer-term outcome. Ku Kluxers were now reorganizing under the name of "Rifle Clubs." Murder and intimidation had returned, "the virus is rapidly extending," and there was an urgent need for renewed penetration orchestrated by a government detective.[24]

The revival of terrorism indicates that the outbreak of law and order in the early 1870s had come about not because of restored southern harmony, but because of federal enforcement. Cutbacks in enforcement happened for reasons other than a sudden southern proclivity for good behavior. Weaker enforcement sprang from government leniency, the expense of high-volume prosecutions, political expediency in the face of increasing Democratic strength, and personal factors.

At the end of 1871, after only eighteen months in office, Akerman resigned. The absence of any official explanation for his departure fed speculation that he had refused to modify his demands for tough enforcement, and had paid the price in a separation that signaled a change in policy. Certainly, the outbreak of federal leniency that followed his leaving confirms the importance to federal law enforcement of firm leadership by the attorney general.

By mid-1872, evidence of policy change was beginning to emerge. The nation was beginning to tire of constant sectional strife, northern politi-

cians like Horace Greeley were calling for national reconciliation, and Akerman's determination was sorely missed by those who were resolved to push
for racial justice in the South. The new attorney general was George H.
Williams, who had sat on the joint congressional committee on Reconstruction in his former capacity as a Republican U.S. senator from Oregon,
but lacked the single-mindedness of his predecessor. In a move that signaled new intentions, Williams sent Whitley to visit Klan prisoners in Albany, New York.

Whitley interviewed forty of them. He reported their predicament to
the attorney general in the most sympathetic terms. Some of them were ignorant, and had been duped into joining the Klan. Others had been forced
to ride because of threats to their families. Many were now showing "contrition" for their atrocities. They also blamed their "leaders, who had managed
to escape from the country, leaving them to bear the responsibility and the
punishment of their misdeeds." The former slave-hunter concluded that
there was a case for issuing pardons, and he opened up the prospect of a
presidential amnesty.

Later that year, Corbin drew Williams's attention to the problem of case
volume in South Carolina. A thousand cases were pending. The number
could soon triple, and it was simply too much work for the courts. He argued that there were other reasons for leniency. The Klan was shattered, and
there was rising sympathy for the plight of those under indictment. Anticipating the rhetoric of Bourbon Restoration and the future glorification of
persecuted Klansmen, he warned that a cult of martyrdom was emerging.
Corbin recommended that resources be concentrated on the prosecution of
those who had taken a leading role in killings; data on those arrested on
lesser charges should be kept on file, but the suspects released on bond.

Williams replied that he agreed, and that he favored restraint. He would
urge U.S. marshals to keep a careful eye on expenditures, and in February
1873 he instructed that there should be no enforcement prosecution "unless the public interest imperatively requires it." In the meantime, Klan
members were being pardoned, and, in the summer of 1873, President
Grant released from jail all those convicted so far of Klan activities.[25]

As the Avery arrest indicates, Justice activities against the Klan did not
cease at that point. On the contrary, the federal authorities reacted with
vigor in that very year. They had little choice in the face of an episode described by historian Eric Foner as "the bloodiest single instance of racial
carnage in the Reconstruction era."

Colfax, Louisiana, was a ramshackle hamlet that represented the extremes of Reconstruction. On one hand, it sat in fertile swampland notorious for its exploitative ways. The novelist Harriet Beecher Stowe visited the area before writing *Uncle Tom's Cabin* (1852), and her fictional slave driver Simon Legree may well be based on a local character. But then, at least for a while, the tide turned. The region became Grant County in honor of the Reconstruction president, and the county seat took the name of Schuyler Colfax, Grant's vice president. Realizing that their enraged neighbors were in a killing mood as Republicans tried to consolidate their grip on Louisiana, local African Americans collected some antiquated weapons, gathered in Colfax, and prepared to defend themselves. Former Confederate soldiers and other local whites then moved against them with modern rifles and a small cannon. On Easter Sunday 1873, with the loss of only two men on their own side, the white supremacists killed an estimated 280 blacks, 50 of them under a flag of surrender. Conforming with established practice, the Department of Justice sent an investigator, J. J. Hoffman, to Louisiana. Once again, the use of unobtrusive detection proved effective. Hoffman gathered evidence, and there were 96 indictments under the enforcement legislation. W. J. Cruikshank and eight others went on trial.[26]

But setbacks continued in the realm of enforcement and criminal detection. By the mid-1870s, the Department of Justice was losing its pristine sheen. Attorney General Williams's reputation took a knock when, nominated for a vacancy on the Supreme Court in 1873, he fell victim to the indiscretions of his wife. It emerged that Mrs. Williams was enjoying a gilded lifestyle. At the government's expense, she had purchased the most expensive carriage in the capital, and equipped it with a liveried footman and coachman. When New York's patronage-wielding Roscoe Conkling wavered in his support for her husband, Mrs. Williams blackmailed him by threatening to reveal how Secret Service funds had been used to assist his election to the Senate. This was an alarming development for President Grant, who had himself dipped into this source. Further stories circulated about Williams's borrowing of departmental funds and immersion in election and business venality. In a display of misplaced loyalty, Grant allowed him to stay in office, and Williams lingered in his post until 1875. Thus, for two years the nation's chief law enforcer was a lame duck and an ideal target for those who wanted to discredit the campaign for racial justice.[27]

Then in 1874, Hiram Whitley fell victim to a campaign of calumny. U.S. Attorney Richard Harrington was accumulating evidence of sweetheart contracts, theft of public funds, and various corrupt practices at the District of Columbia's Board of Public Works. In the course of his investigation, a set of incriminating account books disappeared from his office safe. Officials intent on cutting a deal with the prosecution alleged that Whitley was aware of the identity of the burglar. No evidence was advanced in support of this charge, but Whitley was too controversial a figure to escape unscathed. He was forced to resign on 2 September, and, in a twist of irony, had to undergo a trial for conspiracy, the very charge that had been brought against so many Klansmen.[28]

The local impact of these developments soon became evident. Dispatched to Louisiana to guard against any recurrence of terrorism there, Lewis Merrill was able to identify Klan suspects, but the federal government would not send the major any cavalry to chase them down. Mississippi was also sliding into its former state of thuggery. In northern Mississippi, even without a military presence the rate of conviction on Klan charges had been 55 percent, considerably higher than the national average of 28 percent and well above the latest rates in South Carolina. But in 1875, there was further trouble and a collapse in federal authority. The new attorney general, Edwards Pierrepont, sent in a force of several detectives under the leadership of George K. Chase. Local Democrats promised there would be no election intimidation provided Chase disbanded the black militia and refrained from calling in federal troops. Explaining his collaboration with the Democrats, Chase said his purpose was to ensure "the nigger did not rule the Anglo-Saxon." Intimidation did occur, and in one Mississippi county the Republican vote declined from 2,785 in 1873 to 2 in 1876.[29]

With the return of white southerners to politics and the onset of reform fatigue, the mood of the nation's dominant people was undergoing a change. Speaking in the House of Representatives, Kentucky's James F. Beck articulated an anti-Republican view that would gather strength as his fellow Democrats made electoral advances: "The Attorney General has sent his marshals and secret-service thieves all over the land—to Alabama, Louisiana, South Carolina, and elsewhere—for purposes of wrong and oppression. I repeat, it is a Department of Injustice instead of a Department of Justice." Asserting the civil rights of white people, propagandists made the Secret Service's kidnapping of Rufus Bratton on Canadian soil a cause célèbre. The minority report of the joint congressional inquiry into conditions in the South poured contempt on the efforts of Akerman, Whitley, and the Secret Service. It attacked the latter for having too wide a dominion, for its alleged generation of perjured evidence, and for being "dangerous in the administration of justice." In October 1874 the *Nation*, hitherto noted for its championing of Unionism and reform, retrospectively attacked Attorney General Akerman for having become infatuated with his own power in the South.[30]

The tide was flowing remorselessly against the social-justice ideals of Reconstruction. In 1875, Congress approved a Civil Rights Act giving African Americans rights of access to public services, but it failed to pass a further enforcement law. In the elections of 1874, the Democrats won control of Congress, paving the way for their further gains in 1876, the political compromise that led to "redemption," and a systematic erosion of black rights. In 1894, Congress repealed many of the existing enforcement provisions, and meanwhile southern states introduced Jim Crow laws disenfranchising African Americans and forcing them into a position of social inequality. The Supreme Court set its own seal on the nation's institutional racism. In the 1876 decision *United States v. Cruickshank,* it quashed the only three convictions the government had been able to obtain following the Colfax massacre; in 1883 it declared unconstitutional the Civil Rights Act of 1875; in *Plessy v. Ferguson* (1896) it promulgated the "separate but equal" doctrine that, in effect, sanctioned the removal of educational opportunity from black people. Racial conservatives had achieved their objectives by political and judicial means, but the undercurrent of terrorism remained, and the lynching rate hit a peak in the 1890s.

The Department of Justice and the Secret Service, and especially the link between them, had become politically unfashionable, and they no longer had the resources to counter intimidation in the South. The Secret Service remained available to the department, but it suffered budgetary cuts in the two decades following Reconstruction, and although its agents were quite well paid, there were on average only twenty-five of them in this period. Their first duty was to undertake Treasury work, and, in the 1880s, Congress formally restricted the Secret Service to the investigation of currency and counterfeiting offenses. Even after these restrictions, Congress continued to voice suspicions of the Secret Service. In principle, the attorney general could instead employ U.S. marshals to enforce federal laws, but they lacked the investigative professionalism of the Secret Service detectives.[31]

At the end of the nineteenth century, there was an international resurgence of white supremacy dogmas, and the trend affected the United States. By the first decade of the twentieth century, the Dunning school of historians was writing off Reconstruction enforcement as a bad policy that had failed. The attitude pervaded popular culture, too. Race supremacists acclaimed the publication, in 1905, of Thomas Dixon's novel *The Clansman.*

Set in the hill country of South Carolina, it glorified the Klan as a movement soaked in Scottish tradition and resistance to federal oppression. It excoriated the fictionalized "'Bureau of Military Justice,' with its secret factory of testimony and powers of tampering with verdicts."[32]

The Dixon book furnished the basis for D. W. Griffith's epic movie from 1915, *Birth of a Nation,* whose immense popularity made it all the more galling, to black Americans especially, when it prompted a revival of the Klan. But unlike the novel that inspired it, the movie did not attack the role of federal detectives, perhaps because, by the time it was distributed, the recently formed Bureau of Investigation was oppressing black citizens, not upholding their rights. Instead, Griffith simply ignored the Reconstruction detectives, joining the conspiracy to send them into oblivion.

Further reasons help explain why the story of Reconstruction detection remained untold. Following "restoration," the detectives feared for their safety and that of their families, and some of them had in any case been motivated by duty or ambition, rather than by sympathy for the freedmen. Even Whitley, who had led the well-resourced effort to "crush" the Klan, refrained from speaking out in retrospect. *In It,* his autobiography from 1894, glossed over that chapter in his life. He did refer to a pre–Justice Department investigation he had made of the Klan, to President Ulysses S. Grant's "hearty indorsement" of that work, and to the "bitterness of the rebels" he had brought to trial. But he wrote, "I will not go into any particulars in regard to the case." A brief biographical essay on Whitley published in 1918 studiously avoided Reconstruction. The reluctance of Whitley and his biographer to delve into details of 1871–72 may have reflected his own feelings on racial issues, as much as changes in American culture.[33]

Nor did the soldiers of the Seventh Cavalry who had been dispatched to South Carolina contribute memories of their role. One reason was that many of them perished in June 1876 at the Battle of the Little Bighorn, when their commander Lieutenant Colonel George A. Custer made his ill-conceived assault on the redoubt of the Sioux and Cheyenne. Merrill had been assigned to detached duties elsewhere and survived that episode, but he left no record of any of the events of his colorful career.

But if federal detection was down and almost forgotten, it was not out. A combination of three factors kept it in the frame. One was the policing need created by the continuing consolidation of the nation, and of organized crime. The second was the failure of the private sector to supply the federal government with acceptable detectives. Federal recourse to private agencies did occur for a period. According to the annual reports of the attorney general, private detectives (mostly from the Pinkerton National Detective Agency) were hired on twenty-eight occasions between 1885 and 1892. In the later decades of the nineteenth century, however, it became increasingly apparent that private detectives were habitually in the pay of businessmen who wanted to destroy workers' rights. At the time, there was widespread sympathy with workers' causes, and it was an unwise politician who ignored wage earners' interests. Hiring the Pinkerton agency became impossible after its men engaged in a gunfight with locked-out workers at Andrew Carnegie's steel mill in Homestead, Pennsylvania, in 1892. The following year, in the wake of major inquiries, Congress passed a law banning the use of Pinkertons in government work. From now on, the federal government would have to use its own agents.[34]

The third factor rescuing federal detection from oblivion was the war with Spain in 1898. Suddenly, the nation needed a federal intelligence service. Criticism of government undercover operations gave way to admiration when John E. Wilkie took charge of the Secret Service and, in a well-publicized counterespionage operation, exposed and extinguished a Spanish spy ring. Wilkie's success signaled a revival in the service's prestige. The operations were not yet under the aegis of the Department of Justice, but the gate had been reopened to that possibility.

Nor were the events of the 1870s entirely forgotten. Major Merrill's assistant Louis Post was one of those who kept alive the ideals of racial justice. After a career as a journalist and reformer, he became assistant secretary of labor in President Woodrow Wilson's administration, criticized the Bureau of Investigation for departing from the principles he thought it should be espousing, and published a memoir of his "carpetbagger" days.

Intertwined with the threads of memory were those of expectation. Some citizens never lost their faith in the Justice Department's potential for protecting black people. Departmental files for 1921 contain numerous letters about the resurgent Ku Klux Klan. The great majority were hostile to the Klansmen, and some of the writers expected the Justice Department to once again send its agents against the terrorists. Congressman Harry C. Davis from Ohio shared the sentiments of Reconstruction enforcers fifty years earlier, and recommended the same course of action. He observed: "The organization is moving so secretly here, that it is almost impossible to get definite and exact information except from the operation of the Secret Service. However, since they are meeting and operating secretly, is seems to me that it is right and proper that they should be opposed with their own weapons." Brewster Campbell, editor of the *Michigan Daily*, asked the department to share with him its information on Michigan Klansmen so that he could act against them. Clearly, his expectation was that such files were still being compiled. A pro-Klan writer shared the belief, complaining about pressure exerted on the Justice Department by African Americans, Jews, and Catholics.[35]

Fond memories of the enforcement years lingered for many years, as is evident in the Works Progress Administration's oral history of former slaves, compiled in the 1930s. When speaking of Reconstruction, the now aged freedmen were far from universally bitter. They looked back on that era as a time when possibilities had been demonstrated, and when a good number of African Americans had served with credit in national and local legislatures. There was even cause for hope based on precedent. An Alabama sharecropper who had never in his life been allowed to vote voiced that aspiration: "The Bible says, 'What has been will be again.'"[36]

3

proud genesis: 1905–1909

The FBI gives as the date of its founding 26 July 1908. On that day, the U.S. attorney general issued an order stating that, in future, Department of Justice investigations would be conducted by its own staff. The edict created a permanent force of agents under the attorney general's direct control. Earlier boosts to federal crime-detection activity had been responses to passing crises, the threats posed by the Klan in the 1870s and Spanish spies in the 1890s. In contrast, the 1908 initiative marked a permanent increase in federal police powers.[1]

The immediate occasion of the initiative was a fight between the president and Capitol Hill over the issue of congressional corruption. In 1904, Secret Service detectives on loan to Justice had obtained evidence that led to the conviction of a number of land fraudsters, including U.S. senator John H. Mitchell (R-Ore.). Mitchell died before he could be sentenced. Unhappy about the investigation to which he had been subjected, Congress directed a barrage of criticism at the Secret Service. This culminated, in the spring of 1908, in a legislative ban on the Treasury Department's loan of Secret Service detectives to any other department. Faced with this ban, the executive created the Justice Department's own detective force.

Attorney General Charles J. Bonaparte, however, offered a broader justification than this. In January 1909, he sent President Theodore Roosevelt a thirteen-page letter justifying the creation of the fledgling FBI. He reviewed changes that had taken place since the 1789 act creating the office of U.S. attorney general. Subsequent legislation had given the attorney general the right to supervise and control U.S. attorneys and marshals (1861) and had created the Department of Justice (1870). But marshals were ineffective at collecting evidence, and the 1893 statute prohibiting government employment of Pinkertons or other private detectives meant that Justice had to rely solely on the help of Secret Service men loaned out as special agents.

Now that Congress had banned Secret Service loans as well as the hiring of Pinkertons, something had to be done, but, in any case, Bonaparte thought that reform was overdue. He believed that the use of on-loan Secret Service agents was inappropriate in the investigation of certain crimes such as peonage, which would place them in direct antagonism with local police whose help they would need in other cases (he apparently did not foresee, or chose not to acknowledge, that Justice agents would have the same problem). Similarly, experience of land-fraud cases with their legal complexities demonstrated the need for direct Justice Department control over agents.

According to Bonaparte, the new force would detect crime and enable prosecution at a relatively low cost. A purely Justice-based detective force would "conduce to . . . efficiency of administration." It would specialize, and develop "experts." The cultivation of a professional, properly remunerated and disciplined corps was essential. Detectives would have to frequent the haunts of criminals without acquiring the outlaws' low moral standards; they would have to resist the temptation to manufacture evidence; they would thus need to be distinctly superior to private detectives who were amateurish and, in his view, drawn from the criminal classes. The attorney general was the appropriate person to enforce these high standards.[2]

Bonaparte's letter rang with the tones of Progressivism. The reform movement that swept America in the early years of the twentieth century exalted morality, financial probity, order, and efficiency, and gave a key role to the "expert" in the improvement of society. Bonaparte's justification of the new force that would grow into the FBI echoed faithfully the precepts of contemporary liberal reform.

Yet if Bonaparte was in some ways a Progressive, in other ways he was not. On one hand, he was a Progressive in advocating civil service reform and the imposition of law and order. In an article on lynching, he had argued that it stemmed, in part, from the corrupt practices of local politicians. He advocated a strengthening in the murder laws (though he did not specify that it should be federal legislation). He wanted what a century later would be called the "two strikes and out" approach, the death penalty after two lynching offenses, and advocated the introduction of greater powers for the judiciary at the expense of racist grand juries. It is dangerous to generalize about the "typical" Progressive, but Bonaparte was a recognizable prototype.

Bonaparte was, however, different from others labeled "Progressive." Progressivism was mainly a Protestant crusade, but Bonaparte belonged to its minority Catholic wing. Educated privately and at Harvard, he opposed one of the main Progressive reforms, free, secular secondary school education. Unusually for an American politician, he was of royal descent. His grandfather, the brother of Napoleon I, had been king of Westphalia.

Bonaparte's aristocratic mien and abrasive self-confidence made him enemies. So did his irreverence. When the get-tough President Roosevelt announced at a civil service banquet that he had ordered border patrolmen to undertake target practice, Bonaparte commented in his next speech that he should have required the men to shoot at each other, and given the jobs to the survivors. Such flippancy could cause offense. Bonaparte also shocked the temperance movement. Required under the Pure Food and Drug Act of 1906 to devise proper labels for various brands of whiskey, he proposed a Semper Idem whiskey (vintage) and an E Pluribus Unum whiskey (blend of the best straights). The Anti-Saloon League protested to the White House. In a complementary incident that showed its dry wit, the Joint Encampment of the Knights of Temperance bestowed the title "Camp Bonaparte" on a Madeira cellar it wanted to close down.[3]

Although he was one of the leading personalities behind the founding of the FBI, Charles Bonaparte was a somewhat tactless advocate of a strengthened federal investigative capability. Behind him, however, stood a politically gifted figure. Roosevelt was the nation's most powerful leader since Lincoln. He had become president by accident in 1901, when President William McKinley fell to an assassin's bullet. The old guard in his own Republican Party was horrified by his accession to office. The party of Lincoln had grown conservative; it dominated a Senate largely composed of millionaires who reflexively did the bidding of the giant trusts that had come to dominate American life. To the horror of these legislators, Roosevelt spoke of the social problems affecting newly industrialized America. He demanded a "Square Deal." The first president not to side with capital against labor in a major dispute, he forced coal-mine owners to compromise with their workers in the bitter anthracite strike of 1902. He attacked not only business corruption but also big business itself, launching an antitrust campaign that demanded an end to unfair monopolistic practices and the restoration of competition in the marketplace.

Roosevelt's determination to crack down on bad men stemmed from his personality and background. Having been a weak youth, he had overcome physical infirmities through sheer force of character to become an advocate of outdoor athleticism and a vigorous approach to life. From this sprang his belief in conservation. His pioneering efforts in this regard led him to withdraw 150 million acres of forest from public sale, and his conservationist convictions were an important factor in his prosecution of western timber fraud criminals. His experience of personal adversity also helps to explain his sympathy for the underdog, be he a coal miner or a former slave. To maximize his political support he modified the effects of those sympathies in his second term in office, but at first he seemed a real antidote to government by the rich and privileged. He even defied contemporary social convention and opened the door of the White House to the leading African American of the day, Booker T. Washington.

President Roosevelt was the nephew of James D. Bullock, who, on behalf of Confederate president Jefferson Davis, had secretly commissioned the building of the hit-and-run warship *Alabama* in Birkenhead, England. Proud of his uncle, Roosevelt reveled in the derring-do of undercover work and its converse, criminal detection. He believed ardently in the need for federal police reform. He had established his reputation as a champion of law and order as police commissioner of New York City. When he accepted that position in 1895, brothels and gambling dens had been a political issue. These were the soil from which urban gangsterism was growing. Senior members of the New York Police Department (NYPD) were accepting bribes from the underworld, and the department as a whole suffered from low morale, a hostile press, and recruitment problems. Aiming at the pimps rather than their women, Roosevelt decided on a "no toleration" approach to those who profited from immoral earnings.[4]

Police Commissioner Roosevelt tightened up entry requirements for NYPD recruits. A believer in central authority and top-down reform, he sought to reduce the power of precinct detective forces, and fortified the Central Detective Bureau at NYPD headquarters. He described this as the "right arm of the service," and took pride in the fact that the reformed detective bureau doubled its arrest rate in his first year in office. Both out of personal inclination and because he realized the political advantages, the pre-presidential Roosevelt was firmly committed to the defense of public order and to the use of a centralized detective force in pursuit of that goal.

As governor of New York State and then as president, Roosevelt continued to present himself as an enforcer of law and order. The time was ripe for such a strategy, as there was widespread concern about lawlessness and even social upheaval. Assassins took the lives of three American presidents, including James Garfield in 1881 in addition to Lincoln and McKinley. Gangsterism reared its ugly head in New York and Chicago. Race disturbances continued. Supporters of the business ascendancy worried that European-style class war would spread to America. The bloodily repressed Paris Commune of 1871, the assassination of Tsar Alexander II ten years later, and the spread from Russia of the revolutionary tactic of "propaganda of the deed" did little to allay such fears. A labor movement gained momentum in the United States, its history punctuated by alarming incidents: the Molly Maguires conflict in Pennsylvania, widespread railroad riots in 1877, the anarchist-inspired Haymarket bomb explosion in Chicago in 1886, the Homestead shootout in 1892, and the Pullman strike, a turbulent nation-wide railroad stoppage in 1894. Every major city witnessed confrontations between streetcar corporations and their employees, and dramatic conflicts affected mining operations from Coal Creek, Tennessee, to Cripple Creek, Colorado. National Association of Manufacturers president David M. Parry concluded that "organized labor knows but one law, and that is the law of physical force."[5]

Parry then wrote *The Scarlet Empire* (1906), one of several cataclysmic novels that appeared during the Roosevelt presidency predicting class war and socialist revolution in the United States. Yet, in retrospect, it is plain that there was little danger of revolution. Labor violence was not on the increase as the alarmists claimed, nor was it, as they also claimed, worse in the United States than in other industrial countries. Surviving statistics suggest that crime was in decline in nineteenth-century America, especially in the cities that were supposed to be such dens of vice and violence. Roosevelt's NYPD probably arrested more people simply because he told it to. He was not, it should be noted, alone in his decision to act on the assumption that crime was rampant. The founding of the National Chiefs of Police Union in 1893 had led to the formation of a National Bureau of Criminal Identification whose publication, *The Detective*, provided from 1898 a national forum for discussions of crime. Perversely, however, this increased police activity had no effect on homicide rates, which began to rise after 1890. Increases in police and detective work are not necessarily the results of increased criminality, and they have little provable effect on the crime rate.[6]

Roosevelt did not live in blissful ignorance of such complexities. When he was presiding over the New York police board and claiming to be reforming the police and making the streets safe once again, the newspapers suddenly printed banner headlines announcing a "crime wave." This threatened an early end to his promising career, so he summoned one of the journalists involved. Lincoln Steffens confessed that he and his rival journalist

Jacob Riis had invented the crime wave. Their editors had complained that the news was flat. In time-honored fashion, they had looked at the precinct books of the NYPD, reported a few of the murders contained therein, and then strung them together to create the alarm. Once one newspaper headlined the crime wave, the others had to follow, and the story grew more and more lurid. The actual murder rate did not change during this period. Retractions followed Steffens's confession. Roosevelt was saved. But he was also left to contemplate the facts that crime is not always what it seems, and that it requires skill and vigilance to pose as the champion of law and order.[7]

One interpretation of the motives of Roosevelt and his supporters in reforming police and detective forces rests on a skeptical view of human nature: they manipulated the anxieties of ordinary folk to achieve publicity and to advance their own careers, and to establish new means of social control when social-reform movements challenged the hegemony of the rich. At least in the case of Roosevelt himself, however, this explanation just does not fit. He used Secret Service agents to check capitalist exploitation of the wilderness and to curb business monopolies, not to control working people. At the same time, he was shrewd enough to realize that people value social reassurance. While it may be true that only a minority of crimes are solved, it is comforting even to the skeptic to know that he or she can telephone the police in the wake of a crime, and that, back of the local police, there lies a federal detective capacity. Roosevelt recognized that need for reassurance, and realized that playing the role of national supercop made him popular with the American people.

By the middle of Roosevelt's presidency, the nation was ready for a new investigative bureau. It would be a gradual process, and it is by no means complete today, but Americans were beginning to lose their distrust of the federal government. The "new liberalism" (as distinct from the old laissez-faire, hands-off liberalism) stemmed from a practical consideration. The business corporations that had become so powerful by the end of the nineteenth century required a countervailing force, and, for all its faults, national government and its institutions seemed to offer the answer. Bonaparte's new unit was one of the responses to that perception.

The new faith in government, together with the public's desire for social reassurance on crime and social disorder, were complemented by another kind of changing perception. While the unsavory side of sleuthing was still regarded as offensive, detective work was beginning to acquire a popular mystique. Since the 1890s, there was a vogue for Sherlock Holmes stories. In spite of enduring hostility toward Pinkertons, fiction fantasies about private detectives fueled a public veneration for new techniques like finger-printing. The nation awaited a high-technology federal detective force.

Nevertheless, there was fierce opposition to the Roosevelt-Bonaparte detective-force plans. Ironically, this opposition to gumshoe methods helped shape the final solution. Controversy ruled out the Secret Service as the central agency for law and order. While many Americans revered the Secret Service, which drew fifty applicants for every job vacancy, it also attracted enemies. Even if it helped prepare the public for change, it could not itself become the prime federal agency. This created the void into which would be inserted the Bureau of Investigation.

Much of the controversy about the Secret Service focused on its chief, John E. Wilkie, who, in spite of his provocation of opposition, ranks with Bonaparte and Roosevelt as one of the Progressive-era founders of the FBI. Born in Elgin, Illinois, in 1860, Wilkie joined the *Chicago Tribune* in 1877, working as its police reporter and also becoming its city editor, essentially a business journalist. From the beginning, he exhibited talent and an ability to recognize it in others. It was Wilkie who spotted the brilliance of the satirist Finley Peter Dunne, and gave him a job.

Wilkie rivaled even the creator of the immortal Mr. Dooley in terms of reportage and social insight. In an anonymous article in the *Tribune* in 1890, he broke the story of the Indian rope trick. This story told of a scoop by a local Chicago man with a flair for photography. Fred S. Ellmore (Yale '86) had gone to India to investigate claims that a fakir could throw a ball of twine up into the sky, and then produce a boy who would climb the rope and disappear into thin air. Ellmore set his camera to take a photograph at the critical moment in one of these demonstrations. Result: no twine, no boy, just one fakir hypnotizing the audience.

Or had the fakir fooled the camera? The story set off frenzied speculation among scientists and in the press. One could offer a number of interpretations of the tale and of the fascination it exerted. It furnished evidence both of a healthy American interest in scientific inquiry and of an unhealthy propensity to believe in oriental trickery. Here, it can simply be noted that "Fred S. Ellmore" was a fictitious character with a name that sounded suspiciously like "sell more." Wilkie, at his best, was at one with America.[8]

In 1897, the new administration of President William McKinley turned to Wilkie for help. The Secret Service was in disarray. Its chief, William P. Hazen, had run afoul of the anti-federalist lobby because the service had in 1894 taken on responsibility for protecting the president, and critics who disapproved of the enlargement of federal activities accused him of making unauthorized payments in that regard. The nation faced another crisis, too. A gang of counterfeiters had blanched a quantity of one-dollar bills and then reprinted them as $100 Monroes, forcing the government to withdraw a whole currency issue. Unable to solve the case and already under fire, Hazen had been stripped of his responsibilities and reduced to the ranks.

Wilkie joined the Secret Service with the mission of cracking the counterfeiting ring. William J. Burns of Pittsburgh joined him on the case. Using a corrupt tax collector in Lancaster, Pennsylvania, Wilkie and Burns ran a sting operation. They fed the forgers disinformation that led to their entrapment and arrest. To adulatory headlines in the press, prosecution ran through into 1899 and resulted in thirteen convictions.

By this time, Secretary of the Treasury Lyman J. Gage had promoted Wilkie from a $7-a-day operative to chief of the Secret Service on a salary of $3,500 per annum. In the war of 1898, the new chief assumed responsibility for counterespionage against a Spanish spy ring centered in Montreal, Canada. Not for the first time, the service engaged in some dubious practices, including burglaries disrespectful of the sovereignty of a foreign nation, and a disposition to hound citizens of Latin descent in an ethnically biased manner. On the other hand, Wilkie insisted that his men were honest and efficient, and he made a point of hiring linguists. He frustrated Spanish plans to supply the Iberian fleet with artillery coordinates for commercial and civilian targets along the East Coast of the United States, and established a tradition of counterespionage that the Bureau of Investigation would inherit.[9]

But powerful personalities like Wilkie find it hard to sit back and be passive after each triumph, and, by being so proactive, they can create a hostile climate of opinion. The historian Willard Gatewood wrote a book about the controversies of the Roosevelt administration and observed that the Secret Service was involved in almost all of them. He noted that critics exaggerated the size and reach of the service, assuming that all federal investigators and inspectors were "secret service" agents.

Wilkie showed no inclination to relinquish the job of protecting the president, and, like Hazen, came under fire for unauthorized expenditures. Immediately in the wake of McKinley's assassination, there was criticism of both the service's failure to save his life and its expansionist tendency. Senator George Frisbie Hoar of Massachusetts favored a switch to military protection of the president. Nevertheless, the service increased its protective role, an example of failure generating reward and expansion. In the long term, however, protecting the chief executive and his entourage would become such an important and narrowly defined task that it limited the extension of the service into other roles, and allowed the FBI to flourish instead.[10]

After Roosevelt's inauguration, the Secret Service's practice of lending investigators to other government departments gave it the appearance of having ever-spreading tentacles. Loans to the Justice Department rose to about sixty agents per annum by 1908. Some of the loans were not in themselves controversial. For example, Justice borrowed twenty-three agents in 1902 to help break up a lottery-fixing ring. But the scale of the operations worried advocates of limited government, and some of the operations provoked outrage from powerful interests.

One such operation was against peonage in the South. This "new slavery" was especially prevalent in the turpentine industry. Black workers would be tempted into debt through advances of money. Absconders would be ruthlessly hunted down like their antebellum grandfathers. They were beaten, imprisoned incommunicado, and, in the cases of a number of women, forced into prostitution. Some white workers, mostly immigrants, were also forced into peonage. The labor movement publicized their cause, while doing little to help the black American. It was Booker T. Washington who spoke up for blacks. Some prominent journalists joined him. President Roosevelt backed anti-peonage operations. All three attorneys general who served under him tried to combat white terrorization of the black population of the South. Once again, the Secret Service set out to help the African American; once again, it incurred the wrath of the racist old order.[11]

There was even more trouble when Roosevelt took on big business. He first deployed the Secret Service to investigate the beef trust. In 1906, Upton Sinclair's novel *The Jungle* gave a stomach-churning account of how rats and human parts found their way into cans of meat packed in Chicago. His exposé complemented the Secret Service investigation, and the president secured the pure food and drugs legislation that made America one of the world's safest places to eat. Roosevelt had perceived that consumers were a new animal in American politics, and his action on their behalf made him popular. Nevertheless, certain businessmen joined conservative southerners in opposition to the president's Secret Service methods. The Justice Department's continuing deployment of borrowed agents to investigate antitrust cases rubbed salt into business wounds. A pair of Colorado Fuel Company employees shot dead Joseph A. Walker, the Secret Service agent who was investigating them.

Roosevelt's stand on the principle of conservation provided the immediate setting for the Secret Service crisis. The president was in love with the wild. Camping in Yosemite with the preservationist John Muir in 1903, he shouted out his delight when Muir lit a big fire: "This is bully!" They slept in the open and awoke next morning covered by four inches of snow. "This is bullier!" said Roosevelt. His determination to confront the despoilers of the wilderness was politically astute, and he recognized the potent symbolism of the West in an era when the frontier was newly gone and romance about it flourished. But his commitment was without question genuine, and helps to explain his aggressiveness toward Capitol Hill over the federal police issue.[12]

The land fraud issue involved members of Congress. The Homestead Act of 1862 had given American citizens the right to a quarter section of land in the public domain. Millions of white farmers and their families benefited from the resultant opportunities, but there was also extensive fraud. The Roosevelt administration wanted to tackle the issue, and was especially concerned about the "lieu land" scam in the Far West, whereby, in return for a small consideration, individuals were persuaded to make false claims as putative farmers; they took possession of non-arable tracts of forest and then handed them over to timber businessmen, who made a great deal of money out of each 160-acre section. Certain local and national politicians protected the businessmen from prosecution in return for bribes. The Department of the Interior feared that its own investigators were on the take. It asked Justice for help. In turn, Justice borrowed Secret Service operatives, notably William J. Burns, to secure evidence for the purpose of prosecution, which they did. In 1905, Senator Mitchell and U.S. congressman John N. Williamson (R-Ore.) were among those convicted.[13]

Congressional supporters of the arraigned legislators protested that the Secret Service was being used to secure political ends and to harass members of the national legislature. Some of those indicted for land fraud were found guilty, but others were not. Prominently, Idaho's progressive Republican William H. Borah was acquitted on the eve of his election to the U.S. Senate in 1906. His indictment on unfounded charges no doubt affected his future attitude. In 1910, for example, he sat on a Senate committee investigating allegations that federal prisoners were being subjected to the "third degree" method of interrogation, and accused Wilkie of turning a blind eye to such practices.[14]

As the debates on land fraud rumbled on, the Secret Service became a renewed bone of contention. James A. Tawney, an old-guard Republican from Minnesota and chairman of the House Appropriations Committee, objected early in 1906 to what he saw as the indiscriminate and unauthorized loans of Secret Service detectives to various government departments. He demanded a list of all operatives employed by the Justice Department since 1896, and the list, once produced, showed the steady increase due to antitrust cases and the land fraud investigations.

Inadvertently, however, Tawney was contributing to the idea that the Justice Department should, instead of borrowing from the Secret Service, set up its own investigative force. The attorney general's office made that suggestion tentatively in January 1906, and Bonaparte advanced the idea when he took office in March 1907. His annual report of that year directed Congress's attention to the "anomaly" that the Department of Justice had no permanent detective force under its immediate control.[15]

Mindful of the need for congressional authorization, on 17 January 1908 Bonaparte recommended in testimony to an appropriations subcommittee chaired by Tawney that the Department of Justice should have its own force of detectives. Tawney attempted to wriggle free of this unwanted consequence of his own truculence. He implied that Justice could not be trusted because it had in the past employed disreputable people, and the attorney general had to remind him "we do not employ detective agencies at all."

Tawney had launched a juggernaut that he found difficult to control, as it became open season on the Secret Service. Subsequent hearings revealed, for example, that the Secret Service had been involved in at least one case of sexual policing—it had placed a naval officer under surveillance because he was having an affair with the married daughter of a Washington society lady. Fears were expressed that the Secret Service was spying on the private lives of members of Congress. Tawney was in a dilemma. He was alarmed at the suggestion that there should be a federal bureau of investigation, yet inhibited in his support for the old system of Secret Service loans to Justice by the very sniping campaign he had initiated, and by concerns that Wilkie was an empire-builder who would always exert final control over his men regardless of who employed them.[16]

So strong were the suspicions of the detective loan system that Tawney's committee drafted an appropriations amendment to end the practice. This provoked hostile reactions. Sections of the New York press suggested that timber thieves were behind the amendment. There was outrage in law enforcement circles. The U.S. attorney for the Southern District of New York, Henry L. Stimson, said his work would be "crippled." President Roosevelt wrote to the old-guard Speaker of the House, Joseph "Uncle Joe" Cannon, pleading in vain for the withdrawal of the killer amendment. It would benefit only the "criminal class." Federal detectives were desperately needed to counter anarchists who were plotting "outrages." He knew from his days as police commissioner that intelligence work was essential, and critics' complaints about "spies" were "cheap."

By this time, though, Roosevelt and Bonaparte had formed a dismissive judgment on the mood of Congress. They could see that they had lost the battle for Treasury detectives on loan, and were unlikely to win the fight for congressional approval of an independent federal bureau of investigation. So, once Congress had adjourned, they created the new agency by executive order. A few days after the attorney general's directive of 26 July 1908, nine agents were transferred from the Secret Service to Justice on a basis that was stated as temporary, but proved permanent. By the end of the year, people were referring to this new branch of Justice as the "bureau of investigation."[17]

Tawney's sabotage of agent loans had provoked a decisive response. But although the federal bureau of investigation was now out of the womb, the birth pangs were yet to come. In late 1908 and early 1909, there was a sensational and protracted row over the problems of federal investigation, which ensured that the new agency would be mired in controversy and dogged by misunderstanding.

In his final annual message to Congress, on 8 December 1908, President Roosevelt tore into his critics. He averred that the amendment banning Secret Service loans was the work of political rogues: "The chief argument in favor of the amendment was that Congressmen themselves did not want to be investigated." The amendment "had been, and could be a benefit only, to the criminal class."[18]

Roosevelt's statement may seem rashly confrontational, but it should be remembered that the president was the consummate politician. He had earlier offered Congress immunity from investigation in exchange for approval of the loan system, and this made Cannon's coterie seem intransigent. By hinting that the advocates of restriction were criminals, he now made it difficult for any legislator to oppose his plans. His bold assault may furthermore be placed in the context of his wider reform goals: Roosevelt's private correspondence indicates that he was deeply concerned by what he saw as continuing corruption in Congress. He wanted to rally the American people behind his last-ditch effort to clean up American politics. The investigative powers issue gave him an opportunity of doing that.[19]

Though just two paragraphs in length and buried in a routine message, the president's remarks offended his congressional opponents deeply. Pursuing his personal vendetta with the Secret Service chief, Tawney alleged that Wilkie had sent a Secret Service agent into his district in the 1908 congressional elections for the express purpose of securing his defeat (it was not true; the House appropriations chairman had mistaken a private detective for a federal agent). There was a further complaint that federal detectives furnished Roosevelt with compromising information on his political opponents. Within three days of Roosevelt's message the House had set up a committee of inquiry, and five days later the Senate followed suit.[20]

For the circulation-hungry press, Christmas had arrived early. Not many newspapers could resist the temptation to print stories about government espionage. The *Philadelphia Public Ledger* professed its sobriety by expressing distaste at the way "fiction" stories were blurring the distinction between international intrigue and a Secret Service whose much more mundane job was simply to exercise "eternal vigilance" in the matter of counterfeiting. The same paper then proceeded to dredge up as many colorful incidents as possible from the Secret Service's recent past. Meanwhile, the *Wall Street Journal* thundered its support for the politics-business interests whose integrity had been impugned: the Secret Service was "essentially antagonistic to the ideals of the Republic" and would abet the "expansion of secret and sinister power."[21]

The *Philadelphia Record* launched an attack on Roosevelt that drew on Tawney's criticisms. It pointed to obfuscation over expenditures, and to costs that "never show up in the records." It cited Tawney's guesswork that indicated an expansion from 931 federal agents in 1896 to 3,113 ten years later (the actual aggregate figure for all federal investigators, according to Roosevelt, was 1,900). According to the *Record*, "all departments" were now "infested with detectives," and the cost had quadrupled to well over $4 million. Nor was this to any great avail: "The punishment of crime has not advanced in proportion to the growth in the number of men employed for the purpose and in the money spent for it."[22]

The press was, however, divided. In fact, the historian Gatewood estimates that public opinion was "overwhelmingly" in favor of the president. The *Philadelphia North American* noted that Roosevelt had placed congressmen on the defensive by daring them to oppose potential investigations into their own criminality. It further gave expression to what became an enduring mantra: "He is expected to urge consolidation of all the various detective agencies of the government under one head in the interest of economy and efficiency." Thus, to Wilkie's long-standing argument that the

Secret Service saved the government money through the recovery of defrauded cash and land assets, was added the complementary view that centralization would bring dollar savings.[23]

In the absence of opinion polls one cannot be sure, but perhaps an argument advanced in the *Pittsburg Leader* more surely summed up the sentiment to which Roosevelt successfully appealed. It questioned the motives of "the virtuous congressmen" who complained of the advent of a Russian-style "political secret service" (the press was having great fun with such comparisons, the favorite being with Joseph Fouché, the secret service impresario of Bonaparte's great-uncle, Napoleon Bonaparte). The *Leader*'s editorial stated that such congressmen were "doing a bit of 'secret service' of their own. It is service for the trusts, the railroads, the timber thieves and others of that class." So Progressive partisans of Roosevelt's Secret Service reform could claim that they were on the side of open government.[24]

Having enlivened the approach of Christmas, the debate now showed signs of illuminating the New Year. On 4 January, Roosevelt threw down the gauntlet once again. In a special message to Congress, he attacked his old foe Joe Cannon for having obstructed his attempts at Secret Service reform. Congress must accept, he asserted without proof, that America faced an imminent crime wave, and that federal investigation was the "efficient" way to fight the criminals. Playing to packed galleries, the House debated the issue for seven hours, with the Senate following suit. Both chambers, Roosevelt told his son Kermit, "held a can-can over the secret service." By now a lame-duck president, and resented for his seven years of powerful executive leadership at the expense of Congress, Roosevelt was subjected to abuse, as were his supporters. Cannon and Tawney launched personal attacks on Wilkie of a kind that ruled out that official as a potential future tsar of the federal investigative services. In a parliamentary maneuver that he later claimed was the greatest congressional triumph since the days of Henry Clay, Cannon had the president's message tabled. Never a man to retreat under fire, Roosevelt countered by releasing the text of a letter obtained by the Secret Service indicating that another of his enemies, Senator Benjamin R. ("Pitchfork Ben") Tillman (D-S.C.), had used influence to obtain tracts of Oregonian land for members of his family.[25]

Roosevelt was potentially vulnerable on the Secret Service issue because of the peonage controversy, which had laid him open to charges of hypocrisy, and exposed his administration to attacks from all sides on racial matters. On the one hand, Roosevelt offended conservative southerners by insisting it was the federal government's duty to combat the neoslavery found in several southern states. Secret Service operatives contracted to Justice had made forays into the South to obtain evidence. In 1906, they had built up a case in Florida, and Assistant Attorney General Charles Russell, dispatched to the South with the special mission of fighting peonage, had pressed Wilkie for more action.

But Wilkie, solicitous of local southern support for his work against customs and counterfeiting crimes, dragged his feet. He exposed the administration to the charge of having posed as the champion of black Americans' rights, but for political effect only. Then, in 1908, Bonaparte courted further criticism by not expediting the cause of Alonzo Bailey, a black worker subjected to peonage whose appeal for habeas corpus rights was allowed to drag slowly through the courts.

By this time another tempest, the Brownsville affair, was causing serious embarrassment to the administration. This arose from an accusation against black soldiers of the 25th infantry who had objected to local discrimination, and allegedly ran riot in the small town of Brownsville, Texas, in August 1906, shooting a white man dead. Whether because they were innocent or because of a brotherly code of silence, no evidence was found against the soldiers. Nevertheless, Roosevelt had crudely authorized the dishonorable discharge of the entire black garrison, exposing himself to attack by champions of civil rights. Senator Joseph B. Foraker of Ohio was in the vanguard of this attack. When Roosevelt refused to back Foraker's bid for the Republican Party presidential nomination in 1908, giving his support instead to Secretary of War William H. Taft, the senator mounted an assault that was based partly on principle and partly on revenge.

In a Senate speech in January 1909, Foraker dramatized his cause by focusing on the fashionable issue of the day. He said that Roosevelt and Taft, by now the president-elect, had employed detectives in what he depicted as a ruthless attempt to obtain evidence against the Brownsville soldiers; the president had apparently financed this from the "secret fund," originally set up by President George Washington for special contingencies. Foraker insisted that Taft's action was in breach of the provisions of the 1893 anti-Pinkerton act. President Roosevelt had "become utterly oblivious to all the restraints of law, decency and propriety in his mad pursuit of those helpless victims (the colored soldier) of his ill-considered action." Julia Foraker later offered her version of the atmosphere she and her husband had endured during the "battle for the black battalion." Spies opened the senator's mail, as well as Ben Tillman's. Roosevelt's agents "crashed" her afternoon receptions, and political business could be transacted only after nightfall. Yet darkness was no protection, as "relays" of Rooseveltian spies hung around as her daughters went out to their balls.[26]

At this point, Attorney General Bonaparte issued his justification of the creation of the Department of Justice force of special agents, giving as one explanation the very existence of the Pinkerton Act that forbade the employment of private detectives. This did little to assuage Congressman Tawney's bitter enmity toward John Wilkie. Grilling him in hearings on Secret Service finances on 27 January 1909, the Appropriations Committee chairman accused him of diverting money from anti-counterfeiting operations in a manner that contributed to a rise in forgery. Wilkie responded by saying that he lent his agents only on a short-term basis and for legitimate purposes. One agent, for example, was in El Paso investigating the Mexican Revolution at the request of the State Department. Unappeased, Tawney insisted that counterfeiting investigations were incompetent. He claimed that in one case, an indictment had "hung fire in the courts until the defendant finally pleaded guilty."[27]

Unwittingly, critics like Foraker and Tawney actually contributed to the consolidation of the new Justice Department group of detectives. First, they fell into the trap of appearing to have dubious motives, the result of Roosevelt's shrewd suggestion of corruption on Capitol Hill. Second, the attacks were partisan in that they came from people who had self-evident reasons to oppose the president and his reform policies. Third, they ruled out the existing Secret Service as the agency of central investigation. This was the recommendation of the Senate's corruption report in February 1909, and it prepared the way for the acceptance of the Justice provision. Fourth, they aimed at a regime that had already passed, for Wilkie drew the enemy fire on all "secret service" matters, thus protecting the fledgling new organism in Justice.

In spite of such accidents, the critics did promote a constructive approach to the secret state. When the House committee responded to Roosevelt's attack on corruption, it made no attempt to torpedo the Justice organism, but instead concluded that government detective agencies "should be permanently provided for and their duties defined and limited by law." Swagar Sherley was a member of the House Appropriations Committee who recalled "no instance where a government perished because of the absence of a secret-service force." However, he demanded not the abolition of government espionage, but only "safeguards essential to the preservation of people's liberties." He called for legislative oversight of government detectives: a hiring department "should come to Congress and get authorization from Congress for the employment of this class of men." Though Roosevelt counted Sherley among his enemies, the Kentucky Democrat had offered a potentially confidence-building critique, and was perceptive about the terms on which the American people might in the long run accept secret government activities. In a slightly acid concession of this point, Roosevelt observed that Congress was now advocating as if it was its own idea a proposal he was already making, for a bureau within Justice. He added that he had no problem with oversight. He and Congress were now as one, except on the point that Roosevelt demanded Wilkie should be put in charge of the new agency.[28]

There was no chance of that, but the new president's attorney general, George Wickersham, on 6 March 1909 felt confident enough to give the Justice Department's detective group "the dignity of a name," the Bureau of Investigation. He appointed as its director Stanley W. Finch. Born in Monticello, New York, in 1872, Finch had attended business colleges before joining the Justice Department in 1893 and then rising to the rank of chief examiner, investigating fraud cases while studying for the law degree he obtained in 1908. Since 26 July 1908, he had been in charge of the group of nine detectives who had transferred from the Secret Service to Justice. Finch had made fewer enemies than Wilkie. He forbade his agents from speaking to the press, thus protecting his agency from political accidents. In order to show that bureau investigations were a bargain for the taxpayer, he justified every penny spent. He made a special effort to cultivate good relations with Congress. Finch won acceptance for his bureau, and his tenure as its chief ran through 30 April 1912.[29]

The young bureau did face problems, including opposition by southern states' rights advocates. But by 1910 it had surpassed the Secret Service in both appropriations and number of "special agents" (the term Finch used in his administrative arrangements). In that year, Congressman Tawney again stood for reelection, and Roosevelt, back on the stump and hoping for another term in the White House, campaigned against him, denouncing his past opposition to the Secret Service. Tawney went down to defeat. According to his own estimate, the Secret Service issue did it. If he was right, his demise was a further indicator of Roosevelt's political genius in advancing the cause of federal investigation.[30]

Some of the causes of the establishment of the Bureau of Investigation can be found in the reasons advanced at the time. Undercover investigative powers were needed to combat corruption; existing investigative arrangements were inadequate and controversial; Progressives placed their faith in "experts" who would advance efficiency. The fears of contemporaries who spoke of social upheaval and crime waves were based on distortions, but even so they help explain the support given to the proposal for a national crime-busting agency.

Other causes are clearer in retrospect than they were at the time. These include a growing faith in the role of the federal government in solving social problems and imposing order. Also apparent in hindsight is the significance of conservationism, a campaign that lent force to the demand for a proper detective service. Finally, the bureau owed its existence to strong leadership. Wilkie contrived to make a case both for federal detection and against the existing system, and prepared the way for the new agency. Bonaparte took the specific initiative that was required. President Roosevelt supplied passionate and astute support, a major factor in the creation of the bureau.

What, then, was the nature of the new beast? Critics of Roosevelt and the Secret Service had made some telling points. But the making of the points was in itself an indication that there had been democratic debate. Congress had asserted its claim to the right of oversight, and had given at least implicit sanction to the founding of the bureau. As the continuing popular use of the term "detective" indicates, the bureau was strictly investigative. Its employees did not carry firearms, did not have powers of arrest, and were supposed to abjure political work. Nor was the bureau's director overimbued with abusable powers.

The Department of Justice had been founded in 1870, and had borrowed Secret Service agents to protect those Americans most in need of justice, the former slaves. Over the subsequent decades, the absence of a dedicated Department of Justice investigative bureau proved to be one factor in the attrition of the hard-won civil rights of the Reconstruction era. Whatever their faults, Roosevelt and his allies not only began to rectify this matter, but also gave a wider meaning to justice, bringing to book the robber barons of capitalism and the despoilers of the American wilderness. Undoubtedly, the FBI had a proud genesis.

4

loss of mission: 1909–1924

Belle Schreiber was a woman who worked at Chicago's exclusive all-white bordello the Everleigh Club. In the fall of 1912, Bureau of Investigation agents placed her in protective custody. She sang. Persuaded by her evidence, a grand jury indicted John Arthur Johnson. He faced a charge of having transported Schreiber from Pennsylvania to Illinois—across state lines—for the purposes of prostitution and "debauchery."[1]

On 7 November, policemen under the supervision of bureau agent Bert Meyer smashed through the door of Johnson's room in the Hotel Vendome. They fought their way past his bodyguards and handcuffed him. He was out on bail by midnight, but the arrest was the prelude to seven years of exile and one year in prison. The tide had turned in the fortunes of the first black heavyweight boxing champion of the world.

Jack Johnson was no angel. He dazzled not just with his "golden smile," but also through his less than puritan lifestyle. Those who championed him had to be realistic. The editor of the *Amsterdam News* wrote to President Taft on behalf of "the colored people of New York," demanding an end to Johnson's "persecution by the Federal authorities in Chicago because of his race." But he prefaced the appeal by saying that African Americans "condemn the folly of 'Jack' Johnson."

To some, however, the fighter's human qualities just made him more appealing. The satirist Damon Runyon had a general fondness for the bad, and he made no exception in the case of Johnson. Writing a preface to his friend's autobiography in 1927, Runyon noted Johnson's brilliant defensive qualities in the ring, and his habit of chatting cheerfully with members of the crowd in the middle of a fight. He delighted in the ex-champ's enduring ability to keep in great physical shape, but added: "I don't see why. He never stinted himself in the matter of indulgence."[2]

Whatever the champion's flaws, the Johnson case illustrates what went wrong with the Bureau of Investigation. The bureau of 1909 could be plausibly portrayed as heir to the battle for justice for African Americans. Cloaked in the mantle of Secret Service tradition, it could be represented as neutral between rich and poor, as a key instrument in the fight against corruption, and as efficient in the business of criminal detective work. It was characterized by probity. But by 1924, when a new attorney general finally stepped in to try to stop the rot, the bureau had lost many of these positive attributes.

Within a few years of its foundation, the bureau had become embroiled in financial scandal, turf wars, and the suppression of political dissent. Yet nothing so sharply defined its loss of mission as the volte-face in racial matters that the Johnson case epitomized. One citizen expressed contemporary outrage on this issue in a letter to the White House: "In the name of human justice I ask you to interfere with the framed up case against Jack Johnson which is in the hands of the Federal government."[3]

Why, during its infant years, did the bureau reverse the secret service tradition of fighting racial injustice? It is lazy thinking simply to blame that favorite villain of liberal America, J. Edgar Hoover, whose stewardship of the bureau did not start until the 1920s. It is inadequate also to point too heavily to the sins of other fathers. Hoover's predecessors did contribute to the process of putrefaction, but they did not ruin the bureau all on their own.

Johnson's biographers have offered explanations for his persecution. Randy Roberts argued that "the Bureau of Investigation and the Department of Justice did not so much consciously conspire to get Johnson as express the more general attitude of white society toward blacks who threatened the social order." More recently, Geoffrey Ward offered the contrary view that there was, indeed, an active conspiracy to trap Johnson on interstate charges. He identified the chief conspirators as the Chicago assistant U.S. district attorney Harry S. Parkin, U.S. attorney general George W. Wickersham, and acting bureau chief A. Bruce Bielaski. But Ward, too, saw the driving force as public opinion. The conspirators aimed to satisfy those Americans who wanted Johnson punished for his transgressions with white women.[4]

This invites an explanation of the contemporary mood. In a psychological thesis, the historian John Higham argued that a loss of national confidence led to the "nativist" mood of 1919–24, and that there were already signs of this nervousness during the "happy" Progressivism at the end of Roosevelt's presidency. A Highamite would argue that the bureau's excesses reflected these social currents.[5]

But the political context is also important. Having started as a brave attempt to offer all citizens a "square deal," the Progressive reform movement degenerated into an effort to purge society through oppression. Whereas the Secret Service had reflected the earlier, justice-motivated phase of Progressivism, the Bureau of Investigation became a tool of intolerant Progressivism.

By the time of Theodore Roosevelt's departure from the White House in 1909, the first phase of Progressivism had come to an end. President Taft still pursued big business with antitrust suits, yet the mood had changed. By the time Roosevelt returned to the political arena in 1910, he had become an advocate of the "New Nationalism," which meant embracing not just a regulatory function for the federal government, but also the positive attributes of nationwide capitalist organizations with their marketing efficiencies and economies of scale. Less was heard of conservation and very little of racial equality. Corruption had become a stale issue. Having been created to tackle these problems, the Bureau of Investigation now found itself stripped of its mission. It began to search for a new role, and settled for role reversal.

The Justice Department was about to cut the mainstay of its historic mission. In 1908, there had been a dramatic rise in the number of lynchings in the United States, to 77, from 48 the previous year. The formation in the following year of the National Association for the Advancement of Colored People (NAACP) marked a rejuvenation in the drive for a federal anti-lynching law, and for other actions against lynching. But in April 1910, the department sounded a departure from the premise of Roosevelt's three attorneys general, all of whom had tried to use existing laws to combat lynching. Now, Taft's Justice Department claimed to have "no authority . . . to protect citizens of African descent in the enjoyment of civil rights."

Instead of sending agents into Dixie, the Bureau of Investigation cast about for other roles and undertook sundry minor tasks. While terror gripped the South, its agents chased swindlers carrying forged letters of introduction purporting to have been written by President Taft and former president Roosevelt. While black Americans suffered gruesome deaths, the bureau investigated the alleged theft of a patent for testing alcohol and coloring levels in whiskey. Its men still busied themselves with some of their former functions like antitrust work, and the bureau kept growing—its annual budget increased from an estimated $52,000 in its first year to $290,000 in 1911. But the growth was largely achieved through "shuffling," the absorption of accountants and other personnel from other departments, rather than through dedication to the pursuit of justice. The bureau had surpassed the Secret Service in size, but not in reputation.[6]

Then, in the second half of the Taft administration, the white slavery question rescued the bureau from obscurity and jerked it into reverse thrust. One of Taft's gestures suggests that he remained personally tolerant. His choice of William H. Lewis to be assistant attorney general was a high-level black appointment, and the last such until the Eisenhower administration. However, white slavery became an issue that allowed the bureau to exploit the nation's racial fears. The result of the 1912 presidential election magnified the opportunity, as it placed in the White House a southern Democrat, Woodrow Wilson, whom the NAACP regarded as "anti-negro."

The term "white slavery" derives from the 1830s, when it implied that white workers as well as black chattel slaves were being exploited. But by the early years of the twentieth century, the term had a more specialized meaning, the exploitation of women in the sex trade. Whereas in France the response was a campaign to regulate brothels, in America there was a determined campaign to get rid of them. Public hygiene was a Progressive issue. This included the danger of venereal disease and of its spread by erring husbands to their innocent wives and children. But the media also circulated lurid stories about respectable young white girls being doped, raped, and trapped into debt peonage. Scaremongers ranted about debased morals and "pandering" pimps.

The social reformer Jane Addams pointed out that many prostitutes were "colored girls" imported from the American South. But the campaign against "white" slavery had become a populist bandwagon. In a widely reported address sanctioned by the attorney general, bureau chief Stanley Finch contributed to the campaign. He said the men and madams behind the vice trade could reduce "almost any woman or girl" to "merchandise." They referred to them as "meal tickets" and as "stock." Thirteen-year-old girls were being snatched from the American countryside. Twenty-five thousand women a year were being forced into brothels, he claimed.[7]

Congress had already passed several laws against the vice trade, most recently in 1907, but in 1909 a Supreme Court case, *Keller v. United States,* decreed that it was a violation of states' rights for the federal government thus to determine the nature of criminality within a state's borders. Ever the bastions of states' rights, the southern states opposed any extension of federal powers. Two factors, however, heralded a shift in emphasis. First, the anti-prostitution campaign reached its zenith in 1910 and showed no sign of abating in the short term; it had become politically imperative for Congress to legislate once again. Second, the characterization of prostitutes as property and of prostitution as a trade made it possible to represent the exploitation of women as "commerce." Section 8 of Article 1 of the U.S. Constitution gave Congress the power to "regulate commerce with foreign nations and among the several states." The interstate trade in women gave Congress a constitutional mandate to legislate anew. The Mann Act of 1910 prohibited the transportation of prostitutes across state lines.

Finch could see that the new law offered an opportunity. Aware of the constitutional issue, he gave the interstate commerce clause pride of place in his justification of action. He also cited the Thirteenth Amendment, barring "involuntary servitude." Yet, to begin with, the Bureau of Investigation took little action to enforce the Mann Act. Finch said that his bureau was underfunded, and he demanded more money. He said he needed legislation to empower his men to issue their own search warrants and to "arrest, without warrant."[8]

Political agitation over white slavery increased the chances of larger budgets, if not the wider powers Finch demanded. "American Purity Conference" meetings took place all over the country, and the women's franchise movement, already successful in the western states and on the eve of national triumph, threw its weight behind agitation for enforcement of the Mann Act. The government responded in April 1912. Attorney General Wickersham created a special commission on the slave traffic. He made Finch head of the commission at a substantially increased salary.

Finch's replacement as chief of the Bureau of Investigation was his deputy A. Bruce Bielaski. A minister's son, Bielaski was an athletic lawyer rumored to have been poached from the Bureau of Engraving and Printing in 1907 to bolster the Justice baseball team. A man who did his gardening before breakfast and had a powerful streak of morality, Bielaski complemented Finch, who was a stickler for proper procedures in federal investigations. The two officials combined their efforts in a war against vice. Special agents filed three reports on each case, two going to the bureau's headquarters in Washington, and the third to Finch's office in Baltimore.[9]

Exceptional circumstances had been behind the expansion in federal police power during Reconstruction, namely the depredations of the Klan and the exclusion of the objecting southern states from Congress. Now, in the Progressive era, another exceptional circumstance obtained, hysteria about sex. Few have doubted the importance of the Mann Act to the rise of the bureau. Max Lowenthal, author of a respected study of the FBI, thought it meant its transformation from "a modest agency concerned with the odds and ends of Federal law enforcement to a nationally recognized institution, with agents in every state." More recent historians have agreed with his verdict. Although federal investigation had had its roots in anti-Klan activity, Finch's bureau thrived on the same sexual-racial fears that had driven and still drove so many Klansmen and white lynchers.[10]

The bureau began to establish offices in most of the major cities, relying not just on full-time special agents but also on numerous part-time informants. Finch initiated the creation of a card index of all known prostitutes, establishing a precedent for later techniques of mass surveillance. Attorney General Wickersham as well as Finch saw in the demand for Mann enforcement an opportunity for greater appropriations. "We must have more money," they jointly told Congress in 1911.[11] The money did increase, rising to $400,000 in 1913 and $485,000 in 1915 (Table 2).

White slavery investigations accounted for fractionally less than one-third of the bureau's budget in 1913. But in February of that year Congress began to question the white slavery expenditures. Under threat of scrutiny, Finch resigned his position as the special commissioner on 1 January 1914. Effective the same date, his special division was reintegrated with the mainstream bureaucracy of the agency. Having served no useful purpose, the bureau's index of thirty-eight thousand prostitutes was scrapped.

Table 2. Growth of the Bureau of Investigation, 1911–16

Fiscal year	Appropriation[a]	Expenditure	Number of Agents
1911	$330,000		81
1912	$355,000		158
1913	$400,000	$414,772	335
1914	$475,000	$454,666	122
1915	$485,000	$480,464	219
1916	$510,000		234

[a]Appropriation figures include deficiency payments agreed to by Congress when budgets were exceeded for approved reasons. Thus, the original appropriation for 1911 was $290,000.

Sources: Noakes, "Enforcing Domestic Tranquility," 111–12; Belknap, "Uncooperative Federalism," 26; and Theoharis, The FBI: A Comprehensive Reference Guide, 4.

The drop in the number of agents between 1913 and 1914 reflected the end of a particular crusade, but this was only a temporary setback to bureau expansion. It is notable that expenditures rose even as the number of agents fell, suggesting that the Mann Act was not the only cause of growth. But the Mann Act and the crusade against prostitution did have another important impact. They helped shape the bureau's image and character.

The Jack Johnson episode illustrates this point, sending out as it did the message that the Justice Department was now an instrument of white supremacy. For Johnson had embodied a challenge to that supremacy. As he entered the ring in Sydney, Australia, with the Canadian world champion Tommy Burns in 1908, the titleholder informed him: "Boy, I'm gonna whip you good. I was born with boxing gloves on," to which Johnson offered the amplification, "I have news for you, white man. You're about to die the same way!" Jack London reported on the ensuing fight. "Men are not born equal," he concluded, "and neither are pugilists." Officials stopped the fight in the fourteenth round, making Johnson the victor.

London started agitating to bring back former world champion Jim Jeffries to "remove the golden smile from Jack Johnson's face." The man the press termed "the hope of the white race" agreed to a bout in Reno, Nevada, in 1910 and fought gamely, but he was no match for the great champion and succumbed to a knockout in the fifteenth round. Vengeful white men killed twelve black people in the ensuing riots. For fear of further violence, the movie of the great showdown was never distributed. In the short term, Johnson's 60 percent of the purse made him rich. He collected $120,000. But he was now a marked man.[12]

Johnson's sexual activities with numerous white women made him an even more hated figure, and proved to be his undoing. After a number of unsuccessful attempts, the bureau nailed him over his connection with Belle Schreiber. According to a bureau report from 1921 arguing against parole for Johnson, the boxer started his relationship with Schreiber in 1909, and it continued for three years in spite of the vicious beatings and callous treatment to which he subjected her. Schreiber testified against him, and in May 1913 he was convicted—not for beating her, but for transporting her across state lines for sexual commerce in contravention of the Mann Act. Bail was set at $30,000 pending sentencing. He fled the country. Secretary of State William Jennings Bryan cooperated with the bureau in attempting to secure his return to face sentencing. But Johnson remained abroad, where he traveled extensively. In 1915, he fought Jess Willard in Cuba and was knocked out in the twenty-sixth round, losing his world crown. Not until

1920 did Johnson return to his native land. He entered the States from Mexico, was arrested in California, and was then taken to Illinois, where he was sentenced to one year and a day in prison.[13]

Johnson's critics tended to ignore his physical maltreatment of women and concentrate on the fact that he was a black man having relationships with white lovers. A Detroit journalist, E. Pierpont Tennyson, complained to Taft about the hypocrisy of this. There were millions of mixed-race Americans who were born from the abuse of black women by white men, and in brothels the bosses were characteristically white men and the working women black. Perhaps, as Tennyson's remark suggests, white America's hostility toward Johnson was less to do with the nativist tide than with residual guilt over the multiple rape of black women under slavery. As black men increasingly migrated north to cities like Detroit and Chicago, that guilt generated fear of reciprocal conduct, and aggression. The fear was widespread. In the wake of the Johnson affair, anti-miscegenation bills were introduced in ten of the twenty states that still allowed interracial marriages. The expanding bureau rode on the crest of the wave of fear suggested by that statistic.[14]

Every single one of the anti-miscegenation bills introduced in 1913 was defeated, suggesting that the bureau could not rely on universal support for its expanding role in sexual-racial policing. It is significant, however, that the region where the Johnson trial and his 1912 marriage to "Sweet Lucille" Cameron stirred up the deepest emotions was the South. One of the milder comments came from the governor of South Carolina: "If we cannot protect our white women from black fiends, where is our boasted civilization?" Hitherto, the South had opposed the expansion of federal detective agencies, but the imperatives of racism were now reversed. The Johnson affair encouraged southern supremacists to support the Bureau of Investigation.[15]

Johnson's family charged that his trial was corrupt, with the attorneys on both sides trying to extort money from the accused in exchange for "protection." There is no proof of this, but the champion was justified in saying that his treatment amounted to a "frame up." Fundamental to American law and liberty is the constitutionally enshrined ex post facto principle, whereby you cannot charge someone under a law that was not yet on the statute books when the alleged offense took place. The bureau's own records indicate that Johnson's relationship with Schreiber started in 1909, before the passage of the Mann Act with its interstate provision. There are further indications of government conspiracy. The Mann Act was aimed not at individual transgressions but at organized commercial prostitution. Ninety-eight percent of the cases brought under the legislation were of this character. Johnson's sexual encounters were serial, but they did not constitute organized commerce. Further evidence of discrimination is the fact that, when he was sentenced, the Chicagoan was sent to Leavenworth Prison in Kansas instead of to nearby Joliet. Finally, in its supposedly objective report to the parole board in 1921, the bureau used subjective language and gratuitously accused Johnson of plotting to foment race riots in America while he was resident in Mexico. There is overwhelming evidence that Johnson was the victim of a government conspiracy. On the basis of this prominent case, it was all too apparent that Justice Department detectives, having once been the champions of black Americans, could now act as their ruthless and lawless oppressors.[16]

But the champ had been a soft target. When war broke out in Europe in August 1914, America confronted a real menace, the professional intelligence service of the world's leading military power. In the period of U.S. neutrality, a network of German and Austrian agents operated on American soil, engaging in operations that were sometimes legal, sometimes not. They secretly funded propaganda, attempting to buy up sections of the American press to break the British monopoly of war news. They encouraged and subsidized activists in the Indian and Irish nationalist movements who were trying to overthrow the British Empire from their secure bases in the United States. They organized strikes, sabotage, and bacteriological warfare aimed at disrupting the flow of supplies to Britain, and they planned to place bombs on merchant ships.[17]

Although theoretically neutral, the Wilson government cooperated with British intelligence, thus acquiring an ally against the various agents deployed by Colonel Walter Nicolai, head of the German secret service. But the administration still wanted resources of its own, first to take care of counterintelligence until America entered the war, and then, after the U.S. war declaration in April 1917, to handle both domestic and international intelligence and to try to establish an American independence from Britain's overweening and self-interested tutelage.

Fattened on easy pickings, the Bureau of Investigation was not up to this task. Its personnel were unequal to the cosmopolitan demands of a world war. Many of the people on its payroll, such as the part-time local agents it still used on white slavery cases, were amateurish. The bureau had no counterintelligence experience of its own. The government therefore relied first on the Secret Service, whose chief was now William J. Flynn. He had been in the service when it so efficiently mopped up Spain's Montreal spy ring during the war of 1898. Events would confirm the wisdom of the Wilson administration's faith in the experience and expertise of the Secret Service. Although German intelligence had much greater resources at its disposal than the Spanish spies had sixteen years earlier, barring some spectacular instances of sabotage Flynn's men proved to be effective counterspies.[18]

All of these developments put Attorney General Thomas W. Gregory under pressure. His bureau was larger than the Secret Service, yet less effective than it. Here, a cultural phenomenon may be noted. Apprised of hostile intelligence activity, a counterespionage agency may, to find out more in the interest of national security, let the enemy "run," leaving him free but keeping him under surveillance. But the bureau, in a manner consistent with its location in the Department of Justice and with the view that it should operate within legal constraints, had an "arrest culture." Wanting to make arrests, Gregory complained that he did not have the legal basis to pursue German agents who were trying to undermine American neutrality. This, he hinted, was why the bureau seemed relatively inactive.

A cynic might ask why Gregory was so particular of the rights of German spies that he demanded a legal basis for dealing with them, when his department ran roughshod over the rights of African Americans. Perhaps this was because the kaiser's secret agents were white? At the same time, though, the German agents were the emissaries of a great power that was at war, and not to be trifled with. To avoid gratuitous offense and to uphold the appearance of neutrality, the U.S. government had to proceed with circumspection and observe its own laws. To a certain extent, these laws did need strengthening. One foreign agent who was caught trying to blow up the international bridge between Maine and Canada, for example, had to be charged with nothing more serious than the transportation of explosives across state lines. Gregory's proposed "spy bill," backed by Wilson but defeated in Congress, set forth wide powers, ranging from the criminalization of the unauthorized release of defense information to the censorship of wireless messages and cablegrams.[19]

A rivalry had by now developed between the Justice Department's bureau and the Treasury Department's Secret Service. Bureau agents had from the outset been paid less than their Secret Service counterparts; for their part, Secret Service agents saw their budget being eroded by an organization they thought had lower professional standards. Secretary of the Treasury William McAdoo, a man with presidential ambitions and an appetite for power struggles, began to square up to Gregory, and their combined behavior was unconducive to the harmonization of domestic investigation.

Events soon forced the administration to take another look at its counterespionage capabilities. On 7 May 1915, a German submarine torpedoed the ocean liner *Lusitania,* with the loss of 1,200 lives, including 128 Americans. Wilson sent a note to Germany demanding cessation of submarine warfare. Secretary of State Bryan resigned in protest of the belligerency of the president's note and was replaced by Robert Lansing, a less peaceful official.

In July 1915, a further episode both whipped up more indignation and indicated a need for stronger U.S. counterintelligence. Frank Burke, another veteran of Secret Service counterintelligence in the Spanish-American War, was tailing Dr. Heinrich F. Albert, a senior German spy. Albert dozed off on the New York City elevated, and the quick-thinking secret agent made off with his briefcase. The briefcase contained details of Germany's secret plans for propaganda in the United States.

The Wilson administration leaked the contents of these documents to the press, allowing it to be thought that British intelligence had obtained the evidence. This misinformation hid from the Germans the operations of the Secret Service, and kept the American public unaware of the illegality and unneutrality of the snatch. Newspapers criticized the Bureau of Investigation for not having been aware of the German activities, and, in the inner circle of government, the bureau must have looked second-best, for Bielaski had had no inkling of the German plotting. Then, in September 1915, there came to the government's attention details of another snatch, this time by British intelligence and revealing Austrian plans to encourage walkouts in American munitions factories. Once again, the intrigue was entirely legal. No arrest was possible, and Gregory and his prosecution-oriented Bureau of Investigation were bypassed. As in the Albert case, Lansing had McAdoo turn the details over to the press.[20]

Lansing now decided that counterintelligence had to be reorganized. In a memorandum and covering letter to President Wilson dated 20 November 1915, he pointed to current shortcomings and poor coordination, not just between Justice and the Treasury, but involving also the army and navy departments. Because of the delicate nature of the business, the difficulty of distinguishing between matters that required prosecution and matters that required discretion, and the international repercussions of the whole problem, the State Department should be put in control. He proposed a centralized mechanism whereby intelligence from all sources would go to the second-most senior official at the State Department, the "counselor." Frank L. Polk had just succeeded Lansing himself in this post. Copies of central intelligence memoranda would be sent to both Treasury and Justice. The counselor would be given just two additional staff members, in anticipation that his job would be to "assign" tasks to the subordinate departments and agencies rather than perform the work himself.

According to this plan Ivy League men, the president and top State Department officials, would impose their authority on the law enforcers, whose law degrees usually came from less elite schools like George Washington University. Under the proposal, Justice and its Bureau of Investigation would be given official recognition as accredited players in the counterespionage game, but in a subordinate role.

With Wilson giving the plan his strongest support, Gregory could not oppose it, but he tried to channel the initiative in a way that would boost the authority of the Justice Department. Averse to the idea of written guidelines that might marginalize his department, he told the president the plan could be implemented without an executive order, giving as his reason the need to avoid publicity. Although Gregory convened a meeting of relevant officials who approved the Lansing plan, he still attempted to assert his superior standing by saying he had "delegated" a man to speak to Counselor Polk. If the Bureau of Investigation did not end up at the center of the new American intelligence system, it was not for lack of effort by the attorney general.[21]

As the war emergency intensified, the bureau collected new powers and more money. Gregory approached Congress with a view to broadening the authority it had given the Justice Department in the Reconstruction appropriations statute of 1871. And an event now took place that convinced observers in Congress and beyond of the need for increased vigilance in matters of national security.

Black Tom was an island in New York Harbor linked to Jersey City, New Jersey, by a causeway, and it was used as part of a munitions storage complex. Freight cars lined up on the island and its adjacent areas groaned under the weight of high explosives and ammunition destined for Britain and France. In the early hours of 30 July 1916, an explosion, loud enough to be heard in several states, ripped through the depot. It devastated the local area. Windows shattered all over Manhattan. Up to seven people died, and many more suffered injuries. The nearby Statue of Liberty sustained serious damage.

Suspicion fell on the German secret service, and it is evident in retrospect that Captain Franz von Rintelen and then Friedrich Hinsch did organize sabotage attacks all over North America to prevent strategic supplies from reaching Germany's enemies. But Chief Bielaski at first reported that the explosion appeared to be an accident, and although he initiated inquiries his bureau made no progress in identifying suspects. Like the explosion on the battleship *Maine* that helped precipitate the war of 1898, the Black Tom detonation may indeed have been simply a mishap. But at the time, the blast did encourage people to believe that America's counterintelligence arrangements were inadequate.

An amendment to the appropriation law for the fiscal year beginning 1 July 1916 now allowed the Justice Department "to conduct such other investigations regarding official matters under the control of the Department of Justice or the Department of State, as may be directed by the Attorney General." The understanding was that the bureau could in future investigate noncriminal matters if authorized to do so by the secretary of state, an innovation that made possible political work, the activity that had scared Theodore Roosevelt's critics in the previous decade and that would be vehemently attacked in future decades. The bureau now undertook the compilation of a new type of list, data on 480,000 enemy aliens aged over fourteen and resident in the United States. As soon as America entered the war, Congress approved a $100,000 deficiency payment to the bureau to pay for its new responsibilities and extra agents.

At this point, the bureau rounded up pro-Germans it regarded as dangerous. Bielaski's men also obliged their British friends by swooping on members of the Indian nationalist party, Gadar. The speed and efficiency with which they did so indicated heavy prior surveillance and reflected cooperation with British intelligence, at a time when the nation was ostensibly neutral. Thus, a further group of nonwhite people had been targeted by Justice operations, though in this case the Department of State bore chief responsibility for a tactic that helped alienate the colonized millions of Asia from the United States.[22]

In April 1917, with President Wilson bidding to make the world "safe for democracy," the United States declared war on Germany. Lansing now made a further plea for coordination. He argued that, to be effective, domestic and foreign intelligence should be assessed together. It was now McAdoo's turn to bid for supremacy. He wrote to Wilson recommending a new, coordinating "Bureau of Intelligence." It could be located in either the

State or the Treasury Departments, but, as Counselor Polk would doubtless be busy with foreign intelligence now that America was at war, it would make more sense to choose Treasury.

But Secretary of State Lansing, in his letter to the president, had already given his views on this matter. Because of what Lansing portrayed as a bitter rivalry between the bureau and the Secret Service—he complained that both would give information to State but not to each other—it would be unwise to entrust either Flynn or Bielaski with the coordinating role. His own men would have to remain in charge: "The central office of secret information of all sorts should be in the State Department." But "domestic work" should still be harmonized, and he recommended that a new official, someone other than Bielaski or Flynn, should take this on.[23]

President Wilson allowed State Department coordination to continue, but he refrained from appointing a domestic investigative chief. Whether such a tsar would have been able and willing to exercise a restraining influence is a matter for speculation, but certainly in his absence the bureau expanded in controversial ways. American entry into the war released an enthusiastic bellicosity. New legislation by Congress led to a large expansion in the bureau's pseudo-police activities. The Selective Service Act of May 1917 made it mandatory for young men to register for military service and to carry draft cards. The "slackers" who did not want to serve became objects of public wrath. The American Protective League (APL), a voluntary vigilante-style organization, offered to help the bureau in rounding up alleged evaders. Bielaski recruited 250,000 APL volunteers to help identify and gather evidence on suspects, and local police forces acting in tandem with the bureau made mass arrests. In just three days in early September 1918, the police detained about 75,000 men in New York City alone. The operations were amateurish and had a low yield. Only one in 200 of those detained proved to be a draft evader. But the APL volunteers were proud of their functions and their official badges, and a body of support had been created for future bureau activities.

The Espionage Act of June 1917 was less draconian than its British equivalent, the Official Secrets Act of 1911, but it nevertheless created further scope for bureau expansion. The law made it illegal to oppose the draft and other wartime policies. A number of amendments, forced through against congressional opposition and codified in the Sedition Act of 1918, essentially made it illegal to criticize the government, especially in its prosecution of the war. This proscription exposed African Americans to surveillance and persecution. For although black soldiers had fought for the

United States in every war, questions were being asked in the black community about the appropriateness of a war for "democracy" and "self-determination" when those blessings were being withheld from nonwhites at home. There were no successful German attempts to exploit black discontent, but rumors of black pro-Germanism abounded, and bureau agents were gullible enough to believe them. African American leaders were persecuted not just directly but through neglect. In particular, the impression of the bureau's racial partisanship was confirmed in the aftermath of the East St. Louis race riot of July 1917, when white terrorists killed at least thirty-nine black people and destroyed many African American homes. The bureau made no attempt to investigate this carnage.[24]

The bureau was similarly discriminatory in its treatment of the American Left. When war loomed in Europe in 1914, American socialists shared the opinion of their comrades on the continent, that the conflict was the result of capitalist competition, and working people from all nations should unite to oppose it. But their European comrades deserted the anti-militarist principles of international socialism and supported the war efforts of their national governments. Facing a quandary in the years of American neutrality, the two main U.S. socialist groups, the Socialist Party of America and the Industrial Workers of the World (IWW), finally left it to individual members to decide whether to support the war effort. This produced a mixed response, but by that time it had become all too easy to assert an equivalence between socialism and treason.

A significant number of businessmen seized the opportunity to discredit all labor militants by associating them with unpatriotic tendencies. Not contenting themselves with private vigilante activities against the IWW in the west, businessmen solicited the help of the government. Forgetting the "Square Deal" approach of Theodore Roosevelt, the bureau availed itself of the opportunity to serve the employers' cause, and unleashed its "dragnet inquiry" tactics on the IWW. On the morning of 5 September 1917, its agents led raids on IWW offices and private homes in sixty-four cities, confiscating all records and office equipment in their path and creating the suspicion that their motive was not so much national security as the destruction of American radicalism. According to one estimate, by the end of World War I about half of the bureau's investigations were into political dissent.[25]

Bureau officials had identified a means of capturing popular, not just business, support. Characteristically, they compiled lists of undesirable people, prostitutes, enemy aliens, socialists, and slackers. The creation of the lists gave an impression of busy and efficient activity, even if they were actually inaccurate. They provided the means whereby less reflective members of society could focus on scapegoats for the nation's real or perceived ills, and gave such people a reason to support the bureau.

Congress rewarded the bureau's populist tactics with increased budgets, and consequently a growth in personnel. Appropriations for the bureau rose to more than $1 million in 1918, and to more than $2.7 million in 1920; by the time the United States entered the war in 1917 the bureau had more than 250 agents, and with the Red Scare fully under way in 1920 there were close to 600 (Table 3). The growth was steady, demonstrating that neither the war nor the Red Scare alone accounted for it. Rather, the bureau's leaders had discovered how to milk both the American psyche and the political climate. The Secret Service resigned itself to an involuntary back seat—or at least that was how newspapers interpreted Flynn's resignation as its chief in September 1918. As things turned out, however, he became head of the Bureau of Investigation after Congress finally held Bielaski to account for the excesses of his slacker raids, forcing him to resign in February 1919. Flynn's acquiescence in the move was one more sign that the Justice Department's bureau was now the nation's major investigative agency.[26]

With the end of the war in November 1918, the Feds lost no time in keeping themselves relevant by moving into anti-radical work. In some respects, the Red Scare was a continuation of Progressivism by other means. One of the currents in prewar Progressivism had been the introduction of

Table 3. Growth of the Bureau of Investigation, 1917–20

Fiscal year	Appropriation[a]	Number of Agents
1917	$635,000	265
1918	$1,101,486	225
1919	$2,350,000	301
1920	$2,725,000	579

[a]Appropriation figures include deficiency payments agreed to by Congress when budgets were exceeded for approved reasons.

Sources: Noakes, "Enforcing Domestic Tranquility," 171, and Theoharis, The FBI: A Comprehensive Reference Guide, 4. Where there are discrepancies between the Noakes and Theoharis figures, the former figures are used because Noakes gives a source, the Digest of Appropriations for the Support of the Government of the United States (Washington: GPO, 1900–1930).

social reforms meant to preempt the rise of socialism in America. In 1919–20, Progressives saw an opportunity to harness wartime patriotism to achieve the same goal, now labeling socialism a violent foreign import, with a view to crushing it once and for all. The Bureau of Investigation, a Progressive creation par excellence, seemed the perfect instrument for pursuing this aim. In other respects, though, the Red Scare was a turning away from reform, and the start of a new era of intolerance. The bureau had already deviated from its civil rights mission and was now in danger of being swept along in the reactionary tide.

By 1919, Russian communists were two years into their own revolution and poised to proselytize the rest of the world, America included. At the time, it was possible to think that the United States might be fertile territory. Painful postwar economic readjustment was taking place, and a wave of unrest swept the nation. There were race riots, major stoppages in the coal and steel industries, a general strike in Seattle, and a police walkout in Boston. In the same year, anarchists launched a bombing campaign. Although they were the political enemies of the communists, the anarchists' activities contributed to the perception that a dangerous, hydra-headed radicalism was loose in America. On 2 June, one of the anarchist bombs exploded outside the home of A. Mitchell Palmer, the attorney general. Palmer had been associated with the prewar campaign to end child labor, and was by 1919 a defeat-socialism-by-other-means Progressive. At the same time, he was angling for the Democratic nomination for the presidency. H. L. Mencken observed of Palmer that he was one of a number of politicians who aimed to become "eminent by trying to get . . . victims into jail."

Flynn had already announced a plan to investigate radicals. On 1 August, helped by an additional $100,000 appropriation, he set up a Radical Division, soon renamed the General Intelligence Division (GID). He put a twenty-four-year-old attorney in charge. This was the start of the long career of J. Edgar Hoover. The result was yet another index card list. Hoover was Progressive efficiency personified, and his men compiled 200,000 dossiers. Those considered undesirable were deported. They included some of the best-known figures on the American Left, such as the Lithuanian-born anarchist and contraception advocate Emma Goldman.

Another feature of the GID's work was its surveillance of black radicals. Palmer was convinced that Marcus Garvey's black-pride Universal Negro Improvement Association was a dangerous organization, while Hoover believed that black Americans were flirting with Bolshevism. A black informer, the educator and social reformer Dr. Arthur U. Craig, reported to

Hoover on the activities of Garvey's followers. Additionally, the bureau hired, for the first time in its decade-old history, a black special agent. James W. Jones was a veteran of the war in France, and he investigated the Garveyites until his resignation from the bureau in 1923.

A further wave of arrests, known as the Palmer raids, took place in early January 1920. At first they were popular, and Palmer's presidential hopes must have soared. But questions began to be asked about the legal basis of his actions. The enabling legislation had lapsed at the end of the war, and Flynn had acted in anticipation of the enactment of federal sedition statutes that never materialized. The Logan Act of 1799, the product of an earlier anti-radical scare, was still on the books but could not be used. It did prohibit unauthorized political correspondence with a foreign power, and American communists did exchange letters with Moscow, but they could not be prosecuted because the United States had not recognized the Bolshevik regime, so in American legal terms it did not exist.

In its haste to secure results, the Justice Department had not only acted on spurious grounds but also ignored habeas corpus rights and the right to legal representation. Louis F. Post, the veteran of the anti-Klan campaign of the 1870s in South Carolina and by now assistant secretary of labor, launched an investigation that thoroughly discredited these tactics. Congressional friends of the bureau tried to impeach the former Reconstruction activist, but their attempt backfired. The Red Scare was becoming passé, and public opinion swung to Post's side. Fleet of political foot, Hoover wound down his anti-radical activities, leaving the slower-paced Palmer to flounder in his own mess and ponder the ruins of his political prospects.[27]

The bureau's experience with the Red Scare was important in three ways. First, anti-communism had emerged as a breadwinning gambit that could be deployed whenever the climate was right. Just as the scare had kept appropriations high, so its decline led to a reduction in financial support, from $2,725,000 in fiscal year 1920 to $2 million in 1922. The causal link was plain, and an invitation to future opportunism. Flynn, Hoover, and William J. Burns, the bureau's boss from August 1921 to May 1924, were no doubt genuinely opposed to the Left. For such officials, however, anti-communism was primarily good business. Burns revealed his attitude when trying to convince the House Appropriations Committee of the persistence of the communist threat in 1922: "Radical activities have increased wonderfully."[28]

Second, the Red Scare experience underlined the significance of states' rights sentiment as a brake on the bureau's powers. In the absence of federal anti-radical legislation of a type that would give it legal authority, the Justice Department encouraged state legislators to pass their own sedition laws. The plan was that the bureau would investigate cases, and then cooperate with local law enforcers in securing arrests and convictions. The locals, however, were inclined to be suspicious of the government men.

In one case, Francis A. Morrow, a bureau infiltrator, betrayed the secret plans for a communist meeting in the town of Bridgeman, Michigan. Morrow, or agent K-97, was himself arrested and then led the police and bureau agents to a cache of communist documents hidden in two cracker barrels. The trouble was, though, that local officials felt Washington was bossing them around. A further consideration was that local taxpayers in Michigan and elsewhere had to pick up the tab for the prosecution in cases they saw as having been federal initiatives. This was why the seventeen radicals arrested along with Morrow were never prosecuted. Local resistance meant that lack of constitutionally legitimized legal authority continued to be a problem for the bureau. The absence of such federal authority was one of the factors that induced bureau personnel to undertake irregular missions and ignore due process of law.[29]

The third significant aspect of the bureau's involvement in the Red Scare was its surveillance of those who opposed its own actions and government policy. Hoover pressed his agents across the nation to try to find evidence linking Assistant Secretary Post to the communists or the IWW. The lawyer Felix Frankfurter also came under investigation for trying to defend the legal rights of some of those detained on the bureau's initiative. The bureau spied on black activists, and had files on the peace advocate Jane Addams. There were similar files on prominent politicians, including Senator Robert M. La Follette, the Progressive Republican and war critic from Wisconsin.

Congress had warned against the federal surveillance of politicians in 1908, but because of the corrupt habits of some of its members it had spoken with a weakened voice. In a more robust political climate, the bureau's dubious tactics were sure to attract criticism. They not only endangered civil liberties but also enfeebled the legitimate opposition to communism. Anti-communism was to acquire a bad name in America, and the bureau was partly responsible for that.[30]

In the early 1920s, the bureau, already in other ways removed from the ideals of its founders, became mired in corruption. In a reversal of roles, Congress decided to investigate the bureau's connections with graft. Per-

haps it was inevitable that the scandals of the Warren G. Harding administration (1921–23) would rub off on the bureau, especially as Harding's
attorney general was Harry Daugherty, an official who was eventually acquitted on fraud charges but failed to distance himself from the stench of
public larceny.

When Flynn resigned as bureau chief in 1921, Daugherty appointed
William J. Burns in his place. The first head of the bureau to style himself
"Director," Burns was a larger-than-life personality who did much to color
the style and reputation of the agency. He had been a private eye before joining the Secret Service in 1891. With the service, he demonstrated his capabilities in several cases, ranging from counterespionage in 1898 to the western land frauds and the indictment for corruption of Abraham Ruef, the
city boss of San Francisco. Then, in 1909, he set up his own private detective
agency.

Because the Pinkerton agency had largely withdrawn from the industrial relations scene since its involvement in the Homestead affair in 1892,
Burns soon became one of America's main strikebreakers, supplying "detectives" to infiltrate unions and serve as armed guards. With an eye to publicity and to impressing employers, he set out to detect the perpetrators of
an explosion that took place in 1910 next to the headquarters of the anti-
union *Los Angeles Times*. The blast had ignited the ink supplies, killing
twenty people. Exhibiting scant regard for the truth, he claimed that both
the bridgeworkers' union leader John J. McNamara and American Federation of Labor president Samuel Gompers were involved in the deaths, and
that Gompers was out to assassinate him. In fact, although McNamara confessed to having used dynamite in his union's dispute with the National
Erectors' Association, he was never convicted of the Los Angeles Times
Building murders. As for Gompers, he was a law-abiding man. The conviction of McNamara on a serious criminal charge was never enough for
Burns. He insisted that the conservative Catholic labor leader and his
brother James were out to promote a "great and bloody war between labor
and capital."

Equally controversial was Burns's involvement in the Leo Frank affair.
In a sensational trial in Atlanta, Frank had been found guilty of the murder
of a fourteen-year-old girl. The trial was unfair and notable for its anti-
Semitic overtones. In 1914, Burns asserted Leo Frank's innocence, advancing
evidence that showed another man had committed the crime. Frank went
free, but he then fell victim to a lynch mob, a fate that almost overtook his
vindicator, too. According to his admirers, Burns had shown acumen and

courage, but his critics thought he had played loose with the evidence, bullied his opponents, and exploited the case to publicize his agency.[31]

Burns had come to regard himself as the nation's greatest detective. He was the subject of obsequious commentaries, including *The Exposure of the Land Swindlers,* a movie by Keannan Buel from 1913 starring the sleuth in person. He communed with Sherlock Holmes's creator, Sir Arthur Conan Doyle, who on one occasion posed in a Burns family photograph, hands-on-shoulders with Burns's two sons. But although Burns was an operator who expected even the White House to yield to his demands for patronage, he had made enemies. In 1917, when the William J. Burns agency license came up for renewal in the state of New York, the Pinkerton agency lodged a very hostile objection.

The Pinkertons alleged that Burns was crooked and ruthless. He illegally tapped telephones, intimidated witnesses, and was especially reprehensible in his divorce work. This last was a damaging charge, as the Burns Agency, like most detective outfits, asserted its respectability by denying that it accepted divorce cases. But men from the jealous Pinkerton Agency had been shadowing their rivals and had affidavits to the contrary. One sworn statement by a former employee asserted that an infirm husband had hired Burns detectives to tail his wife while she was having an affair with the Duke of Mecklenburg. She grew suspicious, so she hired her own Burns man to follow the Burns man who was watching her, so the agency "was handling both sides of the case."[32]

The man who took over the bureau in 1921 exhibited several of the tendencies that came to be associated with the darker side of the FBI. However, he was still an inveterate detective. He could not resist a challenge, such as that presented in 1922 by the emergence of evidence allegedly confirming the thesis in Finis Langdon Bates's book from 1907, *The Escape and Suicide of John Wilkes Booth.* Burns launched an investigation that continued into the 1970s. Successive analyses of Booth's left boot and diary in the FBI's case file amount to a mini-history of the development of forensic science. Burns's statement that Bates's "work contains very strong evidence in support of the old belief that Booth did escape and live many years after the assassination of Abraham Lincoln" shows his continuing interest in conspiracy theories, especially of the publicity-creating variety.

Although Burns may be faulted in some areas, he showed a determination to deliver racial fair play that went beyond the Leo Frank case. His bureau moved against the Ku Klux Klan, which had been revived in 1915 and by the 1920s was bullying and murdering its way across not just the South but the nation as a whole, targeting blacks, political opponents, women accused of loose behavior, bootleggers, Catholics, and others who offended its moral and ethnic precepts. Senator David Walsh (D-Mass.) protested to Attorney General Daugherty that there was a criminal conspiracy to deprive citizens of their civil rights contrary to the federal penal code.

Daugherty parried with the observation, "I have no jurisdiction." But Burns's bureau found a way around this. It moved against one of the Klan's top officials under the terms of the Mann Act. On 1 March 1923, the Klan's acting imperial wizard Edward Y. Clarke was indicted for having transported Laurel Martin from Louisiana to Texas, thus across state lines, for immoral purposes. He was convicted and fined in March 1924. In the following year, Indiana's influential Klan boss David Stephenson was imprisoned on rape and murder charges. The reincarnated Klan had been discredited, and it declined through the remainder of the decade.

The events in Louisiana show that the bureau was still determined to fight white terrorism, even if it had succumbed to prejudice in other ways. This dichotomy, wherein it both enforced the law and upheld white racial supremacy, was to become embedded in the ethos of the FBI. It was important to J. Edgar Hoover, who had become assistant director of the bureau in 1921 and succeeded Burns three years later. By the end of the 1920s, Hoover had launched further offensives against the Klan, in Boston and Kansas, for example. But he remained especially fond of recalling his role in the arrest of Klansman Clarke, especially when he came under attack for being hostile to blacks.[33]

The tenure of William J. Burns as Bureau of Investigation director gave America a long glimpse of a born detective. He overshadowed Hoover, who became a dominant personality only in the next decade. He set up a training school for special agents, an innovation that his successor later developed. Burns gave his assistant director an object lesson in how to publicize an agency. But Burns's injection of private-enterprise boosterism into the bureau's affairs came at a cost. He allowed the bureau to become enmeshed in corruption and scandal.

Burns was the architect of his own downfall, and of a slump in the bureau's standing. When he took over the bureau, he made Gaston B. Means a special agent. Means had previously worked for the Burns private detective agency. In a case of playing both sides, he had spied for the Germans while his boss worked for British intelligence. At the bureau, he worked closely with the director on dubious assignments that included spying on Democratic and Progressive critics of the administration. He even arranged for

Senator La Follette's office to be ransacked. Testifying before a congressional committee and then at his trial, Means again tried to put his own interest first by making copious confessions. These focused on the Teapot Dome scandal.

In 1922, Secretary of the Interior Albert B. Fall leased U.S. Navy oil reserves located in Teapot Dome, Wyoming, to private developers Harry F. Sinclair and Edward L. Doheny, in exchange for a bribe of $400,000. When the story emerged and the Senate mounted an inquiry, Daugherty, on the good ole boy principle, refused to hand over Justice Department documents to the congressional investigators. Burns's agents subsequently began investigating not the crime but Daugherty's critics, in an attempt to gag them. This was the reason for the Means-inspired break-in at La Follette's office. Senator Smith W. Brookhart said the objective of such surveillance was "government by blackmail." Clumsy attempts by bureau agents to intimidate newspaper editors produced a backlash, and Daugherty and Burns were forced to resign. Back in charge of his private agency, the unrepentant Burns had his men shadow jury members when Sinclair went on trial. This story hit the newsstands and reminded Americans how William J. Burns had sunk the bureau into a petty venality.[34]

By 1924, the brave new bureau of 1909 had lost its mission. To some extent, the decline may be traced to personalities, notably to Burns and his injection into the public sphere of the ethos of the private detective. But to make scapegoats of individuals is to tell an incomplete story. The decline of the bureau reflected wider tendencies in American society. The imperatives of sex and racism were significant modifiers of the context in which the bureau operated.

On a drier but still significant note, the bureau's mission loss reflected its lack of legislative authorization. The Secret Service had run into that problem prior to 1909. The Mann Act of 1910 and the Harrison Act of 1914 (prohibiting the nonmedical sale of addictive drugs) gave the bureau incipient authority to act, but did not furnish the basis of permanent large-scale operations. World War I legislation authorized more bureau work, but only temporarily. The Volstead Act of 1919, banning the sale and distribution of alcohol, created additional opportunities for organized crime, and thus created work for the bureau by the 1930s, but not before. The Dyer Act, also from 1919, gave it the authority to trace automobile thieves who drove stolen vehicles across state lines, and with the boom in auto production this function became important and the bureau did an impressive job. But this was an exception. In general, the lack of enabling legislation was an open invitation to undertake irregular activities, and to invoke populist sentiment to make sure that the bureau's infringements of civil liberties were overlooked.

For reasons only partly to do with personality, the bureau had already reached a nadir by the time J. Edgar Hoover took over as director.

5

the first age of reform: 1924–1939

The years 1924–39 were a time of reform for the Bureau of Investigation. The period opened with an attorney general's principled ban on the bureau's political surveillance activities. Next came a raft of legislation widening its criminal investigative responsibilities. Meanwhile, a determined effort was taking place to improve the bureau's administrative practices and to upgrade its crime-fighting technologies. Finally, the reform era closed with the Justice Department's creation of a permanent civil rights unit.

The reputation of the times is, however, rather different. Those critical of the FBI and its director J. Edgar Hoover find it difficult to adjust to the possibility that the bureau may have enjoyed something approximating a golden age. Those enamored of the bureau and its director similarly allow thrilling yarns and personality to distract them from some of the era's more important achievements. In both cases, the allure of the war on gangsterism has been a distraction, and that has been for two reasons. One is the eternal attraction of man-to-man combat, the other the determination of Hoover to publicize his personal showdown with the American mobster.

Macabre events can be perversely attractive, as was the case on two occasions when Hoover engineered his own publicity. The first stemmed from an ambush in Florida, where, on 16 January 1935, FBI agents shot dead a sixty-year-old woman, Kate—better known as "Ma"—Barker. They had finally located her because she and the other fugitives the bureau had been tracking were engaged in a conspicuous sport: dragging live pigs behind speedboats across a lake, and machine-gunning the alligators that attacked them.

At the conclusion of the incident in which Kate Barker expired, her son

Fred also lay dead in the luxury cabin where they had made their last stand. He had stopped twelve bullets. Upstairs, the weapon cradled in Ma Barker's arms was still hot as agent Tom McDade photographed the bodies. It was a Model 21 Thompson submachine gun with a 100-shot drum. The Ma Barker gang had been enlivening the middle west with a series of kidnappings, bank robberies, and murders. But the killing of Ma and Fred Barker did not remove the menace, for a dangerous gang member remained at large.

Alvin "Creepy" Karpis had quite a record as a professional gangster. His practice of kidnapping and bank robbery had been punctuated by a term in prison, three further arrests, and as many escapes. He had killed three people in a Minneapolis bank heist, and had murdered a sheriff in West Plains, Missouri. On 30 April 1936, J. Edgar Hoover flew to New Orleans. The FBI had learned that Karpis and a confederate were staying in an apartment on Canal Street. The director and his men surrounded the building and prepared for a siege. Suddenly, Karpis and one of his associates emerged from the building, strolled across the street, and got into an automobile. The FBI men made their arrest.

Hoover's presence at the scene had been carefully orchestrated. It was part of the director's policy to build up his own image, and in the process he focused the attention of friend and foe alike on one particular type of activity. The director was again present for the apprehension of Louis "Lepke" Buchalter. Lepke ran a protection racket in the New York City garment industry, and he presided over the nationwide elimination service known as Murder, Inc. The New York State attorney general Thomas Dewey had had Lepke indicted on charges that could result in the death penalty. The mobster went into hiding, but the authorities turned on the "Big Heat," police harassment of his acquaintances, to prevent him from finding any safe haven.

Pressured and knowing that the Feds also wanted him on narcotics charges that carried a lesser sentence, Lepke arranged to surrender to the FBI. He arrived at a prearranged rendezvous with Hoover on Fifth Avenue at 10:15 p.m. on 24 August 1939. Hoover climbed into his car. Lepke said he was glad to meet him. His relief turned out to be premature, however, for after his conviction on federal charges the government turned him over to be tried in New York State, for murder. He was electrocuted in 1944.

The Karpis and Buchalter arrests mesmerized those who pondered the career of J. Edgar Hoover. To his admirers, they epitomized Hoover's efficiency, his attention to detail, his flair, and his success in destroying gangsterism in its heartland at the height of its power. On the other side, Hoover's detractors tried to deflate his image by noting that Treasury agents had located Karpis, that Hoover did not personally step into the line of fire to capture him, and that both the Karpis and the Buchalter arrests were stage managed in a way designed to shine favorable publicity on the FBI director without exposing him to danger. Skeptics noted that at the time of the Karpis arrest, Kenneth McKellar, chairman of the Senate subcommittee on Justice Department appropriations, had been dragging his feet on budgetary matters and criticizing Hoover for not taking a more direct role in the arrest of hoodlums. The publicity helped the director obtain the appropriations he had asked for—and that only increased the cynicism of Hoover's critics.[1]

The varying interpretations are part of a wider debate about Hoover and crime. To his admirers, Hoover was a genius at detection, at organization, and at that publicity that is so necessary to congressional appropriations. Ranging from the authors Courtney Ryley Cooper in the 1930s to Bryan Burrough in the twenty-first century, such supporters have portrayed Hoover as the true founder of the FBI.[2]

To his critics, Hoover was American democracy's heart of darkness. Here, they said, was a man with an overdeveloped liking for power. He tolerated racial abuse in return for cooperation from southern police forces. According to their indictment, Hoover was a hypocrite who kept ultrasecret files on homosexuals while enjoying a close emotional relationship with his male colleague Clyde Tolson. He engaged in political surveillance, undermined civil liberties, and damaged the principles of free speech and the right to protest. As for his crusade for law enforcement in the 1930s, critics dismissed it as a publicity stunt. There simply was no crime wave. Just like the director's fan club, they fell into the personality trap, and allowed themselves to be distracted by Hoover's manufactured image.

In confronting America's gangsters and pricking the bubble of the Robin Hood myth, Hoover did perform a public service. The spectacle of a government agency terminating major criminality boosted national confidence in a potentially divisive era. But, to arrive at a more balanced appraisal, it is necessary to look beyond the publicity barrage that accompanied those events. Here, the contribution of three attorneys general was vital. Their efforts, to an even greater extent than Hoover's, help to identify the 1924–39 period as an age of reform.

Harlan Fiske Stone was attorney general from April 1924 to March the following year. He joined President Calvin Coolidge's administration having just served a brief period with a prestigious Wall Street law firm. Before that, he had been dean of the Columbia University law school, and, as would be confirmed after his appointment to the Supreme Court in 1928, he was a supporter of strong central government and of the federal role in protecting the rights of African Americans. But Stone recognized that strong government and corruption are a bad mix. He forced William J. Burns to resign as director of the Bureau of Investigation.

Claiming Britain's Scotland Yard as his model, Stone demanded that the bureau's agents should be educated and intelligent "gentlemen" with proper respect for the law, and that they should undergo training. He believed that public servants should be nonpartisan and that the bureau should keep out of politics. "I have always regarded any secret police system at its best a necessary evil, and one to be kept strictly under control and to be limited in its activities to the support of the legitimate purposes of a Government law office," he said.

Stone appointed J. Edgar Hoover as the new director of the bureau. He thought the twenty-nine-year-old would implement his ideals. On 13 May 1924, the attorney general gave expression to these in a notable reform directive: The bureau would be purged of unreliable personnel, and future recruits would have to be of good character and have legal training. Most significantly, the agency would henceforth restrict itself to the investigation of crimes. The bureau dropped its political investigations of organizations like the United Mine Workers of America, the NAACP, and the Women's League for Peace and Freedom. Hoover continued to file informants' reports on such matters, but he explained that this was just a passive activity undertaken "for intelligence purposes."[3]

The Stone initiative was to a certain degree undermined in the next administration, that of the Republican Herbert Hoover, 1929–33. Confronted with the horror of the stock-market crash of 1929 and the ensuing economic depression, President Hoover decided it would undermine business confidence for the federal government to take a proactive role in the economy or in the governance of American society. In the all-important economic sphere, he left poverty relief to local government. Consistent with this approach, his administration shied away from a federal assault on crime.

In 1929–31, George W. Wickersham chaired a federal commission investigating crime. Though remembered as the attorney general who had used federal authority to enforce the Mann Act, Wickersham no longer envisaged a key role for the Bureau of Investigation. His commission did expose malpractices that undermined confidence in local policing, especially the use of "third-degree" interrogations. As an example of this type of questioning, it cited the practice of suspending suspects by their ankles from upper-story windows. Alternatively, the "Chicago telephone book is a heavy one and a swinging blow with it may stun a man without leaving a mark." Wickersham's investigators found that the police used such methods of procuring information and confessions in ten of the fifteen cities they visited. Yet, in spite of such evidence, the Wickersham commission refrained from recommending federal solutions.[4]

The Herbert Hoover administration failed to inspire respect for its localist policy on law and order. It did not address the causes of crime, and it was powerless to enforce the Volstead Act that was supposed to give effect to Prohibition (mercifully for the bureau, that problem was outside its jurisdiction). Held back by the parochial conservatism of his namesake, Edgar Hoover concentrated on preparing the bureau for the greater role he hoped it would enjoy in the future.

Within weeks of his appointment, Edgar Hoover stamped his authority on the bureau by reorganizing its Washington office. He reasserted its primacy over the field offices in different parts of the nation. At the same time, he urged that field offices cultivate good relations with local police forces. This was no easy task, and it is estimated that his success rate was no higher than 50 percent, but he persisted in his efforts to achieve federalism via diplomacy for the remainder of his career. The professionalization of the bureau's workforce was another of the director's declared aims. Stone had called for this reform. Hoover's hiring policies would prove controversial, but he did attempt to create a special culture. In 1927, bureau agents received their first handbook, containing rules of conduct.

Hoover insisted on a conservative dress code, and also on marital fidelity. The handbook promised "summary dismissal" for any agent caught drinking, and stipulated that any obscene material should be placed in a sealed container. In other efforts to improve the quality of his men, Hoover demanded legal training (most recruits from then on were lawyers) and developed the training courses introduced by Burns. In 1935, this effort culminated in the creation of the FBI National Police Academy.

The 1927 handbook cautioned agents to understand their limited role, with one section headed "Power of Arrest, Lack of." Another section told agents to avoid political activities. In this period of circumspection, Hoover also displayed another form of caution. The handbook explained that guns would be issued only in emergencies: "It is not desired that each Agent shall carry arms as a general practice." Hoover continued until the early 1930s to make known his personal reservations about the bureau becoming a tough-guy cop as distinct from an investigative agency, and he advocated gun control: "What excuse can there possibly be for permitting the sale of machine guns?"[5]

When Franklin D. Roosevelt became president in 1933, there was a move to supplant Hoover, a Republican appointee, and replace him with the private detective Val O'Farrell. Protective of states' rights and mindful of Hoover's operations against the Klan, a bloc of southern senators led the campaign for his dismissal, and Roosevelt needed the votes of these Democrats for his New Deal policies. But O'Farrell was a professional strike-breaker, and his appointment at a time of strained labor-capital relations would have been a political risk. Stone urged Hoover's reappointment and, when FDR complied, it seemed to further the former attorney general's aspiration for the bureau to be above politics. However, Hoover's reappointment came at a price. As part of the deal with the objecting senators, the director released almost one-third of his agents, around one hundred men, all of them Republicans. In violation of his usual insistence on high professional standards, he allowed southern Democrats to nominate the replacements. Hoover's force was now open to the charge of being governed by Dixie prejudices, and the director's own racial conservatism only increased suspicions. In an effort to counteract any sectional bias, he circulated his special agents throughout the nation to give them a national perspective.[6]

Hoover encouraged improvements in the techniques of crime detection. In 1932, he created a technical laboratory with capabilities in such specialties as fiber analysis, paint-type detection, ballistics, chemical analysis of bloodstains, and moulage (the reproduction of wounded body parts for display in court cases). Special agent Charles Appel pressed for the bureau to assume central control of criminological inquiry. A typical demonstration of his skills came in early November 1933. Harrington Fitzgerald, Jr., a patient in a veterans' hospital, had opened a Christmas present early, and died after consuming the apparent treat. His sister, Sarah Hobart, fell under suspicion, but the handwriting on the note inside the chocolate box did not match hers. Appel, however, matched the typing on the package label with samples of typing from a typewriter that Mrs. Hobart had tried to conceal.

Keen on administrative reform, Hoover responded when, in 1930, Congress authorized the bureau to collect criminal statistics. Soon, a new system of "uniform crime reporting" identified categories that would make up the nation's major crime index: murder, rape, robbery, serious assault, larceny, burglary, and auto theft. Aiming to improve criminal identification, Hoover established control over all national fingerprinting files. It should be acknowledged that his effort at file centralization took forward a practice that had started in the nineteenth century and progressed under Burns. In fact, some of Hoover's reforms smacked more of boosterism than originality. The organism known as the Crime Records Division released carefully managed statistics and doubled as the bureau's publicity department. Even the National Police Academy was a means of promoting FBI prestige and control.[7]

One of Stone's injunctions had been the reduction in the number of bureau personnel to the lowest level permitted by the effective performance of its duties. In Hoover's reports, bureau officials took pains to show that their organization was cost-effective. They tabulated the sums that the bureau "returned to Treasury" every year from 1925 to 1932, a period when the agency underspent its congressional appropriation by a total of more than $700,000. The reports showed a decline between 1928 and 1932 in the per diem and travel expenses of agents.

But while Hoover trumpeted his efficiency, he was also an expansionist. He was interested in absorbing the Secret Service, and in 1939 he forwarded the attorney general a memorandum supporting the idea that the FBI should take over the Immigration and Naturalization Service, which did become a Justice Department responsibility the following year. Meanwhile, the number of special agents remained fairly stable at just under four hundred from 1925 to 1934, and then climbed steadily to the end of the decade, with expenditures also hovering consistently in the region of $2–3 million until the mid-1930s, and then rising.[8]

Such figures suggest that Hoover was in this period a medium-successful bureaucrat. His agency held its ground when others were in decline. The Military Intelligence Division's personnel slumped from ninety in 1922 to a low of sixty-six in 1936. In the 1920s there had developed a postwar reaction against the business of espionage. In 1927, the State Department gave up its central coordination of foreign and domestic spying. In 1929, Secretary of State Henry Stimson disbanded the American Black Chamber, a government code-breaking unit. The story that he did so on the lofty principle that "gentlemen" do not snoop on each others' mail is apocryphal. After all, Stimson had been upset when Congress tried to clip the Secret Service's investigative wings in 1908, and in World War II he played a proactive role in espionage. But, in the interwar years, the tide did seem to be running against undercover activities. Considered in this context, the bureau did not do too badly. To be sure, the bureau's annual budget remained modest compared with certain New Deal expenditures—notably, the $5 billion given to the Works Progress Administration (WPA) in 1933. It is also true that FDR slapped down some of Hoover's appropriations requests. But, by comparison with his peers in the government investigation business, Hoover held his own.[9]

In 1931, at a time when the economic depression was deepening and the unemployment rate was already 15.9 percent, the Yugoslav socialist immigrant and popular journalist Louis Adamic published his book *Dynamite: The Story of Class Violence in America*. Here, he contended that the racketeering of the Al Capone era was "a phase of class conflict." If ever the time seemed ripe for proletarian revolution in America, it was during the deep social suffering of the early 1930s. The potential political repercussions were considerable. High-profile gangsterism would be especially embarrassing to the new Democratic administration that began in 1933. To the government's left-wing critics, armed robbery could be represented as the cry of the poor and oppressed; to more conservative commentators, any passivity in the face of organized crime offered a welcome opportunity to attack the softness of the liberals now installed in the seat of national power.

One dramatic event after another had underlined the political dilemma. On 1 March 1932, unemployed carpenter Bruno Richard Hauptmann kidnapped the baby son of Charles A. Lindbergh, the aviator who, aboard the *Spirit of St. Louis*, had completed the first-ever transatlantic flight in 1927. The local police made no progress with the case. President Roosevelt ordered the bureau to coordinate the investigation, and Congress ensured that it would have jurisdiction in future cases by passing an act, known as the Lindbergh law, that made kidnapping across state lines a federal offense. The family paid the ransom, the boy was murdered anyway, and then the bureau got its man. In June 1932, after Charles Appel had analyzed the handwriting of three hundred suspects and found a match with the writing on the ransom notes, Hauptmann was arrested. There were complaints about hysteria at the trial, and about tampering with witness evidence, but the Appel analysis held up and the kidnapper went to the chair.

Meantime, the nation's gangsters continued their flagrant lawlessness. In a notorious episode in June 1933, at the railroad station in Kansas City, within sight of a line of unemployed men, Charles "Pretty Boy" Floyd and two associates tried to liberate Frank Nash from the guards who were escorting him to Leavenworth federal penitentiary. At the end of the shootout, one bureau agent and two local policemen lay dead, as did Nash himself, still chained to one of his captors.

The Kansas City shootings justified and inspired bolder federal tactics. The next month, "Government men" apprehended another kidnapper, George "Machine Gun" Kelly, in Memphis, Tennessee. According to FBI mythology, the cornered Kelly called out, "Don't shoot, G-men!" True or not, it gave the Feds a charismatic new name. The time seemed ripe to reverse what had amounted to a media glamorization of crime, with gangsterism portrayed as a reproach to a failed economic system, and the gangster elevated to a cult figure in *Little Caesar* (1930) and dozens of similar movies.

FDR went on to deplore the tendency of journalists to "romanticize" bank robbers, and threw his weight behind the FBI. His new attorney general, Homer S. Cummings, denounced racketeers as terrorists. Cummings, the second of the era's three reforming attorneys general, was a Chicago-born, Yale-educated lawyer who had served as a reforming mayor of Stamford, Connecticut, and as chairman of the Democratic National Committee. During his tenure at Justice, 1933–39, he was a stalwart of the New Deal, guiding Roosevelt through his fight with the Supreme Court in 1936. He had well-developed views on law enforcement.

In a radio broadcast in September 1933, Cummings emphasized that President Roosevelt was "deeply interested" in the problem, and said that the public should take comfort from the fact that America had the best police in the world. In a further broadcast two months later, Cummings called for a "war on crime." He insisted it was wrong to glorify criminals. The lawless should no longer be allowed to exploit the "twilight zone" between state and federal jurisdictions. But Cummings also advanced a softer line. The "environment" was responsible for much criminal misconduct; crime was a "social question," and "prevention" was "even more important than punishment." His suggestion that the new, social-reforming administration would be tough on the causes of crime as well as on the criminals must have reassured many New Deal supporters. The hand on the tiller at a critical phase of FBI's development was, then, that of a federalist, environmentalist liberal.[10]

In his book *Federal Justice*, Cummings acknowledged that there were "sordid chapters and many unhappy and unflattering incidents in the history of federal justice," arguing that it had "followed the main currents of American life." But he also gave the first documented account of Attorney

General Amos Akerman's war on the Klan in the 1870s. Its nonjudgmental tone differentiated his work from the redemptionist writings that had so clouded the historiography of the postbellum South. His narrative is evidence that the thin thread of memory linking the FBI to a reputable past was still intact. It confirmed that Cummings supported strong federal initiatives in the context of the 1930s.[11]

In an address to the American Bar Association in August 1933, Cummings said that local government was failing in its battle against crime, and that the Department of Justice was receiving demands that it advance federal solutions to problems like racketeering and kidnapping. Since the colonial era, in fact "from time immemorial," there had been opposition to the "centralization of power." But the theory of government now lagged behind modern developments. Business organization, air transportation, radio broadcasting, and the movies had had a nationalizing influence, making a "town meeting of America." Crime, too, was now broadly organized, and this required a proportionate response from the federal government. Unlike Stone, Cummings rejected the British model of policing. America, he explained on NBC radio, was different because it was so big, and this dictated an American solution, the integration of federal and local resources. Speaking in North Carolina in 1936, the attorney general denied he was an opponent of states' rights, tactfully claiming that all he asked for was cooperation. His intentions, however, were plainly nationalist.[12]

In 1934, Cummings pressed on with his law enforcement and FBI reform plans. It was at this point that Hoover, contributing to the get-tough approach, introduced the Public Enemy Number One concept. This was akin to the Wild West technique of posters proclaiming, "Wanted: Dead or Alive." The campaign was a reaction to depictions of the gangster as a kind of glorious reincarnation of the western gunslinger, notoriously, for example, in the movie *The Public Enemy* from 1931, in which James Cagney had charismatically portrayed a character in the Chicago gang wars. The idea was to reverse the image.

In 1934, there were various candidates to be the first Public Enemy Number One. The bank robbers Clyde Barrow and Bonnie Parker were shot dead in May, trying to drive through a police posse near Sailes, Louisiana. That left John Dillinger, who had robbed ten banks and killed a policeman. His confederate Harry Pierpont explained that "banks steal from the people," but public sympathy for such sentiments was evaporating. Dillinger escaped from prison in 1934 but, in making his getaway in a stolen sheriff's car, crossed a state line, giving the FBI jurisdiction under the Dyer Act. On

April 22, a bureau ambush in Little Bohemia, Wisconsin, failed, with one agent left dead. Cummings instructed the bureau to "shoot to kill." On 22 July, three agents challenged the killer outside an East Chicago movie theater. Dillinger reached for his Colt revolver one last time, and too slowly. The G-men shot him dead.[13]

The Public Enemy Number One idea had a nationalizing impact, drawing the country together in a manner that was supportive of federal anti-crime initiatives. The Dillinger drama publicized the need for reform just as Cummings was making his proposals. One of these involved the establishment of a new, island-fortress prison to house the "public enemies" convicted of serious crimes. The former military prison on Alcatraz, in San Francisco Bay, served this function from 1934 to its closing in 1963.

On 19 April 1934, Cummings announced a package of measures leading to the enactment of twenty-one laws. They defined and created a range of interstate crimes, including new racketeering offenses, over which the bureau would have jurisdiction; they gave agents the powers to carry guns and make arrests; they provided for still closer federal-local cooperation and established an Interstate Commission on Crime; they tightened the rules on personnel selection, "professionalizing the service."[14]

In the afterglow of the Dillinger episode, Cummings called a conference to publicize his program. He thus started a public relations juggernaut favoring law and order. The government acquired new images, and the bureau a new and highly effective name. In 1932, the Bureau of Investigation had been rebranded the United States Bureau of Investigation. Then in 1933 "Division of Investigation" became the official designation, even if it was rarely used in public discourse. On 1 July 1935 the organization acquired its modern title, the Federal Bureau of Investigation, or FBI.

That same year, the Warner Brothers movie *G-Men* appeared. In this film, Cagney acted as the same type of tough guy he had in *Public Enemy,* but this time on the other side of the law. He was now a brash, college-educated, machine-gun-toting FBI agent, an action hero who had trouble with his rules-obsessed boss and with his neglected girlfriend. In one respect, at least, he represented a real change in the FBI. A six-page section on firearms in its 1936 manual noted that the "bureau is supplied with the most modern and best equipment procurable," including Thompson submachine guns. Special agents were instructed to keep them clean, and to practice shooting regularly.

Hoover cemented the FBI's relationship with the moviemakers and took pains to keep the media sympathetic. He reached out to opinion makers by delivering public addresses. In a departure from Cummings's more liberal approach, he warned Women's Clubs in 1938 not to be beguiled by the American female's "zealous desire to live upon a higher plane than has currently existed." For it was "not necessary to coddle our prisoners, as is too often done, to reform them." Cannily, he noted in another address that year that although crime was receiving great publicity, it should be recognized that it was an eternal and ineradicable problem. Clearly, he was aware of the danger of raising public expectations and then being unable to satisfy them. Nevertheless, he went on to warn against the danger of becoming "philosophical" about crime: "When crime or a disregard for law and order attains definite proportions, the state itself deteriorates." His shrewdly calibrated message was that continuing the effort against crime mattered as much as the success or otherwise of crime busting.[15]

Hoover went on the stump to inspire sympathy for his agents and their activities. He told a group of businessmen in Tulsa, Oklahoma, in 1939 that twelve FBI men had "joined their fellows where the rattle of machine gun fire is unknown." He was looking after their families, and seven of the widows had desk jobs at the FBI. All G-men were dedicated to the public cause. Even when they were not being shot on duty, they were suffering impairment of their health through overwork. Investing his special agents with an aura of martyrdom, he urged his listeners to support the bureau. His appeal to America's heart was more than an ego trip. Hoover aimed to inspire sympathy in juries who would vote to convict in federal trials, and to obtain more powers and a larger budget from the people's representatives in Congress.[16]

A snapshot of FBI activities in 1939 shows the bureau reflecting Hoover's confident leadership. In January, the director celebrated the opening of the tenth session of the FBI National Police Academy, noted the booming demand for places, and announced that its eleventh and twelfth sessions would meet in May and July. In May, Hoover reported to the attorney general that John Torrio, languishing in a federal penitentiary after surviving a feud with Al Capone, was speaking of an assistant U.S. district attorney in New York who could be "reached" by members of the criminal fraternity. His report suggests that the FBI was attempting to penetrate the recesses of judicial corruption. In August, Hoover showed his concern for federal-local relations and his flair for publicity by asking the attorney general to attend the FBI's baseball game with the Baltimore Police Department, a "friendly rivalry" fixture that had taken place for several years. Should he accept, there would be a police escort through the city of Baltimore. The FBI was starting to behave like royalty.[17]

This air of confidence was one of several factors that made 1939 a turning point in the legal history of race relations. Earlier in the decade, there had been unpromising signals on this issue. Federal inaction had been conspicuous in a case in Scottsboro, Alabama. In an unfair trial, a group of black boys and young men were convicted of the rape, in 1931, of two white girls on board a Chattanooga-to-Memphis freight train on which all concerned were traveling illegally. The brutal punishment of the innocent convicts became an international cause célèbre, but the federal government did not act. In 1934, white terrorists kidnapped another imprisoned black man, Claude Neal, from an Alabama jail, tortured him, and hanged him in Florida. But the Department of Justice again took no action, citing the technicality that the kidnappers had demanded no ransom. Then in 1937, a southern filibuster defeated the latest congressional attempt to make lynching a federal crime. Time, it seemed, was standing still.

Yet there were signs of a change in the legal climate. Attorney General Cummings knew that the Justice Department had been formed to fight white terrorism. Stimulated by the growth of black participation in the legal profession, lawyers were searching for grounds on which the federal authorities could take action. After a double lynching in 1933 facilitated by the presence of an Alabama sheriff, for example, the NAACP's Charles Hamilton Houston argued that, under the Fourteenth Amendment and the Reconstruction Enforcement Acts, the federal government could step in when a state engaged in racially discriminatory action, as indicated in this case by the sheriff's participation. The Department of Justice was cautious about such arguments to begin with, but a new judicial wind was beginning to blow.[18]

President Roosevelt's wife, Eleanor, openly campaigned for racial justice. Her husband took a more political approach, but here, too, developments were taking place. Badly hit by the depression, the South had benefited more than other regions from his New Deal policies, and this engendered electoral loyalty to Roosevelt. Thus, he could at least consider taking the risk of helping the black citizen. Meanwhile, African Americans who had moved north in the Great Migration had become an electoral bloc worth cultivating, and they had already in the 1936 election begun to desert the party of Lincoln for the Democratic standard. These domestic pressures for a change in racial policy occurred before 1939; after that, they were supplemented by international pressures, first the need to articulate a case for tolerant democracy against the racism of the Nazis, and then the need to appeal to the emerging nations of Africa and Asia in face of Soviet propaganda that emphasized racism in the United States.

In January 1939, FDR's appointment of Frank F. Murphy to replace Cummings marked a change in approach. The third attorney general to reform the FBI's mission, Murphy was a Michigan politician of some standing. As governor of his state, he had mediated in the 1937 sitdown strike at the General Motors plant in Detroit, showing a regard for the rights of organized labor that augured well for his approach to civil liberties in general. He had helped bring about the 1934 agreement that led to the independence of a nonwhite nation, the Philippines. His track record of supporting the NAACP moved African American leaders to greet his appointment with enthusiasm. Like Stone, Murphy spent only a short time in his post before becoming an associate justice of the Supreme Court (in January 1940). In a further similarity with his predecessor, he used his few months at Justice to effect a significant change.

On 3 February 1939, there came into being in the Justice Department a civil rights unit, renamed the civil rights section in 1941 and gaining the status of a division in 1957. At twelve lawyers and three assistants, the size of the unit was modest. But it had the backing of the president, and it was potent enough to raise reactionary hackles. One Mississippi congressman said it was a "Gestapo for the persecution of white people throughout the South." Murphy set the unit the task of scouring the statute books for laws authorizing federal action, and lawyers pored once again over the Reconstruction statutes, especially the Civil Rights Act of 1866 and the Enforcement Act of 1870.

Government lawyers now accepted the course advocated by Charles Houston. They also revived arguments put forward in 1904 by Thomas Goode Jones in *Ex Parte Riggins*. A federal judge for the northern district of Alabama who had fought for the Confederacy, Jones had at a time of great racial tension successfully urged an all-white grand jury to indict members of a lynch mob that had burned the Huntsville jail in order to kidnap and lynch a black man, Horace Maples. When the lynchers appealed on the basis that their habeas corpus rights had been infringed, Jones wrote an opinion justifying his action, arguing that the Fourteenth Amendment required equal treatment by the states, so there was a right of federal intervention when that equal treatment was not forthcoming at the state level. When Attorney General Bonaparte presented the case to the Supreme Court in

United States v. Robert Powell (1908), the justices of that era had been un-sympathetic, but the Jones argument remained useful for future civil rights lawyers, who were by the 1940s hopeful of a change of heart.[19]

The real impact of the civil rights unit, however, was more on attitudes than on outcomes. At first, to be sure, Murphy's FBI seemed destined to take a proactive role. In the summer months of 1939, the FBI busied itself with cases that seemed to have no obvious interstate dimension, suggesting that there would now be vigorous federal intervention. In June, for example, Hoover reported to Murphy on a rape case in Arlington, Virginia. Six black men had defiled at knifepoint six white girls aged fifteen to seventeen. Two of the girls had contracted gonorrhea, and a third was thought to be preg-nant. Not surprisingly, perhaps, the bureau had made no progress in the case, but at least it had investigated. In August, the press in Buffalo, New York, found out about a planned FBI raid on the local brothels and plas-tered the news on the front pages, causing the surprise operation to be aborted. Again, this appeared to be a case with no obvious interstate dimen-sions, even if it ended in failure.[20]

Another series of events in 1939 suggests that, in certain circumstances, the FBI was capable of taking the part of African Americans. It stemmed from Murphy's response to a rash of strikes on Works Progress Administra-tion projects. The WPA provided employment through public works schemes, airport construction, hospitals, schools, and so forth, for millions of workers who found themselves out of a job because of the depression. In spite of its support for labor union rights as a general principle, the Roo-sevelt administration's view was that WPA workers should consider them-selves fortunate to be earning at all, and should accept modest conditions of employment. The renewed WPA act for 1939 required 130 hours of work per month; it set payment rates for skilled laborers at seventy cents an hour, well below union rates.

Union objections led WPA workers to go on strike against the WPA Sewing Project in Minneapolis–St. Paul, Minnesota, on 5 June 1939. There was fighting on the picket line, and on 10 July a policeman was killed. Two days later, the project reopened under police protection, and further rioting occurred. Murphy now declared his position: there should be no "strikes against the government."[21]

In response to local demands that his bureau "clean up [the] Min-neapolis WPA mess," J. Edgar Hoover stated that "the sole function of the Federal Bureau of Investigation inquiry at Minneapolis into the WPA strike situation is investigative and is to determine whether any federal statutes making intimidation of WPA workers a criminal offense have been violated." However, on the same day he reported to Murphy in tones that betrayed his own attitude and, perhaps, told the attorney general what Hoover thought he wanted to hear. The director's memorandum was about another WPA strike, this time at the scene of the notorious 1917 race riot, East St. Louis.

Hoover said the "WPA workers want to go back to work," but he meant black workers especially. For the local WPA director had warned of "serious difficulty anticipated Monday when colored will make attempt to return to work. Communists and others not employed on WPA causing major portion of trouble." In 1939, then, Hoover conceived of a situation where communists would stir up *white* workers. He expected black citizens to be loyal American employees.

This might be taken to indicate that the New Deal FBI was benign in its attitude toward African Americans, confirming that the Roosevelt administration was more favorably disposed to black citizens than is sometimes supposed. The historian Nancy Weiss analyzed bureau files on the NAACP and other black organizations, and concluded that Hoover and the FBI took no action against black radicals until they began to suspect communist infiltration of the African American movement in the 1940s—they "virtually ignored racial matters before 1941."

The picture was not quite that rosy. Before the arrival of Hoover, the bureau had persecuted Jack Johnson. Hoover had complained in 1919 that some African Americans were "seeing Red." He then secured the imprisonment (in 1923) and the deportation (in 1927) of the Jamaican-born back-to-Africa promoter Marcus Garvey. Black Americans had enjoyed only a relative respite from the attentions of the FBI. A more realistic claim might be that, between the creation of the civil rights unit in 1939 and the arrival of new paranoia in 1941, American justice allowed black Americans their first glimpse of the sun since Reconstruction.[22]

However, even in the immediate aftermath of Murphy's reform, there were grounds for pessimism. The civil rights unit's first chief, Henry Schweinhaut, directed U.S. attorneys' attention to the need to enforce Fourteenth Amendment rights, but, in mid-1940, the Justice Department faced a significant challenge to this policy in the case *United States v. Sutherland*. W. F. Sutherland was a policeman in Atlanta, Georgia, with a history of brutal behavior toward black suspects. When he burned a sixteen-year-old African American with a hot iron in order to extract a burglary confession, a local judge ruled that he had violated the boy's Fourteenth Amendment rights. Sutherland lodged in his defense an assertion of good character, and the local U.S. district attorney, R. W. Martin, asked the FBI to secure evidence of general brutality by the Atlanta Police Department.

Hoover objected to this request, saying it would disrupt the friendly relations between the FBI and the Atlanta police. Southern politicians lent their support, insisting that the protection of civil liberties was a matter for the several states, not the federal government. Deputy Attorney General Matthew McGuire concurred: "It is questionable whether a right not to be beaten is secured by any provision of the Constitution or any Federal Statute. It is secured by State laws." Were the FBI to investigate, McGuire observed, it would impair the federal-local cooperation on which effective law enforcement depended. In the absence of evidence, a mistrial was declared.

Martin now used his own resources to obtain witness statements on Sutherland's beatings of black suspects, but wartime dislocation was given as a reason for trial postponement, and the prosecution was dropped in 1944. As in the *Ex Parte Riggins* case and with the same principle involved, a courageous southern attorney had been let down, but this time by the Department of Justice itself, not the Supreme Court.

When the United States went to war against an Asian nation, Japan, it faced a new challenge. Allied to Britain and its potentially rebellious colonies, particularly in Africa, America had to try to demonstrate racial tolerance at home. This would test anew the principles behind the civil rights unit.

In January 1942, a white mob in Sikeston, Missouri, killed Cleo Wright, the first lynching since Pearl Harbor. Murphy's successor as attorney general, Francis Biddle, assigned the FBI to the case. Yet again, the finding was that no federal offense had occurred.[23]

Appreciating the urgency of the matter, Roosevelt directed the Justice Department automatically to investigate "in all cases of Negro deaths where the suspicion of lynching is present." The new chief of the civil rights section asserted a "Federal right not to be lynched." Some investigations did take place, but again results did not match the hopes of civil rights advocates.

As World War gave way to Cold War, the disappointing results continued. One setback followed a lynching episode in Monroe, Georgia, in July 1946. A mob of twenty white men murdered four blacks, and the FBI was asked to investigate with a view to turning over evidence to the local police. Hoover was under pressure because of the hue and cry in the press at a time when the future of the FBI and the rest of the security/intelligence community was under debate. Should the FBI fail to deliver, it would appear to be ineffective at doing its job.

Hoover showed that he was troubled by his bureau's failure to make headway. He worried that the government had been "completely ineffective" at investigating lynching and that the bureau might therefore lose "prestige." His frustration and concern confirm that the civil rights unit, while relatively ineffective at achieving results, was at least influencing attitudes.[24]

The historian must try to gauge the significance of the 1939 reform, not just for the FBI, but also for the history of race relations. In terms of FBI history, it confirms the durability of that thread of memory going back to the Justice Department's war on the Klan in the 1870s. In terms of the reform's impact on 1940s race relations, the picture is suggestive of several possibilities. Once the FBI renewed its work in the field, the Justice Department was deluged with complaints about its inadequacy, evidence of disappointment, but also of rising expectations. And it is possible that the bureau and the lawyers at the back of it had after all sent a message to southern policemen. The local U.S. attorney thought the *Sutherland* case "had a wholesome effect on the Atlanta Police Department."[25]

The argument can be made that federal intervention produced a deterrent to the violent persecution of African Americans. Noting that the annual rate of lynching had declined to single figures by the 1940s, the historian Adam Fairclough suggested that this was because of federal intervention, or the fear of it, with the civil rights unit and the FBI playing a significant role. It is very possible that the FBI's renewed efforts contributed to a mood of confidence among southern black people, and ultimately to the civil rights activities of the 1950s.

Certainly, the nation accepted the greater degree of federal policing arranged in the New Deal reforms. Writing in 1950, the constitutional authority Edward S. Corwin even claimed that the 1930s federalization of the law on such matters as racketeering and kidnapping had shifted the balance of power in America, and that the Supreme Court had "definitely discarded" the Tenth Amendment doctrine of reserved powers.

But the South moved in its own way, and for its own reasons. The presence of Democratic presidents in the White House and the enactment of legislation favorable to the welfare of the region softened the stridency of the region's states' rights pleas. The South had always maintained that it could solve its own race relations without interference from Washington. Less embattled than at any time since the antebellum days, it had begun to find a new voice, for example through the work of the Association of South-ern Women for the Prevention of Lynching, which in the 1930s launched a crucial attack on the myth that lynchers were defending the honor of white women. One student of the decline in white terror, Gail Williams O'Brien, has noted the effect of post-1945 prosperity and geographic mobility on southern communities—instead of turning inward and keeping silent about atrocities, they began to laugh at the posturing men in white robes. If the FBI contributed to social change after 1939, it also reflected it.[26]

It may be concluded that the FBI underwent three types of reform in the years 1924–39. Attorney General Stone's clampdown on political work would be tested time and again in the ensuing decades, but it did lay down a marker. The drama of the challenge to Ma Barker and her kind should not distract from a second significant reform, a widening of the bureau's com-petence backed by enabling legislation. Finally, the formation of the civil rights unit institutionalized the bureau's war on white terrorism. Hoover's FBI was reluctant to employ African Americans as agents and would soon start harassing black militants, but at least it took an unequivocal stand against murder.

6

counterespionage and control:
1938–1945

World War II was a time of profound change for the FBI. It received a renewed mandate in the counterespionage field. The director immersed himself in bureaucratic power struggles, and attempted to dominate the U.S. intelligence community. He acquired a Latin American empire, and seemed well positioned to expand his role with the return of peace. Hoover might even have succeeded in gaining wartime intelligence preeminence for the FBI but for his profound misinterpretation of President Roosevelt's intentions.

The counterespionage story began thousands of miles away in the Scottish city of Dundee, where a local postman, or "postie," demonstrated the virtues of an inquiring nature. One of the postie's clients was a fifty-one-year-old hairdresser, Jessie Jordan. Described by a local journalist as "a small and full-figured blonde," Mrs. Jordan was a puzzle to the postie. She had told her landlady that her mother lived in Canada. Some of her mail did arrive from there, but the postie could think of no reason why she should also be receiving letters and parcels from France, Holland, South America, and the United States. With Stalinist spy trials in full swing in the Soviet Union and espionage scares sweeping the nation, he was alert to the possibilities. In July 1937, he reported Mrs. Jordan as suspicious.

MI5 moved in. The British counterintelligence agency found that Mrs. Jordan was the widow of a German soldier who had been killed in World War I. She had made frequent trips to Germany, where she met top Nazi officials. It further established that her address was a mail drop. She was working for German military intelligence, the Abwehr.

The British authorities did not immediately arrest Mrs. Jordan. However, they decided to warn the U.S. War Department of an impending plot, for some of the letters passing through the Dundee mail drop came from a person in New York City who identified himself as "Crown." The letters indicated that Crown and his confederates were planning to lure to a room in the MacAlpin Hotel on Broadway an unsuspecting army colonel, in circumstances where he would be carrying the nation's East Coast defense plans. There, agents of the German secret service would overpower him, steal the plans, and leave behind a trail of false clues indicating that communists were behind the plot.

On 30 January 1938, the case was turned over to Leon G. Turrou, an agent in the FBI's New York field office. Born in Poland, Turrou spoke several languages. Perhaps it was this cosmopolitan background that moved him to say "the British have a real intelligence service; America has virtually none." He noted that British intelligence had the "decided advantage" of being able to open people's mail. Turrou constructed a profile of Crown: a man who was fluent in English and German, who had served in the U.S. Army, and who was chronically short of money. On 24 February 1938, the New York police arrested a man they suspected of trying to steal blank passports. Turrou interrogated him, and found that he matched his profile.

It was now time for the Dundee police to make their move. On 2 March they arrested Mrs. Jordan under her other name, Jessie Wallace. In company with Colonel Hinchley Cooke from the War Office, they searched her premises and the cellar and drains beneath, seized a number of documents, placed her in a car, drove her around the nearby region of Fife, stopping at the naval base at Rosyth, and then returned her to a prison cell in Dundee. She was found to have made sketches of military installations and was charged under the Official Secrets Act of 1911, which made such sketching a crime where the intention was to assist a potential enemy. She appeared in court for one minute, "attired in a smart black coat with fur collar and a little green hat adorned with a feather," and looking "pale and anxious." Nine days later she made a further, four-minute court appearance to be charged under a 1920 law with failing to register with the Post Office as a forwarder of mail. For the local reporter who was following these events, the trail now went cold. The suspect was removed to Edinburgh, where she was tried in camera at the High Court and received a four-year prison sentence.

Back in New York, Turrou's prisoner turned out to be Guenther Gustave Rumrich, an Austrian-American U.S. Army deserter. Under interrogation, Rumrich confessed to being "Crown," and to being the man behind the defense plans plot. That plot had never come to fruition, but Rumrich was evidently someone to take seriously. The "Rumrich" spy ring, so called in spite of the fact that Rumrich was a minor cog in it, was, in fact, ambitious. Rear Admiral Wilhelm Canaris had taken over the Abwehr in 1935 and reinvigorated foreign intelligence. American-based German secret agents sent Canaris's office a stream of information, for example the blueprints for a wide range of military aircraft, military cartographic secrets, naval construction plans, and secret details of U.S. radio devices. The German intent was not necessarily hostile: Hitler was still in transit from his 1928 view that Americans were "a young racially select people" to his 1938 opinion that the USA was "a Jewish rubbish heap." Rather, the Germans were interested in U.S. technology and wanted to steal it. Still, by any standards, this was serious, offensive espionage.

Hoover accepted the job of hunting down the other members of the spy ring, but with a degree of reluctance. His hesitation is understandable, as the case had been compromised: the press had publicized Rumrich's arrest, and it could be assumed that the bigger birds had flown.

Undeterred, Turrou pressed on with his inquiries. Revealing again their penchant for hairdressers, German intelligence had recruited the services as courier of Johanna Hofmann, an attractive young assistant who worked in the beauty salon of the transatlantic steamer *Europa*. Acting on information supplied by Rumrich, Turrou arrested Hofmann when the *Europa* docked in New York, and she revealed under interrogation the name of the true master of the Rumrich spy ring. He was Dr. Ignatz T. Griebl, who had served as an artillery officer in the German army in World War I and then studied medicine at New York's Fordham University.

At first, Dr. Griebl held out under interrogation, but Turrou discovered inside a matchbook belonging to him a secret code Hofmann was known to use. Griebl now confessed. In all, eighteen members of the spy ring were indicted.

At this point, newspaper publicity combined with poor coordination by the American authorities ruined the outcome, allowing most of the spies to escape. Even Dr. Griebl was let out on bail. He duly slipped his FBI tail and embarked for Europe on the steamer *Bremen*. Only four members of the ring were brought to trial, none of them a major figure. Turrou resigned from the bureau, and then tried to sell his own story to the press.

This earned him presidential censure, but the Rumrich episode did help to persuade President Roosevelt that America needed a stronger counterespionage provision. It highlighted an immediate national security problem, and sparked a debate that has reverberated since. Poor coordination suggested a need for centralization, prompting questions about government power and who in the intelligence bureaucracy should wield it. Did government power inevitably mean more initiatives taken by the White House, or would Congress and the courts be involved? In Roosevelt's third term, government by "executive order" and "presidential directive" became commonplace, generating a long-running controversy. The Roosevelt administration is sometimes seen as having originated a "national security state."[1]

Further issues also arose. Out of counterintelligence grew the practice that critics of the FBI and its predecessors had always dreaded, political surveillance. Was such surveillance little more than a wise precaution in light of the threats to American security posed by the rise of fascism, or did unscrupulous politicians and a compliant FBI seize on the international emergency as a pretext for the advancement of an intrusive domestic agenda? Not stopping there, did FDR and the FBI plan to extend their political hegemony to Latin America?

But these questions lay in the future. In the late 1930s, Hoover must have seemed unstoppable. The FBI's ascendancy is apparent from the outcome of a meeting early in the evening of Wednesday, 2 November 1938. At FDR's bidding, the director had boarded the presidential train at Pennsylvania Station, New York, just after its arrival from Washington. The ever-artful president had not informed Hoover of the agenda for their meeting, but he suddenly launched into the matter of counterespionage funding. He intimated that military intelligence would receive $50,000 for this purpose, naval intelligence a similar amount, and the FBI $150,000. There was no mention of the Secret Service.

The chief executive in this way gave the FBI primacy in counterespionage fully three years before America entered World War II. The following April, Attorney General Murphy pressed the FBI's claim to continuing support. Refuting Nazi claims that soaring American crime rates were evidence of social decomposition, he asserted that the FBI was doing a great job. In similar booster style, Hoover told a House appropriations subcommittee that his agency's counterespionage work had escalated dramatically, from an average of 35 cases per annum before 1938 to 634 in that year, and even more in 1939. Congress responded by doubling the counterespionage appropriation proposed by Roosevelt.[2]

In September 1939, Hoover and Murphy set forth the FBI's claim to support. Hoover warned that "forces alien to American peace and democracy are seeking to burrow deep into our social order" and insisted that "these exponents of foreign isms have no moral right to bite the hand that feeds them." Murphy acknowledged that the FBI's fight against communism and fascism involved the use of secret methods that laid it open to the charge of undermining the values it purported to defend. But, anticipating Cold War rhetoric, he warned that although openness and constitutionalism may have been the bedrock of American liberty, they also laid America open to enemy penetration. In cherishing equal rights and justice for all, "we have known that . . . we were giving the enemies of democracy a perfect field of operation."[3]

At least in the short run, the campaign succeeded. Roosevelt reaffirmed his backing for the FBI's authority on a number of occasions. In June 1939, for example, he told relevant cabinet members that he was instructing the FBI "to take charge of investigative work in matters relating to espionage, sabotage, and violations of neutrality regulations."

Roosevelt's pro-FBI stance provoked potentially formidable opposition. The Texas Democrat Martin Dies, for one, was unhappy. Dies chaired the House Un-American Activities Committee (HUAC), which he had helped to establish in 1938. In June 1940, he called for the creation of a "Home Defense Council," a threat to the FBI's jurisdiction that perhaps foreshadowed the twenty-first century's Department of Homeland Security.

Hoover said that the idea signified Dies's ignorance of the provisions already made through the FBI. To the director, FBI expansion was the most desirable solution. In September 1940, he asked for 500 more agents, 200 more fingerprint personnel, and a $2 million increase in appropriations. He wanted to take on ever-increasing responsibilities. In October 1941, for example, Attorney General Francis Biddle endorsed his request that the FBI should be given the job of doing security checks on all federal employees, a move apparently calculated to forestall any attempt by HUAC to take over that function.[4]

A success in 1941, in the Sebold-Duquesne operation, further strengthened the FBI's grip on counterespionage. William G. Sebold was the name used by one William Debowski, who had served a prison sentence in his native Germany before emigrating to America and becoming a U.S. citizen. The Gestapo knew that Sebold was vulnerable to blackmail, because he had a criminal record and had failed to declare it to the U.S. naturalization authorities. When Sebold returned to Germany for a family visit in 1938, Hitler's secret police told him that if he did not spy for the Abwehr, they would expose his criminal past, send him to a concentration camp, and eliminate members of his family. Sebold accepted expense money and told the Nazis he would do their bidding.

But he had other ideas, and in Cologne he approached a U.S. consular official. After establishing his credibility, the FBI took him on as a double agent. The bureau now found itself in an "arrest or follow" quandary. As a law enforcement agency with strong links to orthodox police forces, it generally had an "arrest and convict" philosophy. But the preference in counterespionage is to follow someone around even if you know he is guilty, in the expectation that he will reveal his contacts and methods, perhaps become the unconscious purveyor of disinformation to the people who sent him, and serve as an indicator of what his people know about your own secrets and methods.

In New York, Sebold was contacted by Frederick, or "Fritz," Duquesne, who headed a German spy ring based in the city. At first, the FBI followed Duquesne and his associates. With secret help from the bureau, Sebold set up an office in Manhattan that was prewired for eavesdropping—he was the bait that attracted German agents whose activities could now be monitored. With similar help, he established a shortwave radio station in a house in Centerport, Long Island. Morris H. Price then learned to impersonate Sebold. Price was an FBI agent from Milwaukee who was skilled in radio transmission and the handling of codes. Price conveyed doctored information to Sebold's German controllers and in reply received lists of the Abwehr's spying requirements and instructions for the Duquesne spy ring. The cat-and-mouse game lasted for sixteen months. Then, on 29 June 1941, the Feds pounced, making thirty-three arrests.

The resulting prosecution presented the Justice Department with a further quandary. One of the key charges against the accused was the theft of the Norden bombsight plans—the bombsight was an accuracy-enhancing piece of American technology whose details the U.S. Navy was determined to deny to the nation's potential enemies. The plans had been recovered in time to prevent their falling into the hands of the German authorities, but could the spies be convicted without producing the Norden plans as evidence in court? A legal memorandum requested by the Justice Department's G. Mennen Williams noted that "the Navy would, of course, prefer losing the prosecution to making public the bombsight plans." Once again, a clash loomed between sound security practices and the arrest-and-prosecution culture of the FBI. Citing British law cases as precedents as well as executive privilege, the memorandum concluded that the spies could be prosecuted on the basis of secondary as distinct from "best" evidence: "The plans taken can be identified as bombsight plans without production in evidence of the plans themselves."

Success in the Duquesne-Sebold case and the publicity surrounding it kept the FBI's fortunes buoyant at a time when a renewed struggle was taking place over who should have overall control of American intelligence. In 1927, Secretary of State Frank Kellogg had ended the central control exerted by the Department of State. But in the late 1930s, Assistant Secretary of State George Strauser Messersmith wanted to reinvigorate U.S. counterintelligence. Reacting to the Rumrich case, he recommended the creation of an interdepartmental committee to coordinate counterespionage, with the State Department in control and the FBI denied any direct access to intelligence agencies in foreign countries. Hoover, however, demanded FBI control over a wide spectrum of counterespionage activities, and, mindful of the lessons he thought could be learned from the Rumrich case, demanded in October 1938 that the FBI should be able to investigate foreign espionage cases "without notifying the Secretary of State."[5]

Hoover wanted intelligence coordination, but on his terms—he explicitly rejected plans based on the World War I arrangement whereby the State Department had been in control. His feud with the diplomats therefore rumbled on. In March 1939 he told the attorney general of the work of the FBI's recently revived General Intelligence Section, which correlated information on subversive activities. The military branches of counterintelligence already relied on the FBI to investigate civilian matters, a secret "plan of cooperation" had been developed after careful study, and "the President [was] in accord with the general substance of the plan." Four days later, Messersmith met the bureau's Edward Tamm and other officials and pressed for State Department leadership and coordination. Hoover rejected the plan outright in a further memo to Murphy, insisting that "centralization" should be in a single agency, the FBI.

Just as he had backed FBI appropriations, President Roosevelt for a considerable period supported the bureau's claim to ascendancy in the struggle for overall intelligence control. A directive he issued on 26 June 1939 to relevant cabinet members gave the FBI primacy by naming it first: "It is my desire that the investigation of all espionage, counter-espionage, and sabotage matters be controlled and handled by the Federal Bureau of Investigation of the Department of Justice, the Military Intelligence Division of the War Department, and the [O]ffice of Naval Intelligence of the Navy Department."

Upon the outbreak of war in Europe, Attorney General Murphy wrote to Roosevelt: "Existing conditions make it essential that matters relating to espionage and sabotage be handled in an effective, comprehensive and unified manner." In response, Roosevelt requested "all police officers, sheriffs, and all other law enforcement officers in the United States" to hand over to the FBI any information relating to espionage. Here, the emphasis was slightly different, in that the directive addressed the issue of state-federal authority as distinct from the issue of ascendancy within the Washington bureaucracies, but the intention was still to give presidential backing to the FBI.

By the spring of 1940, Assistant Secretary of State Adolf A. Berle had inherited the intelligence coordination assignment. His diaries give the impression of a vacillating official. He was wary of Hoover's ambitions, but unwilling to push for a reinvigoration of the coordinating role previously exercised by his own department. After one meeting in Hoover's office in May, he noted "we had a pleasant time coordinating, though I don't see what the State Department has got to do with it." A few days later, however, he claimed to have converted the FBI and Military Intelligence Division (MID) to a plan that would "transfer some of this paranoid work into positive and useful channels" leading to the creation of "a secret intelligence service" such as "every great foreign office in the world has."

The next day, 5 June 1940, Hoover responded by circulating a proposal for the coordination of the FBI, MID, and Office of Naval Intelligence (ONI), a proposal that had the backing of the new attorney general, Robert H. Jackson. Under his plan, the bureau would "act as the coordinating head of all civilian organizations furnishing information relating to subversive movements." Its operations would be domestic, but its writ would run in the U.S. territories, except for Guam, Samoa, the Philippines, and the Panama Canal Zone.[6]

Hoover had already positioned the FBI in a manner that would enable him to take over significant aspects of foreign as well as domestic intelligence. He had benefited when, in April 1940, William Stephenson visited the United States. Stephenson was a conservative Canadian businessman who would be the lynchpin of British intelligence operations in the Western hemisphere. He would revitalize British intelligence efforts under cover of the passport control office in the British Purchasing Commission in New York. Though the United States was still neutral, and to the dismay of Berle, Roosevelt gave his backing to the development of cooperation between Hoover and Stephenson.

Hoover's expansionism made enemies for the FBI. In September 1940,

General Sherman Miles of MID complained to Berle that the bureau was failing in its job of counterespionage. Jabbing at the debilitating homogeneity of the agency, he said the FBI was proving incapable of penetrating ethnic groups. It was also refusing to pass on information that the MID needed, forcing Miles's men to duplicate investigations already conducted by the bureau. Disinclined to pursue an emollient course, Hoover retaliated by complaining to the White House that "the Military Intelligence authorities are inclined to overstep their proper jurisdiction," notably by setting up offices all over America to handle civilian matters.

Complaints by Miles and others did not matter, so long as the FBI had executive backing. Here, there was little cause for concern in the fall of 1940. On 30 October, Berle gave official approval to an FBI mission to London for the purpose of studying intelligence and internal security matters. The mission consisted of Hugh H. Clegg, who had been the first head of the police academy and was now responsible for training and inspection, and an assistant, Lawrence Hince. Clegg and Hince spent December and January in England, and their presence and function there signified the high standing of the FBI in all intelligence matters.

In the meantime, however, Hoover had received a memorandum that presaged an end to the prospects for FBI intelligence domination. Edward A. Tamm was its author. Tamm had thought up the acronym "FBI" in 1935, and was Hoover's trusted assistant. He had attended more than twenty-five of the meetings between Hoover and the president, and he was thought to be a skillful Roosevelt-watcher. But, in his memorandum of 3 December 1940, he made a serious error.

According to Tamm's memorandum, the British connection was about to founder. "The President," he wrote, "is reported to be less and less sympathetic towards the British cause in the present war but cannot publicly do an about-face at the present time because of the very positive nature of his previous statements and acts of friendliness towards Great Britain." The U.S. ambassador in London, Joseph P. Kennedy, had convinced FDR that the British request for loans on the ground of being broke was duplicitous. The British had major assets in Latin America, where, moreover, they were in ruthless competition with American businessmen. The British had irritated Roosevelt over a number of issues, such as their poor regard for protocol when their ambassador, the late Lord Lothian, had appealed to American public opinion over the head of the president. Tamm predicted that FDR would not declare his distrust of the British publicly, but would "endeavor to manipulate matters to his own satisfaction without disclosing his viewpoint."[7]

Tamm had completely misunderstood the inscrutable president, who was concealing his support for the British, not his distrust of them. As for Hoover, it would not take much to bring to the surface his suspicion, widely shared in America, that London had manipulated the United States during World War I and could never be entirely trusted. Such mistrust of the British could only drive a wedge into the hitherto cozy Roosevelt-Hoover relationship.[8]

When Hoover, drawing on the work done by Clegg and Hince, reported to the White House on British intelligence arrangements, he did have some positive things to say. Their effort, he noted pointedly, was fully financed. British foreign intelligence, MI6, received $14 million per annum, almost as much as the FBI. The British were a bulwark against the spread of communism, and their counterintelligence services suffered from no excessive qualms over the use of microphones, mail and wireless interception, and wiretaps. But, he noted, in an implied assertion of American superiority, MI5 had inadequate control over local police forces. He further stated that British officials believed intelligence work would be more effective if MI5 and MI6 were combined.[9]

These remarks conform to Hoover's ambition for a unified American intelligence system. His analysis may well have encouraged the idea of central intelligence. But his desire to become the overall tsar of a super-espionage agency would be realized neither during the war nor after it.

Roosevelt danced to a different tune from Hoover's, and was determined to support British military resistance to Nazi Germany. He formed a secret bond with Prime Minister Winston Churchill. At home, he turned increasingly to William J. Donovan for intelligence advice. Donovan had headed the criminal division in the Justice Department in the 1920s. Though a Republican, by background and social milieu he had much in common with the president. A Columbia graduate and Wall Street lawyer, he was a match for Hoover both as a Washington insider and in the wider publicity game, and, for the duration of World War II, became his arch rival in the world of intelligence.

As FDR knew in advance, Donovan held views that were likely to please the president. Sent to London in 1940 to inquire into Joe Kennedy's view that England was about to sink, he returned home with an obligingly contrary interpretation. Sent back to Europe on a further investigative mission, he reported in glowing terms on the merits of British intelligence. This put him in a strong position to cultivate Stephenson and further endeared him to Roosevelt.

Feuding in the intelligence community was by now chronic. In a cabinet meeting in April, the frustrated president proposed that there should be a "Mister X" to mediate in intelligence disputes, claiming, on no good evidence, that this was how the British ran things. In a move he would later regret, General Miles proposed that Donovan should be Mister X. Roosevelt now determined on the creation of an Office of the Coordinator of Information (COI). Hoover objected on the ground that coordination already existed, but on 18 June FDR issued the order for the creation of the COI with Donovan in charge, and on 15 July the new agency came into existence.

Hoover and his colleagues responded by revving up their anti-Donovan campaign. Tamm trained his guns on Donovan's sponsors, the British. He objected to the arrogance of British intelligence "basking in the light of its own brilliance," and to the influence that its agent Stephenson exerted over Donovan. According to Berle, the FBI regarded information coming from British intelligence as "subject to check." The rifts in the intelligence community were widening just when the Roosevelt administration was trying to pull things together.[10]

Pearl Harbor exposed the fissures in the U.S. intelligence system. The attack provoked a barrage of criticism, some of which hit the FBI. One charge against Hoover was that he ignored the "Tricycle" warning of the impending attack. Tricycle was the MI5 code name for a Yugoslav double agent, Dusan Popov. Piecing together information he had gleaned from his German controllers about the coming raid and adding his own deductions, Popov warned British intelligence, which informed its American counterparts, and, on 14 August 1941, the FBI's agent in charge in New York, Percy Foxworth, briefed the director. Apparently, Hoover passed the warning neither to COI nor to any other government colleagues. He met Popov, took a puritanical dislike to the high-living agent, and decided he was untrustworthy. Popov subsequently discovered that the FBI had bugged his Manhattan apartment. Several British intelligence agents viewed with contempt the "police" mentality that led Hoover to treat Popov as a criminal instead of as an asset who could be used for feeding disinformation to the Germans.[11]

In Hawaii, too, the FBI made enemies and showed itself to be one of a number of poor team players. The bureau participated in the surveillance of Tadashi Morimura, who was chancellor at the Japanese consulate in Honolulu but also Tokyo's chief secret agent in the region. Between March and

August 1941, Morimura supplied Tokyo with logistical information on local U.S. military aircraft and on ships entering and leaving Pearl Harbor.
Over the next few months, he supplied the location of naval targets. Japanese pilots used a bombing-and-torpedo chart of "Battleship Row" supplied by the Japanese agent as they closed on Pearl Harbor on 7 December.
On the day before the attack, Morimura had tipped off Tokyo that U.S. barrage balloons and torpedo nets seemed to be out of position: "a considerable opportunity is left for a surprise attack."[12]

Navy intelligence was suspicious from the outset and, with Hoover's
approval, conducted its own investigation on the "follow" as distinct from
the "arrest" principle. Meanwhile, however, the FBI ignored the juris-
dictional agreement and watched Morimura independently. His own suspicions of Morimura growing, Hoover demanded access to naval code-
breaking output on the case. Refused permission, he condemned the navy's
"uncooperative attitude" and ordered the FBI to withhold cooperation
from the navy. By 16 June, the FBI had identified Morimura's role on the basis of its own inquiries, and Hoover informed Berle on 7 August. If there had
been better intelligence transmission, Japanese intentions might have been
deduced and American forces in Hawaii might have been in a better state of
alert. But such intelligence coordination never was achieved, for "turf war"
reasons that involved a variety of organizations, the FBI included.[13]

The FBI escaped major censure over Pearl Harbor because it was a minor player in the area of military intelligence. Before and after the disastrous
raid, the bureau was, in fact, receiving a good press because of its success in
the Sebold-Duquesne case, which culminated in fourteen convictions on 12
December 1941. But in another way the attack was bad news for the bureau.
It ensured the entry of the United States into the war, which resulted in
a higher profile for the military and for the Office of Strategic Services,
formed in 1942.

America's entry into the war in significant ways consigned Hoover to
the sidelines. One indication of this was the FBI's exclusion from policy
planning. On 3 December 1941, the military had formed a Joint Army and
Navy Intelligence Committee, subsequently known as the Joint Intelligence
Committee, or JIC. A top-level organism, JIC represented the U.S. Joint
Chiefs of Staff on the British-American Combined Intelligence Committee.
Donovan sat on the JIC, but Hoover's request for membership was denied.
In the words of intelligence historian Larry Valero, "J. Edgar Hoover and the
FBI were never permitted to sit at the big intelligence table."

In June 1942, Hoover suffered another reverse. It should have been a good month for him. When, on a dark and foggy night, a German submarine landed a team of saboteurs at Amagansett, Long Island, the FBI rounded them up in smart fashion. But Hoover had in the meantime learned of plans to consolidate intelligence under an arrangement that did not give the FBI primacy.

The plot to sideline Hoover and his bureau stemmed not just from institutional rivalries, but also from a quarrel over professional standards. Lieutenant General John L. DeWitt, commander of the Fourth Army on the West Coast, claimed that Japanese Americans loyal to Tokyo were engaging in sabotage and secretly signaling to submarines, enabling them to attack American ships. He demanded the internment of the Japanese American population. Hoover insisted that FBI investigations showed there was no proof of espionage or disloyalty. The army was "getting a bit hysterical" in cases "where power lines were sabotaged by cattle scratching their backs on the wires." Hoover's professional judgment that Japanese Americans were not engaging in espionage or sabotage against the United States has stood the test of time.[14]

However, in a victory for DeWitt, and not wishing to take a military risk, President Roosevelt on 19 February 1942 issued Executive Order 9066, giving the general the authority he needed to implement the notorious ethnic purging of a whole section of California's population. This left a bitter taste for Hoover and his allies. More than a year after FDR's order, James H. Rowe, Jr., assistant to the attorney general, still fumed with undiminished anger. He noted that his department's Civil Rights Division was standing up for African Americans, but "why are we willing to take on the whole Southern delegation and yet quail before the General who has nothing to do but appear before subcommittees." Hoover tried to follow a pragmatic course. In the words of Justice Department attorney Edwin J. Ennis, he took a "neutral" stance and did not "urge any course of action." But his standing had clearly been undermined.

In spite of the setback, Hoover attacked the proposal to create a "central agency" as archaic and reminiscent of World War I. But on 13 June, the very day of the Amagansett landing, President Roosevelt issued an executive order creating the Office of Strategic Services (OSS). The OSS did not supplant the JIC and never did achieve a dominant role in American intelligence, but its creation and the appointment of Donovan as its director were visible indications of the relative marginalization of the FBI.[15]

Hoover had in some ways become a pathetic figure. His unrealistic ambitions in the realm of foreign intrigue and his continuing failings as a team player contributed to that image. In spite of the director's reputation for success in the New Deal's war on crime, FDR from the outset seems to have scorned him as an informant on foreign affairs. For example, when Hoover reported to him in March 1939 that the former German consul in New York, Dr. Paul Schwarz, was plotting with a high-ranking compatriot to achieve Hitler's downfall, the president issued one of his put-downs: "Thank you for the information about Dr. Schwartz. Never heard of him."

That is not to say that the FBI failed to contribute in useful ways to the war effort. It must be remembered that Hoover, like most Americans in the intelligence game, was on a learning curve. British intelligence officers who dismissed him as a mere policeman ignored the fact that the United Kingdom had entered the war earlier, and therefore learned their tricks sooner than the FBI. Like the rest of the U.S. intelligence community, the bureau became more sophisticated with the passage of time.

In 1944, for example, W. Mark Felt, a young FBI agent, developed a disinformation asset, the defecting German agent Helmut Goldschmidt. A lack of restraint in sexual matters had earned Goldschmidt the code name "Peasant," and the British had discarded him for being morally flawed. The less fastidious Felt told Goldschmidt to remain in England, and had FBI agents in Washington assume his identity. In a deception operation, the G-men sent radio messages to the Abwehr in Hamburg containing both military misinformation and, for the purpose of demoralization, accurate information on American factories' formidable production of multi-engined aircraft. The Germans mistrusted Goldschmidt and were not wholly taken in, and the episode was in any case a minor one. Nevertheless, the running of Peasant was Tricycle upside down, with the Americans forgetting about prudery, and disseminating disinformation in a manner that trumped the British.[16]

In spite of the setbacks he endured, Hoover throughout the war clung to the hope that the FBI would assume worldwide responsibility. And he did succeed in one large area, Latin America. Entrusting him with that region may have been a way of propitiating him politically. But it also made sense, for the reason that the bureau already had experience south of the Rio Grande.

In the presidency of Theodore Roosevelt, Mexico had been one of the very first preoccupations of the newly formed detective force within the Department of Justice. In the second half of 1908, the Justice Department had a surrogate secret agent based in El Paso, Texas. In a vain attempt to avoid congressional censure, José Priest was nominally employed and paid by the

Department of State, but he ran a team of Justice Department detectives to investigate what Secret Service chief John Wilkie was already calling "the Mexican revolution" (the revolution proper took place in 1910). In 1911, Bureau of Investigation agents worked with the army and Texas Rangers to disarm and disrupt a faction operating across the Mexican border with the aim of thwarting the revolution led by Francisco Madero. Worries about instability in Mexico fomented by the Germans and later the communists ensured continuing bureau interest. In 1920, some issues of Hoover's Weekly Bulletin of Radical Activities were entirely devoted to Mexico.

In the 1930s, German economic rivalry in South America gave the United States renewed cause for concern. Nazi propagandists cultivated South Americans of German and Italian origin just at the point when Spain, the major cultural influence on the region, fell to fascism. The possibilities of revolution and even stab-in-the-back diplomacy could not be dismissed. But, at the Pan-American Conference of 1933 in Montevideo, the Roosevelt administration had foresworn overt military intervention.

In this context, police and intelligence intervention seemed to make sense. In 1938, Congress passed a law enabling the government to lend civilian experts to other American republics. The administration sent U.S. police missions and FBI advisers to various Latin American countries. When Brazil asked for help in countering the efforts of secret operatives from Axis countries, Hoover sent in FBI agents to establish a training school with a view to establishing a Brazilian clone of his own bureau.[17]

Against this background of FBI know-how, it came as no surprise when, on 24 June 1940, Berle issued a directive on behalf of the president giving the FBI responsibility for "foreign intelligence work in the Western Hemisphere," or, as Hoover more dramatically expressed it the next day, the "entire Latin American portion of this hemisphere." Hoover responded by creating a new counterintelligence unit, the Special Intelligence Service (SIS). He told Attorney General Jackson that he would be recruiting candidates with "linguistic ability," and would have to relax some of his other criteria.

All of this infuriated military and naval intelligence officials. Hoover complained to Jackson that they seemed to regard the FBI "as somewhat of an octopus." They did not realize that civilian control of intelligence within the United States was essential, and that he had neither sought nor wanted the hemispheric assignment. What Hoover had, however, he was determined to hold. In the wake of Pearl Harbor, Donovan made a determined bid to supplant the bureau in Latin America, but Hoover fought him off and pursued his mission with vigor.[18]

Although the bureau already had exposure to Latin America, it had to hire additional agents to meet the nation's wartime needs. This meant rookies who had to learn their trade. One SIS agent later recalled how green he was at the start of his assignment. He attended a dinner party in Chile posing as an American businessman. After a few brandies, his host revealed that he knew he was working for J. Edgar Hoover. His evidence was sartorial. A slave, no doubt, of the director's dress code, the agent looked just like the G-men exhibited in the pages of *Time* and *Newsweek*.[19]

Of course, every professional player is a rookie at one time in his life. The real question is, how effectively did FBI agents learn their trade in the war? Mexico is a significant test case. The USA's southern neighbor was a center for Nazi intrigue, and a conduit for secret intelligence en route to Germany from other Latin American nations. According to the historian María Emilia Paz, FBI failings in Mexico went beyond the wearing of gabardine topcoats and snap-brim hats. She believes the bureau played a limited role, and that navy intelligence did the main work because of its code-breaking expertise.

But the FBI could point to achievements even in the realm of code breaking. SIS's radio intelligence division set up twelve listening stations, and these passed on intercepted Abwehr messages from all over Latin America to the cryptanalytic section of the bureau's technical laboratory. It turned out that the cipher used in messages to control Sebold was similar to those used in South America, so the FBI was off to a flying start and was reading virtually all Abwehr traffic on the eve of the Sebold spy ring arrests in June 1941.

In Mexico City, the FBI had an agent whose experience predated Pearl Harbor. From 1939 to 1943, Gus T. Jones worked directly for the bureau and then as a legal attaché, standard FBI cover. In some ways, Jones's anti-Nazi work was less effective than it might have been. He complained of red tape and of superiors who, in the run-up to Pearl Harbor, turned deaf ears to those working in the field. His energies were also diverted into anti-communist activity. In August 1940, for example, Jones was at the deathbed of Soviet dissident Leon Trotsky, and he then interviewed Jacques Mornard van den Dreschd, the man who had driven an alpine climber's axe through Trotsky's head on the orders of Soviet dictator Joseph Stalin. Jones's interest is understandable in that the United States was not yet at war with Germany, and not yet a wartime ally of the Soviet Union. But Hoover's interest in the Mexican left was obsessive, and the FBI continued for years to trail such left-wing Mexican figures as the artists David Alfaro Siqueiros and Diego Rivera.

Regardless of such distractions, however, Jones reported on the Nazi threat from the very start of his mission. In October 1939 he warned that most members of the Mexican government were anti-American and potentially pro-German, and supplied a list of those Mexican officials who were more likely to be friendly toward the United States. FBI operations gradually expanded. By August 1941, the bureau had eleven agents in Mexico, six of them in the capital.

As the Abwehr ran seamless operations in Latin America and the USA, it was an advantage to U.S. counterintelligence that the FBI operated both at home and abroad. The logical nature of this provision did not, however, prevent outbreaks of turf warfare. The intelligence branches of both of the armed services disregarded FDR's instruction to cede control and jurisdiction. Navy intelligence actively opposed FBI expansion. Army intelligence launched its own operations without telling the FBI, and withheld data from the bureau. One example is its denial of information on German expertise in microphotography. The U.S. military attaché learned in December 1940 that the Abwehr had a new technology, the capacity to reduce photographs of three pages of documents to the size of a pinhead, so data could be sent disguised as the dot on the "i" in an innocuous-looking letter. But the U.S. military apparently did not tell the FBI, which seems to have become aware of the new technique only in April 1941.

In spite of this lack of cooperation, however, the FBI fastened onto the trail of the head of German intelligence operations in Mexico, Georg Nikolaus. Bureau agents identified Nikolaus in part because he had a bent arm, which betrayed him as the person who had been shot in an earlier incident in the Panama Canal zone. Nikolaus was further undone because he had whispered indiscretions to his Mexican mistress Teresa Quintanilla who, on finding that he had dumped her, passed them on to the Mexican authorities. Now under surveillance but still at large, Nikolaus continued to operate. In mid-December 1941, he sent Berlin details of U.S. Navy movements after Pearl Harbor. The Mexican authorities arrested him in February.

Mexico was not yet at war with Germany and wanted Nikolaus to have safe passage to Europe. As he waited in New York to embark for Lisbon, the U.S. authorities were obliged to look for evidence of a crime committed on American soil, so that they might detain him. Because it had the domestic as well as Latin American remit, the FBI had the authority to look for this evidence. By now, the bureau was aware of miniaturization technology, and a search of the German agent's shoes revealed a hidden set of microdots. Nor was this the only Mexican-related success in 1942. From his sanctuary in Mexico, Gerhardt Wilhelm Kuntz had been directing Nazi activities in the United States. Gus Jones had Kuntz arrested in Mexico, and a United States court later convicted him. By the war's end, German intelligence operations in Mexico had been neutralized.[20]

Sartorial naïveté did not, in the event, undermine the FBI's effectiveness in Chile. J. Edgar Hoover had identified that copper-rich nation as important to the U.S. war effort. Like its neighbor Argentina, Chile had a substantial population of German extraction and was a target of Nazi intrigue and propaganda. Alfredo Kleiber's cover story was that he worked for a German bank, but his spy ring was transmitting secret intelligence by radio. The Chilean authorities arrested and interned him in the fall of 1942. The Germans then used another radio station to transmit secret messages, but in February 1944 the Chilean police stopped the operation by arresting more than ninety Nazi agents in Santiago. The FBI did not play a lead role in these events, but Hoover claimed that, from April 1941, the FBI was able to intercept and decode all Nazi radio messages sent from Chile to Hamburg. The FBI kept the White House informed, in this way making a contribution to U.S.-Chilean relations.[21]

The FBI's southern operations were not confined to Mexico and Chile. By the start of 1943, 156 SIS agents disguised as embassy attachés, businessmen, or *Newsweek* correspondents operated throughout Central and South America. The number rose to 369 by the war's end. In some ways, the SIS shared its parent body's habit of measuring its success in terms of the number of arrests. In May 1944, Hoover reported to the White House that there had been many arrests in Brazil, a hotbed of Abwehr activity, leading to 86 convictions. By August 1945, SIS claimed to have identified over 800 spies across the whole of Latin America, and half of these had been apprehended.

In the Caribbean and Gulf of Mexico areas, the SIS used both the arrest tactic and intelligence gathering to try to counter the threat posed by German submarines. U-boats were menacing the approaches to the Panama Canal, an essential U.S. naval conduit as America fought a two-ocean war, and disrupting the transit of militarily essential raw materials like aluminum ore and petroleum. Between February and November 1942, U-boats sank 609 Allied ships in the relatively small region, a loss of 10,000 tons per day. In the realm of counterintelligence, the FBI participated in the investigation leading to the arrest of Heinz August Lüning, an Abwehr agent accused of transmitting information on Allied shipping movements. A half-Jew who served the Nazis out of opportunism rather than conviction, and whose talent was for boozing and fornication rather than espionage, Lüning is rumored to have been the inspiration for Graham Greene's anti-heroic novel *Our Man in Havana* (1958). At a nadir in Allied military fortunes, when any boost to morale was welcome, the American press was able to trumpet the downfall of what the *New York Times* called a "key German spy." Lüning was executed by a Cuban firing squad on 10 November 1942. Meanwhile, the SIS rather more quietly engaged in positive espionage. In Colombia, there was an effort to discover the details of U-boat refueling operations with a view to stopping them. Hoover personally briefed Berle on the matter.

One of the main aims of the bureau was to inform, and not all of this work was clandestine. In 1943, midway through the U.S. war effort, the bureau produced a comprehensive digest of Latin America, organized by nation. The volume "Totalitarian Activities in Argentina Today," for instance, came in two parts. Part 1 was a factual introduction, called "Argentina—The Nation," covering history, demography, and geography; Part 2 was on "The Axis in Argentina."

The country-by-country reports did not exhibit a sophisticated cultural awareness, and given the riven nature of the intelligence bureaucracy, it is doubtful whether they commanded a significant readership. The FBI could not match the glittering array of intellectuals hired by the OSS, which could employ experts on a temporary basis because of the wartime emergency. The majority of special agents did not show any marked enthusiasm for learning foreign languages. But in June 1941, special agent Joseph E. Santoiana, Jr., received a commission to start an FBI Spanish-language training school, and the program continued for several decades. This was evidence of Hoover's long-term international ambition.[22]

Although Hoover had been excluded from the JIC, the acquisition of the Latin American fiefdom seemed to give him at least a pale green light. He envisaged an FBI-based international intelligence agency that would continue to operate in peacetime. As the war's end approached, he sought to ensure that role. In August 1945, two weeks after the surrender of Japan had brought the war to a close, he declared that the FBI's experience in the Western hemisphere meant that it was the agency best qualified to operate a "world-wide intelligence service."[23]

At the end of 1945, the FBI had no real rival on the domestic front, and even states' rights had taken a back seat during the war emergency. In Latin America, it had gained some valuable experience of foreign intelligence. The death of President Roosevelt removed from office a leader who had partially sidelined the FBI. Then in September 1945, the new president, Harry Truman, disbanded the OSS. This eliminated from the scene not just an institutional competitor, but also Hoover's arch rival William Donovan. With the arrival of peace, furthermore, the FBI's exclusion from the JIC might become less important, for the military would surely lose influence. The FBI seemed in some ways poised to become America's ascendant peace-time intelligence agency. But it was not to be.

7

the alienation of liberal america: 1924–1943

Until World War II, the FBI could still be seen as an artifact of American liberalism. To be sure, it had faltered in its mission during the Taft, Wilson, and Harding administrations. But it was a child of Reconstruction, and the agency had then taken shape in two progressive administrations, those of Theodore and Franklin D. Roosevelt.

After World War II, however, the FBI became a target for a liberal assault. It was open to attack from that quarter because, in parallel with the reforms of the 1924–39 era, there had taken place a counterreformation. This culminated, by the early 1940s, in federal police practices that redemptionists and conservatives had condemned in the past, but which were now more repulsive to liberals. Some of the reforms endured, such as the improvements in FBI training and technology, and the investigations of white terrorism. Others, however, withered. The ambitions and prejudices of J. Edgar Hoover partly accounted for this. But so did the exercise of power by Franklin D. Roosevelt, who believed firmly in executive privilege and, like most Americans at the time, thought that the wartime emergency justified extraordinary measures. America's greatest liberal president thus shared some of the responsibility for the alienation of liberal support from the FBI.

The 1940s surveillance boom that offended liberals as well as a number of conservatives was the culmination of an incremental tendency. Even in the immediate wake of Attorney General Stone's May 1924 pronouncement, the FBI had continued to spy on the American Civil Liberties Union. In September 1924, the bureau's Los Angeles field office reported that it had recruited an informer on the ACLU's board and was following the activities of one of the ACLU's supporters, the socialist novelist Upton Sinclair.

Hoover in 1925 established an "Obscene File" that contained sexual gossip. Together with the "Confidential File" that also stored personal data, it contained information that could potentially be used to intimidate or blackmail politicians.[1]

The later 1920s was ostensibly a period of transparency and idealism. The State Department central intelligence unit, first established in 1915 under Frank Polk but gradually reduced after the war, was abolished in 1927. Under Calvin Coolidge's successor, Herbert Hoover, the code-breaking unit known as the American Black Chamber was also dissolved.

In reality, however, the second half of the Republican decade was a period of continuing government surveillance. In 1927, President Coolidge's Bureau of Investigation opened a file on Theodore Dreiser, an American writer whose unorthodox views were as unpalatable to the bureau as they were to the Communist Party, which refused him membership. Nor did the bureau neglect its by now time-honored target, the ACLU. The bureau feared that the ACLU was doing a reverse investigation and building a file that would expose the pointlessness of the Feds' white slavery work, still a staple item in annual appropriation requests. One of the bureau's last acts under Coolidge was to ransack the ACLU's New York office in a vain search for the white slavery exposé files.

Under President Hoover the bureau investigated dissent regardless of provenance. In November 1929, in the wake of the great crash, it launched a noncriminal inquiry into a right-wing group, the Sentinels of the Republic, who opposed what they saw as Hoover's plans to centralize power in the hands of federal government. In the following month, the bureau generated reports on two further voluntarist groups, this time critical of the administration from a liberal perspective. These were the Foreign Policy Association and, once again, the ACLU.[2]

These activities do not mean that Herbert Hoover's bureau was running out of control. The presidential hand is visible, in spite of efforts to preserve what a later generation would call plausible deniability. President Hoover's closest aides regularly asked the bureau for help. One such was Lawrence Richey, who had worked for Herbert Hoover when he was secretary of commerce, and then continued as his personal secretary in the White House. Formerly a Secret Service agent and a keen detective buff, Richey logged the activities of the president's critics, investigated press leaks, and was reputed to have a defamatory file on the private lives of Democratic politicians.

Richey belonged to the same Masonic lodge as J. Edgar Hoover and had been a supporter ever since advocating his appointment as bureau chief in 1924. Richey would go to considerable lengths to protect the president. In May 1930, the White House received information that the Democrats had compiled their own dossier of data on the president and his administration. Operating through an intermediary to avoid accountability in case of discovery, the White House engaged the services of ONI officers to break into a Democratic Party center of operations in New York. The ONI burglars achieved this without detection but also without result: the room had been stripped of its contents before they arrived. Even when they followed the political operator allegedly responsible for the derogation file, the ONI men had to confess to Richey that the trail remained barren. Nevertheless, the episode throws light on the history of the FBI, as it shows that political inquiries were very much on the White House agenda in the Republican years and were not invented by J. Edgar Hoover.[3]

Herbert Hoover's bureau continued its political surveillance to the bitter end of the Republican era. One of its last targets was the Bonus Expeditionary Force, the organization behind the march on Washington by patriotic but impoverished World War I veterans in search of economic relief. Neither the Chicago nor the New York field offices found evidence to support the contention of the two Hoovers that the Bonus army was a communist plot.

Would the election of a Democratic president make a difference? In 1934, Congress passed the Federal Communications Act, making wiretapping illegal. It is tempting to see this as evidence of a new liberalism associated with the Democratic administration and the New Deal spirit, a flirtation with open government before the gathering of the war clouds.

But the executive's urge to snoop continued regardless of the advent of a Democratic administration. The Justice Department claimed that the 1934 communications act did not apply to federal agents, and launched into a struggle with the Supreme Court on the issue. Well before the advent of serious worries about Hitler and for reasons that had nothing to do with fascism, the Roosevelt administration showed itself ready to spy on its political opponents. In December 1934 the White House solicited a report on the ACLU, which wanted to meet Roosevelt to discuss the rights of labor and its campaign for an anti-lynching law. FDR needed the support of Dixie for his New Deal reforms and was looking for ways to avoid the anti-lynching issue. Hoover obligingly advised that the ACLU was conducting a "vicious" campaign and that a presidential statement in response to its demands "might offend many who hold to conservatism and law enforcement." The president duly refused to meet with the civil liberties advocates.[4]

The foregoing catalog of political surveillance confirms that, even in the post-Stone peacetime era, investigations of a noncriminal character did occur. No mechanism existed for the rigorous enforcement of the Stone principles and, with the passage of time, they gradually eroded. This erosion did not take place for any one reason to the exclusion of others, though the Big Brother character of modern U.S. government played its part, as did the influence of individual personalities. By the time the scale of the totalitarian threat to democracy had become apparent, the White House was already disposed to take even more forceful measures.

FDR kept no written record of his private meeting with the FBI director on 24 August 1936. He had no wish to be saddled with the reputation of having established an American police state. But for Hoover, the dictates of prudence were different. He did not want to be left vulnerable to the charge that he had taken the bureau down an unauthorized path. So he created a unilateral paper trail.

According to Hoover's record of the event, he reminded the president in this private meeting that the FBI had from time to time collected intelligence about various right-wing figures such as Father Charles Coughlin, the anti-Semitic "radio priest." However, his current concern was with the communist menace. He told Roosevelt that the communists were behind the West Coast longshoremen's union, whose leader Harry Bridges had recently led a general strike in San Francisco; they were plotting to take over the United Mine Workers of America; they were infiltrating government departments, notably the National Labor Relations Board. Yet, while the FBI had some information on these activities, no single agency existed to collect systematic intelligence on such developments.

The communist activities alarmed Roosevelt. He asked Hoover to undertake the necessary investigations. Hoover replied that, as the Communist Party was a legal entity, he lacked the authority to do so. Instead he volunteered the view that the Appropriations Act of 1916 might be helpful. Passed in the era when the State Department coordinated intelligence activities, it authorized the FBI's precursor to undertake noncriminal work when requested to do so by State. Moscow directed the activities of the American communists, so the problem was international in character and it would be appropriate to approach Secretary of State Cordell Hull on this occasion.

In a meeting with Roosevelt and Hoover on 1 September, Hull agreed to issue the request. When Attorney General Cummings duly received this, he gave Hoover the authorization he required, but again not in writing. To reinforce his paper trail, the FBI director wrote a further memo to Tamm, confirming the attorney general's "authority upon which to proceed in the conduct of this investigation."[5]

The historian Katherine Sibley has referred to FDR's early "naïveté about the scope of Soviet intentions," and his administration did, in the late 1930s, pay more heed to the fascist brand of totalitarianism than to its communist equivalent. However, the manner of the revival of the 1916 Appropriations Act suggests that he and Hoover were fully aware of the communist problem in 1936. What is missing from the discussion is any reference to espionage, which Moscow conducted through its trading mission Amtorg and through the Communist Party USA, and which was a more potent threat to U.S. interests than labor agitation. But FDR's exchanges on FBI authorization do confirm that he wanted the FBI to engage in political investigative work against the Left.

There were changes not only in the authority to undertake political work, but also in the means by which such work might be conducted. The FBI in 1936 included in its agents' manual a four-page section on "sound equipment." It gave technical instructions on eavesdropping with the use of electronic devices, on the planting of concealed microphones, and on the installing of equipment to record the telephone numbers dialed by a particular person under surveillance.

The bureau's aptitude in these matters only slightly anticipated a changing legal and political climate. In the case *Olmstead v. United States* (1928), the Supreme Court had ruled that wiretaps were not in themselves a breach of the Fourth Amendment protecting the right of citizens against unreasonable search, but that Congress could legislate to make evidence secured through wiretaps inadmissible in court. In the light of the 1934 law, the Supreme Court duly confirmed, in *Nardone v. United States* (1937), the inadmissibility of such evidence. But there now occurred an exchange of views between Attorney General Cummings and Senator Burton K. Wheeler (D-Mont.), chairman of the Interstate Commerce Committee and a seasoned critic of FBI abuses. Cummings assured Wheeler that he was against the "indiscriminate use of wire-tapping," but went on to observe that the matter involved "a question of balance which is peculiarly within the province of the legislative branch of the Government."

Wheeler seemed prepared, in principle, to amend the 1934 law to allow telephone tapping in cases of suspected felonious behavior (as distinct from less serious misdemeanors or political dissent). In 1939, there came an apparent setback when the Supreme Court confirmed its 1937 ruling on the inadmissibility of wiretap evidence. However, this did not stop the wiretappers. With the war clouds gathering, the president in May 1940 affirmed (and both he and Congress later confirmed) the FBI's right to wiretap "in cases of suspected subversive activities." A doctrine of secrecy developed—wiretapping was permissible, with the proviso that the information derived from it was for the use of government officials only. The upshot of all this was that discreetly organized wiretapping for *information* (not prosecution) was deemed to be legal. It was a charter for counterespionage, but also a carte blanche for surveillance of noncriminal political activities.[6]

Meanwhile, the application of such techniques in a widening sphere received continuous presidential backing. In November 1938, Roosevelt had approved a Hoover memorandum that noted how espionage was repugnant to the American people, and how important it was to give no ground for popular protest on this issue. The avoidance of public opprobrium was to be achieved not through abstinence, however, but through the exercise of "the utmost degree of secrecy." In June 1939, President Roosevelt hardened his policy in another respect when he authorized the FBI and military intelligence to investigate cases "potentially" involving espionage.

In March 1940, the new attorney general, Robert H. Jackson, banned all wiretapping by the FBI. A dismayed Hoover protested that this "materially retarded" espionage investigations, and could result in a "national catastrophe" with the Justice Department being blamed for "its failure to prevent some serious occurrence." With Nazi "fifth column" panic sweeping through the nation, the president again intervened. In May, he authorized the use of "listening devices" to monitor the activities of "persons suspected of subversive activities against the government of the United States," a decision that, in Jackson's view, defied the Supreme Court ruling in *Nardone,* and indicated how "the President's patience failed" when confronted with congressional refusal to legislate in favor of wiretapping.

Roosevelt also asked Jackson to try to find a legal basis for a mail-opening program. Once America was in the war, the president became even more security minded, though he did not entirely lose his sense of irony, on one occasion asking Hoover, "Have you pretty well cleared out the alien waiters in the principal Washington hotels? Altogether too much conversation in the dining rooms!"[7]

Although the reasoning behind wiretapping and mail opening was couched in terms of squashing German espionage, there were other targets. This was why there was such a hostile reaction, at the end of the war, to the suggestion that the FBI might take on wider duties. The anti-intervention-ists are a case in point. Between the start of the war in Europe in 1939 and America's entry into it two years later, these people argued in a legal and democratic manner against U.S. belligerency. Although they lost the debate, they had widespread support to begin with, and would become influential again at the conclusion of the war—and unsympathetic to the FBI.

Charles Lindbergh used his celebrity status to promote the anti-inter-ventionist cause. When Britain and France declared war on Germany fol-lowing the German invasion of Poland, Lindbergh was aghast, and started work on a radio address to the nation appealing for nonintervention. Roo-sevelt heard about this and offered to appoint Lindbergh to what would be a special new post, Secretary of Air, on condition that the aviator did not publicly oppose the administration's foreign policy. This only increased Lindbergh's determination to speak out. Roosevelt now set out to smear his critic. He described him to cabinet colleagues as a "Nazi" and compared one of Lindbergh's speeches to the outpourings of Hitler's propagandist Paul Joseph Goebbels. It was on the very day of this denunciation (21 May 1940) that FDR authorized the use of "listening devices" to monitor the activities of suspected "subversives."

The Roosevelt-Lindbergh feud continued. In his State of the Union ad-dress on 6 January 1941, FDR announced his Lend-Lease program extend-ing a financial lifeline to the embattled British. Lindbergh was prominent in the attack on the supportive House Resolution 1776, and in April he joined the anti-interventionist America First Committee. Established in the sum-mer of 1940, America First was a formidable pressure group with an esti-mated membership of 850,000 opposing involvement in the war.

In July 1941, Lindbergh recorded in his diary his suspicion that the gov-ernment was tapping his telephone conversations with America First. Hoover was too prudent to have done that, or at least to have left a record of it. However, the bureau in Lindbergh's case did cross the line between polit-ical surveillance and covert political action, in that it set out to discredit the American hero. It made an abortive effort to show that the flier had ob-tained American war plans and leaked them to the isolationist *Chicago Tri-bune*. It also sought the means of sexually discrediting Lindbergh, whose media image was that of a family man who had suffered the tragic kidnap and murder of an infant son. Here, the bureau missed an opportunity. Only decades later did the world learn that Lindbergh had a mistress in Germany, a woman who bore him children whom he visited in secret over the years.

But the bureau did collect other evidence on Lindbergh's alleged indiscretions. One report filed in June 1941 claimed that he had associated with prostitutes in Butte, Montana, in the 1920s. Perhaps the bureau anticipated prosecution under the white slavery law, but the intent behind the investigations of Charles Lindbergh was less to do with law enforcement than with politics.[8]

Hoover acted as a kind of political spy for the president. In February 1941 he reported to FDR on the progress of the Lend-Lease debate in the U.S. Senate. Then in May that year, he sent to the White House a painstakingly typed out reproduction of a public opinion poll about to be published in *Look* magazine, indicating strong disapproval of most forms of American interventionism, including 80 percent opposition to the use of U.S. ship convoys to save Britain from defeat. A few days later, he told the White House he had been "confidentially advised" that the American Peace Mobilization group would hold an anti-convoy demonstration outside the White House. The use of the coded euphemism "confidentially advised" may well have been an indication of phone tapping. While in other respects there was nothing pernicious in this kind of reporting, it did show that Hoover was acting outside his brief. Opposition to U.S. foreign policy in peacetime was neither illegal nor subversive. Hoover's active involvement in politics was a sign both of his desire to please the president and of his ambitions for the bureau's future role.[9]

Roosevelt demanded vigilance against opponents of Lend-Lease. In February 1941 he learned of America First's distribution of a circular criticizing the proposal, and he told his press secretary Stephen Early to "find out from someone—perhaps FBI—who is paying for this." The bureau's investigation revealed that the money came from voluntary contributions within the United States. But, like so many politicians, Roosevelt found it difficult to accept that opposition to his policies may have been genuine. In November, with congressional opposition to his foreign policy persisting, FDR directed the attorney general to inquire further into the "money sources behind the America First Committee." Once again, the FBI launched an investigation, spending months chasing a lead suggesting that America First was German financed. Once again, the quest was in vain.[10]

The bureau's investigation of America First finances spread beyond their provenance into the realm of expenditure. So Hoover was able to report to the White House that with the help of America First money the FBI scourge Burton Wheeler was stumping the nation speaking against intervention. When Senator Wheeler addressed an enthusiastic rally of eleven thousand in Los Angeles, a man from the bureau took notes both on his speech and on those listening to it.

Senator Gerald P. Nye (R-N.D.) was another target of FDR-FBI political investigation and attempted smear tactics. In 1934–36, Nye had headed a high-profile inquiry into the role of munitions manufacturers and financiers in prompting American entry into World War I. The inquiry had helped create the climate that led to the enactment of neutrality laws in 1935–37, laws that tied the hands of the administration when it came to dealing with the international Nazi menace. When World War II started in Europe, Nye was a leading opponent of U.S. involvement. He fell under the watchful eye of the bureau, and Hoover seemed determined not just to monitor his political activities but also to discredit him.

Acting on a tip from a local U.S. attorney, the Indianapolis branch of the bureau investigated an allegation that Nye had been involved in a "shady deal" connected with the sale of stock in a North Dakota newspaper. The agent in charge of the case, S. J. Dayton, hinted that the allegation was a reaction to Nye's principles, not his actions, and reported the view of one person (whose name is blanked out from the declassified FBI report) that Nye was "a very sincere, honest, trustworthy and high-type individual." Apparently this was not the right answer. Hoover told the agent in charge "immediately" to interview the complainant (name also blanked out, but presumably the attorney), stating, "I must insist that you give this matter your personal attention."

Emboldened by America's entry into the war, the FBI stepped up its surveillance of Nye and opened his mail. One such intercept was a letter to Horace J. Haase of the New York School of Democracy. In the letter, the senator criticized the inefficient conduct of the war and attacked "Union Now," a movement that advocated a strong federal bond between the United Kingdom and the United States. There was nothing incriminating or subversive about the spied-on correspondence of Gerald P. Nye.

Hamilton Fish was a third prominent legislator investigated by the bureau. This New York Republican had virulently opposed the New Deal for its socialistic tendencies. Upon the outbreak of hostilities in 1939, he formed the National Committee to Keep America Out of War. He challenged Lend-Lease and other cornerstones of FDR's foreign policy. For a while, his views carried authority, not least because he had been decorated in recognition of his bravery fighting with the 369th Infantry regiment in World War I. He was a political encumbrance to the Roosevelt administration because he was the ranking minority member of the House Foreign Affairs Committee. The FBI monitored Fish's political activities and sought evidence to discredit him, dredging up details of his associations with the right-wing dictator Rafael Trujillo of the Dominican Republic and unsuccessfully hunting for evidence of income-tax evasion, which would have allowed him to be bracketed with Al Capone and similar American villains.

In the summer of 1941, the FBI looked into allegations that Wheeler, Nye, and Hamilton had abused their franking rights to send out millions of politically charged postcards attacking U.S. foreign policy. It turned out that they were innocent. The Nazi agent George Sylvester Viereck, with the aim of sowing discord on Capitol Hill and demoralizing the interventionists, had organized the franking plot out of the German embassy. But the starting assumption of the investigation was that congressmen voicing dissent should be suspected of subversion, and even treason.[11]

If the FBI's harassment of politicians spelled trouble at the end of the war, so did its pursuit of intellectual and literary figures. Harry Elmer Barnes was such a case. His treatment illustrates how the bureau courted unpopularity among liberal intellectuals. For although the anti-intervention movement received substantial support from the Right (America First was predominantly conservative, as were Lindbergh and Hamilton Fish), it also had a significant left wing, of which Barnes was a member.

Barnes was a revisionist historian with criminological interests. His book *The Genesis of the World War* (1926) had questioned the official view that Germany alone should bear the burden of guilt for the outbreak of the 1914–18 conflict. His writings contributed to the questioning of America's role in that war and, by extension, underpinned the Nye investigation and congressional neutrality legislation in the 1930s. Barnes supported FDR's New Deal, and was in favor of uniform crime reporting. But, in spite of having claimed in a 1931 book that the volume of crime in the USA was "scandalous," Barnes offended Hoover by claiming that the agency was scaremongering on the law and order issue. In 1938, a leftward-leaning group attracted Barnes's attention. The Keep America Out of the War Congress had the support of Socialist Party of America presidential candidate Norman Thomas, as well as of other people as diverse as Gerald P. Nye and the architect Frank Lloyd Wright. Barnes joined it. He was an anti-interventionist in whom Hoover would take a particular interest.

Between December 1942 and March 1943, the FBI director sent four reports on Barnes to the Criminal Division of the Department of Justice. The objective was a possible prosecution for sedition. Hoover quoted the Albany field office on Barnes: he had "long associated with Communist Front Organizations and isolationist movements" and was "strongly anti-British and opposed to President Roosevelt." The Criminal Division found no cause for prosecution, underlining Hoover's inability to distinguish between free expression of opinion and sedition.[12]

The FBI's hostility to creative writers stored up trouble for the future and meant it was out of step with New Deal policy. Through the Federal Writers' Project and similar programs for theater, music, and art launched in 1935, the Roosevelt administration had shown a tolerant and friendly face to potential rebels, if with a view to cooption. In contrast, the FBI turned a philistine countenance on those who dared to differ. Theodore Dreiser was by no means the only author on its files. The bureau consistently maintained literary files long before, as well as during, the international crisis of the late 1930s. It monitored the thoughts and activities of Sinclair Lewis (his file was opened in 1923), Sherwood Anderson (1932), Upton Sinclair (the Feds forgot to destroy the transcript of a 1934 wiretap on him), Clifford Odets and Ernest Hemingway (both 1935), John Steinbeck (1936), Pearl Buck (1937), and William Faulkner (1939). Some writers only scraped onto the list later on, posthumously in the case of F. Scott Fitzgerald (1951), but it would seem that virtually every significant interwar fiction author came under surveillance.

Not even the progeny of distinguished writers escaped. The Nobel Prize–winning Thomas Mann, a refugee from Hitler's Germany who arrived to lecture at Princeton University in 1938, is today best remembered for his novel *Death in Venice* (1913), whose evocation of illicit love was the theme of Luchino Visconti's eponymous movie in 1971, set to the strains of Mahler and starring Dirk Bogarde. But Mann's daughter Erika and her brother Klaus were both homosexual, and this made them the target of FBI surveillance.

The affair became a chapter in the history of Hooverite prurience. The FBI's large file on the leftward-leaning Klaus Mann pointed not just at his homosexuality but also, rather improbably, at his alleged incest with his sister. Klaus Mann never did learn precisely why he failed to achieve his goal, an official role in the intelligence and propaganda war against Germany, though he probably suspected why. In an effort to achieve respectability and employability, he tried to pass himself off as heterosexual, asking a female acquaintance to supply him with "a beautiful girlfriend . . . with naked shoulders, bedroom eyes and all." Resorting to another tactic, he gave the

FBI an unsolicited confession regarding his sexuality. All this was to no avail, and America did not use a promising intelligence asset.

Hoover was already embarking on what would become a great homosexual scare. His copious file on another case confirms this. It concerned one of the brightest stars of American diplomacy, Undersecretary of State Sumner Welles. In 1941, Welles's career rival William C. Bullitt tipped off the president about Welles's indiscretions with porters on a train trip. At FDR's behest, the bureau looked into the matter and found that Welles had been propositioning young black men at random, and was in danger of becoming a liability to the interventionist cause and the administration generally. Indeed, Hoover warned FDR that Bullitt had alerted Senator Wheeler about the matter at the height of the Lend-Lease debate. Although Wheeler seems to have kept the story to himself, the story leaked, and with a congressional probe in the offing by 1943, Welles resigned. It is still too early to speak of resentment at anti-gay prejudice as a factor undermining support for the FBI, but Hoover's tactics did earn him condemnation. Secretary of the Interior Harold Ickes, one of the architects of the New Deal, had little doubt that Hoover had been instrumental in undermining Welles.[13]

What more surely stored up trouble for the FBI, however, was the way Hoover was becoming an anti-left and anti-liberal legend. The FBI director had studied communism, and prided himself on being anti-left from an informed perspective. Hoover watchers fastened on the trivia of his anti-socialism, including the disclosure that the driver of the director's Cadillac was under instructions to make no left turns (the real reason was that Hoover had once been involved in an accident when making a left). FDR had a more practical objection. In May 1942, Attorney General Francis Biddle told Hoover: "During a conversation I had with the president yesterday, he told me in his opinion the Federal Bureau of Investigation was spending too much time investigating suspected Communists in the Government and out, but particularly in the Government, and ignoring the Fascist minded groups both in the Government and out."

In a factual rebuttal, Hoover gave examples of the bureau's investigations of "pro-Axis individuals." He stated: "Since the entrance of the United States into the current war, searches have been made of the residences and business establishments of 13,872 individuals, and actual apprehensions have been effected of 2,860 Germans, 1,356 Italians and 4,611 Japanese, a total of 8,827. All of this applies to the combating of the pro-fascist element as differentiated from the pro-Communist."[14]

Hoover's record does indicate he was prepared to investigate the Right. When the HUAC held sensationalist hearings that exaggerated the degree of communist infiltration in America, thus implying administration incompetence in dealing with it, Hoover investigated its chairman, Martin Dies. Thereafter, Hoover treated Dies as a foe partly out of self-interested loyalty to the White House and partly because he saw in the Texas Democrat a rival in the populist publicity stakes. Hoover's attitude toward HUAC during the Roosevelt presidency is one of several illustrations of his ability to be pragmatic over the issue of communism.

But Hoover's habit of keeping files on prominent liberals was deeply ingrained, and provocative. One such file was on Attorney General Frank Murphy. Another detailed the activities of Felix Frankfurter, one of the main promoters of the New Deal and later a justice of the Supreme Court. Perhaps most significant of all in revealing Hoover's prejudices and vulnerabilities, there was a file on the president's wife, Eleanor Roosevelt.[15]

Hoover disliked Mrs. Roosevelt. She was not just a liberal, but a liberal who criticized the FBI. Potentially, ER thought, the bureau should be capable of acting in character with American ideals, and that it should be able to offer professionalism in place of the ideological and emotional accusations emanating from the Dies committee. But she was displeased by the FBI's inquiries into the Abraham Lincoln Brigade of American volunteers fighting for the democrats against the fascists in the Spanish Civil War. Only a few members of the brigade were left wing, but the FBI tended to tar them all with the same brush. The bureau's interest in this group suggested to ER a parallel with the Gestapo. Mrs. Roosevelt was further infuriated when she discovered that the bureau had investigated the sex life of her secretary, Edith B. Helm.

Even more provocatively, in the private cabinet behind his office desk, Hoover kept files purporting to document ER's own sex life. Some of the "evidence" in these files came from the army's Counter Intelligence Corps (CIC). The allegations should have been suspect for that reason, as the CIC notoriously contained right-wing Roosevelt haters. Nevertheless, Hoover hoarded CIC matter and all kinds of rumors about ER's allegedly loose behavior, both heterosexual and lesbian.

In March 1943, CIC agents, without consulting her husband, bugged ER's room at the Hotel Blackstone in Chicago. They hoped to record her in flagrante with her good friend Joseph Lash, who was hated by the Right for having fought for the democratic cause in Spain, and who was booked into a room adjoining Mrs. Roosevelt's.

The FBI already had a recording of Lash in action. This had been at the Hotel Lincoln earlier in the month, when the woman in the young serviceman's arms and on the CIC tape was his lover, Mrs. Trude Platt. ER's role was in reality confined to consoling Lash, many years her junior, on the tribulations of his love life. The Hotel Blackstone staff having tipped off ER about the bug in her room, FDR soon learned of the matter, and his emphatic response was to dissolve the CIC. This major agency was not revived until the presidency of his successor, Harry Truman. However, some spurious materials found their way into Hoover's file via his CIC liaison agent. Because Trude Platt's vocal emissions in one hotel had been improbably confused with the voice of ER in another, the president had to go through the tedious process of listening to the FBI director telling him something he already knew to be false. FDR's son later remarked that the affair left a question mark over the true purpose of Hoover's confidential files.[16]

ER's commitment to the campaign for civil rights for black citizens triggered another type of FBI investigation. It took place against the background of a white southern panic. There was a fear that the wartime demand for labor would attract black servants to the North, and away from their southern duties. In 1941, Mrs. Roosevelt visited Alabama's Tuskegee Institute and mixed socially with black women. Stories reached the FBI about how this had inspired southern black women to form "Eleanor Roosevelt Clubs." In November 1942, southern field offices looked into the rumor that one Eleanor Roosevelt Club was promoting the slogan "not a cook in the kitchen by Christmas." The agent in charge in Memphis, Tennessee, concluded that there was no such conspiracy, and a contemporaneous non-FBI inquiry by Howard Odum revealed that the Eleanor Clubs were a figment of southern imagination. The following year, nevertheless, Hoover requested a further inquiry into whether black female domestics were demanding better conditions, this time deploying the slogan "a white woman in the kitchen by Christmas."[17]

The FBI was nervous about the possibility of black revolt or disloyalty. The black community did not greet with unalloyed pleasure the outbreak of war against Japan, a nonwhite nation. W. E. B. Du Bois claimed that "every Negro" was unhappy about the fight with Tokyo. This was an exaggeration. Only a small number of African Americans joined Du Bois in protesting against the internment of the Japanese American population in the spring and summer of 1942. African Americans represented only 2.6 percent of the conscientious objectors in America. But there was still a widespread feeling that democracy had to be proved at home as well as enforced abroad. While

Hitler was clearly a racist and every African American knew about his fury at black sprinter Jesse Owens's successes at the Berlin Olympics in 1936, the full extent of the führer's racist holocaust in Europe was not yet universally realized, and the Japanese actively promoted the idea that black Americans' sympathy should be with them, even if not with the full Axis. All this gave jittery government officials reason to worry about African Americans' loyalty.[18]

The FBI launched a number of hostile investigations that formed a counterpoint to the Justice Department's civil rights work. In January 1941, the FBI filed reports indicating that Paul Robeson was a member of the Communist Party (he was not). Billie Holiday was another black singer who fell under suspicion. Hoover humorlessly complained to the White House about her nightclub rendition of the song "The Yanks Are Not Coming" (a communist slogan during the Nazi-Soviet pact years of 1939–41). Following FBI investigations in Chicago after the start of the war, Black Muslim leader Elijah Muhammad and sixty-three other members of the Temple of Islam were arrested. Hoover hoped, in vain, that they could be charged with sedition because of their pro-Japanese views. Harlem politician and Baptist minister Adam Clayton Powell, Jr., was kept under surveillance. In 1943, charges of communist infiltration led to an investigation of the recently formed Congress of Racial Equality (CORE), although the organization was in fact Christian pacifist in composition.

Beginning in 1941, and then with renewed vigor after the Detroit race riot of 1943, there was intensive FBI surveillance of the March on Washington Movement and its leader A. Philip Randolph. Instead of seeing Randolph for what he was, a man playing poker with the White House in pursuit of wartime concessions to black America, Hoover chased his communist-conspiracy phantoms. The movement, he reported at the outset of the FBI investigation, was a protest against Jim Crow and imperialist war and was endorsed by James W. Ford (a communist, and the first African American to run for the U.S. vice presidency).

Hoover downplayed the racial and social elements of the Detroit disturbance. He looked instead for outside influences. The bureau amassed 385 volumes of reports and correspondence in its file on "Foreign-Inspired Agitation Among the American Negroes." In his letter transmitting a 714-page summary report to the White House, Hoover explained that the FBI had for two years been receiving "reports and allegations of forces with foreign influence and with anti-American ideology working among the Negro people of this country as well as exploiting them." The report criticized the black press for stirring up discontent. It alleged that the *Baltimore Afro-American* was pro-communist. It cited the *Pittsburgh Courier* for suggesting that African Americans would be no worse off under the Japanese. It quoted the view of FBI agent W. G. Banister on the 19 September issue of the *Oklahoma City Black Dispatch:* it was "of a rather biased nature and [was] sprinkled with such well-worn Communist phrases as 'Civil Liberties,' 'Inalienable Rights,' and 'Freedom of Speech and of the Press.'"[19]

Hoover hoped that there would be prosecutions of the black press for sedition. But he ran into what historian Patrick Washburn described as "the unwavering constitutional views of Attorney General Biddle." Leading members of the Justice Department were more sensitive to the civil rights cause than Hoover and his FBI colleagues. Assistant Attorney General James H. Rowe, Jr., noted that his department's civil rights section was taking on "the whole Southern delegation" and urged that the Japanese Americans' cause be given similar support. He told FDR it was essential to hire more black attorneys, and not just in a token manner. Otherwise, the Democrats would be in danger of losing the black vote. Against this background, there were no sedition prosecutions of the black press, but the FBI was not in good odor.[20]

The bureau's reluctance to hire black agents was a further aggravation to some of its liberal critics. There was no absolute ban on such agents. To take a well-documented example, James E. Amos served the bureau from 1921 to 1953. He worked on the Garvey case, but also against non–African American targets such as Murder, Inc., and the Duquesne spy ring. Amos was in some ways a throwback to an earlier era; the conservationist Gifford Pinchot was one of his referees, and it was Burns who hired him, on the strength of Amos's previous performance working for the Burns detective agency. But even the famously conservative Hoover promoted some of his African American personal staff, such as chauffeurs, to be special agents. They were not properly trained, and perhaps the director acted out of paternalistic concern for their welfare, or to ensure their loyalty, or to secure their exemption from the draft, or because he wanted them to be armed the better to protect him, but, nevertheless, he trusted them. The overall statistics are resistant to inquiry because official monitoring did not occur until later, but FBI historian John F. Fox has unearthed records of fifteen African Americans hired between 1919 and 1956, and there was also a handful of Hispanic agents, the first of whom, Manuel Sorola, enlisted in 1916.

Biased though it was, the FBI's hiring policy was no worse than that of other government agencies. There has been a running debate over the question of whether the New Deal agencies discriminated against black job applicants. When America entered World War II, most employers as well as the more conservative labor unions held to the color line. Government training agencies would not take on blacks because they said they would not be hired, and defense contractors denied jobs to blacks on the ground that they had not been trained. The problem with the FBI was not that it lagged behind in its hiring practices, but that, because of the nature of its work, it needed to be ahead of the game, and was not. In a commentary in July 1943, the *Nation* got it slightly wrong, but conveyed the depth of resentment: "J. Edgar Hoover, who has steadfastly refused to include Negroes among his 4,800 special agents, has a long record of hostility to Negroes."[21]

Although tempered by more enlightened views in the Justice Department and by its own anti-terror work, the FBI's attitude to black Americans damaged that section of the nation. However, it also injured the bureau. To be sure, the FBI focused its more repressive tactics on the relatively powerless. Gays and leftists, too, were easy pickings, while anti-interventionists were vulnerable to the charge of being unpatriotic, at least as long as the war lasted. But a coalition of the aggrieved can be dangerous, and America's liberals, even those in government, were losing patience with the agency. By the war's end, America was ready for its great Gestapo panic.

8

gestapo fears and the intelligence schism: 1940–1975

In 1947, President Harry Truman and the U.S. Congress reorganized the American security apparatus, for the first time giving the nation a major peacetime intelligence capability. Truman's motive was the detection of military threats from the Soviet Union. Congress had a more general approach, wishing to prevent another Pearl Harbor–style attack from any quarter. Virtually all commentators agreed that America needed a more centralized intelligence system.

The National Security Act of 1947 established the Central Intelligence Agency (CIA), whose very name indicated the direction in which the government intended to go. Moreover, the director of the CIA would wear a second hat, that of director of central intelligence in charge of the entire intelligence effort, military, signals, and FBI included.

But while the new arrangement aimed to unite, it also separated. The CIA would be allowed to operate only in the foreign sphere. The FBI had to give up foreign work, surrendering its Latin American assets in the process. It would in future operate only on the domestic front. Thus, flying in the face of the call for centralization, there appeared an intelligence schism. Its problematic nature was immediately apparent. For example, Wilmoore Kendall, later a prominent neoconservative philosopher but at the time head of the CIA's Latin American intelligence division, referred scornfully to the mentality of the "three mile limit," whereby foreign and domestic intelligence were not integrated.[1]

Why did President Truman restrict the FBI to domestic work? The explanation is more political than administrative. The recent conduct of the FBI having aroused suspicions that it was undertaking political work, the bureau was already vulnerable to the charge that it resembled an American Gestapo. Then there came a major Gestapo scare in 1945, the outcome of which was that nobody wanted so much as a hint of that genocidal organization in America. The FBI had a compromised reputation on the racial issue, and did not seem to be the proper conduit for American values. That public perception made it too risky for Truman to consolidate or expand the bureau's powers.

The problem first became apparent at the time of an earlier Gestapo scare. On 5 February 1940, the bureau swooped on a number of homes in Detroit. This was after a secret indictment had been issued to authorize the arrest of a number of individuals on charges of having recruited men for the Abraham Lincoln Brigade. One of those arrested, Leon Davis, had fought in Spain. Some of the people on the list were communists. Davis and others were members of the United Automobile Workers union.

The arrests came at 5 a.m., leading some of the victims to conclude that gangsters were kidnapping them. The suspects' homes were searched without warrants, and the prisoners were held incommunicado for lengthy periods without access to lawyers. After an uproar in the press, the arrestees were released, and none were charged. But the matter did not end there, for the FBI's arbitrary action had sent out shockwaves in Detroit and throughout the nation. Dr. Henry Hitt Crane, pastor of the Central Methodist Church of Detroit, observed, "the American people will not countenance even the first steps toward the establishment of a secret police that will in any way resemble the despised German Gestapo or the hated Russian Ogpu."[2]

The Detroit raids were a gift to the bureau's critics in the Senate. New Deal supporter George Norris took the lead. The Nebraska Republican had first asked questions about the bureau's accountability back in 1913. He now drew on the advice of Max Lowenthal, a lawyer who had been studying the FBI and its authorizations since the late 1920s. On 22 February, Senator Norris lodged a formal protest with the attorney general. He attacked the revival of the bureau's General Intelligence Division (GID), which had been the instrument of the notorious Palmer raids of 1919.

Letters of support poured into the senator's office. The press sided with him. The *Nation*, a liberal journal already noted for its criticisms of the FBI, denounced its Gestapo tendencies, choosing the heading "Our Lawless G-men." The *Philadelphia Inquirer* announced that the "G" in G-men now stood for Gestapo, and claimed that Attorney General Jackson was appalled at the FBI's conduct. Hoover furiously retorted that the paper's proprietor,

Moe Annenberg, was taking revenge on the bureau for an indictment the previous summer. But even the conservative *New York Daily News* warned of Hoover's "building up [of] a secret police organization of un-American complexion."

Eleanor Roosevelt demanded, through her secretary, the "truth" on Detroit. The historian Mary Beard entered the fray. She complained that Hoover and the GID were about to repeat the excesses of 1919 by setting up "an incipient Ogpu or Gestapo." FBI lawyer Alexander Holtzoff replied. He claimed that Hoover had disapproved of the Palmer raids and appealed to "liberals" to support the director. Forced into responding, the Justice Department announced an in-house inquiry. Henry Schweinhaut, the assistant attorney general then in charge of the department's civil rights division, headed an investigation that, after a few weeks, cleared his colleagues of any wrongdoing. In the *Washington News,* journalist Ludwell Denny announced a "whitewash," though he did caution "liberal critics" to remember that FDR and the attorney general made policy, not J. Edgar Hoover. In his view, Congress too should share responsibility for Gestapo-like practices, and Hoover was likely to become the scapegoat for the more powerful elements in national government.[3]

Burton Wheeler did his best to rein in the bureau. The senator from Montana stated that while the G-men claimed to be stamping out un-Americanism, they were in reality persecuting "thousands of poor, ignorant, helpless people." He admitted he was "prejudiced" against the bureau because it had raided his office "time and time again." He had been down to the Department of Justice where he found a file on himself. He said the FBI had "files on this Senator and that Senator, . . . on Senator Robert M. La Follette. . . . They have gone through the offices of every liberal Senator."

For a while in 1940, it looked as if Hoover would indeed become a scapegoat. Wheeler was chairman of the Interstate Commerce Committee that had jurisdiction over wiretapping, and was about to launch an inquiry into that issue. However, the "Gestapo" protest of 1940 fizzled out. Much though the Senate loves a row, a majority of its members on this occasion supported the administration and, however reluctantly, the drift to interventionism. Not long after the Detroit raids, Congress indicated the majority mood by enacting the Smith Act, making it a crime to advocate the violent overthrow of the U.S. government or to belong to an organization deemed to have that overthrow as its objective. The need for national consensus on security matters in a time of international crisis exerted a powerful influence. Even Senator Wheeler refrained from carrying through with his committee's promised investigation of wiretaps. Although "Gestapo" mutterings continued, the issue laid relatively dormant until the end of the war.

In the meantime, however, events were taking place that would intensify Gestapo fears. The Nazis saw the outbreak of war as an opportunity for the "Final Solution" to what they called the Jewish problem. Beginning at Chelmno in 1941, the German government applied factory mass production techniques to the killing of Jews. Although the Nazis ran a closed and secretive society, the scale of the murders was such that news began to leak, and a press conference organized by the Polish government-in-exile in July 1942 revealed that 700,000 Jews had been gassed or starved to death, a prelude to the murder of millions. For reasons that ranged from disbelief to anti-Semitism, the genocide at first received little publicity in America. However, when U.S. troops stormed Europe and entered the death camps, the reality and scale of the Holocaust became evident. The shock was profound.[4]

The Gestapo issue would turn the tables on J. Edgar Hoover's ambitions. It influenced Harry Truman's decision making, not least because the new president had other reasons for looking askance at the bureau. He had bruising memories. Although personally honest, Truman had been a protégé of the corrupt Pendergast machine in Missouri. The FBI had helped to put Tom Pendergast behind bars, and Truman must have had mixed feelings about this, as he remained loyal to his old boss and attended his funeral in 1945 even at the cost of being wrongly associated with graft.

There were other personal factors, too. Truman was well acquainted with Senator Wheeler, and with Max Lowenthal. As a senator in 1939, Truman had co-sponsored the Wheeler-Truman bill, leading to the Transportation Act of the following year that addressed the problematic finances of the railroad industry. Senator Wheeler had set up a subcommittee to study the issue, on which Lowenthal was a counsel. Lowenthal and Truman became good friends, and Lowenthal was very knowledgeable about the FBI's shortcomings.

As if this were not enough, the White House's new resident had a record of pressing for the welfare of black citizens, a sizable bloc of voters in Missouri. The FBI's racial record would have troubled him even before the Gestapo became a political issue, and that issue could only have concentrated his mind.

The Gestapo parallel again came to public attention in February 1945. FDR's press secretary Stephen T. Early released the genie from the bottle. He leaked to Walter Trohan of the *Chicago Tribune* a confidential memorandum drafted by General Donovan, in which the OSS director proposed a permanent peacetime central intelligence agency, which, everyone assumed, he would wish to direct. Trohan's account in the *Tribune* spoke of "spying at home" and a "super Gestapo," and other newspapers repeated that language. Hoover had combined with other Donovan-haters to shape Roosevelt's thoughts and cause him to authorize the leak, and their activities proved fatal to the OSS chief's ambitions. Donovan pleaded with Roosevelt that some newspapers supported his proposal, and assured him that his hoped-for new agency would have "no police or law enforcement functions," but FDR had other things on his mind and was a sick man. He died on 12 April, and his successor President Truman dismissed the wounded OSS director at the war's end.[5]

That seemed to open the way for the FBI. In September 1945, Attorney General Tom Clark presented "A Plan for U.S. Secret World-Wide Intelligence Coverage," essentially a proposal for extending the FBI's Latin American work to the rest of the world. He said there were advantages in combining domestic and foreign work. Claiming that the FBI's record of respecting civil liberties had been "highly praised even by the American Civil Liberties Union," he argued that the "Gestapo" charge could be resisted.

But, while Truman conceded the advantage of domestic-foreign integration, he cited an operational objection. This was that the FBI's work in Latin America had been police/legal in character, and was too narrow to be described as intelligence. Then, at a meeting with Hoover's emissary, Morton B. Chiles, Truman chose to advance a more political and therefore more lethal objection. He stressed his anxiety that Hoover's brainchild would be denounced as an American "Gestapo."

In the late fall of 1945, Truman warned repeatedly against "building up a gestapo," and he was adamant in his opposition to anything that smacked of a "police state." This meant, according to his aide George Elsey, that he wanted "no single unit or agency in the federal government" to have excessive power. Only his loyalty to his attorney general Tom Clark prevented him from cutting back drastically the FBI's budget.

The anti-FBI campaign continued without letup. In April 1946, for example, the Washington insiders Joseph and Stewart Alsop noted the foreign ambitions of the bureau in their *Washington Post* column, and recited with gusto the reasons why Hoover was being excluded from discussions for the centralization of intelligence. They said the FBI had too little experience of the world outside the United States and Latin America, and had alienated the British, whose help (in the Alsops' opinion) was essential in intelligence matters. Above all, the addition of foreign responsibilities to the FBI's portfolio would create the very real danger of an "American Gestapo." Only dictatorships like Germany and Russia had "a secret service with the responsibility for both foreign espionage and internal security."[6]

It was now the FBI's turn to be a wounded beast, and, to cap his misery, Hoover lost Latin America. In April 1946, Congress cut $3 million from the FBI budget specifically in order to end bureau operations outside the United States. The annual appropriation had climbed from just over $6 million in 1939 to a wartime peak of $44 million in 1945, but it would now descend to a low of just under $35 million in 1947. Against this background, SIS agents began to desert to the Central Intelligence Group (CIG), an interim foreign intelligence agency formed by Truman after his abolition of the OSS.

Ed Tamm visited Admiral William Leahy, Truman's chief of staff, and expressed fury at the CIG's delegation of some of these ex-FBI men to liaise with the bureau. Although SIS officially continued to operate until 31 March 1947, all parties concerned now wanted a rapid FBI exit from Latin America. Leahy told CIG director Hoyt Vandenberg that Hoover needed his agents back in America. To "avoid offending Mr. Hoover," CIG should hire neither current nor former FBI agents, even if that would result in a "temporary reduction of efficiency" in Latin America.

In the background, Hoover fumed at his humiliation, and complained of having been "virtually evicted" from South America. It must remain a matter of guesswork whether the FBI would have acquitted itself well in South America if it had been permitted to continue there. Would it have tolerated the "rat line" operated by Army intelligence and then the CIA, whereby Nazi war criminals like Klaus Barbie were allowed to live unmolested in South America in return for intelligence cooperation against the communists, or would the bureau's arrest culture have prevailed?

Setting aside such speculation, Hoover undoubtedly scrapped an entire intelligence network just when America was starting to worry about international communism. Within months, an outbreak of violent unrest in Bogotá, Colombia, threatened to disrupt the founding of the Organization of American States and was a serious embarrassment to the United States. The *Washington News* attributed this to a predictive failure arising from the withdrawal of five hundred FBI agents from South America. In the wake of Bogotá, the CIA beefed up its Latin American operations, but in a manner that would further embarrass the United States.[7]

Tensions between the bureau and the CIA now developed to a troublesome degree. To be sure, there were retrospective denials of the problem by officials with a vested interest in proclaiming a united front. CIA directors were also national intelligence chiefs, and supposed to deliver harmony. CIA boss Allen Dulles claimed in 1963 that stories of FBI-CIA discord were mere "rumors" and that there was "no failure of coordination." Nine years later, his successor Richard Helms claimed that the "bad relationship between the Agency and the FBI" was one of those "hoary-headed" myths that "stick like barnacles." Two years after that, another CIA director, William Colby, insisted the CIA relationship with the FBI was "in good shape." However, such denials only confirmed the existence of a problem. Even Helms realistically conceded in his 1972 remarks that there had been "some trouble back in the '50's and so forth," and that "Mr. Hoover himself had a certain antipathy toward the [Central Intelligence] Agency." This was an understatement. In a handwritten instruction in 1970, Hoover ordained that "direct liaison" with the CIA was to be "terminated," and any future communications were to be "by letter only."[8]

Resentment at the loss of Latin America was one source of Hoover's hostility. Hoover had insisted in the 1940s that the CIA could not hire a former FBI agent in Latin America unless that individual had held another job in the interim. But there was fighting back as well as obstruction. In spite of the Truman administration's decision, the bureau appears to have held on by its fingernails to the lost continent. Newspaper reporters commented on the number of FBI agents still operating in Latin America under "legal attaché" cover.

With the CIA engaging in James Bond–type adventurism in Guatemala, Guyana, and Cuba, there were suggestions that the bureau would better perform the analytical role. With Cuban and other Latino populations swelling inside the United States, there seemed to be a logical counterespionage berth for the FBI in Latin American affairs. When a crisis in the Dominican Republic caught the CIA napping in 1965, there was speculation that President Johnson trusted the bureau more than the agency, and that he was playing one off against the other. The press returned to the issue after Hoover's death with rumors that, in the wake of revelations about CIA shortcomings, FBI operations would be permitted in Latin America.[9]

FBI-CIA rivalry was by no means confined to Latin American affairs. From the beginning, it was part of the culture of the two institutions. Mutual disregard manifested itself over significant issues, such as the Intelligence Advisory Committee (IAC). The IAC was established in 1947. It operated under the chairmanship of the DCI (director of central intelligence), a coordinating official who in practice was always the CIA director. The armed forces and the State Department were represented on the committee, but, not wishing to be subservient to the CIA director, Hoover refused to sit on the body. He sent a representative to attend its meetings, only for that official to inform the DCI that as the FBI had been banned from foreign intelligence, he would not play an active role. Having been excluded from the wartime intelligence high table, the FBI was now refusing to join it in peacetime.

The formidable General Walter Bedell Smith, head of the CIA from 1950 to 1953, made a renewed effort to persuade Hoover to join the IAC. The FBI chief remained intransigent on the IAC matter, but he did agree to meet Smith for lunch from time to time. One day, Hoover declared himself deeply interested in "flying saucers," and demanded every scrap of information on the phenomenon from the IAC. The redacted CIA minute on the matter records Smith's reaction: "DCI has said pungently that **** . . . should attend IAC meetings so he could get dope." Double entendre or not, the reproving tone was obvious.

Hoover deserted the team in other ways, too. In spite of his anti-communist pedigree, in March 1950 he withdrew the FBI from the Interdepartmental Committee on International Communism, known as the "JIGSAW committee." The director of naval intelligence was dismayed at the damage this caused. Arguing that "many of the subversive actions of the Communists are directed against the internal security of the U.S.," he recommended "reorganization of the JIGSAW Committee with FBI participation, which is considered highly important." From the reactions of his peers, it is plain that Hoover's willful refusal to cooperate was no trivial matter.[10]

Just as ominous was the FBI's obstruction of security procedures. Upon the establishment of the CIA's predecessor, the Central Intelligence Group, the FBI had agreed to carry out security checks on prospective CIG employees. It would review one hundred cases a month and receive a hundred dollars per case, promising a result in every instance within two weeks. However, Alex Rosen, assistant director of the bureau's Investigative and Accounting Division, told the CIG that the FBI could conduct only overt checks, making no discreet inquiries; nor could the Feds undertake surveillance of CIG personnel already in post.

Then in January 1947 Hoover complained that the FBI was having to handle many more than a hundred cases per month and would in future need up to thirty days per clearance. CIG found all this to be unsatisfactory and set up its own investigative group to handle the more sensitive and urgent cases, in this way undertaking surveillance of U.S. citizens within the United States. In vain did the CIA later try to paper over the cracks with an observation that carried a sting in its tail: "At this point in time, CIG-FBI relations appeared to be cordial with CIG being most circumspect in its dealings with the FBI."[11]

According to the CIA, Hoover started to become difficult from the moment the DCI made arrangements for the CIG takeover in Latin America. On 30 September 1947, "without warning," the FBI director said his bureau had too much work and that the newly formed CIA would have to take over security checking by 15 October. In an effort to change Hoover's mind, DCI Admiral Roscoe Hillenkoetter wrote him a placatory letter:

> Our mission is the foreign intelligence one. We certainly do not wish to build up, even for the purpose of investigating our own candidates, an organization which could even be accused of duplicating or overlapping the function of the FBI, as an example, I feel the very fact that there exists in our investigative files the FBI reports on myself . . . is a protection to the Government and myself. This is in accord with the democratic process of checks and balances and dispels all accusations of "Gestapo" to either of our Agencies.[12]

FBI-CIA relations at this point became so acrimonious that, even with declassification in 2001, the CIA blanked out an entire page of its record of the proceedings. Hoover did extend his deadline, but the FBI ceased its checks in 1948, and the CIA established its own Employee Investigations Branch. In December of that year, the FBI resumed security checks, but in December 1950 it again and finally withheld its services. The CIA account of that event reads: "Hurried, and to a degree, frantic efforts were instituted to compensate for the disruption in Agency staffing caused by the FBI withdrawal."[13]

In the early years of the Cold War, the Feds threatened to place in jeopardy the government's attempt to reorganize the intelligence establishment and thus to counter the threat posed by the Soviet Union. The FBI in this period refused to accept the authority of the DCI, would not join the rest of the intelligence community in the defense of national security, obstructed the security checking of key intelligence personnel at a time when the communists were known to be running a major espionage offensive, and got away with it.

The degree to which FBI obstruction continued in and beyond the 1950s cannot be properly measured because the bureau destroyed some of the evidence and much of the rest of it remains classified. Counterintelligence, a sensitive area because it has to do with Americans betraying their friends, does not easily lend itself to declassification. Efforts at cooperation took place, with the FBI undertaking some complementary domestic work to help the CIA with its counterintelligence efforts. However, the indications are that resentment was never far below the surface. For example, in 1970 the CIA annoyed Hoover by probing into the FBI's sources relating to the agency's asset Professor Thomas Riha, who had apparently defected to communist Czechoslovakia. In retaliation, the FBI director disbanded the FBI's CIA Liaison Office and reduced mail opening and other domestic programs carried out on behalf of the CIA.

Whatever the difficulties, it was always important politically to aim at a show of cooperation. The bureau and the agency had to demonstrate to congressional appropriations committees that they were making the effort to get along together. Under Hoover's aegis, FBI personnel attended a counterintelligence course run by the CIA. After his death, the CIA agreed to supply the FBI training school with teaching material consisting of "copies of unclassified samples" of its work. But on this occasion the author of the policy-determining agency memorandum was at pains to indicate that the samples would be generic not specific, that FBI people would not attend the CIA senior personnel training program, and that there would be "cooperation in only the broadest sense." FBI-CIA suspicions were mutual, and outlasted J. Edgar Hoover.

Searching common ground for the purpose of a display of amity, the FBI and the CIA could at least agree on the importance of secrecy. At a two-hour meeting to discuss requests for files under recent freedom of information legislation, officials agreed that the FBI would deny knowledge of CIA documents in its custody, and vice versa. This was in the 1970s, when the scandal-ridden intelligence community was under the microscope. Jointly under attack, the CIA and the FBI sometimes made common cause. Yet the relationship remained chronically parlous. When the CIA rallied to advise the Feds about their retirement provision when personnel cuts were in the offing, it simultaneously spied on FBI pensions arrangements, a practice that the bureau reciprocated.

Efforts to patch things up continued to indicate the existence of an underlying problem. In 1980, the directors of the two agencies launched Operation Courtship, an attempt to mend the rift in at least one significant sphere, the initiative to "turn" Soviet intelligence officials based in Washington, D.C. But the rivalry rumbled on, surviving even seismic events like the end of the Cold War and 9/11. In 1994, both the National Security Council (NSC) and the Senate Intelligence Committee reviewed poor liaison that had allowed the CIA's Aldrich Ames to spy for Moscow. When the NSC recommended that the FBI should have a relative increase in counterespionage responsibility, CIA director James Woolsey reacted furiously and lobbied against the proposed arrangement on Capitol Hill. In 2003, a Congressional Research Service report based on careful comparative study concluded that the FBI-CIA relationship was less well coordinated than that between MI5 and MI6. It might have added that the MI5-MI6 partnership was itself one of legendary fractiousness.[14]

The unification of American intelligence, a major theme after 9/11, was already deemed desirable in the 1940s. Only powerful feelings could have brought about the FBI-CIA schism in the face of such thinking. Lingering states'-rights, white-ascendancy sentiment was still a factor in opposition to federal policing and counterintelligence, but it had become a minor one. More important, the erosion of liberal support for the bureau led to the ascendancy of the view that the FBI should not be given too much power. But the reputations of the OGPU and the Gestapo were key short-term factors. The murderous ruthlessness of the OGPU was not yet universally appreciated, but the Gestapo was already widely detested for its trampling on human rights well before the end of the war. When news arrived from the concentration camps, the shock of the Gestapo's genocide inevitably became the final catalyst in the divide-and-weaken fissuring of American counterintelligence.

Yet the anti-FBI reaction, while understandable in emotional terms, was illogical. To equate the Gestapo and the FBI was to engage in a misinformed game of copy and paste. The FBI had not killed millions of people, and was not about to. The bureau had played its part in the curtailment of personal liberties in World War II, but wartime restrictions were nothing new, and bore no comparison with events in Germany. Whatever commentators said at the time, the Gestapo was a domestic agency and did not centralize foreign and domestic intelligence. In banning the FBI from foreign work in defiance of its centralization creed, the Truman administration made the FBI more like the Gestapo, not less.

Political decisions are not, however, always based on logic. The Gestapo comparison would not have held up to cool scrutiny, but it was especially damaging for the FBI because of the bureau's reputation in matters of race. Politicians did not overtly complete the Gestapo-FBI-race equivalence triangle, but they did not have to. The Holocaust did it for them.

FBI-CIA rivalry is usually regarded as deeply regrettable, and that implies that the 1947 split was a mistake. However, certain qualifications are in order. First, there were other aspects of the 1947 reform that can be regarded as even more unfortunate, such as lumbering the CIA, an intelligence agency, with a covert-action mission that undermined its main function, not to mention its reputation. Second, as President Truman noted, the FBI had limited foreign expertise. Third, FBI-CIA noncooperation stemmed not just from petty rivalry, but also from weak, divide-and-rule presidential leadership and repeated failures to back the DCI's authority over America's giant intelligence community. Finally, there can be no systemic formula for the preemption of surprise attacks, every one of which is by definition different from the last one.

In one area, however, FBI-CIA bickering was very damaging. This was the area of "intermestic" intelligence, work that had international as well as domestic dimensions. Examples of intermestic intelligence are counterespionage, anti-drugs work, and anti-terrorism. The FBI would enjoy successes in all these areas, but it also suffered setbacks that might have been avoided with better coordination. By neglecting the ideals of Reconstruction and thus laying itself open to emotional charges of being an American Gestapo, the bureau lost not just a South American empire, but also the opportunity to operate intermestically. The nation would pay a price for that.

9

anachronism as myth and reality: 1945–1972

By the 1960s, some Americans regarded the FBI as an anachronism. J. Edgar Hoover, who entered the eighth decade of his life on 1 January 1965, seemed to them to be a spent force. At the end of 1959, supporters of John F. Kennedy urged the president-elect to fire the director. JFK refrained from doing that. But, according to his adviser Arthur Schlesinger, Jr., this was only because he needed a "strategy of reassurance" and realized that Hoover was still a national icon. The perceptions of anachronism persisted to the eve of the Boss's death. In a book published in 1971, former special agent William W. Turner claimed that Hoover "was still living in the long-faded Dillinger days, when the FBI legend was born."

In significant ways, the anachronism charge is understandable. Between the end of World War II and the director's demise in 1972, the FBI participated in an overblown anti-communist witch-hunt that resembled the shooting of a dead horse. The bureau's harassment of civil rights campaigners showed it to be out of tune with the times. The same can be said of its persecution of homosexuals. The Feds failed to keep up with the slick nationwide drug-pushing tactics of the Mafia. And then the bureau seemed hopelessly adrift in the radical 1960s.

But in some ways Hoover was far from anachronistic. On particular issues, he parted company with conservative opinion. He advocated gun control, for example, and his bureau renewed its assault on white racism. Nor was Hoover anachronistic in the sense of being out of step with public opinion. The American people supported his anti-communist policies. In general, the FBI remained one of America's most popular institutions until the 1970s. The director may have been conservative in supporting the "law and order" rhetoric of the 1960s, but here he was more in touch with public opinion than the liberals who failed to keep up with the national mood and then lost the law-and-order debate in the 1968 election, which propelled Richard Nixon to the White House. Even at the very end of his life, Hoover kept his finger on the public pulse. He did not genuflect to the (at first) popular President Nixon. In refusing to allow his bureau to become enmeshed in the surveillance malpractices that led to the Watergate scandal, he demonstrated that his political antennae remained superior to those of some much younger men.

Hoover's hunt for Red spies did degenerate into an overblown obsession. But this was not before the FBI had chalked up some achievements. The successful side of the bureau's counterespionage work in the early Cold War is evident in the career of Robert J. Lamphere. This talented special agent encapsulated an FBI paradox. His work was effective yet counterproductive, a triumph, but a triumph that led to excess.

Described by a communist newspaper as "baby-faced and hard-lipped," Lamphere's powerful build and aggressive looks disguised his underlying intelligence while underlining his determined character. His dedication to hunting down communist spies is at least partly explained by a family background of public service. Grandfather Lamphere lost an arm fighting for the Union, became the Treasury Department's chief administrator, and, with his remaining arm, wrote a book on the organization of the federal government. Robert Lamphere grew up in the Coeur d'Alene mining district of Idaho, a region deeply riven by class conflict. Through the influence of his mine-manager father, he had a college-vacation job working underground. He refused to join the union.

Lamphere arrived in Washington in 1940, where he completed his law degree, joined the FBI, and received his standard issue .38-caliber pistol. Events now took place that would pitch Soviet intelligence, the NKVD, into deadly rivalry with the FBI. The Soviets spied on America even when the United States was a wartime ally, as they wanted scientific and technical expertise to help them fight Germany. As U.S.-USSR Cold War tensions developed, each side conducted espionage against the other, but this time as avowed adversaries.

In November 1941, the NKVD's New York station chief Pavel Pastelnyak warned Moscow that U.S. and British scientists were working on an atomic bomb. His controllers launched operation "Enormoz," an espionage project in the USA, Canada, and the U.K. intended to uncover the secrets of nuclear research.

The nuclear scientist Klaus Fuchs became a Soviet informant. Fuchs was a German who had opposed the rise of Hitler and had associations with the anti-Nazi underground resistance movement. Like many members of the resistance movement, he was a communist. He left Germany in 1933 to avoid arrest, and in the war years he was mainly associated with Edinburgh University in Scotland; meanwhile, his sister Kristel attended Swarthmore College in the States. In 1941, Fuchs volunteered his services to the NKVD. In furtherance of research and of his espionage mission, he traveled to the United States as a member of a British team whose object was the joint development of a nuclear weapon. In America, he gained familiarity with the research at the Manhattan Project and Los Alamos. According to GRU (Soviet military intelligence), he sent his controllers 570 sheets of valuable data between 1941 and 1943.

In September 1945, Igor Gouzenko finally confirmed beyond doubt that communists with access to defense information were a security risk. In that month, Gouzenko, a defecting code clerk in the Soviet embassy in Ottawa, told his story to the Royal Canadian Mounted Police. He said that the Soviets were operating spy networks in Canada, Britain, and the United States, and were using local communists as agents. Alan Nunn May, a British scientist who had visited U.S. research laboratories and worked in Canada, passed to GRU not just classified information on atomic research but also an actual sample of enriched uranium.

Gouzenko's debriefing by MI5 with the assistance of the FBI did not in itself lead to the decryption of Soviet diplomatic messages. This was because the messages were enciphered in addition to using code words. The Soviets used the one-off pad system. Enciphering and deciphering personnel had pads of four-digit numbers and employed each four-digit set just once, so codebreakers could detect no patterns in runs of letters. Army codebreakers working at a facility in Arlington Hall, in northern Virginia, confronted a formidable obstacle. Then they discovered that, in a breach of security procedure, some overworked Soviet encryptors were using the one-time pads more than once. The Arlington Hall people developed techniques for identifying repetition and, as a result, were able to read a considerable number of Soviet diplomatic messages sent from 1942 to 1948. Moscow knew through its agent William Weisband, a Russian-language consultant on the periphery of the U.S. Army code-breaking program, that an effort was being made to read its traffic. But the Russians were unaware of the critical breakthrough until February 1950. In that month, they received a tip-off from Kim Philby, the British official who was responsible for

British-American intelligence liaison but was at the same time a member of the notorious Soviet-run Cambridge spy ring.

The work at Arlington Hall was known by the code name "Venona." It was clear from Venona that Gouzenko's claims were true, and that Soviet diplomatic traffic had been the means of organizing espionage activities inside the United States. But Venona's product was fragmentary, and a great deal of forensic work needed to be done.

It was here that Lamphere played a significant role. The Venona messages made it plain that the Soviets had had a spy in New York's Manhattan Project. Piecing together information from the Gouzenko case, from a captured Gestapo document, and from Venona, Lamphere identified Fuchs as the most likely suspect. Fuchs was by now head of the theoretical physics division at the British Atomic Energy Research Establishment in Harwell, England. Lamphere alerted MI5, who already had their suspicions, and Fuchs was arrested on 2 February 1950.

At first, there was a problem with the prosecution. If Venona messages were used in court, the Arlington Hall operation would be revealed to the Soviets, who were assumed to be unaware of it. But, under British interrogation, Fuchs himself resolved this dilemma. He had developed doubts about the Soviet system and about his role as a communist spy, and confessed. It would no longer be necessary to divulge Venona.

FBI-MI5 relations were not at this time in a state of prime health. The British were developing their own nuclear bomb, and trying to conceal their activities from disapproving American eyes. The United Kingdom authorities rightly suspected that the Americans were holding out on them with regard to nuclear research information. For his part, J. Edgar Hoover fumed at "the sly British" for denying the FBI access to the Fuchs interrogation process. The British were being difficult with good reason. Fuchs disliked the American nuclear monopoly and, having assisted the Soviets, had been feeding U.S. data into the British atomic research program. To keep the relationship sweet, the British encouraged Fuchs to believe that he might be favorably treated, and he was be released from prison at the relatively early date of 1959. It was in the British interest to encourage Fuchs to impart American secrets, not British ones, and to keep the impatient American interrogators at bay.

When, in May 1950, Lamphere at last traveled to London to question Fuchs on behalf of the Americans, he had to do so in company with an FBI minder whom he cordially disliked, Assistant Director Hugh "Troutmouth" Clegg, co-author of the 1940 FBI report on British intelligence, and an American official who did not go down well with MI5. Lamphere, how-ever, overcame the mutual distrust, and the American interrogation pro-ceeded.

The U.S. scientific establishment hoped the Lamphere-Clegg interro-gation would reveal the extent of Fuchs's information betrayals, and the Atomic Energy Commission framed some questions it wanted them to an-swer. But Lamphere and Clegg were not qualified to ask follow-up ques-tions about atomic science, and they concentrated on police work. They simply wanted to know who, in the United States, had spied for the Soviet Union. Fuchs was uncooperative until Lamphere suggested that things might go badly for his sister in America if he did not change his tune. Kris-tel was already in hospital, due to acute nervous distress. Lamphere and Clegg asked about specific individuals. Presented with a list of suspects that included Albert Einstein, Robert Oppenheimer, and Edward Teller, Fuchs revealed nothing of a compromising nature. But he did provide informa-tion that led, after a process of deduction by Lamphere, to the identification of some American traitors.[1]

It could be argued that Lamphere's achievement came too late. It did not protect U.S. national security secrets because the Russians already had their information from Fuchs by the time he confessed. What he told the Soviets about the atomic bomb program helped Moscow accelerate its pro-duction of a nuclear weapon. The test explosion conducted in 1949 caught the West off guard, and the later Soviet development of a hydrogen bomb may also have derived partly from secrets that Fuchs disclosed.

According to one school of thought, the FBI's obsession with subver-sion as distinct from espionage prevented it from catching the Soviet atomic spies in time to prevent serious damage to U.S. national security.[2] But, in defense of Lamphere's personal performance, he was put onto the case at a stage when it was too late to achieve prevention. He helped to crack what was probably the most serious single case of espionage ever conducted against the United States. His success contributed to the plugging at least of similar leaks in the future. The FBI may not have been visionary in its antic-ipation of different types of future threat (counterespionage agencies rarely are), and its success was confined to halting the Russians, a predominantly white, European nation with much more in common with 1940s America than either side dared admit. But, in spite of these qualifications, in the case of Lamphere the bureau had produced an ace.

However, in its desperation to win back the ground it had lost in turf wars, the FBI distorted its counterespionage mission. On the pretext that some spies had been communists, the assumption was made that treason was generically leftist in character. This was an archaic assumption, as Soviet spymasters, once having been rumbled, decided it would be foolish to continue with readily identifiable, ideologically motivated spies. In future, most American traitors would betray their country for money, not principle. FBI spy catchers either could not see that or would not see it, as they had another agenda. The Canadian political scientist Reg Whitaker has identified a process he called "Cold War alchemy," whereby government officials processed spy cases to make them look like subversion, and to justify political repression.[3]

The FBI's contribution to McCarthyism helped to drive millions of Americans into cringe mode. It contributed to a climate of opinion that helped the bureau to escape public censure. Its infractions of civil liberties, its reluctance to fight organized crime, and its obstruction of national security coordination—all these went unchecked at the height of the McCarthy era.

The origins of this dark story are to be found in the Venona and Robert Lamphere successes. Lamphere's interrogation of Fuchs forced the British scientist to identify a trail that led to David Greenglass, a soldier serving at the Los Alamos laboratory. Greenglass's sister Ethel was married to Julius Rosenberg, an American communist and Soviet spy who controlled Greenglass and other agents. The FBI arrested the Rosenbergs on 17 July 1950, and told the husband that he had to identify other agents if he wanted Ethel, the mother of his two small children, to live. Julius Rosenberg refused. He and Ethel Rosenberg were executed in June 1953.

Ethel probably guessed the nature of her husband's activities but was herself innocent of espionage. As for Julius, he was of rather minor assistance to Moscow. But the Rosenberg case was sensationally reported. It had the effect of reinforcing popular fears of the Red menace, and liberal belief in the iniquities of McCarthyism.[4]

As a cause célèbre dividing Left and Right in American politics, the Rosenberg case built on the impression created by the conviction of Alger Hiss a few months earlier—this, too, had been connected to Venona evidence. Alger Hiss had served in the New Deal and then worked for the State Department. At a hearing before the House Un-American Activities Committee (HUAC) in August 1948, FBI informer Whittaker Chambers accused Hiss of having delivered secret State Department documents to his Soviet controller (Chambers himself) in 1938. Hiss was charged with perjury for denying this under oath (the statute of limitations meant he could not be directly prosecuted for espionage undertaken more than a decade previously). He was convicted in January 1950, and went to prison.

The significance of the case arose less from the spying Hiss was supposed to have done than from the symbolism of a New Dealer on trial, and from his supposed work as an agent of influence standing at the president's elbow—would America have ceded half of Europe to Stalin at the Yalta summit but for "the whispered pleas from the lips of traitors" (Joe McCarthy's words) insinuated into Roosevelt's ear? Hiss supporters insisted that he had received an unfair trial. The affair gave rise to a false-debate syndrome, with Right and Left arguing for decades over Hiss's guilt on the illusory premise that a single verdict could win a political argument.

Declassification of Venona materials in the 1990s led to claims that Hiss's Soviet-intelligence code name—allegedly "Ales"—could at last be verified. But Hiss defenders questioned the interpretation of Venona given by neoconservative scholars, recruited Russian intelligence veterans to their side, and even impugned the integrity of those who defended the guilty verdict. The continuing vigor of the Hiss debate is testimony to the longevity of the McCarthyist controversy, and to the alienation from the FBI even of some of those New Deal liberals who had presided over its expansion in the late 1930s.[5]

Strictly speaking, the McCarthy period is scarcely an "era," extending according to narrow definition merely from the start of 1950, when Joseph McCarthy claimed that the State Department was infested with communists, until the Senate vote in December 1954 to "condemn" the by now discredited Wisconsin Republican. The political columnist Richard Rovere described this phase of the senator's career as "mercifully short." But, when defined less literally, the great scare later given McCarthy's name can be traced to the creation of HUAC in 1938 and the passage in 1940 of the Smith Act, which forbade any conspiracy to overthrow the government by force or membership in an organization dedicated to the government's overthrow. And although McCarthy faded from the scene in the mid-1950s, McCarthyism lasted longer. Some historians have portrayed the federal government as being at the heart of post–World War II intolerance, and have assigned a critical role to the FBI. The historian Ellen Schrecker has not been alone in suggesting that "Hooverism" might be a better term for the elongated phenomenon. As evidenced in the Hiss controversy, the debate about McCarthyism-Hooverism lasted even longer, outliving the famous director.[6]

By the 1950s, the great panic consisted of a Lavender Scare directed against homosexuals, a Red Scare directed against the Left and liberals, a Pink Scare aimed at assertive women, and a Black Scare conducted against the civil rights movement. Congressional committees promoted headline-grabbing investigations: most prominently HUAC, the Senate Internal Security Subcommittee (SISS), and McCarthy's own organism, the Permanent Subcommittee on Investigations of the Committee on Government Operations, whose broadcast hearings made an inquisition out of television. At the height of McCarthy's popularity, a Gallup poll indicated that half of America approved of his tactics with only 29 percent against; the chief justice of the Supreme Court observed that, if the Bill of Rights were put to a vote, it would lose.[7]

With American values disintegrating before her eyes, Eleanor Roosevelt said the FBI should be doing HUAC's job. Here was a New Deal liberal who tried to keep the faith with an agency her husband had fostered, but which in reality had become conservative. Adlai Stevenson, the Democratic contender for the presidency in the 1952 election, also believed the job of ferreting out disloyal communists should be left to the professionals in the FBI. No doubt he hoped that the bureau's involvement would lower the political temperature and take the sting out of McCarthyism. As in the Theodore Roosevelt and New Deal eras, there was an elitist faith in professionals and experts, and a dwindling minority of liberals stubbornly hoped that the thoroughly trained G-men would be able to see off the populist orators. Pro-FBI liberals tended to be staunchly anti-communist, and the historian William Keller has advanced this as a reason why they allowed the bureau its "autonomy."

But the FBI secretly betrayed these stalwart liberals. It kept files on both ER and Stevenson, whom Hoover perceived as a Hiss sympathizer and soft on communism; the FBI withheld support from the police in Stevenson's home state of Illinois, and spread the rumor that "Adeline" was a homosexual. Neither ER nor Stevenson realized at the time that the FBI was, in Ellen Schrecker's words, "at the heart" of the system that facilitated McCarthyism.[8]

Misplaced liberal support for the FBI came most significantly from President Truman. In March 1947, he established a loyalty-security program designed to combat both espionage and conservative and Republican attacks on the alleged softness of his administration. The FBI was assigned the task of making security checks on government employees, including atomic scientists and, until the bureau-agency split, CIA personnel. In a further effort to satisfy public opinion in the wake of the fall of China to communism and of McCarthy's accusations about treason in the State Department, the administration encouraged loyalty hearings by a Senate foreign relations subcommittee chaired by Millard Tydings (D-Md.). China expert Owen Lattimore was dragged before the committee and would be forced to leave America in a welter of hysterical innuendo, one of several indications that Truman's effort to propitiate the Right was a tactical error that backfired.

Hoover was reluctant to help the Tydings committee. He watched its deliberations with interest, sending FBI agents to the Hill to make personal notes on the proceedings. But when asked to make FBI reports available to the committee, he refused. He said that FBI files often contained unverified information that, in the wrong hands, could be used to distort the truth. Furthermore, there was a need to protect FBI sources. An editorial writer for the *Cincinnati Post* agreed with these views, stating that Senator McCarthy, in particular, could not be trusted with that kind of information, as he was "too much given to shooting off his mouth."

Hoover was delighted with this editorial, and with the fact that Senator Tydings had received a copy of it (possibly at Hoover's instigation, but this cannot be confirmed because the record is partly redacted). He remained wary even after Peynton Ford of the attorney general's office had reached a compromise with Seth Richardson of the Loyalty Review Board. According to this compromise, the Tydings committee would see reports only after the excision of sensitive information, including that on "espionage investigations, such as Lattimore." The FBI director instructed his negotiator: "Analyze [Richardson's 24 April 1950 memorandum] carefully and be certain there are no 'jokers.' We must protect our own interests—[no] one else will—certainly not Ford nor Richardson." The director appears to have had trouble trusting an inquiry that had as one of its purposes the preemption of further inquiries.[9]

Hoover treated other investigative committees with caution, too. He was wary of McCarthy's committee. The Wisconsin senator had the habit of citing FBI data rather too freely for comfort, and McCarthy's assistant Roy Cohn committed the further gaffe of saying that the committee was enacting an FBI agenda. Nevertheless, the director did give information to the committee. A common enemy, not the Soviet Union but the CIA, bonded him and the senator. McCarthy shared Hoover's intense dislike of that agency, considering it to be stuffed with closet communists and liberals. In 1953, he tried (unsuccessfully) to subpoena the CIA official William P. Bundy, who had offended him by making a donation to the Alger Hiss defense fund.

Hostility to gays was another bonding factor. Hoover had started sur-veillance of gays in 1937, depicting them as subversive and vulnerable to blackmail when in sensitive government posts. In spite of the fact that no American homosexual has ever been blackmailed into espionage, by 1977 the "Sex Deviate" files ran to 330,000 pages. But the Lavender Scare was not based on evidence. Clyde Hoey (D-N.C.) headed a 1950 investigation into the alleged problem, in the course of which CIA director Roscoe Hillen-koetter delivered fabricated testimony on the invidious role of the homo-sexual spy in history. When FBI gossip prompted McCarthy to query the ap-pointment of Charles Bohlen as ambassador to the Soviet Union in March 1953, and to ask if this defender of the Yalta accords was a homosexual, Hoover obligingly reported that Bohlen was "a very close buddy" of the U.S. consul general in Munich, who was a "well-known homosexual." This caused Charles Thayer, the official in question, to resign his Munich post rather than face a public inquiry and embarrass Bohlen, who was, indeed, "close" to him, as he was his brother-in-law.

But the innuendos also prompted the Senate Foreign Relations Com-mittee to insist, on this occasion, on access to FBI raw reports. These reports showed the rumor cupboard to be bare of evidence. So, the Foreign Rela-tions Committee confirmed Bohlen in his appointment, and Hoover suf-fered the indignity of an all-out attack. This came from committee member J. William Fulbright, a former FBI supporter who now saw McCarthy as a budding Hitler and the bureau as his secret police. It was at this point that Hoover finally decided that McCarthy was an unreliable ally and withdrew his support, anticipating a sinking ship as he had done in the case of the Palmer raids more than three decades earlier.

However, like other aspects of McCarthyism-Hooverism, the persecu-tion of gays would continue beyond the 1950s. Supreme Court cases in 1965 and 1969 established equal rights for gays in federal employment, but this, along with other aspects of sexual liberalism that swept through 1960s America, left the FBI untouched. The bureau's anti-gay policy was anachro-nistic and unlikely to yield higher appropriations, but it carried its own logic. It diverted attention from the persistent rumors that the director might himself be homosexual, and gave Hoover information that could be exploited politically or passed on to his political masters.

The FBI file on Henry Cabot Lodge, Jr., demonstrates that the bureau's interest in homosexuality had little to do with espionage. Lodge served as President John F. Kennedy's ambassador in South Vietnam. The bureau had earlier investigated him when he was President Dwight D. Eisenhower's nominee to be U.S. ambassador to the United Nations. On that occasion, previous allegations of homosexuality garnered by Louis B. Nichols, head of the FBI's Crime Records Division, were found to be unproven. Nichols's anonymous informant had accused an unlikely array of public figures of being homosexual, including President Roosevelt. But the false testimony about Lodge remained in Hoover's files, one more unsubstantiated rumor to be deployed if advantage beckoned.

The FBI file on homosexuals continued to be both active and actively deployed into the 1970s. For example, in 1970, with the administration increasingly under siege by critics of the Vietnam War, President Nixon's White House aide H. R. Haldeman asked Hoover for a list of Washington reporters who were homosexual, and the FBI was able to oblige within forty-eight hours. Although the 300,000-page sex deviates file was destroyed in 1977, its existence was not publicly admitted until 1990, an indication that the FBI's archaic values were by no means entirely a consequence of Hoover's influence.[10]

Hoover hated to trust any politician with original FBI reports, and by choice he informed through paraphrases, and only those whom he thought would be discreet about their source. Thus, he obstructed Tydings and gave McCarthy only qualified support. He assisted Francis E. Walter when the Pennsylvania Democrat was in charge of HUAC (1955–63), whereas he had been less enthusiastic about some of his predecessors, especially HUAC's first impresario, Martin Dies (1938–44).

The director helped the Senate Internal Security Subcommittee when it was under the aegis of its first chairman, Senator Patrick McCarran. The McCarran committee wanted to know if the U.S. radio propaganda station, Voice of America, was staffed by "sexual deviates." The FBI cleared one official of a charge of homosexuality, but it reported that allegations of "sexual perversion" had been recorded against three other VOA employees. However, when William Jenner inherited SISS and made reckless accusations against former Democratic presidents, the FBI terminated the relationship—only to resume in 1955 when Senator James Eastland, already a Hoover confidant, took over. All this confirms that while Hoover strongly favored the anti-communist crusade and circulated smears to further that cause, he was also a pragmatist—a quality that helped him to survive long after he had become an anachronism.[11]

Presidential authorization fortified the FBI in its pursuit of gays, leftists, and civil rights leaders. Under Hoover's guidance, President Truman in July 1950 instructed that the FBI "should take charge of investigative work in matters relating to espionage, sabotage," and, in phraseology that amounted to a carte blanche, "subversive activities and related matters." President Eisenhower issued a similar directive. President Kennedy devolved the matter to the office of the attorney general. In 1964, his brother Robert F. Kennedy (RFK), who had been an assistant to Joe McCarthy and was now attorney general, confirmed the instruction and retained the reference to subversion.[12]

There was reinforcement on the legislative front. Congress in September 1950 approved a measure that expanded the authority already vested in the FBI through the 1940 Smith Act. The Internal Security or McCarran Act required communist organizations and communist "front" organizations to register with a federal subversive activities control board, and made new provisions for the deportation of subversive aliens and the detention of subversive American citizens. The measure was another indication that President Truman had started a process he could not stop, for it passed in spite of his veto.

The United States Supreme Court, however, challenged these developments. Under the terms of the Smith Act, a series of prosecutions starting in 1948 meant that most officials of the Communist Party USA (CPUSA) faced prison sentences, but the increasingly liberal court began to review some of these cases. Its decisions, notably in *Yates v. United States* (1957), determined that a doctrinal commitment to the overthrow of the government was insufficient for conviction; proof of actual intent would be required. This rendered the Smith Act ineffective.

This forced the bureau to be circumspect, but a great deal of damage had already been done. By January 1953, the FBI had checked on 6 million citizens with the help of 5,000 paid informers. It compiled a hard-core list of 26,000 people to be detained in an emergency, and discreetly tipped off any employer in the public or private sector who planned to give a job to any of those individuals. A hidden terror pervaded the land, with millions protecting themselves against dismissal, if not by informing on their neighbors and colleagues, at least by conforming to the precepts of intolerance in the name of a sham kind of freedom. The work was a form of job creation for the bureau, which began to recover from the shocks administered to it by the loss of Latin America and the National Security Act of 1947. The number of agents and the amount of money needed to sustain them almost doubled and more than doubled, respectively, between 1946 and 1952 (from 3,754 to 6,451 agents, and from $37.1 million to $90.7 million).

The FBI's war on disloyalty took a variety of forms. For example, it fed politically useful information to a privileged group of supporters. This happened in the case of "little HUACs" in several states. It also occurred nationally. The Feds, possibly showing their liking for the more conservative Republican Party, supplied names of individuals in its files to past president Herbert Hoover and to the aspiring presidential candidate Thomas Dewey. Nichols leaked derogatory information on a range of dissidents to friends in the media. A core of newspaper journalists refused to be intimidated, and McCarthy bitterly criticized the press. But most journalists went along with McCarthyism, either because they were anti-communists and agreed with the purges, or because of the climate of fear. Those complicit in Nichols's clandestine defamation tactics included prominent members of the press corps, among them Walter Winchell, Drew Pearson, Jack Anderson, Victor Riesel, and the ever-peppery Walter Trohan.

Grassing on one's fellow citizens had once again become a national pastime. Informers like former Screen Actors' Guild president Ronald Reagan helped with the compilation of the notorious Hollywood blacklist. In an echo of its use of the American Protective League in World War I, the bureau recruited the help of the American Legion both as a source of informers and as a convenient disseminator of FBI educational materials. In a semi-humorous letter to "Comrade" Hoover in 1964, Trohan noted that the patriotic organization had become "an adjunct of the FBI." The American Legion Contact Program had started in 1940, and continued its work until March 1966.[13]

The FBI deterred the exercise of free speech by ruining the careers of dissenters and those who supported dissenters' constitutional rights. The bureau's "Responsibilities Program" ran from February 1951 to March 1956. It systematized the process of leaking derogatory information about job applicants who were deemed loyalty risks in the public services, especially school teaching. An estimated four hundred people lost their jobs through being "fingered" in this way. The FBI further bullied the articulate into silence through the use of informers and spies on America's college campuses. The conservative William Buckley, Jr., for one, was an FBI informer at Yale, and the bureau kept files on the student newspaper the *Harvard Crimson*.

In its efforts to define a role for itself after its 1947 reverse, the bureau tilted at windmills. It wildly exaggerated the domestic Red Menace at a time when the Soviets no longer used American communists as spies, and when, in any case, American communism was in a state of terminal collapse. The CPUSA had had an estimated seventy-five thousand to eighty-five thousand members in 1945, and then declined from that small base. Beginning in 1948, prosecutions under the Smith Act proceeded with the assistance of testimony by party member and FBI informer Herbert Philbrick. They resulted in the conviction of ninety-three of the party's leaders. But this was just one of the CPUSA's problems. The FBI's compilation of a special Communist Index, the arrest of Soviet spies, anti-communist propaganda, the repulsive Soviet crushing of Hungary's uprising in 1956, and the awful realization that Stalin had murdered millions of his fellow citizens all combined to demoralize the CPUSA and reduce its membership to about three thousand by 1971. Real support was weaker still, as a considerable portion of the remnant consisted of FBI infiltrators.

The communists were no longer a credible subversive threat. The bureau faithfully shadowed a dwindling band of survivors, but it was a farcical exercise. For example, the communist historian Herbert Aptheker had an FBI tail who babysat for him when he was out for the evening undermining American democracy (i.e., giving a lecture). By the mid-1960s, Aptheker no longer needed a babysitter and had been generationally marginalized. Now known as the father of a famous daughter (Bettina was a fiery leader of Berkeley's protest movement against the Vietnam War), Aptheker still retained his personal FBI sleuth. Flying in the face of the evidence, discriminatory practices endured. For example, Philip Foner, whose books were published by New York's Soviet-financed International Publishers, was barred from being a professor in the 1950s because he was a communist, and in the 1960s because he lacked teaching experience. Such hypocrisy underscored the outmoded nature of FBI methods and assumptions.[14]

As ever, Hoover was aware that he ran the risk of making enemies, and, as in the 1930s, he mounted a propaganda blitz. Although the American public in general still supported his agency, the director dealt savagely with any critics. When Max Lowenthal's critical study *The Federal Bureau of Investigation* appeared in 1950, Hoover's congressional ally George Dondero compared the author to Benedict Arnold; HUAC summoned Lowenthal to testify, and attempted to dissuade former senator Burton Wheeler from representing him. The bureau also continued with publicity of its own, including "histories" by chosen journalists like Don Whitehead (*The FBI Story,* 1956). Like the director's 1930s propagandist Courtney Ryley Cooper, Whitehead focused on Hoover as the progenitor of all that was good in the bureau. His best-seller was serialized in 170 newspapers and inspired a 1959 Hollywood movie. Not until 1964 did another critical work appear, Fred Cook's *The FBI Nobody Knows.*[15]

Whitehead's rehearsal of Hoover's virtues as a crime fighter helped the director to refute claims that he was unable to counter the Mafia. He needed to do so in order to satisfy conservatives who increasingly supported the FBI, but who worried about problems with law and order. By the 1960s, he also had to be on guard for the further reason that some liberals were charging that the FBI's obsession with the communist issue caused it to neglect its duty to fight crime.

One such broadside came from Robert Kennedy. The ambitious Democrat had attacked President Eisenhower's Department of Justice for its "lack of action" over racketeering activities in the International Brotherhood of Teamsters, one of the nation's most powerful labor unions. Then he became attorney general in his brother's administration. According to the Kennedys' house historian, Arthur Schlesinger, Jr., once RFK was installed in Justice, "Subversion was out. Organized crime was in." RFK pushed for the investigation and prosecution of the Teamsters' leader, Jimmy Hoffa. Convicted for the attempted bribery of a grand juror, this tough-guy militant duly went to prison in 1967 and, after his release, went missing, presumed dead.[16]

RFK was far from alone in finding fault with the FBI's anti-mobster record. Ramsey Clark, attorney general at the end of the administration of President Lyndon B. Johnson (LBJ), similarly complained that the bureau "came slowly to the organized crime field," saying this was because it had concentrated on the Communist Party "long after there was any risk to national security from that source." The attack on Hoover's anti-crime record has been multifaceted. He has been charged with being sweet on the Mafia, gullible when his mobster friend Frank Costello told him the Mafia did not exist, a victim of Mafia blackmail and thus inactive in its pursuit, and unequal to the task of taking on an outfit that was tougher and cleverer than the rural bandits the G-men had hunted down in the 1930s. Hoover's straitlaced agency was widely held to be anachronistic in that it was unable to handle the post-1940s underworld with its culture of gambling, drugs, and manicured fingernails. William H. Webster, FBI director from 1978 to 1987, barely concealed his contempt for the Hoover years: "I hope we won't go back to the days, Mr. Chairman, when our agents walked into bars and ordered glasses of milk."[17]

The politicization of the organized crime issue had its roots in a televised crusade in 1950. McCarthy had not been the only senator to exploit the visual medium in that year. Tennessee Democrat Estes Kefauver held colorful hearings into the underworld's involvement in gambling. He allowed television cameras into sessions of his Senate Special Committee to Investigate Organized Crime in Interstate Commerce, and his parade of gangsters wearing business suits attracted 30 million viewers. In its report the committee identified "a nationwide crime syndicate known as the Mafia, . . . the cement that helps bind the Costello-Adonis-Lansky syndicate of New York and the Accardo-Guzik-Fiscetti syndicate of Chicago."

But visions of a crime-ridden society did not at the time accord with the Cold War view that America had to show a united front in the face of the ideologically cohesive Soviet Union. In the battle for international opinion, unfortunate realities like slavery, labor conflicts, and organized crime had to be brushed out of the central narrative of the history of a great nation. Sociologist Daniel Bell contributed to the debate. In 1953, he offered an interpretation that amounted to a kind of politically correct Toryism. Italian Americans should not be pilloried and did not monopolize organized crime. There was an "ethnic ladder" which all immigrant groups climbed at some stage in their history. Crime, by no means a Sicilian preserve, was just a rung on that ladder, a glint in the American Dream.

Mafia denial became a respectable refrain in political discourse, and Hoover added his voice to the chorus. Whether out of belief or convenience, he claimed there was no such a thing as a nationwide, cohesively organized crime syndicate. The FBI prioritized its goals accordingly. As late as 1959, the FBI had only four agents investigating organized crime in New York, compared with four hundred investigating communists.

By this time, an event had taken place that should have dealt a mortal blow to Mafia disbelief within the bureau. One Saturday morning in the fall of 1957, New York state trooper Edgar Croswell watched the traffic entering a discreetly located estate in the mountain village of Apalachin, next to the Pennsylvania border. A sequence of black Cadillacs and Lincolns bearing out-of-state number plates entered the property. His suspicions aroused, Croswell thought of a minor legal pretext and organized a roadblock. Tipped off, the conferees made a run for it, but sixty-three were apprehended and had to identify themselves before they were released. Here were Vito Genovese of New York, John Scalisi of Cleveland, Joseph Zerilli of San Francisco, Joseph Civello of Dallas, Santos Trafficante of Miami, and fifty-seven others of similarly Italian extraction (the sixty-third was a servant caught up in the contagion of the escape). Nobody believed their story that they were retired businessmen. It was an interstate Mafia meeting. The FBI did not know about the conference, could not identify the conferees, and had been caught napping.[18]

Publicity about the Apalachin episode reinforced images of racketeering already popular in the movies. Most famously, Elia Kazan's *On the Waterfront* (1954) had played on the theme of violently enforced corruption in the labor movement. Kazan had named names to HUAC, and *On the Waterfront* glorified the role of the informer, but crucially the movie opened up new territory, that of organized crime. In the wake of Apalachin, Senator John McClellan of Arkansas chaired the committee that, with RFK as chief counsel, investigated labor racketeering. RFK presided over a staff of a hundred, at that point the largest in investigative history; former FBI man Joe Maher was his chief investigator; to RFK, he and other ex-Feds who worked for him were all "heroes." In 1963, Joseph Valachi testified to a further McClellan investigation and dispelled any remaining doubts about what the long-serving mobster dubbed "Cosa Nostra" (Our Thing). The slightly face-saving new terminology helped Hoover to make an implicit admission that the Mafia had existed all along, but he could not shake the mafiosi out of the public consciousness. Mario Puzo's 1969 novel *The Godfather* and its filmic sequel threatened to restore the American gangster to his 1920s status as charismatic anti-hero.

As a crime-fighting agency, the 1960s FBI was anachronistic in four ways. First, it was preoccupied with communist subversion, a phenomenon that no longer represented a threat to America and which proved a distraction from crime fighting. Second, its men were too good for the job: clean-cut special agents could not hope to penetrate the Mafia. Third, the bureau was insufficiently diversified ethnically, and unacquainted with the ways of Italy south of Naples. Fourth, Hoover was handicapped by being ill attuned to liberal thinking on crime. According to one strain in liberal thought, the Mafia debate was but a distraction from the dire social conditions that really lay at the root of allegedly soaring crime rates: in Ramsey Clark's words, "the essential action is to create a wholesome environment." Hoover resisted this line of thinking and was tough on crime itself, not its causes, making him out of touch with progressive thinking.[19]

However, it would be a mistake to belabor the archaic and inadequate nature of Hoover's performance. The liberal approach to law and order was unpopular, and Hoover was in tune with the majority view. In fact, in some ways he continued to provide imaginative leadership in the war on crime. His flair for recruiting public support in the fight against crime showed no signs of diminishing. In 1934, the bureau's publicity campaign had focused on "Public Enemy Number One." In 1950, the FBI introduced its Ten Most Wanted Fugitives program, based on photographs and word portraits. This was an inspired public relations exercise. It made Americans feel more secure, and also a part of the law enforcement effort: by the year 2000, citizen recognition had accounted for thirty-four Top Ten arrests. Tourists visiting the FBI Building in Washington made two of the identifications—a potent symbol of the American people bonding with their bureau.

The makeup of the Top Ten list suggests that the bureau was capable of changing in at least some ways: bank robbers dominated the list in the 1950s, "revolutionaries" (the FBI's word) in the 1960s, organized crime suspects and terrorists in the 1970s, and serial murderers and drug barons in subsequent decades. A cynic might say that the art of making up a Top Ten list is to insert only those whom you know you can capture. Nevertheless, it was reassuring to Americans worried about law and order that, of the 458 fugitives identified in the first half-century of the program, 429 were tracked down. Fugitives had reason to fear the bureau. Murderer Rudolph Alonza Turner apparently did not relax during the nine months he spent on the list. "I knew you'd get me sooner or later," he told the agents who arrested him in 1974.[20]

And while it is true that Hoover's FBI failed to arrest the mafiosi, there is an extenuating circumstance. The Democratic administration that took over from the Republicans in 1961 spewed forth civil rights and anti-mobster rhetoric. The press credited RFK with advances. The number of FBI agents in race-torn Mississippi rose from 3 to 153, and RFK assigned 60 attorneys to the crime-busting effort. But the civil libertarian Victor Navasky suggested that the attorney general's "blood line to the White House" made him subordinate the interest of American justice to the political interest of his brother the president. RFK may have had, in Navasky's telling phrase, an "incorruptible self-image," but in reality the Kennedy brothers were only verbal crimebusters, and, writing in 1971, Navasky did not know half the story.

For the Mafia had them in an armlock. This was for three reasons. First, former ambassador Joe Kennedy, the orchestrator of the dynasty that bore his name, had ensured that Sam Giancana, a leading Chicago mafioso, would help deliver cash and labor votes to his son's cause in the close-run presidential election of 1960. When the Mafia does you a favor, you cannot forget your obligation. Second, Sam Giancana had a more intimate connection with Jack Kennedy. They were both acquainted with Judith Campbell Exner. On one occasion, Exner defended her ethics by saying she refused to have another woman join her and Frank Sinatra in bed. But her sexual relationship with Jack Kennedy, which started when he was a senator and continued well into his presidency, was inconsistent with the family image projected by the president and his wife. The time-honored press conspiracy not to mention presidential infidelities would have been sorely tested in the case of a mobster's moll.

Third, Hoover may well have been aware that the Kennedy White House engaged Giancana and hit man John Rosselli in a bungled attempt to assassinate President Fidel Castro of Cuba. The idea had originated with the CIA at the end of the Eisenhower administration but had not then been implemented. Hoover's awareness that the plan now had more concrete presidential support is suggested by the fact that Exner was under FBI surveillance when she conveyed sums of cash directly to Giancana. Regardless of how Hoover joined the dots, it was clear to him that the prosecution of Giancana could implicate the Kennedys in the most serious crimes. In the understated language of Exner's FBI shadow William R. Carter, the realization that she was having sex with the president as well as with Giancana and Rosselli was "demoralizing."[21]

In LBJ's presidency, Hoover cited a further reason for the FBI's sluggish performance against organized crime, the continuing restrictions on wiretapping. Hoover engaged in a spat with Attorney General Nicholas deB. Katzenbach over the propriety of bugs, and, for a while, scaled down surveillance of the Mafia for fear of being arraigned for malpractice. Not until 1968 did the Omnibus Crime Control and Safe Streets Act provide for court-ordered electronic surveillance in specific cases. This was followed by the Racketeer Influenced and Corrupt Organizations Act of 1970, making it possible to prosecute Mob collectivities without tracing responsibility to an individual. Aimed at circumventing the Mafia's code of silence, the law illustrated the nature of the detection problem, and is a reminder that no such legislation had existed earlier to help the Feds.

The enactment of a law does sometimes point to the existence of earlier shortcomings. A notable example is the approval of a bill, in August 1965, making it a federal crime to kill the president. The need to legislate in such a way illustrates the enduring difficulties the FBI faced in a federalist nation: the bureau collected statistics on murders, and a 1934 law made it a federal crime to flee from one state to another to evade prosecution for murder, but, significantly, murder remained a state, not a federal, felony. In the mid-1960s, even allowing for the statistically distorting effects of race riots and the propensity of the FBI to exaggerate, there was a boom in violent crime. But the FBI could do little except ask for more money. The legislative deficit made the apprehension and prosecution of murderers a sluggish affair in certain critical cases.[22]

An example is the fatal shooting, in June 1963, of Medgar Evers, a field secretary for the NAACP in Mississippi. The killer, a segregationist named Byron De La Beckwith, obligingly left a palm print on the murder weapon, and together the Jackson police and the FBI solved the crime. But the FBI's authority to investigate derived from Reconstruction legislation, the charge being that Beckwith had deprived Evers of his civil rights. It fell to the state authorities to prosecute on the more serious charge of murder. However, the state-funded Mississippi State Sovereignty Commission gave under-cover support to Beckwith's attorneys as they weeded out Jews and civil rights sympathizers from successive juries. Racist and perjuring local po-licemen and racially packed juries made it difficult to convict under state law. Beckwith remained free until 1994 when, at the age of seventy-three, he finally went to prison.

The anti-assassination law addressed only one type of murder. It also failed to stem a rush of damaging allegations that the FBI had passed up op-portunities to prevent Lee Harvey Oswald from killing President Kennedy, and then covered up the evidence of its own incompetence. On the whole, these allegations were without basis in fact. Nevertheless, the Kennedy as-sassination became part of the litany of complaints about an agency that no longer seemed up to the job.

The FBI was in a no-win situation. If it had ignored Oswald, it would have been seen as negligent. Because it *had* kept him under surveillance, it was charged with not preventing what was preventable. The bureau watched Oswald from 1959 as a potential Soviet spy, and accumulated a file on him. Its Dallas office in May 1960 reported that Oswald had gone to Moscow and renounced U.S. citizenship, and that his mother was sending him dollar drafts from the First National Bank of Fort Worth. Another Dal-las report just weeks before Kennedy's assassination indicated that Oswald was a communist and a Castro sympathizer, adding that he was a person who reportedly drank to excess and beat his wife "on numerous occasions."

U.S. intelligence agencies always have such reports on file and receive numerous false rumors. Nevertheless, it is conceivable that better liaison with the CIA and with the FBI's older rival the Secret Service might have caused the identification of Oswald as a threat and led to his removal from Dallas on the day of the fatal tragedy. In recognition of this, the FBI and the Secret Service reached an agreement in 1965 to share information necessary to the protection of the president.[23]

But the FBI's most serious error of judgment in the assassination affair was its support of investigative closure. Chief Justice Earl Warren headed a commission of inquiry into the murder. The Warren Commission accumulated a mountain of evidence, and waded through a great deal of it. But, with the support of the septuagenarian Warren, who was feeling his age, and of Attorney General Katzenbach, Hoover advised that the inquiry into the deeply distressing affair should come to an end.

Psychological closure was the aim, but the premature halt had the reverse effect. The decision to end the investigation and publish only partial findings had left too many stones unturned. In November 1969, it was estimated that one-third of the commission's 28,000 documents still remained classified. The situation was an open invitation to conspiracy theorists who claimed that Oswald had not been the sole assassin, and that a range of suspects ranging from the CIA to Fidel Castro had been responsible.

By 1966, 50 percent of Americans believed that Oswald had not acted alone; the figure rose to 81 percent over the next decade. In 1976, it emerged that Hoover had known that the CIA had been plotting Castro's death, giving the Cuban dictator a motive to kill Jack Kennedy preemptively. The revelation that Hoover had not passed that information on to the Warren Commission fanned suspicions that there was a cover-up conspiracy. In 1993, a book by lawyer-turned-author Gerald Posner debunked the conspiracy theories and drew attention to the thoroughness and impartiality of the FBI's investigation of Kennedy's murder—its 25,000 interviews supplemented the 1,500 conducted by the Secret Service. Posner's book, *Case Closed,* was well received, but within two years another book appeared claiming that the Warren Commission suppressed FBI information submitted to it. As his Ten Most Wanted exercise shows, Hoover had a gift for social reassurance. But, in the case of the Kennedy assassination, he failed in an area where in the past he had succeeded.[24]

COINTELPRO actions further contributed to the idea that the FBI was a dinosaur blundering about in a modern age. The term COINTELPRO is a compression of the words "counterintelligence program." The program originated in a National Security Council meeting held on 8 March 1956. Set up in 1947, the NSC generally concerned itself with such foreign issues as Soviet missile strength. It had authorized the CIA to conduct an array of covert operations, including the overthrow of elected leftist governments in Iran (1953) and Guatemala (1954): in the convoluted logic of the Cold War, democracy and freedom could sometimes be best defended by destroying them. At NSC meeting number 279, Hoover requested authorization for COINTELPRO, the domestic application of methods hitherto applied only against foreigners in distant nations. President Eisenhower asked him what techniques he proposed to use. Hoover listed an array of tactics, ranging from misinformation to trash inspection, with which the NSC was already familiar. Neither Eisenhower nor his colleagues on the NSC objected at the meeting to the importation of dirty tricks, and Hoover was left to get on with the job.

The first COINTELPRO, launched on 18 May 1956, was against the communists. Hoover realized the CPUSA was on its knees, but he aimed to reinvent it by painting it in menacing colors. This invited criticism from those who thought he was just trying to raise appropriations or distract attention from the bureau's shortcomings, but the director still saw advantage in playing the anti-communist card. The COINTELPRO against the CPUSA lasted longer than any other, from 1956 to 1971. It consisted of 1,388 separate actions out of a total of 2,370 reported COINTELPRO operations, more than half the total.

Some of the COINTELPRO weapons used against the CPUSA were from the old armory, for example mail interception, electronic surveillance, and "snitch jackets." These last were forged documents designed to indicate that a target was an FBI informer when he was not. CPUSA national committee member William Albertson was stitched up in this way, and never recovered his standing within the party. There were also newer, more proactive methods. With cooperation from the Internal Revenue Service (IRS), for example, the Feds practiced tax harassment. IRS audits were run at inconvenient times on the finances of communists or other radicals.[25]

On 12 October 1961, a new COINTELPRO was launched, this time against the Socialist Workers Party (SWP), a small communist faction that had split from Moscow and adhered to the views of Leon Trotsky. One of the FBI's targets was Morris J. Starsky, a tenured philosophy professor at Arizona State University in Tempe who was active in Trotskyist and other radical causes. The bureau forged anonymous letters expressing outrage at Starsky's activities. Sent to the university's committee on academic freedom and tenure, they falsely claimed to be the work of outraged alumni. The associate professor lost his post at Arizona and was blacklisted at other universities.

On 25 August 1967, the FBI launched its COINTELPRO against "Black Hate." Its targets were the Nation of Islam, the Congress of Racial Equality, the Student Nonviolent Coordinating Committee, and the Southern Christian Leadership Conference. The Black Hate COINTELPRO showed the FBI to be thoroughly out of tune with the spirit of an America that had just seen increased black voter registration in the South and the demise of racial segregation.

The Black Hate COINTELPRO formalized the bureau's time-honored actions against black civil rights leaders. Its files on celebrities like Paul Robeson and Malcolm X were so voluminous that they have been a boon to biographers. But it was its treatment of Dr. Martin Luther King, Jr., that reached a new level of viciousness and made the bureau a byword for racism.

The bureau set out to destroy a man who was the hero of the civil rights movement, an opponent of the Vietnam War, and a campaigner for poor people. King was a target because of his prominence and success. *Time* magazine's "Man of the Year" in 1963, he next year won the Nobel Peace Prize for his civil rights efforts. William C. Sullivan of the FBI's Domestic Intelligence Division disbelieved Hoover's contention that King was a communist, but he crumbled in the face of the director's ire and an explicit authorization from Attorney General Robert F. Kennedy. Sullivan aimed "to take [King] off his pedestal and to reduce him completely in influence." He could have succeeded in this aim if he had been better informed. Exposure of the fact that King's Ph.D. from Boston University in the 1950s was considerably based on plagiarism would have ruined the great leader's reputation, as alas would evidence to reveal his prodigious womanizing. But lacking black agents and obsessed with communism, FBI penetration of the civil rights movement was less intelligent than it might have been.

The FBI bugged King's hotel rooms in a desperate effort to document sexual indiscretions. To the suggestion that King was unlikely to misbehave when protected by police bodyguards, Hoover replied, "I don't share the conjecture. King is a 'tom cat' with obsessive degenerate sexual urges." Lacking proof of what they knew to be true, Sullivan and his Domestic Intelligence Division now manufactured it in FBI laboratories. With Hoover's consent, Sullivan arranged for forged tape recordings of nonexistent sex orgies to be sent to King with threatening notes, in an attempt to unnerve him and even drive him to suicide.[26]

And yet, the FBI was still capable of acting in character. The "White Hate" COINTELPRO was very much in keeping with what federal agents had tried to accomplish in the 1870s and several times thereafter. The aim was to prevent white men from terrorizing black people. Not for the first time, Hoover showed his willingness to confront white violence, and this time he was ruthless.

On 30 July 1964, the FBI launched "counterintelligence and disruption tactics" against the Ku Klux Klan, which was undergoing another revival and was behind many beatings and murders of civil rights workers. This

COINTELPRO also targeted racist organizations like the American Nazi Party, the White Knights of Mississippi, and the National States Rights Party. The operation reduced the power of the Klan, which declined from a membership high of fourteen thousand in 1964 to forty-three hundred in 1971.

However just its objective, the story of the White Hate COINTELPRO is not a pretty one. For example, COINTELPRO agents ran a "snitch jacket" operation to label as an FBI informer the assistant head of the Louisiana Klan. As for the activities of FBI informant Gary Thomas Rowe, they were positively sinister. Rowe was a former Marine reserve who had joined the Klan. In the aftermath of the Selma-to-Montgomery protest march led by King in 1965, Alabama Klansmen murdered Viola Liuzzo, the only white female civil rights worker ever thus killed, and Rowe supplied the evidence that led to their rapid apprehension. But, to protect his real identity as an undercover agent, the FBI turned a blind eye to his unstable and mendacious character, and to the vicious violence he himself perpetrated against various civil rights workers and African Americans. When Rowe later told a congressional committee that he had demoralized the Klan by sleeping "with as many wives as [he] could," legislators were left wondering whether this was true and, if it was, whether it could possibly be an instance of altruism.[27]

The White Hate operation was partly for political and tactical reasons. The Klan revival was a potential threat to Hoover's cherished relations with local law enforcers. It had, for example, developed a disturbingly close connection with the police force in Birmingham, Alabama. The need to propitiate liberals in the 1960s was a further factor inducing the FBI to be tough on white racists. RFK and LBJ had both encouraged the idea of applying COINTELPRO tactics to White Hate, and while there was no love lost between Hoover and RFK, the director had a warm relationship with the president. The historian Richard Powers sees the program as having taken place in the context of "Lyndon Johnson's greatest achievement as president," the destruction of "legally tolerated terrorism against blacks in the South." Although the initiative did come from politicians, the bureau undoubtedly played its part in this achievement, in a manner that both reflected and ended a tradition. The Klan has not risen as a threat to black people in the South since.[28]

If that success was as timely as it was timeless, the bureau's record on student protest showed it to be seriously out of kilter with the 1960s. Accustomed as it was to dealing with communists for whom organization was axiomatic, the bureau had difficulties dealing with students whose composition changed with every freshman intake and whose activities were as undisciplined as their ideologies.

The FBI was not alone in being out of touch. To President Johnson, it was a Texan certainty that those who opposed America's military involvement in Vietnam were disloyal and the pawns of Moscow or Beijing. In April 1965, he told Hoover he was certain that the communists lay behind the antiwar protests. Hoover knew he could not prove this. Instead, he fueled LBJ's worries by claiming the campus turmoil opened the door to communists who "feigned" sympathy with the right to dissent, and were "jubilant over these new rebellious activities." Hoover also pointed to Students for a Democratic Society (SDS), founded in 1960 and by 1966 the main campus organization protesting the war. FBI reports were careful not to state that the SDS was communist led, but they argued that communists were active in it and that its protests furthered communist goals. The bureau set out to disrupt the activities of the SDS, using disinformation to drive a wedge between the students and their allies, running secret smear campaigns against student leaders, and then launching on 28 October 1968 its New Left COINTELPRO, a formalization of its existing surveillance and harassment of protesters that was applied to all kinds of protest groups, including veterans opposed to the war.[29]

The bureau's failure to find evidence of subversion only fanned LBJ's suspicions. The frustrated president had already in 1967 ordered the CIA to investigate the protest movement, and on 15 November CIA director Richard Helms had delivered his report based on CIA, FBI, and National Security Agency files. Helms complained that he was "woefully short of information" and that the campus protest groups were "highly mobile and sometimes even difficult to identify." He said the FBI needed to do more work. But he wrote that there was "no evidence of any contact between the most prominent peace movement leaders and foreign embassies, either in the U.S. or abroad. Of course," he added, "there may not be any such contact."[30]

President Johnson ignored this indication that antiwar protest was spontaneous and American in character. In the fall of 1967, he decided to press on both with the war and with the investigation of domestic dissent. His advisers told the FBI to find out "how and why demonstrators are so well organized." Hoover obliged, and the New Left COINTELPRO followed, even though the FBI had already contributed indirectly to the CIA's finding that the protests were not communist inspired.[31]

In significant ways, by the 1970s the FBI had become an anachronism. It kept tilting at the illusory communist menace. It ran a sleazy campaign against homosexuals. It floundered in its perception and pursuit of the modern Mafia. It persecuted black citizens just when much of America was trying to help raise them up. It could not understand youthful protest. Yet, as Hoover aged visibly in his reclusive office, he managed in several ways to keep in tune with the times. Overall, the Feds remained popular with the American people. And the Boss's agents finally achieved what Hiram Whitley had begun. They put an end to large-scale white terror in the South. That achievement, at least, was in keeping both with tradition and with the spirit of the time. It meant that the bureau was not beyond redemption.

10

a crisis of american democracy:
1972–1975

In the 1970s, Americans were shocked to learn that their government had destroyed democracy in several foreign countries, and was now undermining it at home. Disillusionment with government reached a critical level, and a precipitous decline in respect for the FBI contributed substantially to that result.

Much of the disillusionment was with the conduct of foreign policy. The costly Vietnam War was waged against nonwhite people in support of an unelected government in Saigon, and disproportionately fought (according to its critics) by blacks, Latinos, and other underprivileged Americans. Meanwhile, it emerged that the CIA had propped up some of the world's most invidious dictatorships, and had conspired in the overthrow of elected governments in Iran, Guatemala, Guyana, Chile, and Australia.

These foreign events framed the debate on America's democratic shortcomings, yet they were not the crux of the matter. What really goaded people into action was the undermining of democracy at home. Revelations that the CIA had spied on Americans inside the United States through its CHAOS program, in contravention of its 1947 charter, helped destabilize American politics. President Richard Nixon's disgrace in the Watergate affair intensified concerns over the right of Americans not to be burglarized by their own government. When it was discovered that the FBI had violated the democratic rights of Americans through COINTELPRO and other activities, the bureau, too, became a target for public opprobrium.

The bureau's contribution to democracy's crisis was just one factor among several. It was still significant, however, and invites scrutiny. Prior criticism of the bureau, new revelations in 1972–75, the death and replacement of J. Edgar Hoover, and the unfolding of the 1974–75 intelligence "flap" all help to explain both the crisis in general and the particular nature of the FBI's intense discomfiture by mid-decade.

Criticism of the FBI and its precursors was an established tradition, and had many strands. It had been chiefly conservative in character until the bureau lost sight of its equal justice mission in the World War I era, and then it was mixed, with widespread liberal disillusionment setting in by the end of World War II. McCarthyism-Hooverism alienated more liberal and left-leaning citizens, as well as some conservatives.

Fred Cook's 1964 book, *The FBI Nobody Knows*, concentrated the minds of liberal critics. Cook was a journalist whose previous activities were of a character to have been recorded in Hoover's Confidential and Personal files. The author of a book defending Alger Hiss, he had also excoriated the FBI in articles in the *Nation*. He noted how the bureau had tried to sabotage Max Lowenthal's 1950 critique and then pink-smeared its author when the book came out anyway. FBI intimidators delayed publication of Cook's own book. When it appeared, he was unsparing in his judgments of Hoover and his agency: the bureau stood "four-square in the corner of the white supremacists," and the congressmen of the Teddy Roosevelt era who had feared the rise of a Fouché-style secret police had been justified in their suspicions. Like his mentor Lowenthal, Cook overlooked the conservative stance of those Progressive-era critics. He devised a menu with liberal flavors and ascribed many of the FBI's ills to a single individual, J. Edgar Hoover.

Though Cook's publication received a muted reception, it signaled a progressive erosion of public confidence in the bureau. In 1965, the popular writer Rex Stout published his novella *The Doorbell Rang*, about the bureau's reprisals against a fictional millionairess who had had the temerity to support Fred Cook. In the same year, the West Coast Catholic magazine *Ramparts* published an exposé of the FBI by one of its former "bag job" specialists (the bags in question stowed the tools carried by electronic "buggers"); William Turner subsequently published a book on FBI malpractices. As his apostasy implies, morale within the bureau was in decline. The archaic survival of sexual surveillance of FBI employees—one of them sued the bureau after he was fired for having a girlfriend stay overnight in his bachelor apartment—stimulated an exodus of personnel. At 34.4 percent per annum, staff turnover in the FBI was the highest in the U.S. government, whose overall turnover rate was only 19.7 percent. Externally, the FBI's public approval rating at first remained buoyant. It dropped from 84 percent in 1965 to a still impressive 71 percent by the end of the decade. By 1975, however, it was down to 37 percent.[1]

With the bureau slipping from its pantheon, investigative journalists looked for stories to satisfy the public's thirst for scandal. The emergence of a new generation of young reporters, a management cadre that saw profit in exposé, and the emergence of watchdog organizations all contributed to a critical climate. Events played into the muckrakers' hands, sometimes in a direct manner. On 8 March 1971, for example, a group styling itself the Citizens' Commission to Investigate the FBI broke into an FBI office in Media, Pennsylvania, and removed hundreds of files. Hoover reacted furiously and tried to prevent their contents from leaking into the public domain. But the illegally obtained information seeped into the newspapers, and the nation became aware of the COINTELPRO efforts. More indirectly, the muckraking impetus also arose, rather cruelly, from one of the Nixon administration's successes, détente with the Soviet Union. The apparent reduction in the Soviet threat meant one could criticize American institutions without seeming to contribute to an unpatriotic weakening of U.S. national security.

The COINTELPRO evidence was damaging because it confirmed what many people had already suspected about the bureau's activities. One file, for example, listed 100,000 "subversives" the FBI suspected had been responsible for the race riots of the previous decade. The great majority on this list were black. A Los Angeles weekly noted: "Minority groups need never be reminded that such a list exists. They know. But it has taken a handful of stolen documents to awaken snug 'Anglos,' who can now simmer and squirm while trying to figure out what's next." Because of the Media break-in, Hoover had to close down the COINTELPRO operation.[2]

The firing of the number-three man in the bureau confirmed the disaffection that existed within the agency. Assistant to the Director William C. Sullivan had served the bureau since the start of World War II, when he had undertaken a special mission to Spain. He regarded himself as a loyalist and a potential successor to Hoover as FBI director. But, unusually for a top bureau official, he had had the courage to express differences with the Boss. He questioned one of Hoover's key premises, the notion that the CPUSA was behind the civil rights movement. Sullivan believed that Hoover, now past the normal retirement age for public servants, was finally losing his grip. Though legendary for his bureaucratic skills, the "old fox" was no longer alert to new challenges on the personnel and statistical fronts. The ambitious Sullivan complained that the Boss's autocratic tendency was getting out of hand, and that it stifled initiative in the bureau.

According to Hoover's staid criteria, "Crazy Billy" had always been a misfit. A senior colleague remarked that the number-three man was moody, and sartorially "professorial." In the fall of 1971, Sullivan took a step too far when he ingratiated himself with the White House by offering to organize a separate presidential surveillance service, using bureau assets to effect "national security" wiretaps. Hoover waited for Sullivan to go on vacation. Then, on 30 September, he changed the locks on Sullivan's office and removed his nameplate, thus ending a thirty-year career. In a slightly incoherent letter, he then explained to Sullivan that he had been fired because he had "views" that differed from Hoover's own. The abrupt nature of Sullivan's departure fed speculation that there were problems at the bureau.[3]

It was becoming open season on the FBI. The bureau's McCarthy-era victims seemed to be rising from the grave. One such was the literary leftist Lillian Hellman, who organized a Committee for Public Justice. Former attorney general Ramsey Clark attended its November 1970 launch and remarked that the FBI's investigation of the CPUSA was a waste of money. Princeton University and the ACLU then invited the bureau to participate, in October 1971, in a conference to evaluate FBI practices. The aging director refused on the ground that the Princeton inquiry was partisan. He had the conference organizers investigated, and circulated rumors impugning their loyalty. But such tactics were losing their effectiveness, and new critical organizations kept springing up: in 1974, the Center for National Security Studies, advocating the protection of civil liberties via controls on the FBI and the CIA; in 1977, the National Lawyers' Guild's Campaign to Stop Government Spying.[4]

The bureau now had to face detailed and thoughtful criticism. The journalist Walter Pincus contributed to the Princeton conference and to the 1973 book based on its proceedings. Pincus argued that Hoover misspent FBI funds, referring inter alia to the "fabled Hoover limousine, which in 1970 cost $30,000." The bureau budget had doubled in four years, and there was collusion with the House Appropriations Committee, which was able to borrow special agents for its own purposes. Hoover issued deceptive budget figures that appeared to indicate that the FBI was investigating civil rights cases, whereas in fact it was investigating African Americans. In an effort to change the mindset of the people who mattered, Pincus ripped into the supine attitude of Congress, where the bureau enjoyed an "almost sacrosanct status."[5]

Then, things really began to change. At breakfast time on 2 May 1972, four black people awaited the appearance of J. Edgar Hoover. But his house servants and limousine driver were in for a shock. After forty-eight years in charge of the FBI, the Boss lay on the floor of his bedroom, dead from a heart attack.

Hoover had exerted a big influence on the FBI in his lifetime, and his death inevitably had a destabilizing effect. There was an immediate leadership problem. In quick succession, two acting directors presided over the bureau. The first was L. Patrick Gray, a Texan who had served in the navy in World War II and had become a Nixon-supportive official in the Department of Justice. It soon became apparent that an era was at an end, for Gray relaxed the FBI's dress code and lifted the restriction on women serving as field agents. When Gray became a casualty of the Watergate scandal and had to resign, former Environmental Protection Agency chief William Ruckelshaus took over temporarily. The rapid turnover in leadership was both a symptom and a cause of the malaise affecting the FBI.

Clarence M. Kelley arrived at FBI headquarters on 9 July 1973 as the first permanent director of the post-Hoover era, and his appointment offered the possibility of some kind of recovery. Kelley seemed to have credentials for the job and brought a glimmer of hope for some kind of redemption. He hailed originally from Kansas City, and had joined the FBI straight from law school. By the late 1950s, he was special agent in charge of the Birmingham, Alabama, field office. During his time there, Birmingham's infamously racist "commissioner of public safety," Eugene "Bull" Connor, continued his reign of terror against black Americans, and he set police dogs on civil rights marchers. As usual, the instructions from Hoover's Washington were that the FBI should not interfere with the local police. Kelley was thus confirmed in his critical view of the director: as early as 1940, he had noted that Hoover, on visiting the FBI National Academy in Quantico, Virginia, "was quite taken" by recruits with southern accents. Though by no means a rebel by temperament, Kelley was his own man.

In 1961, Kelley quit the FBI to become chief of police in his native city. He set out to modernize the force, and acquired the nickname Dick Tracy because of his fondness for information technology and gadgets. He made a big effort to integrate the (hitherto 95 percent white) Kansas City police and to improve police-community relations, but he learned a lesson that would be powerfully reinforced once he became FBI chief—namely, that you cannot fully control events. In 1968, his force used tear gas against a crowd of children demanding the closure of their schools as a mark of respect for

Martin Luther King's funeral. In the ensuing riots, six African American men were shot. Though blessed with good intentions, Kelley came to his federal post with a less than wholesome reputation.[6]

Kelley set out to reform the FBI in purely police terms. He deemphasized the fight against property crimes that were relatively easy to solve, and boosted the investigation of crimes of violence. This meant that the practice of presenting cosmetic statistics that placed the bureau in a good light ceased to be such a prominent goal. But Kelley was hampered by an adverse mood in the nation, by his wife's illness, and, of course, there was no respite from the usual train of traumatic events that dog a director's day.

As Kelley struggled to lead and reform the FBI, then, he had to struggle with a job that remained as challenging as ever. Yet another problem was that, although he had not immediately succeeded J. Edgar Hoover, he remained in the shadow of that fabled director, whose stature had by now been literally set in stone, in the shape of a new FBI headquarters building that dwarfed the Justice Department across the street on Pennsylvania Avenue. Kelley had to contend with a particularly difficult Hooverite legacy. For, with Hoover dead, the FBI had lost both its capacity to strike fear into its potential critics, and the old man's guile.

The bureau had entered a period when the deceased leader's judgment might have proved useful. Hoover had known when to hold back, as, for example, in the case of the Huston Plan. In 1970 Nixon had been so angered by "New Left" attacks on his policies that he had asked Tom Huston (formerly president of the Goldwaterite Young Americans for Freedom) to prepare a scheme to dig out information on his tormentors. The Huston Plan proposed the relaxation of restrictions on mail opening and the revival of "surreptitious entry," including a scheme to burglarize the Brookings Institution, a Washington think tank. Hoover was canny enough to sabotage the plan, telling Attorney General John Mitchell that it would invite the attention of the "jackals of the press" and that, once on the prowl, these journalists might find out all kinds of things. Such prescience was an asset that would be sorely missed in the remainder of the Nixon administration, and might just have saved the FBI from contamination in the Watergate affair.[7]

Watergate was Kelley's most difficult inheritance, and it contributed materially to the mid-1970s intelligence flap and to the discomfiture of the FBI. The bureau had little apparent connection to Watergate. But this was a poisoned era in which two elected leaders, Gough Whitlam in Australia and Harold Wilson in the United Kingdom, lost or quit their positions amid a welter of suspicions over secret service involvement in plots. A third democratically elected leader, Salvador Allende of Chile, died violently in the course of an outright coup d'état in which the CIA and Nixon were implicated. The massive publicity concerning Watergate, its cover-up, and the accompanying cluster of political scandals took place against a background of widespread political disillusionment, and was deeply damaging to the bureau.

Early on the morning of 17 June 1972, a security guard at the Watergate office complex in Washington, D.C., alerted police to a break-in at the suite rented by the Democratic National Committee. The five men arrested at the offices were in possession of telephone-bugging devices. Even after extensive inquiries, the aims of the incompetent burglars never became quite clear. Probably they were never very clearly thought out in the first place. But in due course it transpired that the burglars had connections with the Committee for the Re-election of the President, known as CREEP.

The bureau was not directly implicated in the Watergate break-in. Hoover's fastidiousness had in this sense paid off. But Hoover's scrupulous avoidance of risk had indirectly contributed to the Watergate fiasco, for it had forced Nixon and his cronies to go private.

The private initiative stemmed originally from the White House's determination to control the debate over the Vietnam War. In February 1971, the *New York Times* had obtained a classified seven-thousand-page archive from the Defense Department on decision making about the Southeast Asian conflict. It began publishing selections from these volumes, which came to be known as the Pentagon Papers. The chosen excerpts tended to show that the Johnson administration had made foolish errors. Aides to the furious Nixon gave a White House investigative group the job of discrediting the man who had leaked the papers, Daniel Ellsberg. This unit burglarized the office of Ellsberg's psychiatrist. They found nothing of interest but left a trail of clues; the disclosure of their action eventually led to a declaration of mistrial when Ellsberg was charged with the theft of the documents. In the meantime, the anti-leak group, the "Plumbers," continued to operate. This was the unit the police caught red-handed at the Watergate complex.

The District of Columbia police inferred from the tapping equipment carried by the Watergate burglars that there had been an infraction of federal laws on communication interception. They called in the FBI, which organized a trace on some of the dollar bills found in possession of the Plumbers. The currency trail led to Mexico. The White House now prevailed on the CIA to claim that because of its foreign dimension the matter was within its exclusive jurisdiction, and to request that the investigation be stopped on (apocryphal) grounds of national security risks. The cover-up had begun in earnest, and it would lead to the ruination of Richard Nixon and those associated with him.

When the Watergate burglars were convicted in January 1973, there was no immediate indication of higher-up complicity in their offense. One of them, however, former CIA officer James W. McCord, made allegations of further crimes, and of the involvement of top officials. The United States Senate set up a Select Committee on Presidential Campaign Activities, popularly known as the Senate Watergate Committee. Congress was in an increasingly adversarial mood, and the searchlight of suspicion fell on acting FBI director Gray. It transpired that, in an excess of loyalty, Gray had colluded with the White House in the destruction of evidence linking Watergate to the administration. Seeing Gray as a White House stooge, the Senate Judiciary Committee refused to recommend his confirmation as FBI director.

Matters did not improve for the FBI when Ruckelshaus took over in late April. In the summer of 1973, members of Vietnam Veterans Against the War, the "Gainesville Eight," were on trial in Florida on charges of having allegedly conspired to disrupt the 1972 Republican National Convention in Miami. Local police had caught the FBI bugging confidential consultations between the Gainesville Eight lawyers and their clients. Stories like this fanned public suspicions of the bureau and blurred any meaningful distinction that might have existed between the unofficial Plumbers and the FBI.

Throughout this period, the press was powerfully reinforcing the congressional inquisition, with Carl Bernstein and Bob Woodward of the *Washington Post* to the fore. W. Mark Felt was their main informant. Since his days as a World War II disinformation specialist, Felt had risen in the FBI. Hoover had taken a special interest in his welfare (even counseling him to eat bananas to ward off heart complaints), and Felt was a Hoover loyalist. After the Boss's death, Felt was an unhappy number two to Acting Director Gray. He had resented Nixon's appointment of a crony to succeed Hoover, and did not like some of Gray's counter-Hooverite reforms, such as the employment of female special agents. More importantly, though, he was disgusted by what he saw as the corrupt practices of the Nixon administration, not just the Watergate burglary but also its sleazy accompaniments, including attempts to politicize the FBI. The inside information he supplied was of crucial assistance to the *Post*'s reporters, who privately dubbed their source, after the title of a blue movie, "Deep Throat."

Realizing that he would be impeached if he remained in office, Nixon resigned from the presidency on 9 August 1974. The FBI had featured in the

House Judiciary Committee's impending articles of impeachment. The second of these cited the presidential abuse of FBI wiretaps, the concealment of wiretap records, the blocking of the FBI investigation of the Watergate burglary, and the use of FBI-derived intelligence against Nixon's partisan opponents. Such revelations not only doomed Nixon, but also left the FBI perilously exposed.[8]

The Senate Watergate Committee demanded and obtained FBI documents on wiretapping. Minority (Republican) staff members questioned Sullivan and learned of COINTELPRO-style operations that had taken place under Democratic administrations. These details were omitted from the final report of the Watergate Committee, but the cat was slipping out of the bag.

The climate of scrutiny was further darkened by a General Accounting Office (GAO) inquiry. Founded in 1921, the GAO was an independently run congressional support agency with nationwide field offices charged with ferreting out waste and fraud in federal programs. In 1974–76, it investigated the FBI's efficiency, the scope of its inquiry making it a sequel to the Pincus critique. The GAO investigation sought documentation on 797 domestic-intelligence (as distinct from criminal) investigations of individuals, chosen at random from ten field offices.

Americans living through the mid-1970s could be forgiven for taking a jaundiced or even cynical view of their government. One distressing story followed another. Two of them broke in a single day, 8 September 1974. First, newspapers confirmed that Nixon's CIA had secretly connived to overthrow the government of Chile, Latin America's oldest democracy. Later on the same morning, President Gerald R. Ford announced his pardon of any crimes Nixon had committed while in office. His intention was to draw a line under the Watergate affair. But he laid himself open to the suspicion that he had made a deal with his predecessor in return for the presidency.

Revelations about CIA abuses were to punctuate the year ahead, destabilizing the political context in which the FBI operated. The CIA flap reached crisis proportions when, on 22 December 1974, journalist Seymour Hersh broke the story that the agency had, contrary to the terms of its charter, spied at home, in that its CHAOS program had kept tabs on domestic protesters against the Vietnam War. Americans were particularly upset that their foreign intelligence service had misbehaved on U.S. territory. The CIA's popular approval rating sank to a new low of 14 percent in the Gallup poll.

The FBI was licensed to operate domestically. But, because they affected U.S. citizens living in America, disclosures about the bureau's malpractices were potentially alarming. And, by the time of Hersh's CIA story, the FBI was already the subject of such revelations. Noticing the program descriptor COINTELPRO on a document from the Media break-in, journalist Carl Stern initiated Freedom of Information Act inquiries and obtained additional records. With awkward questions being asked, the Justice Department prepared a report. In November 1974, Attorney General William Saxbe released twenty-one pages of the twenty-nine-page document. The surviving portions of the text showed that COINTELPRO had been a major program. Like its cousin across the Potomac, the FBI could now expect serious criticism.

An incipient split opened up between the Justice Department and the FBI. Saxbe said that he was asking the Civil Rights Division to investigate the COINTELPRO issue, and would prosecute FBI agents if appropriate. Kelley, however, was reluctant to condemn the program. Acknowledging past operations against the CPUSA, the Ku Klux Klan, and New Left groups, the FBI director swung into the counterattack. Those targeted in Hoover's day, he stated defiantly, had been "violence-prone groups whose publicly announced goal was to bring America to its knees." It would have been an "abdication of its responsibilities" for the FBI not to have taken action.[9]

On 4 January 1975, Ford created the Presidential Commission on CIA Activities Within the United States under the chairmanship of Vice President Nelson A. Rockefeller. The executive hoped this preemptive move would calm the public mood. But there was no respite for the White House. On 19 January the *Washington Post* came out gunning for the FBI, with Ronald Kessler taking the lead investigative role.

According to historian Kathryn Olmsted, the *Post* acted in part out of rivalry with the *New York Times*, whose reporter Seymour Hersh seemed to have scooped the *Post* with his story about the CIA and CHAOS. Whatever the motive, Kessler's revelations were politically dangerous for the FBI. They focused on the bureau's practice of keeping files on members of Congress. Former FBI official Cartha DeLoach called Kessler a "journalistic prostitute," but, at the end of February, Attorney General Edward Levi acknowledged that the Kessler revelations were true.[10]

On 29 January, the U.S. Senate established a Select Committee to Study Governmental Operations with Respect to Intelligence Activities. Under the chairmanship of Frank Church of Idaho, a Democrat, it conducted the nation's largest-ever public inquiry. The House followed suit on 19 February, setting up its own Select Committee on Intelligence. Another Democrat, Representative Otis G. Pike of New York, served as its chairman. Already under scrutiny by the GAO and the Rockefeller inquiry, the CIA and the FBI now found themselves under intense congressional scrutiny.

In the spring and summer of 1975, the Church committee conducted closed hearings and engaged in a constitutional struggle with the executive, trying to force the White House and its agencies to release documents and allow intelligence officials to testify on matters ranging from FBI surveillance of American feminists to its infiltration of Christian groups. Then, in August, Pike held open hearings. His committee's interlocutors pummeled bureau witnesses on what they regarded as inadequate auditing procedures, and on other issues that included COINTELPRO, the rationale for its 58-million-strong index card system, the necessity or otherwise for keeping files on individuals like Joan Baez and Jane Fonda, and the FBI's alleged tendency, apparently evidenced by the fact that it had eighty-three agents serving abroad under the "legal attaché" program, to flout its charter by engaging in "foreign intelligence."

In the fall, it was the Church committee's turn to hold open hearings, many of which focused on the FBI. In mid-November and early December, the most extensive hearings of the entire Church investigation were about the bureau exclusively. Then came the reports. The FBI escaped relatively lightly from the censures of the Rockefeller Commission (June 1975) and the Pike report (leaked illegally in February 1976). But it encountered a full frontal blast of criticism from the GAO report (February 1976) and the Church report (April 1976).

A vigilant U.S. Congress was determined to expose and reform. In response to Kessler's original story, Representative Robert W. Kastenmeier (D-Wis.), chairman of the House Judiciary Committee's courts, civil liberties, and administration of justice subcommittee, introduced a Freedom From Surveillance bill specifically aimed at FBI malpractices. Other legislators stressed a variety of issues: Senator Edward Kennedy (D-Mass.) proposed a bill on wiretapping, Representative Charles Mosher (R-Ohio) a Bill of Rights Procedures bill. Introducing a bill to provide "joint congressional oversight of [the] U.S. intelligence–law enforcement community," the Senate's Democratic floor leader Mike Mansfield (Montana) noted the steep ascent of the FBI's budget (in 1971, $294 million; in 1975, $440 million) and the relative absence of congressional scrutiny: the Senate and

House judiciary committees had jurisdiction in this regard, but together they had held only three days of hearings in the specified period of budget elevation.

The FBI had become a significant issue in the clash between the legislative and executive branches of government, and it continued to be a bone of contention in the early months of 1976. Bella Abzug (D-N.Y.) confronted the Ford administration in her capacity as chairwoman of a subcommittee of the House Committee on Government Operations. She had demanded information on government interception of telegraph and telex messages. Attorney General Levi told her that compliance with her request would damage national security, but he would not reveal how. When FBI agents appeared before her subcommittee, they would not supply the information she wanted, saying that President Ford had ordered them not to comply and citing executive privilege. Abzug retorted: "Executive privilege went out with the American Revolution."[11]

For the press, the "Year of Intelligence" was a cornucopia, a time when the reading public could be effortlessly entertained. Conspiracy stories multiplied. Speculation about the Kennedy assassination was especially vigorous, with the FBI coming under suspicion both for incompetence in the tracking of Oswald and for collusion in cover-up. The conjectures flourished anew when, on 20 June 1975, unidentified gunmen assassinated Sam Giancana, the gangster who had been involved in the U.S. government plot to kill Castro that, according to a popular conspiracy theory, had given the Cubans a motive to kill the American president as a preventive measure. The timing of the hoodlum's demise seemed like a sinister extension of the 1960s cover-up, as he was about to testify to the Church committee.

The Castro story simply would not die. "FBI Knew of CIA Plots on Castro," ran a *Washington Post* headline on 21 May 1976, its story indicating that Hoover had personally withheld Castro-plot information from the Warren Commission in spite of the possibility that it suggested a possible preemption motive for the president's killing; not only that, but the FBI had again neglected to supply the documents when Senator Church requested that type of information in the spring of 1975; they had been discovered recently only as an accidental consequence of cross-referencing by Church committee inquirers. The story was powerful enough to stimulate yet another congressional investigation into assassinations.

Former victims of the FBI joined the fray. Efforts to calm them down only added to the press furor. For example, in May 1975, the new head of the New York City FBI office, J. Wallace LaPrade, rather courageously addressed, in the words of a *New York Times* report, "a group of old-line left-ists, trying to convince them that the days of J. Edgar Hoover are over." The "half-hearted clapping" at the end of LaPrade's talk was greatly exceeded in volume by the cheers that greeted a member of the audience, ACLU board member Algernon D. Black, who said, "You still have the image of a Gestapo." Legislation in 1974—amendments to the Freedom of Information Act and a separate Privacy Act passed in response to the revelations about the FBI's domestic spying—had made it possible to request one's own files. Black demanded that his FBI file be shown to him, and not to conservatives out to destroy him.

At the same meeting, Princeton University professor H. H. Wilson, a veteran critic of both McCarthyism and Hooverism, said "they've planted guys in my courses for years" and complained that the FBI was stalling over the production of his file (this was standard practice—the bureau falsely told Joseph Lash that its only file on him was the one containing Lash's letters requesting his file!). Wilson added: "Mr. Hoover said I was an absolute liar and a disgrace to the academic profession, so I assume they must have some information on me, and I'd like to see it."[12]

Editorially, the *New York Times* showed no inclination to depart from the censorious line of its rival the *Washington Post*. In August 1975, it demanded stronger supervision of the FBI from within the White House and the Justice Department, but its most powerful injunction was aimed at Congress, which had a "prime responsibility: to cut back the FBI's jurisdiction and define it sharply." The *Times* repeatedly demanded that Congress exercise diligent and permanent oversight, reflecting the desire of the Church and Pike committees and alarming the administration. Attorney General Levi warned of the danger that "Congress might try to manage" the FBI and other security agencies and urged that there should be no "unwarranted and debilitating restraints." Levi said, "There's no reason to believe that the Department of Justice in the normal course cannot effectively handle violations of the law."[13]

On 23 February 1976, the GAO submitted to the House Judiciary Committee its 230-page report, eighteen months in the making, on the efficiency and effectiveness of the FBI. Its quantitative approach gave its findings an air of objectivity. The GAO charged that many bureau investigations were based on "soft" evidence, such as the way a person looked, or car license plates spotted in proximity to a political demonstration. In 86 percent of 300 soft cases it had reviewed, no connection at all was made with extremist groups, yet the data collected—for example, a wiretap recording of two women discussing which men they would like to bed—were not only re-tained but passed on to third parties. The FBI had secured convictions in only 8 of the 797 domestic intelligence investigations scrutinized, and all of these 8 were for offenses that could have been treated as straightforward criminal cases, without any need for a contra-subversive apparatus. The GAO doubted that the bureau even had the legal authority to conduct do-mestic intelligence work, and urged Congress to clarify the matter.

The Pike committee also finished its report early in 1976. The commit-tee had inquired into the FBI and its budgetary arrangements, but it con-centrated on foreign intelligence performance. This was a serious topic but also a genuinely sensitive one from the national security point of view, and the committee had become mired in controversy when a shadowy person of unknown motive started leaking some of the sensitive information. A disil-lusioned Congress then voted to suppress the final report, but it was smug-gled via the journalist Daniel Schorr to the Lower Manhattan alternative publication the *Village Voice*. The *Voice* published the Pike report as a spe-cial supplement on 11 February, making its recommendations publicly known.

Pike recommended that there be a permanent House intelligence over-sight committee, and that there should be regular GAO audits of intelli-gence agencies' financing and management. Recommendations specifically aimed at the FBI called for an end to warrantless infiltration of domestic groups, an eight-year limit on the tenure of the FBI director, a refocusing on counterespionage instead of subversion, and tight Justice Department con-trol over counterterrorist activities aimed at domestic groups.

Book 1 of the Church committee's report in April 1976 was on "Foreign and Military Intelligence" and ran to 651 pages, but, at 396 pages, Book 2 was also substantial, and was backed by Book 3, 989 pages of staff reports. Entitled "Intelligence Activities and the Rights of Americans," Book 2 largely concentrated on the FBI. It called for the repeal of the Smith Act. Like the Pike report, it recommended that a director should serve for no more than eight years, adding that the tenure of the assistant director for the Intelligence Division should also be limited. Such demands aimed to end Hooverism, and reflected traditional congressional concerns about civil lib-erties. In similar vein, the Church committee recommended curtailments of the bureau's domestic intelligence operations. It proposed a permanent Senate intelligence oversight committee, specifying that it should have ju-risdiction over the FBI as well as the CIA. However, the committee also stressed heavily the responsibilities of the attorney general to oversee and actively supervise the FBI.

However, the Church committee was more concerned with rights than with effectiveness. It took a conservative line on how counterintelligence should be organized, confirming that the FBI should have jurisdiction only in the domestic sphere, from which foreign and military intelligence agencies should be excluded. In this way, its researchers had revisited the reasoning of the 1940s, recent scandals having reinforced doubts about the trustworthiness and racial tolerance of the FBI. There were no proposals for a wider FBI mandate, and no serious discussion of unification of the intelligence services.[14]

The mid-1970s investigations of the FBI had mixed fortunes. The GAO established itself as a responsible inspectorate, and, by the end of the century, was reporting on the FBI with some frequency. But the Pike committee was to a considerable extent discredited by its history of leaks. When the FBI was asked to investigate who had given Schorr his copy of the report, the Watergate wheel had turned full circle and the Plumbers were back in business, but this time officially.

The Church committee report was taken more seriously. On its staff were experts and scholars who not only commanded respect at the time, but also fostered understanding of the committee's work in years to come through their own publications and, in one case at least, the publications of their students. Engaged by John Elliff to scour presidential libraries for FBI records, Athan Theoharis later joined the faculty at Marquette University, where he supervised a stable of masters and doctoral students who wrote about the civil liberties record of the FBI.[15]

Yet the Church inquiry, too, met with its share of criticism. Senator Church was a contender for the Democratic presidential nomination, and he and some of his fellow committee members were seen as ambitious headline grabbers. The Democrat-dominated committee incurred censure for being allegedly partisan, and also for being affected by liberal bias.

The committee was, perhaps, justified in spending so much time exposing FBI abuses against the Left. Eighty-five percent of COINTELPRO operations had been against such targets as the CPUSA, Black nationalists, Martin Luther King, Jr., and the New Left, while only 15 percent of them were aimed at White Hate. Whereas the FBI had needed little invitation to proceed against the Left, it had required the intercession of Democratic politicians, Robert Kennedy and LBJ, to arrange the White Hate COINTELPRO. In that the FBI's operations against the Left had been more ruthless than those against the Right, the committee's extra condemnation of anti-Left dirty tricks may also have been justified. The suspicion nevertheless remained that the Church committee was short on objectivity. Its FBI guru, Michael Epstein, who had stronger political connections than his nominal boss, John Elliff, believed the bureau might have had a hand in Martin Luther King's death.

As the years passed, those sympathetic to the recommendations of the Pike and Church committees had other reasons to be disappointed. The idea that there should be some kind of legislative framework or "charter" for the FBI was debated throughout the Carter administration (1977–81), but came to naught. House and Senate intelligence oversight committees were set up, but in due course they became "institutionalized," their members developing a cozy relationship with the agencies they were supposed to be scrutinizing. One disillusioned comment on the 1970s congressional inquiries came from Martin Luther King's biographer David Garrow, who charged that they had taken an unreconstructed approach to racial reform. Writing in 1981, he drew attention to the "seemingly total disinterest in bureau recruitment and personnel policies among the reform advocates of the 1970s."[16]

By the middle of the decade the FBI was a demoralized agency that had lost the confidence of the American public. Revelations about the Hoover era only partly account for its plunge into infamy. Hoover's death, Watergate, détente, media opportunism, CIA scandals, and congressional assertiveness all contributed to the FBI's problems. The media portrayed American democracy as being in a state of crisis. Legislators pronounced the FBI part of that problem. They advanced some reforms, but constructive remedial action had to come also from an unheralded source, the Ford administration and its Department of Justice.

11

reform and its critics: 1975–1980

The Ford administration launched a program of executive reform to improve the conduct and image of the FBI. The reforms were not all embracing. They addressed neither the unification of counterintelligence nor the bureau's lack of diversity. But they did curtail some of the bureau's controversial practices, and refocused its effort on criminal rather than political cases.

Support for reform came from Congress, from Democrats, from liberals, and, beginning in 1977, from the Carter White House. However, much of the initiative came from a moderate Republican executive in the years 1975–76. President Gerald Ford endorsed reform partly to calm the political storm, and partly out of an earnest desire to put improvements in place. His Justice Department formulated solutions to the FBI crisis. Not for the first time, a Republican attorney general was instrumental in shaping federal police policy.

Civil libertarians protested that Ford's reforms did not go far enough. There was also criticism from a different quarter. After 9/11, conservatives attacked and reversed the 1970s reforms on the ground that they had gone too far, allegedly shackling the bureau, making it risk averse, and interposing a legalistic "wall" that blocked special agents' efforts to get at evil plotters. But such rhetoric had its origin a quarter century earlier, in the immediate aftermath of the Ford reforms, when some conservatives mounted a defense of the old-style FBI. Their objections proved significant, as they prepared the way both for the adoption of Ronald Reagan as the Republican presidential candidate and for the restoration and enhancement of FBI powers under future Republican presidents.

Edward H. Levi had enjoyed seven relatively tranquil years as president of the University of Chicago when, in January 1975, he entered the national political maelstrom. In that month, at a time when criticism of the FBI was reaching a crescendo, President Ford appointed him attorney general. Levi was to endure a troublesome year. At the end of it, he appeared on the CBS television program *Face the Nation.* His interrogators launched into him with some ferocity. What was the FBI doing about its unsatisfactory investigation of the 1968 assassination of Martin Luther King? What was he doing about allegations of corruption in the bureau? Were the G-men out of control? The attorney general replied in measured tones. The Civil Rights Division of the Department of Justice was reviewing around ninety files on the King murder; his department was looking into the allegations of corruption. While neither he nor the FBI director could be expected to know everything that was going on in an organization as large as the FBI, he was confident that it was not a "runaway agency." To guard against any future abuses, he was working on a set of guidelines to steer the organization's future conduct.

A few months later, the press reported on the curbs to be imposed on the FBI. Inappropriate investigations of citizens with radical opinions would be eschewed. Instead, the targets would be gangsters, terrorists, and spies. Legislation would define the powers of the FBI, it would limit its investigations to advocates of violence, there would be closer oversight of its activities by the Justice Department and Congress; the collection of damaging information on individuals would be restricted; electronic surveillance would be more tightly regulated; the tenure of future directors would be limited to prevent a recurrence of the Almighty Hoover phenomenon.[1]

FBI reform was the major preoccupation of Levi's Justice Department. To be sure, there were other concerns. The effort to integrate American high schools by busing students from one neighborhood to another had sparked a riot in Boston in December 1974, and Levi had to justify his apolitical, noninterventionist stance on the issue. As for the FBI, it had to be business as usual regardless of the political storm. There was the Patty Hearst case, for example. Kidnapped by revolutionaries, the publishing heiress became one herself. Not realizing this, the FBI tried to rescue her, shooting dead five of her comrades. She eventually went to prison for armed robbery. Finally, it should be noted that the FBI was improving its police practices independently of any external pressures. There was the "message switching" program whereby the bureau's National Criminal Information Center would set up computer storage of all criminal data, whether federal or state in origin. A further advance in criminal detection was "psychological profiling"; also in the 1970s, the American public first made the chilling acquaintance of the term "serial killer." Yet none of these riveting events displaced political reform as the item dominating the attorney general's agenda.

Levi was variously criticized for being aloof, for disdaining to master the terminologies of intelligence, and for being conservative. But he brought special qualities to the job of FBI reform. He was a leading academic authority on the law, and had been at one time counsel to the Federation of American Scientists, the conscience of the scientific profession and a sponsor of open government.

One of those who admired Levi's reforming activities was John T. Elliff, the nation's leading academic authority on the FBI. Under the imprimatur of Harvard University, Elliff had in 1971 published a study of the FBI and civil rights. With the encouragement of Kelley and support from the Police Foundation, he embarked in 1974 on a three-year research project culminating in a book published by Princeton University Press, on FBI reform. In the meantime he served as chief of the FBI Task Force for the Church inquiry. Potentially, this put him on a collision course with Levi, but on the contrary, he came to believe that the attorney general made "landmark efforts to establish guidelines for FBI intelligence investigations," and that the FBI "underwent significant change in the 1970s."

In the spring of 1975, Levi alerted Congress to his reform intentions, in testimony not to the Church committee but to a subcommittee of the House Judiciary Committee that had traditional oversight responsibility for the FBI. The chairman of the Subcommittee on Civil Rights and Constitutional Rights was San Francisco Democrat Don Edwards, an early critic of the Vietnam War and floor manager for the recent Equal Rights Amendment proposal. Levi aimed to pull liberals like Edwards into his reform consensus, while at the same time conserving the FBI's freedom to operate. He next created a committee to draft FBI guidelines, chaired by Mary C. Lawton. Deputy Assistant Attorney General since August 1974, Lawton would now be responsible not only for drafting guidelines but also for developing policy on what documents the Church committee would be allowed to see, especially in cases where those documents were private in provenance, as in the case of the records of communications corporations.

Domestic wiretapping was one of the most politically charged issues that Levi and his colleagues had to address. The Omnibus Crime Control and Safe Streets Act of 1968 had stipulated that a judicial warrant was required for any domestic electronic eavesdropping on wire or oral communications, except in cases where the White House deemed there was a threat to national security. In the *United States v. U.S. District Court* case from 1972, commonly known as the Keith decision, the Supreme Court reserved judgment on whether the president had the constitutional authority to order warrantless surveillance in foreign counterespionage cases "where there is collaboration in varying degrees between domestic groups or organizations and agents or agencies of foreign powers." It was hoped that legislation might clarify this point. The aim of such reforms, Elliff later recalled, had been "to institutionalize the concerns for freedom and legality, so that they are not easily cast aside or forgotten under the pressure of some future crisis or emergency."

In August 1975, Levi announced a first and partial draft of new FBI guidelines. They introduced controls to prevent White House assistants from requesting electronically obtained information for partisan political purposes. Henceforth, all requests to the FBI had to be in writing and from a named and approved official; investigative files from the FBI and the White House were to be subject to safeguards against unauthorized dissemination.

Pondering an array of impending restrictions, Kelley now wanted to know in what circumstances the bureau would be able to operate. For example, what authority would it have to act in terrorist kidnappings and airplane hijackings? After some pondering, Levi said that in some circumstances the bureau would be able to act in a preventive manner, even if a crime had not yet been committed. These circumstances included foreknowledge of impending violence, or of plots by non-U.S. intelligence agencies against American national security.[2]

Levi's curtailment of FBI powers was too limited to satisfy the more trenchant bureau critics in Congress. He had difficulties with the Church committee, now largely dominated by another ambitious politician, Walter F. Mondale of Minnesota, who would be elected vice president in 1976. Testifying to the committee on 11 December, Levi invoked the injunction of his predecessor Harlan Fiske Stone: the bureau should not intervene in politics, but should investigate only infractions of the criminal law. But, he insisted, this could not be an absolute rule, and he acknowledged that foreign counterintelligence provisions "are now being debated within the guidelines committee." Mondale was not happy: "When I look at these vaguely defined guidelines, I have to ask, would they stand up under direct orders to the contrary from a President of the United States?"

The tone of the exchange now deteriorated. Mondale demanded to know why the FBI was dragging its feet in handing over COINTELPRO documents to the Church committee, when the CIA had proved to be compliant in regard to similar materials. Levi said he could not speak for the CIA. Was that a good answer? asked Mondale. As good as the question, replied Levi. "Well," said Mondale, "I think that kind of arrogance is why we have trouble between the executive and the legislative branch." Levi apologized for appearing arrogant but only conditionally, noting that "someone else was being arrogant." The exchange made a vivid impression in the media and on the Hill. Levi had to explain on television that the FBI was not a "runaway agency," and that he really did want legislative backing for his guidelines.[3]

Though unable to mollify all of his critics, Levi continued to advance his reforms through consultation and by incremental degrees. On 18 February 1976, President Ford issued an executive order governing intelligence agencies. The section on the FBI still assigned to it responsibility for the detection and prevention of "subversion," and gave it the power to use unwarranted electronic surveillance "in support of foreign intelligence collection requirements of other intelligence agencies."

On 10 March, Levi amplified the Ford reform program by issuing his own guidelines. Those of the Levi guidelines that governed counterintelligence and foreign espionage remained classified, but the domestic security provisions, already having been widely anticipated, were announced publicly. Guidelines committee chairwoman Mary Lawton explained that the right to take "preventive action," asserted in the previous year but heavily criticized, had been removed. She said the guidelines prohibited such practices as the anonymous dissemination of information designed to expose individuals to public scorn and derision. In general, intrusive surveillance would be directed only at cases involving violence and/or crime. In special cases, the attorney general would have to give his prior approval in writing, and that approval would be subject to time limitations.

In a complementary move in midsummer, Kelley transferred domestic security cases from the bureau's Intelligence Division to its Criminal Investigative Division. Because of the latter division's mandatory observance of due process, this had the immediate effect of a reduction in intrusive surveillance. In an editorial anticipating the changes, the *Washington Post* contrasted the attorney general's boldness with the hesitation of most of his predecessors. The guidelines incorporated the right principles. However, they "may be effective as long as Mr. Levi is in office, but could be scrapped by any future Attorney General." Legislation was still needed.[4]

But Levi and the FBI were now running into further troubles, troubles that reduced the possibility of permanent reform legislation. Ominously for the moderate Republican reformers, criticism did not come only from liberal and leftist quarters. In October 1975, White House aide Michael Raoul-Duval deplored the "increasingly partisan" nature of criticism. The administration had endured the barbs of the Democrats, but he also wondered "how long it will be before we hear from Reagan."

Some American right-wingers either did not know, or wanted to forget, that the FBI was not an entirely happy contributor to the American gun culture. Before the advent of Prohibition-era gangsterism, special agents had not carried guns. Levi's FBI reckoned that, between 1963 and 1973, handguns killed 84,000 Americans, compared with a more modest estimate of 46,000 U.S. mortalities in the Vietnam War (historians more recently say it was more than 58,000 in Vietnam). The attorney general suggested a restriction on handgun ownership in high crime areas. This was not music to the ears of Reagan, the former governor of California who was shaping up to challenge Jerry Ford for the Republican nomination in 1976. Goaded by support from the *Los Angeles Times* for Levi's position, Reagan warned that the attorney general's plan to disarm law-abiding citizens would only help criminals.[5]

Reagan-style conservatives were annoyed with Levi and his reforms because they really wanted to defend the FBI in its old, undiluted form, and uphold it as an icon of the American Right. They approved of its contribution to law and order and to national security, and, ignoring its liberal provenance, thought of it as an inherently right-leaning institution. The latter assumption largely stemmed from the FBI's targeting of the Left in the 1950s and 1960s. Conservative columnist William F. Buckley, Jr., had defended the bureau's "bugging" activities when they came under fire in 1966. Representative John Ashbrook (R-Ohio), who had sat on HUAC and regretted its passing, would launch a similar attack in 1979 against his fellow legislators who persisted in trying to enact an FBI charter that would make it impossible to hunt down subversives and would enshrine the reforms of the preceding Republican administration. His voice was that of a conservative who put principle above party loyalty.

Ashbrook's comments received favorable coverage in *Human Events*, a conservative magazine that reflected Reagan's views and numbered him among its admirers. According to *Human Events*, "far left" groups supported the FBI charter, which, if enacted, would be a "boon to subversion." The magazine was convinced that the Carter administration's stance on the

FBI would doom its efforts to capture "middle America" in the 1980 presidential election. In the event, other issues like the economy and abortion were to overshadow FBI reform in that campaign, but Reagan still managed to position himself on the bureau in such a way as to appeal to those conservatives who were increasingly ascendant in the Republican Party. Periodic attacks on the FBI by remnants of the Klan and other white supremacist organizations made his support for the bureau seem quite reasonable, and, once elected, he could present himself as having a sensible agenda for the bureau.

Reagan took a genuine as well as political interest in the FBI. He drafted in his own hand a series of masterful radio broadcasts on the need to revive the intelligence community. According to one of his broadcasts, the prevailing attitude in Washington was that "our liberties will be safe if we can just keep the FBI and the CIA from doing what they are supposed to do." He reminded his listeners that some of the people under FBI surveillance were actually a greater threat than the FBI. It was a shame, he added in another broadcast, that congressional committees had given up investigating subversion in favor of investigating the FBI.

Group Research, Inc., a Washington press organization dedicated to recording the activities of the American Right, tracked the conservatives' strengthening interest in the FBI. It noted in June 1977 that FBI defenders were raising money. The Citizens' Legal Defense Fund for the FBI helped special agents accused of criminal surveillance, and included "a real corner of the right wing" among its supporters, for example, William Buckley's brother James, who had recently represented New York in the U.S. Senate, and the former congresswoman and ambassador Clare Boothe Luce. A few months later, Group Research noted the emergence of several more pro-FBI groups. One of these was the Committee to Help the FBI. Herbert A. Philbrick, an anti-Left columnist whose account of his own exploits as a bureau informant in the labor movement had inspired a television series in the 1950s, chaired the committee.[6]

Conservatives were in this period able to exploit an issue that had started life as a cause célèbre of the Left. In March 1976, FBI officials found in a New York bureau office twenty-five volumes of records on break-ins that occurred in the years 1954–73, evidence that discredited bureau claims that surreptitious entries had ceased in 1966. Local officials had ignored Hoover's "do not file" instructions. The records of the illegal operations had not been sent to Washington to be destroyed along with like files from other regions, and they constituted a unique window into the world of clandestine intrusion. The documents proved that FBI burglaries ran not to the few hundred admitted to Congress, but to many thousands.

By means of a lawsuit, the Socialist Workers Party was able to obtain documents showing that the FBI had burglarized its offices on dozens of occasions in the period up to 1973; subsequent revelations showed that illegal break-ins were still taking place, the latest in Denver in July 1976. The disclosures were news to the apparently unwitting Kelley, who in 1975 had assured the American press, the Church inquiry, and the Ford administration that, except in national security cases, no illegal entries had taken place since 1966. The Civil Rights Division of the Justice Department now launched yet another inquiry into FBI misdeeds. Presidential counsel Philip Buchen warned Ford: "This investigation is particularly critical because unlike the break-ins learned about previously, the ones being investigated fall within a period for which prosecution is not barred by the statute of limitations."

Media commentators roasted Kelley. In an interview for CBS television, the director abandoned the principle of loyalty to his predecessor and blamed illegalities on the "turkeys," a minority of Hooverite mavericks still working in the bureau. Kelley stated that he had been "deceived" over the non-cessation of burglaries, admitted he did not know who the deceivers were, and declined to be more specific on the ground that the FBI was conducting an inquiry into the affair. Columnist Garry Wills unleashed his scorn: "Suddenly, the FBI can't find its own files," and "I thought bureaus of investigation were supposed to specialize in information." Sanford Ungar, one of Kelley's CBS interviewers, could not understand why the bureau was pursuing archaic agendas when real problems needed to be addressed. He asked why the SWP was still under investigation, and suggested there were agents in the FBI "who have not been told that the red scare is off."

The FBI was reportedly split over Kelley's internal inquiry, with younger agents frustrated by the ill-repute that aging bureau cowboys conferred on them, and the older hands feeling that they had received no preoperational briefing on the illegality of certain types of break-in. The *New York Times* reported resentment at the new inquiries by "street agents," who felt they were about to be "sacrificed." With a further inquiry under way into the allegedly corrupt award of FBI surveillance equipment contracts, there was good reason to fear continuing censure from liberals and the Left.

But the American Right saw things in a different light. Conservative commentator Pat Buchanan instructed the FBI not to apologize, and warned critics not to demoralize an agency that, one day, America might need. Acting associate director W. Mark Felt and Assistant Director Edward Miller were unrepentant when they were in due course convicted and fined for authorizing illegal break-ins. Felt justified the activities he had approved against revolutionary groups like the SWP and the Weathermen: "Terrorism is one of the worst problems in the world and that's what we were combating," he insisted. The Citizens' Legal Defense Fund and other conservative organizations upheld the convicts' cause. Ronald Reagan treated them as martyrs. *Human Events* exaggerated when it suggested that the Felt-Miller trial would "cripple" Carter's reelection chances, but Reagan did make intelligence revitalization an issue, if one of several, in the 1980 presidential campaign. He pardoned Felt and Miller soon after his inauguration as president.[7]

In the long term, then, criticism from the Right blighted the prospects for acceptance of Attorney General Levi's moderate program of FBI reform. During his period in office, however, the viability of his reforms was already under threat for reasons other than partisan criticism. Charges of FBI bungling and top-level corruption undermined the prospects for the attorney general's success.

Demoralization was widespread, and every crisis now took its toll. Centered on the "badlands" of South Dakota, one such emergency gave civil rights advocates an opportunity to resume their attack. On the Blue Ridge reservation, memories lingered of the Seventh U.S. Cavalry's artillery attack on a Sioux village in 1890, resulting in the deaths of two hundred men, women, and children at the "battle" of Wounded Knee. When local native people formed the American Indian Movement (AIM) in 1968, the FBI, which had jurisdiction in federal reserves, labeled the organization dangerous and subversive. Two AIM militants died in an FBI siege in 1973, and the bureau lost two agents in a further shootout in 1975. The Feds launched a manhunt for four suspects in the latter case, inserting more than a hundred combat-clad agents into the area and incurring criticism for ignoring due process.

But the problem did not end there. On 24 February 1976, Roger Amiott was out fence mending near his ranch seventy miles from Wounded Knee. At 3 p.m., he came across the partly decomposed body of a woman. It lay in plain view, just fifty yards from a well-traveled state highway. W. O. Brown, a pathologist who was unpopular with reservation dwellers, said, "It's fairly common for Indians like these to die of an overdose," and he arranged a drug analysis. When the tests proved negative, Brown concluded that the cause of death was exposure. In a display of stunning insensitivity, the remains were interred minus the woman's hands, which had been severed and sent to Washington for fingerprint identification.

Efficient as ever in this area, the FBI determined that the dead woman was Anna Mae Aquash. She was a thirty-one-year-old AIM militant from Nova Scotia under indictment for a shootout with policemen in Oregon. She knew the four men wanted for killing the FBI men and had been preparing to testify in their defense. Her Canadian family insisted on a further autopsy. In the course of this, it was discovered that Aquash had been shot in the back of the head, close-range and execution-style, with a small-bore weapon. The new, independent pathologist said the wound should have been obvious at the first autopsy. Brown defended his earlier conduct with the observation that "a little bullet isn't hard to overlook." But activists speculated variously that Aquash's murder was meant to avenge the deaths of the FBI agents, that it was an attempt to suppress evidence, and that there had been a further cover-up of the real cause of her death. As journalist James Goodman put it, the Justice Department was "letting the FBI 'solve' a crime that the FBI itself might be involved in."

The controversy did not prevent the FBI from getting its man. In 1977, Leonard Peltier was convicted on a charge of double murder for killing the FBI agents. He remained in prison in spite of appeals that lasted into the 1990s. But his incarceration achieved closure only for the FBI, and did nothing to promote confidence in the bureau's commitment to racial justice. As Brown lamented of Aquash, "I suppose the Indians will never let that woman die." The badlands had bred many unsavory memories, and now the FBI had become one of them.[8]

The reputation of the FBI was in decline. Executive aide Raoul-Duval in October 1975 remarked on some "key constraints" in a manner that suggested lack of sympathy for the bureau. He deplored the lack of cooperation within the intelligence community. He alleged that the soundest overall grasp of intelligence was to be found not in the FBI or the CIA, but among the staff of the community's interlocutors, the Church committee. Assessing the agencies' receptiveness to change, he claimed that "the CIA is cooperating the fullest, and the FBI the least."

By 1976, the CIA was benefiting from the leadership of George H. W. Bush, an experienced Washington insider who was visibly reviving the morale of the bureau's old rival, throwing the FBI's problems into unwanted relief. In a snub whose origins stretched back to World War II, the FBI was marginalized at the high table of American intelligence. On 30 January, a White House proposal on "intelligence community leadership" afforded primacy to foreign intelligence, giving the FBI director the status merely of "observer," and then only "as appropriate." Kelley did not even attend the meeting, though George Bush did, on his very first day in charge of the CIA.[9]

The affair of the valances then blew up into a political scandal. In mid-1973, workmen from the bureau's Exhibits Section had installed two plywood valances in the windows of Director Kelley's apartment in Bethesda, Maryland. According to a report later submitted to the attorney general, the bureau subsequently developed the habit of supplying Kelley with some items to permit him to work at home, as his wife was ill with cancer—she died on 9 November 1975. For security reasons, private contractors could not be allowed into the Kelley dwelling, so help from government workers was only proper. The director, however, had neglected to pay for the various small jobs and items. This news leaked in the summer of 1976 at a time when Kelley was contending not only with other crises but also with pain from a displaced disc; in mid-August, he underwent a lumbar laminectomy in a Kansas City hospital.

Kelley explained that he had been busy with FBI problems, that the valances had been his wife's idea, and that he had no knowledge of them at the time. He said he had inadvertently neglected to pay for items running to a total of about a thousand dollars, but that he would now settle his debts. When he failed to pay up by the end of August, there were, according to the *Washington Post*'s Bob Woodward and other reporters, calls within the administration for his resignation. Ford asked Levi for a further evaluation of Kelley's alleged misconduct. Kelley blamed the press for his misfortunes, claiming that he had a policy of openness that had worked well when he was police chief in Kansas City, but that the same policy on behalf of the FBI was meeting with systematic abuse from the national press. The FBI director was in danger of becoming a political liability. In mid-October, Buchen and Levi had to pull him off a TWA flight bound for Albuquerque, having gotten wind that, at the height of the presidential election campaign, Kelley was going to threaten noncooperation with the media in a speech he had not cleared with the White House.

But this slap on the wrist was too little too late. The FBI problem was already an ingredient in the electoral damage that the intelligence flap had inflicted on the Ford administration. In mid-August, Senator Mondale, now speaking as the Democratic vice-presidential candidate, had attacked Levi and Kelley for presiding over a runaway bureau tainted by corruption and abuses of power.

The Democratic presidential candidate Jimmy Carter weighed in with similar rhetoric. When Kelley failed to extricate himself from the valance affair, Carter said he was a "disgrace," that he would fire him if he was president, and that the cancer story was just an attempt by Ford to cause a distraction. Ford accused Carter of lacking compassion, but his riposte was not as effective as it might have been: just days before Carter's swipe, Kelley had reentered the ranks of matrimony—his new wife was Shirley Dyches, a former nun.

To the *New Republic,* the Kelley "perquisites" affair confirmed that the Ford administration consisted of "an oafish group of politicians," the FBI director being, like the president himself, amiable, open, honest in a clumsy sort of way but, above all, "inept." At the end of September, Buchen told Ford that such publicity had delayed finalization of Levi's plans for constructive changes at the FBI, and that the time had arrived to press ahead with reform. But, for the Ford administration, the opportunity had irretrievably gone.[10]

Jimmy Carter's election victory in 1976 put into the White House a president who thought the 1908 arrangements for legislative control of federal investigation had been inadequate, and in his campaign had called for a legislative charter governing the FBI's affairs. He favored an equal rights amendment for women, wanted more black judges, and promised there would never again be harassment of the type inflicted on Martin Luther King. In another implied swipe at the Hoover era, he called for a concerted effort to crush the nation's heroin-peddling mafiosi. In some senses, Carter favored the bureau, for example by advocating the subordination of the Drug Enforcement Agency to the FBI. His rhetoric did not sharply differentiate him from FBI reformers in Congress and in the preceding administration, and this opened up the possibility of a bipartisan consensus on how the FBI should be mandated and governed. In office, however, Carter met with indifferent success, and his political weakness left the way open for a conservative surge in the political life of the nation, and for future reversals of the 1970s reforms.

The advent of a Democratic president seemed to augur the imminent departure of the wounded Kelley as director of the FBI. Such would be the fate of the CIA's George Bush. But early in 1976 there had been earnest talk of the need to depoliticize the FBI issue, and Kelley had vowed not to submit his pro forma resignation to coincide with the end of Ford's term. The idea was that the bureau should neither intervene in politics nor become a party political football. Once the election was over, Carter respected this principle, and Kelley stayed on until February 1978. At this point, the president had to appoint under new circumstances. The job had been undergoing reform. The Omnibus Crime Control law of 1968 required Senate confirmation of a nominee, and a 1976 law imposed a ten-year maximum term. Carter's initial choice was Frank M. Johnson, Jr., a federal judge from Alabama with a record of supporting civil rights for both African Americans and women. When Johnson withdrew because of ill health, Carter looked elsewhere for a principled candidate who could do the job and satisfy the Senate.[11]

The successful nominee was William H. Webster. A native of St. Louis and a graduate of Amherst College, Webster owed his rise to Republican administrations; President Nixon had named him a U.S. district court judge. But his appointment by a Democratic president signaled that he was a nonpartisan public employee, and, after Carter's defeat in 1980, Webster continued to serve under two Republican presidents, as bureau chief and then, from 1987 to 1991, as director of the CIA.

Having made an issue of some of the FBI's deficiencies in the election campaign, Carter made moves in the direction of reform. Ford's executive order in 1976 governing the activities of the FBI had still allowed the bureau to engage in the prevention of "subversion." Carter's equivalent order of January 1978 dispensed with that term. Congress passed in the same year the Foreign Intelligence Surveillance Act (FISA), which established a special court that would meet in secret to review and approve government requests for the electronic surveillance of U.S. citizens and resident aliens. It was this FISA restriction on unwarranted wiretapping and bugging that would come under intense attack after 9/11, when critics maintained that it sacrificed security on the altar of due process.

There was a contemporary reaction, too. The nation was tired of the constant refrain of reform, and Congress was becoming more conservative and less inclined to enshrine FBI restrictions in a legislative charter strong enough to survive the next bout of national hysteria. Nor would it have been prudent to launch renewed attacks, as the bureau was exhibiting a timely vigor, with Webster authorizing a sting operation against corrupt congressmen. The FBI set up a front organization called Abdul Enterprises, Ltd., yielding the code name Abscam. One senator, Harrison A. Williams, Jr. (D-N.J.), and six U.S. representatives proved willing to accept bribes from an agent posing as an Arab sheik, and eventually they were successfully prosecuted and convicted of bribery and conspiracy; Williams went to prison. The operation would have delighted Teddy Roosevelt, and it cheered modern Republicans, too. As *Human Events* pointed out, seven of the eight indicted lawmakers were Democrats.[12]

This did not mean that debate about the FBI died a sudden death. Webster was an expansionist, and there were waspish comments about the inverse relationship between the rising crime rate and the number of FBI agents, and about the progression from one agent per spy suspect in 1972 to four agents per spy suspect in 1982. There was also concern that sleazy sting operators had now taken the place of the too-clean-cut agents of the Hoover years, especially where drug operations were concerned. In February 1981, the House subcommittee on civil and constitutional rights held oversight hearings on FBI undercover guidelines, and, in his testimony, sociologist Gary Marx painted a picture of new intrusive techniques using lasers, parabolic mikes, periscopic prisms, truth serums, and other potentially disturbing devices.[13]

The degree of ethnic and gender diversification in the FBI was beginning to emerge as a thorny issue. Levi was conscious of the need to make progress. He reported in March 1976 that in recent years 104 blacks had been recruited as agents, together with 117 Latinos and 41 women. With the advent of the Carter administration, expectations were high, and the new president did appoint African Americans to federal posts in larger numbers than at any time since Reconstruction. Whereas President Johnson had appointed seven blacks as federal judges, for example, and President Nixon three, President Carter appointed thirty-seven. His solicitor general and his assistant attorney general for civil rights were both African Americans.

In November 1976, civil rights campaigner Jesse Jackson declared that there should be 750 African American FBI agents. There were 8,619 special agents at the time, so he was requesting recruitment at a modest rate in proportion to the number of black citizens in America (on the same principle, women, making up more than half of the population, should have had more than 4,300 posts, not just 650). However, the tide was beginning to run against positive discrimination, as was demonstrated in the *Regents v. Bakke* case in 1978, in which the Supreme Court struck down racial balance as a criterion for medical school admissions selections. The chairman of the Congressional Black Caucus, Parren J. Mitchell (D-Md.), complained that African Americans under Carter were "almost going through the same kind of tokenism as . . . before." The FBI did make some changes. In 1979, Director Webster appointed the first African American and the first Hispanic to promoted posts; they became special agents in charge. But the sense of urgency communicated by Carter's judicial appointments was less evident in the bureau.[14]

The reformers of the 1970s tried to insist on the traditional principle that surveillance should be apolitical. Congress instituted greater oversight and passed the Foreign Intelligence Surveillance Act, but it failed to agree on a legislative charter that would enshrine American civil liberties. Attorney General Levi's strengthened executive guidelines in the short term filled the space vacated by the legislators, but these were subject to the vagaries of American politics. With conservatives developing the view that some liberties needed to be sacrificed in the name of the greater defense of democracy, challenges to the 1970s reforms were on the way sooner rather than later.

The Ford-Carter FBI had critics on the Left who thought it could be reformed further, and critics on the Right who thought it should be made a tougher instrument of government. Seen with the wisdom of hindsight, though, these contrasting sets of critics had common shortcomings. Neither offered a pragmatic critique of the absence of diversity in the bureau. And neither the Left nor the Right advocated moves to improve coordination of the counterintelligence and counterterror effort.

12

mission regained: 1981–1993

In the penultimate decade of the twentieth century, the FBI recovered its sense of mission. In part, this was a psychological process, a bourgeoning in confidence springing from the bureau's restored prestige. But the recovery was also based on observable phenomena. The FBI scored spectacular successes against organized crime. The end of the Cold War and the collapse of communism in Europe eliminated the bureau's traditional antagonist, the KGB, giving a sense of victory. Although the Feds' oldest mission, fighting white terrorism, had lost its prominence, that was because the battle had been virtually won, and on a parallel front, that of diversity in hiring, the FBI made progress.

The bureau's psychological recovery owed much to the presidency of Ronald Reagan. When he departed the scene, and especially during the presidency of Bill Clinton, its star seemed once again to be on the wane. Lapses in competence, feuding between Clinton and his FBI director Louis Freeh, and controversy over ethnic profiling led to a renewal of criticism that reached a crescendo by the start of the new century. The new attacks obscured some of the virtues of the modern FBI, as well as the political achievement whereby it survived the demise of its Cold War raison d'être, the communist threat. But they also throw into higher relief the reconstructive accomplishments of the Reagan administration.

Right-wing groups such as the Western Goals Foundation had called for a revitalized FBI in the course of the 1980 election campaign, and President Reagan was happy to comply. He had long been a fan: "As a young man, I used to thrill at the FBI story." In his Hollywood days, he had worked as a political informer for the bureau. As president, he was a bureau booster. To commemorate its seventy-fifth anniversary in 1983, for example, he announced an "FBI Day." All of this came easily to Reagan because it conformed to his more general philosophy. His support for the FBI's war on crime gave him an opportunity to take a swipe at liberal theories. He said that criminality could not be blamed on "underprivileged backgrounds." He wanted to deploy G-men, not social spending, against the "dark, evil enemy within."[1]

Reagan was careful to preserve those aspects of the FBI that met his approval. Notably, he kept William Webster on as director. This was a defiant decision, mainly because of controversy resulting from the FBI's Abscam investigation, which had snared mostly Democratic lawmakers. On Capitol Hill, there were protests about partisanship and entrapment in the Abscam sting, and calls for curbs to be placed on undercover probes. However, like his Republican predecessor Theodore Roosevelt, Reagan outfaced his critics, and Webster stayed.

But in other respects, Reagan overturned the existing order, sometimes emphatically. This was partly a matter of gesture politics. Pardoning FBI convicts Mark Felt and Edward Miller in the first weeks of his presidency, he insisted that they had served the bureau "with great distinction." Yet Reagan gradually changed the FBI in more concrete ways. He increased its powers, and removed certain restrictions. In December 1981, for example, he issued an executive order governing intelligence matters. It authorized the bureau to collect foreign intelligence in the United States, in this way chipping away at the domestic-foreign, FBI-CIA split that had been intended, in 1947, to prevent the emergence of an "American Gestapo."

Early in the following year, Attorney General William French Smith boosted the bureau's prestige when he made the Drug Enforcement Agency (DEA) subordinate to the FBI. This was a bold decision, but the need for action had been evident. Established in the Justice Department in 1973, the DEA had enjoyed only indifferent success. With teenagers in America's affluent suburbs falling prey to narcotics hitherto associated only with the ghetto, the backbone of Republican political support was in a state of panic and had to be propitiated.

The move to strengthen the enforcement of prohibition did not satisfy everybody. According to one neoliberal school of thought, decriminalization was the answer, as market forces would then drive down the price of legalized drugs, and, with no profit on offer, gangsters would stop pushing them. The prohibition-induced high price of cocaine was further held to be a factor in the destabilization of Latin American politics, to the disadvantage of the United States. In tension-fraught congressional hearings, there were objections to the FBI running anti-drugs wars in South America, as CIA covert operations in that region were already bringing the USA into disrepute.

But with crime fighting high on the Reaganite agenda, and with organized crime syndicates making so much money out of drugs, it was good politics to boost the FBI's anti-narcotic capabilities. In the Republican heartlands, a war on drugs had a stronger appeal than a campaign for legalization. It made operational sense to coordinate the resources of the two leading agencies. The administration's solution did not give the FBI complete control over the DEA, but the new arrangement was nevertheless a visible boost to the FBI's authority and standing.

In March 1983, Attorney General Smith relaxed the guidelines governing the FBI's conduct of domestic security and anti-terrorism investigations. The annual number of such investigations had declined in the previous seven years from 4,868 to a mere 38. Webster attributed the decline to the Levi guidelines of 1976. No doubt with the Felt-Miller convictions in mind, he said that proper guidelines "are important to law enforcement because they tell us if we function within those parameters, we will not be the subject of successful lawsuits and prosecutions." The new Smith guidelines introduced a degree of permissiveness into the conduct of preemptive inquiries. They could now proceed in cases where two or more people were suspected of plotting violent criminal activity, or of advocating such activity. In a relaxation of current regulations, the FBI would no longer be required to notify the attorney general in advance of such probes, having a duty to notify only the Justice Department's Office of Intelligence Policy of their existence.

The impact of the Smith guidelines is open to question. Former FBI assistant director W. Raymond Wannall complained in 1990 that agents were still in a Catch-22 situation: they could investigate only if they had evidence of a crime, but the only way to get such evidence was to investigate. In the same year, the Senate Intelligence Committee received a report from a panel chaired by Eli Jacobs, owner of the Baltimore Orioles and formerly an arms control adviser to President Reagan. On the basis of a review of recent espionage cases, the Jacobs panel recommended increased powers for the FBI, such as access to unlisted telephone numbers and, in an echo of the 1941 Sebold-Norden bombsight case, legislation to enable prosecution for secret document theft without production in court of the secret document in question.

In Wannall's view, congressional intimidation had contributed to investigative timidity in the bureau. He argued that the House Judiciary Subcommittee on Civil and Constitutional Rights, which he called the "extreme anti-intelligence wing in the House," was in the 1980s unduly influenced by its chairman, Don Edwards. A Democrat from the Peninsula area south of San Francisco, Edwards had been an FBI agent in 1940–41 and had his own ideas about the bureau's proper mission. Chairing a further FBI-DEA merger hearing in September 1983, he made no secret of his opposition to the enhancement of FBI powers. He impeded attempts to increase the number of agents allocated to the investigation of domestic terrorism, and opposed the deployment of FBI agents to investigate political opposition to the Reagan administration's foreign policy initiatives in Central America.[2]

Clearly, the congressional investigative fervor of the 1970s had not evaporated upon the entry of Reagan into the White House. Critical questions were being asked on a broad front. One, for example, was about the FBI's surveillance of Reagan's foreign-policy critics. The *San Francisco Chronicle* later estimated that this program had affected over a hundred organizations.

Most controversial was the bureau's monitoring of Central American groups and their U.S. sympathizers, especially in the case of Nicaragua. One of Reagan's main foreign policy aims was the removal of the government of that country, which was democratically elected but too left wing for his liking. He promoted secret support for the "Contra" armed opposition movement, and continued to do so even when Congress banned that support. Ultimately, his administration circumvented Congress by illegally selling arms to Iran and diverting the funds to the Nicaraguan terrorists.

The FBI became the domestic face of the Iran-Contra operation. In 1984, the bureau refused to provide details of what a local journalist called "brownshirt" break-ins at a church in Cambridge, Massachusetts, where documents were stolen that shed light on membership of the Christian organization Sanctuary for Central American Refugees. Later, the FBI admitted to having been behind ninety-three such burglaries, with targets ranging from church sanctuaries to a children's daycare facility, but, at the time, it made every effort to keep its operations secret.

In February 1987, details of the break-ins began to emerge. At a two-day hearing before the House Subcommittee on Civil and Constitutional Rights, it became clear that the FBI had infiltrated the Dallas branch of one of the larger Central American groups, the Committee in Solidarity with the People of El Salvador (CISPES). This organization opposed the government in El Salvador, a dictatorship that shared Reagan's goal of assisting the Contras. According to the conservative journal *Human Events*, CISPES was a "client" of the "far-left." Witnesses testifying to the subcommittee accused the group of plotting the assassination of President Reagan. However, adversarial witnesses accused the FBI of assisting Salvadorian death squads. The *New York Times* acidly noted that the FBI had interviewed one of the chief Iran-Contra conspirators, Oliver North, but had "lost" the transcript. In due course, the FBI investigation cleared CISPES of any involvement in terrorist activities. Under pressure, the bureau had to issue a denial that it targeted only leftist organizations.

But if the hounds still brayed, they brayed less loudly than in the 1970s. Even the supposedly inquisitorial Congressman Edwards approved of the "latitude" that the guidelines on "domestic terrorism" gave the FBI. When the Senate Intelligence Committee reported on the CISPES affair in 1989, it similarly gave the bureau fundamental support. It deplored the addition of 13,198 names to the FBI files and the surveillance of organizations like the United Automobile Workers and the Southern Christian Leadership Conference, and concluded that the entire investigation had been a mistake. However, it exonerated the FBI, and described the whole affair as an "aberration."[3]

Meantime, a further civil liberties issue had come to light. The Library Awareness Program generated controversy that would dog the footsteps of the FBI for years to come. Since 1962, the FBI had been asking librarians to report their suspicions, for example, if someone with a foreign accent inquired about scientific books. By the 1980s, there was a spreading realization that, in an age of computers and in a nation that prided itself on being an open society, it was an easy matter for the Soviet Union and its allies to pillage technical journals or simply to download scientific information that might be of assistance to their commercial and military ambitions. The Reagan administration resolved to tighten up U.S. scientific counterintelligence.

An attempt, in 1984, to persuade scientists to deny "sensitive but unclassified" information to foreign competitors was unpopular and had to be abandoned in March 1987. But, by this time, the FBI had stepped up its Library Awareness Program. When two FBI agents turned up at Columbia University's Math and Science Library to ask questions about the library's users, it sparked an uprising of librarians across the land, invocation of a document not every American knew about, the "Library Bill of Rights," and, in 1988, the inevitable hearing before a committee chaired by Don Edwards. While the CISPES and Library Awareness incidents may have demonstrated to some that the FBI had been reinvigorated, to others they proved that the bureau was once again engaging in political work.[4]

Supporters of the Reagan administration and the ensuing administration headed by his former vice president, George H. W. Bush, were able to ride out such criticism. In large measure, this was by pointing to their successes. In a peaceful election in February 1990, Nicaraguans voted into office a new government that was more congenial to American conservatives. Reagan-Bushites in the following year claimed victory in the Cold War with the Soviet Union. The "victory" claim is controversial, with Poles and others arguing they needed no U.S. encouragement to oppose communism. In any case, the halo effect soon wears off in politics. The Cold War had inspired national unity, but the removal of the communist threat caused divisiveness, and a disposition to challenge iconic Cold War institutions like the FBI. Nevertheless, "victory" brought at least short-term popularity for Reagan, Bush, and their institutions, as well as the possibility of a reduction in military expenditure that would yield a "peace dividend" and make civilian agencies more affordable.

If President Reagan's political skills and the ending of the Cold War contributed to the FBI's restitution, so did the bureau's achievements in fostering a greater sense of justice in American society. There was progress on the racial and ethnic fronts, with a further hint of cosmopolitanism in the FBI's willingness to engage in international cooperation. There was a new tolerance toward women, with evidence of enlightenment on the pragmatic advantages of racial and gender outreach. In addition to this, the FBI scored its best-ever successes against Big Crime, demonstrating in a tangible manner that the bureau was there for the protection of the little guy, not just the rich and powerful.

The FBI's success in combating organized crime was one of the healthiest indicators of its post–Cold War performance. Gone were the days when just four special agents were pitted against the might of the Mafia, when sociologists tried to explain away the Sicilian connection, and when G-men in suits drank glasses of milk in downtown bars. During the Reagan presidency, the bureau flexed its anti-mobster muscles. In the 1984 "Pizza Connection" arrests, FBI agents exposed a ring of international heroin traffickers who had distributed their goods nationwide via pizza parlors. Working in tandem with district attorney Louis J. Freeh, they secured a number of convictions, including that of the former Sicilian Mafia leader Gaetano Badalamenti, who was trapped, Freeh later recalled, "in the ether, at the far end of one of the phone lines we had tapped."

In 1987, another FBI investigation based on electronic surveillance and the testimony of informers resulted in the arrest of Philadelphia's Mafia boss, Nicodemo Scarfo. "Little Nicky" and sixteen of his associates were convicted on charges of extortion and murder. Even more spectacularly, in 1988, following a coordinated FBI-DEA inquiry, the Panamanian dictator General Manuel Noriega was kidnapped in violation of the sovereignty of his own country and put on trial in the United States for drug and money laundering offenses.

In 1992 there came a key conviction, that of John Gotti, up until then known as "the Teflon Don" because of the inability of prosecutors to make a case against him stick. His imprisonment brought one major branch of mobsterism into disarray. Gotti was convicted on an array of charges that included the murder, in 1985, of Paul Castellano. After being arrested in 1957 at the Apalachin raid along with Carlo Gambino, Castellano had spent years in prison. After Gambino's death in 1976, Castellano received his reward for his observation of *omertà,* the Mafia's code of silence, and assumed leadership of the Gambino crime syndicate. In that role, he prospered from such rackets as the sale of stolen American automobiles in Kuwait. Gotti had him shot down because the old-school Castellano disapproved of Gotti's heroin trafficking, and because Gotti wanted to take over the Gambino clan. But, by this time, scarcely a whisper in the Gambino operation went unrecorded by the FBI's omnipresent and sophisticated listening devices. Gotti's second in command, Sammy Gravano, turned informer, and scores of Gambino mobsters went to prison along with their chief.

Gravano testified in a Brooklyn courtroom, and predicted a terminal decline for organized crime. As he anticipated, there was no abatement in the bureau's war on the Mob. In 1996, nineteen members of the Genovese crime family, perhaps America's most powerful racketeers, were indicted on charges ranging from murder to tax evasion. By 2002, there were seventy-five Feds working on Mafia cases in New York City alone, and press conferences to announce mass arrests had become a common occurrence.[5]

Things still went wrong. There was the affair of James J. "Whitey" Bulger. According to his former associate Eddie Mackenzie, Bulger had "a stare of blankness, no compassion in his eyes," and "the toughest guy" would "almost go to the bathroom in their pants in his presence." An Irish American mobster, Bulger perpetrated murder and general mayhem in his native Boston, where he was a foil to his brother Billy, president of the Massachusetts state senate. In a belated attempt to combat Italian American crime, J. Edgar Hoover had recruited Whitey Bulger as an informer against the

Boston Mafia, giving him immunity from prosecution. But the special agent assigned to handle him, James Connolly, became a member of the South Boston Irish American mob. A "Southie" who had grown up with Bulger, Connolly tipped him off whenever the FBI seemed to be getting curious about his activities.

By the 1990s, several additional FBI agents had been corrupted, and it was becoming apparent that bureau informants were committing major crimes while on the federal payroll. The Massachusetts state police and the DEA had become disillusioned with the Boston FBI office and no longer cooperated with it. The stench of corruption finally reached Washington, and in 1995 federal racketeering charges were lodged against Bulger and another long-term FBI informer, Stephen "The Rifleman" Flemmi. Flemmi eventually received a prison sentence. Bulger was indicted for twenty-two murders, but, a master of disguise with millions of dollars at his disposal, he evaded capture. While the bodies of his terminated rivals continued to be disinterred until well into the following century, the blank-eyed mobster could be sighted only on the FBI's Ten Most Wanted posters.[6]

Even though the bureau was not universally triumphant, it was more successful against organized crime than at any point in its past. Perhaps affected by the 1980s renaissance of American individualism, mafiosi began to abandon the collective code of *omertà* and sang with increasing frequency. For its part, the FBI did not simply stand still and let the ripe fruits of good fortune fall into its lap. Its proficiency continued to be in the technological vanguard—by 1990, its experts were making effective evidentiary use of DNA to confirm identities in murder and rape cases, and, following the Digital Telephony Act in 1994, they were able to track criminal activities on the Internet. As ever, such developments could be open to abuse, but without them the FBI would have been a less formidable detective and law enforcement agency.

In the 1980s and 1990s, the FBI became more diverse in its employment practices. By the time Reagan became president, even the most conservative politicians had to make politically correct gestures. When twenty children were murdered in Atlanta and the newly inaugurated Californian was accused of reacting slowly because they were black, he retorted that "this administration is totally color blind" and gave the FBI an extra $4 million to help the investigation. Reagan was opposed to affirmative action and refused to set quotas in federal employment. Whereas 12 percent of President Carter's federal appointees had been African American, the corresponding figure for the Reagan administration declined to less than 4 percent, even though the number of blacks in nonfederal management jobs continued to rise during his presidency. However, the figure for Reagan's FBI bucked the trend, being slightly higher than 4 percent and rising.[7]

A number of reasons account for the FBI's increasing diversity. One of these was the bureau's success against the Ku Klux Klan and other white hate organizations. This had helped to create a climate in which civil rights workers could operate free of intimidation, and their efforts had resulted in legislation. The Civil Rights Act of 1964 prohibited job discrimination and set up an equal employment commission whose remit was widened, in a 1972 law, to include jobs in federal government. According to Dr. Elsie Scott, executive director of the National Organization of Black Law Enforcement Executives (NOBLE), lawsuits arising from this legislation increased minority employment "more than any other factor."

Another factor was the accelerating diversity of American society. According to a projection by federal statisticians, America's nonwhite citizens were on course to account for almost 30 percent of the population by 2050, and the Hispanic-Latino proportion of the population was already approaching 13 percent by 2000. Such changes could provoke xenophobia, but they also invited Americans to think again about who should be working for federal agencies.

Another factor causing people to think about diversity was the disappearance of distractions. The intelligence flap of the 1970s had focused attention on other issues, and its subsidence had the indirect effect of concentrating minds on recruitment reform, with the bureau playing catch-up in this area.

The Cold War had been a further distraction from the need for diversity in hiring. The rivalry with the Soviet Union had encouraged support for civil rights on a merely opportunistic basis. Communist propagandists had made political capital out of American segregation and discrimination and, in the struggle for the hearts and minds of the world, U.S. leaders had perceived the need for racial reform to be in the self-interest of the white majority. The end of the Cold War, however, promoted reform in a more constructive way. With no apparent threat to their nation, white Americans were more prepared to tolerate women, gays, and blacks in sensitive national security jobs. Feeling more included, minority members who had previously shunned the FBI were more inclined, in turn, to apply for jobs at the bureau.

There had always been a pragmatic case for hiring such people: the larger the pool of talent, the better your recruits will be; as they are called on to investigate all kinds of people, police or intelligence agencies do a better job if characterized by ethnic and gender diversity; just hiring practices make an organization more acceptable to a greater number of people, and that promotes the public support that is helpful to effective detective, police, counterterrorism, and counterespionage work. Yet, in spite of these sound reasons for political correctness, the prejudiced attitude lingered on until the end of the Cold War that it would be too risky to employ "emotional" women, gays subject to blackmail, or blacks with attitude problems and maybe left-wing sympathies. The election of Bill Clinton in 1992 brought to the White House one of American history's most noted presidential friends of the African American, and Clinton no doubt contributed to the new spirit of tolerance. But times had changed, as well as the politicians.

In 1988, the House Subcommittee on Civil and Constitutional Rights held hearings on affirmative action and equal opportunity in the FBI. Once again in the chair, Congressman Don Edwards explained that this was in reaction to a series of challenges: a class action lawsuit by Hispanic agents employed by the FBI who claimed racial discrimination in promotion, a claim of racial discrimination by a black agent named Donald Rochon, and charges of gender-based harassment by a female agent. The chairman claimed that the bureau had "come a long way from the days when the only black Special Agents were the Director's personal servants." In her testimony, Elsie Scott retorted that many in the bureau still had "the same mindset as Hoover." While the number of black agents in the "Ivy League" of law enforcement had increased, she argued that the FBI still lagged behind municipal police forces as well as certain federal employers, such as the DEA. In raising the numbers and relativity issues, the NOBLE leader had created potent criteria. The FBI responded by supplying figures showing, for the period 1982–87, a 51 percent increase in the number of African Americans it employed. The corresponding figure for Hispanics was 48 percent, for Asian Americans 73 percent, for women 93 percent, and for whites 17 percent.[8]

If the FBI's psychological profilers had turned their attention to the typical special agent of the 1930s, they would have identified a white Protestant male from a comfortable if not affluent parental background, a person of some athletic ability with modest educational attainments, and often a southerner. From the 1940s, Irish American Catholics began to make substantial inroads, just as they had done in urban police forces and other occupations. Their combative ascent of the ethnic ladder forms part of the background to the story of Whitey Bulger, his FBI handler, and the bureau's decision to team up with the Irish American underworld to target the Sicilian Mob. But if these events and struggles seemed dramatic to insiders, to outsiders the FBI special agent still looked the same until the 1980s. He typically remained white, and male.

While J. Edgar Hoover had been widely accused of racism, he also had a reputation as a male chauvinist. On 26 May 1924, after just sixteen days as director, he requested the resignation of two of the bureau's only three female special agents. The third (Lenore Houston) resigned in 1928, and forty-four years were to elapse before the next woman became a special agent. At the time of Hoover's death in 1972, there were sixty-one black agents in the FBI and fifty-nine Hispanics, but there were no female agents.

Already, however, a federal court was dealing with a lawsuit brought by two women who claimed they had been denied employment as special agents in violation of their constitutional and legal rights. With Hoover out of the way, the bureau gave ground and took on Susan Lynn Roley, formerly of the U.S. Marine Corps, and Joanne E. Pierce, formerly a nun. Special agent posts were now open to all, in principle, but the gap between principle and attitude attracted comment. For example, Diane Wang and Cindy Jaquith of the Socialist Workers Party took issue with the chauvinist language of special agent reports that described radical women as "making a real attempt to be unattractive," and that characterized their debates as "bickering."

In a significant change in policy, FBI directors William Webster (1978–87) and William Sessions (1987–93) became proactive in the recruitment of women and members of minority groups. Webster kept tally on a card he carried around with him in his wallet: 413 minority agents and 147 female at the start of his tenure, and 943 and 787 at the end. As for Sessions, his policy of hiring minorities and women was so vigorous that it was rumored to have spurred reactionary colleagues to plot his dismissal in 1993.

The 1980s and 1990s still witnessed expressions of minority discontent. Whenever the FBI moved against prominent black targets, it could expect a firestorm. Such was the case in January 1991 after the arrest of Mayor Marion Barry of Washington, D.C., on a charge of narcotics possession. The FBI's videotaped evidence of Barry and a female friend smoking crack cocaine in a hotel room reawakened fears of persecution. When, in July 1991, the FBI revealed that there had been charges of sexual harassment against Supreme Court nominee Clarence Thomas, the nation went through a further period of collective angst.

Expressions of discontent did not indicate regression, but, as had so often happened in the past, rising expectations gave rise to frustration. There were protests against what was portrayed as the slow speed of change, and these protests contributed to a deterioration in the FBI's image in the 1990s. Across the Potomac in Virginia, three hundred CIA women brought a class action that proved discrimination and resulted, by 1995, in retroactive promotions and salary payments. Back in the District, FBI women were also alert to evidence of discrimination and belittlement, and found plenty of it. Candice DeLong, who had been a senior nurse before joining the FBI, was told in training she would be unable to handle the stress of some of the more gory work. When she laughed, she was reported for insolence. Her autobiography records the fact that you can cry and still be tough, and accepts with pride the epithet "bitches in badges."

Frank Buttino had been with the bureau for twenty years when, in 1990, he was fired from his post at the San Diego office after an anonymous tip-off to his bosses that he was gay. Buttino sued, and expanded his lawsuit into a class action on behalf of all gay agents who were being forced by the FBI's ban on homosexuals to remain in the closet and to lie about their sexual orientation. When the trial began in a U.S. district court in San Francisco in December 1993, Attorney General Janet Reno lifted the ban on gays in the FBI. Buttino won compensation including pension rights. However, reservations remained about the FBI's policy, which was that gays were subject to blackmail and a security risk unless they came out—bureau officials would visit their parents to make sure that they had done so.

Minority lawsuits exerted a constant pressure on the government and the FBI to hire a more diverse workforce. Bernardo Perez filed a class action on behalf of himself and more than three hundred other Hispanic special agents, arguing that they had been assigned to restricted missions, typically on the "taco circuit" of the southwest, thus being deprived of promotion opportunities. A federal court found in favor of Perez and his fellow litigants, and, in 1990, Sessions compensated them. Hispanics' complaints echoed black agents' concerns that they were being put to work chiefly on African American cases. The perception was that the FBI had learned how effective minority agents could be in ethnic communities, but not how to utilize their talents more broadly.

Just before the Perez settlement, Sessions had agreed to a million dollars' compensation for special agent Donald Rochon, who had been racially harassed at the bureau's Chicago and Omaha offices. This did not appease the bureau's black agents. In April 1991, 250 members of Black Agents Don't

Get Equality (BADGE) planned a class action alleging discrimination in assignments and promotion. Sessions heard about their move, and arranged a meeting with BADGE. This provoked a rebellion by the FBI Agents Association, originally formed to support Felt and Miller following their convictions, and by this time representing 6,500 of the bureau's 9,500 special agents. The association went to court in an attempt to join the negotiations, but a judge ruled against it, and Sessions cut a deal that promoted six black agents.[9]

Meanwhile, Webster's pocketbook statistics were being overtaken by change. At the conclusion of his tenure in 1987 there had been 943 minority agents. Ten years later there were 1,651, or 15.3 percent of the agent workforce; by 2003 the figures had declined to 1,575 and 13.5 percent. By 1997, Webster's 787 women had become 1,617, 15 percent of the agents. The figure for 2003 was 2,109, a rise to 18.1 percent. Thus, in the case of racial diversification, the bureau peaked in the 1990s, whereas the number of women serving as agents kept rising in the next decade. It could be argued that both minorities and women were underrepresented in the 1990s, as they were about 20 percent and 50 percent of the U.S. population, respectively. On the other hand, in the early 1990s only 9 percent of journalists were minority members, and only 2 percent of major law firm partners were nonwhite. In the speed of change and the relative outcome, the FBI was in the vanguard of progressive hiring in the 1990s—in spite of all the criticism, and no doubt in part because of it.[10]

In the meantime, the FBI showed that it still allowed no latitude to the kind of intimidation that had, for so many decades, retarded the realization of civil rights in America. By the 1990s, FBI investigations of hate crimes had become routine, and citizens had as much reason to expect justice without favor from their government as at any stage since Reconstruction. The Hate Crimes Statistics Act of 1990 and its subsequent amendments required records to be kept of crimes and the actions taken against them, and broadened the definition of hate crime beyond its original racial connotation, additionally taking into account criminal abuse of citizens arising from religious, ethnic, disability, or sexual orientation bias. In 1999, the bureau logged 19 crimes arising from disability bias. This compared with 828 ethnic, 1,317 sexual orientation, and 1,411 religious cases; the largest category included 4,295 cases arising from racial bias.

The number of race hate crimes may have been a reflection of the nation's continuing racial problems, but it also indicated a determination to record what was going on, and to act against racists. A case in point occurred in Oklahoma on 19 April 1995, when a terrorist bomb exploded and killed 169 people at the Alfred P. Murrah Federal Building in Oklahoma City. The FBI amassed evidence against the perpetrators, Timothy McVeigh and Terry Nichols. The case became controversial because of procedural and laboratory mistakes made by the FBI. But there was another underlying message. When an Oklahoma trooper arrested McVeigh ninety minutes after the explosion, he had in his possession a right-wing novel, *The Turner Diaries*, that detailed a fictional bombing of the FBI building in Washington, an event that would, in the Turner story, trigger an Aryan revolution. Actions against such right-wing terrorists and racists became an operational trademark of the FBI, as once again illustrated, for example, when Shawn Adams and three other white supremacist terrorists were arrested in 1997 for conspiring to sabotage a natural gas plant and commit robbery. The 1990s may not have been characterized by the strident tones of feminism, civil rights, and gay rights campaigns in the 1960s and '70s, but there was a realistic expectation that the FBI would fight for justice.[11]

In a development that complemented domestic multiculturalism and anti-racism, the FBI showed an interest in foreign activities and cooperation. The bureau's foreign activities were not new; it already had a long history of engagement in the Western hemisphere. In 1935 Hoover agreed to furnish information on criminal fugitives to Interpol, then based in Austria. The National Security Act of 1947 aimed to freeze the bureau's international activities, but the Pike investigation in the 1970s unveiled fairly extensive FBI foreign operations. At that time, an estimated eighty-three FBI personnel worked abroad, fifty-four of them as legal attachés. Assistant Attorney General Eugene W. Walsh said that the overseas FBI offices mainly sought exchanges of criminal information, through liaison with local police forces.

Under Reagan, the bureau took a further step in the direction of cosmopolitanism. Although the FBI had established a Spanish-language training school in 1941, agents had hitherto undertaken translations from other languages on an ad hoc basis. But the FBI now hired some specialist linguists. What began as a small band in 1983 expanded to a workforce of eleven hundred by 2002, with translation expertise covering many of the world's languages.

The Democratic president Bill Clinton supported the principle of international intelligence cooperation, even though the Iran-Contra affair had made the FBI's international work highly controversial. When the Mafia murdered Giovanni Falcone, a prosecuting judge in Sicily who had worked with Louis Freeh on the Pizza Connection case, Clinton put the FBI's DNA analysts at the disposal of Italian officials and sent Freeh, now director of the FBI, to Palermo, Sicily, to arrange more powerful liaison. In a speech delivered on the steps of the Palatine Chapel of the Palace of the Normans, Freeh honored the memory of his friend Falcone, defied the Mafia, and challenged all Sicilians to embrace the rule of law. Thereafter, he made an annual pilgrimage to the scene to reinforce the point. Centuries of Sicilian tradition did not die a sudden death, but life would not be the same for the mafiosi in future. When the "boss of bosses" Bernardo Provenzano was arrested in Corleone in 2006, he had been on the run for many years, much of the time living in conditions of squalor.

Clinton made a general promise to share information with friendly foreign nations, so long as it did not betray U.S. operational methods and undercover personnel. In 1995, he found a further international use for the FBI. Through electronic intercepts, he received an intimation that the CIA was planning to assassinate the Iraqi dictator Saddam Hussein—on its own initiative, and without consulting the White House. CIA officials faced charges of disobeying executive orders and murder-for-hire. Clinton asked the FBI to investigate, and in the following year it was able to report that the whole episode had stemmed from Iranian disinformation.

The evidence of transnational activity is more than episodic. The degree to which the FBI had developed an international perspective is seen in its Ten Most Wanted Fugitives list. The original list in 1950 was made up of Americans, mostly from the world of organized crime. But, by 1997, eight of the ten fugitives were of international derivation. In a message marking the fiftieth anniversary of the list in 2000, Freeh gave special attention to the globalization of crime in the previous decade, and to the FBI's matching commitment to international activity.[12]

The FBI had not only rediscovered its historic mission but had also begun to renew that mission, engaging in multicultural hiring practices and embarking on international enterprises. Yet, by the start of the new millennium, its reputation was largely in tatters. The unraveling process began because of the political problems that beset the Clinton administration.

13

strife and slippage: 1993–2001

For much of the presidency of William J. (Bill) Clinton, the FBI continued to succeed, and to live up to its founders' ideals. But political strife affected the administration more and more, complicating the bureau's work and affecting its morale. And, by the end of the decade, it was beginning to slip into some recidivist habits.

Although the end of the Cold War brought benefits to the United States, it also prompted uncertainty and questions about the apparatus of the secret state. Senator Daniel Patrick Moynihan (D-N.Y.) advocated the abolition of the CIA. Though he took a more benign view of the FBI, the bipartisan commission on government secrecy that he chaired took an unsettlingly close look at the bureau. By the time his inquiry was over, Clinton had lost his majorities on Capitol Hill, and was in political trouble. Early in 1998, the Monica Lewinsky affair surfaced and played into the hands of those who wished to destabilize his administration. Clinton's panicky denials of his sexual relations with the White House intern opened the door to a ferocious attack led by the Republicans' leader in Congress, Newt Gingrich. The president was impeached in the House, and tried and acquitted in the Senate.

With Gingrich increasingly in the ascendant, the FBI was potentially in trouble. Its cause had not been helped by the discovery in 1996 that the bureau had given the White House Democrats its files on four hundred Republicans. By 2000, an investigative panel had concluded that the affair was the result of nothing more sinister than bureaucratic incompetence, but Gingrich was sufficiently annoyed by "Filegate" to oppose additional wiretap powers that Freeh had requested for anti-terrorist operations.[1]

In the 1990s, personality issues affecting the FBI reached an unusual degree of intensity, and undermined the reputation of the bureau. They were by no means confined to Clinton and Gingrich. For a start, William S. Sessions departed the directorship in 1993 via a vale of tears. The son of a clergyman, a moderate Republican, a federal judge under President Ford, and then a worthy promoter of fair hiring practices in the FBI, Sessions appeared to be a sound and even straitlaced public official—until he allowed investigative journalist Ronald Kessler privileged access to help him write a book on the bureau.

Kessler charged that Sessions had taken advantage of his position. Special agents ran errands for his wife, Alice. An official plane carried a batch of Sessions firewood from New York to Washington. The director kept an unloaded gun in the trunk of his car so that he could claim it as a law enforcement vehicle and accordingly deduct mileage from his taxes. Buttressed by a damning report on Sessions from the Justice Department's Office of Professional Responsibility, Kessler's articles and subsequent book made the director's position untenable. Clinton received a no when he asked the in-denial Sessions to resign, so he fired him.

Needing a clean-cut successor to Sessions, Clinton plumped for Louis J. Freeh. The nemesis of the Mob in the Pizza Connection case, Freeh had the image to appeal to all parties. He carried in his pocket the worn prayer book he had received as a Catholic altar boy. His wife, Marilyn, bore him six sons—he had met her when she worked for the bureau's Civil Rights Division. His former crime-fighting colleague Rudolph Giuliani said he was the "straightest guy" he knew.

However, from the perspective of the Clinton administration, the straight arrow would turn out to have a poisoned tip. Freeh proved to be adroit at handling Congress, and took care to mend fences with the Right after his brush with Gingrich. Consistently with this, he had a spat with his boss, Attorney General Janet Reno, who was anathema to the Right. The president had appointed Reno to encourage gender balance, and to bring a breath of fresh air to an overly cryptic branch of government: as he declared in his nomination statement, "she has a listed telephone number."

Freeh had different people to call. With Clinton's star on the wane in his second term, the director made a move that would please the Republicans. When a story circulated about China making financial contributions to the Democratic Party, Freeh urged Reno to appoint an independent counsel. He then leaked his own memo to the press, and put three hundred agents on the case, making it the largest investigation ever, until 9/11 came along. No administration officials were indicted, and Clinton's assistant Sidney Blumenthal later complained that some of the agents had been taken off counterterrorism assignments. Clinton wrote that in this case Freeh had advanced his own interest "even if it damaged our foreign policy operations." In his autobiography, he accused the FBI director of having taken "an adversarial position toward the White House." Freeh, in his counterpart memoir, claimed he had "fallen off the A-list" at the White House, partly because Clinton disliked his Boy Scout image. The remarks underline the personality difficulties that clouded the history of the FBI in the final years of the Clinton administration.[2]

Not only did political problems arise, but also the FBI began to show, once again, its frailty in the matter of racial tolerance. This weakness helped spoil the FBI's counterespionage record, which, for a number of years, had seemed to be good. President Reagan had boasted that his administration had dramatically improved on the spy-catching performance of the Carter years. In 1985 especially, several significant spies were caught. Among those the FBI arrested in that "Year of the Spy" were John Walker, for selling navy codes to the Soviets, and Jonathan Jay Pollard, for betraying naval secrets to the Israelis. When it became apparent that the KGB had a "mole" in the CIA, the FBI launched yet another counterespionage probe, code-named NIGHTMOVER. After some initial obstruction by jealous CIA personnel, the agency cooperated with the bureau's investigation, and, in 1994, the FBI was able to arrest Aldrich Ames, a senior CIA officer who had been betraying his country for money. Possibly because of a decline in social cohesion that affected the whole of society and not just Sicilian Americans, there seemed to be a rash of spy episodes, but the FBI seemed to be on top of the case.

Nevertheless, there were those who worried, and their worries began to focus on Asia. One of the FBI's arrestees in 1985 had been Larry Wu Tai Chin, who had been spying for communist China. In 1996, Robert Chaegon Kim, a computer expert at the Office of Naval Intelligence, was arrested for passing secrets to South Korea. It was another bumper year for FBI counterespionage arrests.

Not all those apprehended were Asian. There was also the CIA's Harold J. Nicholson, who spied for the KGB and its post-communist successor, the Russian Foreign Intelligence Service. Also caught was one of the bureau's own, special agent Earl E. Pitts, who had similarly obliged the Russians. But, although Asians were a minority among arrestees, there were those who saw the People's Republic of China, in particular, as a new Red Menace. In 1998, with the Republicans in control of both houses of Congress and baying for

Clinton's blood, Gingrich sanctioned a special investigation of technology transfers to China. To chair the investigation, he chose Christopher Cox, a Republican congressman from California's affluent Orange County who was known for his work on limiting government expenditures and for his 1995 law curtailing the right of appeal against death sentences. The Cox committee scoured the recent past for details of Red China's intelligence activities against the United States.

The hunt for Chinese agents in the United States intensified. Suspicion fell on Wen Ho Lee, a mechanical engineer employed at the Los Alamos National Laboratory, New Mexico. Lee worked on computer codes for simulation exercises connected to the development of W88 nuclear warhead technology. This was the research program that produced a miniaturized hydrogen bomb with thirty-two times the force of the weapon that had destroyed Hiroshima. But for his race, it would seem unlikely that Lee would have attracted suspicion. He was a Taiwan-born American citizen and a confirmed anti-communist. His wife, Sylvia Lee, had helped the FBI since 1984. Born in mainland China, she was a computer technician who doubled as a translator in Los Alamos. She supplied her bureau handler Dave Bibb with information on Chinese Americans who worked in Los Alamos and visited China, and on Chinese scientists who visited the U.S. facility.

But Wen Ho Lee's ethnicity meant he could ill afford to step out of line, and his cavalier disregard for security procedures got him into trouble. He did not report all of his trips to China as regulations required. An FBI investigation revealed that, again in contravention of security stipulations, he had downloaded 430,000 pages of documentation and taken them home. Although New Mexico FBI agents thought of him as merely naive, and in January 1999 urged caution on headquarters in Washington, details of the case were leaked to the media, and pressure mounted for action to be taken. In March, Lee lost his job.

Amid mounting hysteria, the *New York Times* (which Lee regarded as one of his prime persecutors) reported that China had stolen U.S. nuclear secrets and had by this means upgraded its technology from its 1950s level in one fell swoop. A few days later, on 25 May, the Cox report was released. According to a *Times* editorial, it proved the "serial hemorrhage" of nuclear secrets to China over two decades. There were dissenting voices. Senator Bob Kerrey (D-Neb.) complained that the report created the erroneous impression that Chinese nuclear espionage was a greater threat than its Russian equivalent. But such voices were drowned out in what *Nation* journalist Bill Mesler described as a media frenzy orchestrated by the opportunistic

Right. In April 2000, a poll confirmed the existence of the new nativism, finding that 32 percent of Americans believed Chinese Americans to be more loyal to China than to America.

In September 1999, Freeh recommended Lee's indictment on fifty-nine counts of injuring America to the advantage of China. Not wishing to be outdone, Attorney General Reno had instructed that additional charges be brought under the provisions of the Atomic Energy Act, charges that, if proved, would carry a life term. After some months in pretrial detention, the arrested scientist was subjected to 278 days in solitary confinement and special restrictive measures. After a while, these were relaxed and he was allowed to kick a soccer ball around the prison exercise yard for one hour a day, but with his feet still chained together.

Lee was released on 13 September 2000, having entered a guilty plea to just one, relatively minor, charge of breaching security. Freeh later complained that "political correctness" had hamstrung the judicial process. But Robert Vrooman, a former security official at Los Alamos, charged that Lee was originally singled out because of an unfair process of "racial profiling." Fourteen prominent Asian American groups seized on this point in drafting a joint statement protesting his treatment and condemning an investigation "flawed by negative ethnic stereotypes and fueled by anti-Chinese hysteria." Lee unsurprisingly concluded that one could not trust the FBI. After the FBI failed to produce any convincing evidence against Lee in court, the trial judge, James A. Parker, appeared to agree. The judge blasted the Department of Justice and, in an unusual statement, apologized to Wen Ho Lee for his indefensible treatment. In 2006, Lee won a $1.65 million settlement for invasion of privacy because of the government and press smears against his reputation.[3]

Treason by one of the FBI's own served only to highlight the absurdity of racially motivated suspicions. The exposure of Robert P. Hanssen cast a terminal shadow over Freeh's career. Hanssen worked as a Russian specialist for various divisions of FBI foreign counterintelligence; in 1991–92, he was a program manager in the Soviet Operations Section, with responsibility for countering KGB efforts to acquire U.S. technical and scientific secrets. He had first offered his services to the KGB in October 1985, and for many years he was well placed to send his Moscow controllers information that damaged U.S. national security. On one occasion, he divulged details of the Continuity of Government plan, the arrangements for the safety of the president and other key officials in the event of nuclear attack. Conceivably, this knowledge might have helped and inspired the Kremlin to devise a precision strike to take out the U.S. command and help them win a nuclear war. On another front, Hanssen betrayed the identities of a number of agents working for the United States. General Dimitri Polyakov was one such agent. The Russians executed him for espionage in 1988. News of such executions played badly in the American media, with their interest in the human side of events.

So did the FBI's failure, over several years, to discover Hanssen's betrayals. Up to a point, the traitor was cunning. Although he received hundreds of thousands of dollars for his treachery, he spent modestly. Yes, he bought a used Mercedes for an exotic dancer with whom he had a physically unconsummated relationship, but generally he lived a lifestyle one would expect of a family man and father of six on a relatively modest income ($120,000 a year). But, in 2003, a Justice Department report prepared by Inspector General Glenn A. Fine debunked the theory that Hanssen's crimes had been undetectable. He had repeatedly violated security procedures, and he had taken risks. In 1990, for example, the mole's brother-in-law, also an FBI agent, found $5,000 in cash in a dresser drawer in Hanssen's house. He reported his suspicions to the bureau, but no action was taken. Caught accessing a computer without authorization a couple of years later, Hanssen managed to persuade his superiors that he was running a security check, hacking in to see if he would be caught.

According to Fine's report, FBI officials just could not believe that someone who conformed to their own social norms was capable of behaving in such a manner. A practicing Catholic, Hanssen appeared to have no ideological motivation for betraying his country. He seems, rather, to have been inspired by the mystique of betrayal (he told his Russian controllers he was fascinated by the Kim Philby case); rather like "old money" families, he was glad of his wealth but did not display it. Not black, not Asian, not gay, not female, not socialist, not Muslim, Hanssen was an obvious patriot— until his arrest.

On the afternoon of 18 February 2001, an FBI surveillance team finally caught up with Hanssen as he drove his silver Ford Taurus to a dead-drop site in Tysons Corner, Virginia, there to deposit a black plastic bag illegally containing confidential materials. "Freeze!" they said as they placed him under arrest, but, instead of producing a gun, he asked a question: "What took you so long?"

Freeh had not been director at the time of Hanssen's worst transgressions, but he had to bear the brunt of the case, and of the FBI's renewed overall unpopularity. The Hanssen affair was only one of several FBI scandals. Bureau agents had shot dead the wife of a wanted white supremacist in Ruby Ridge, Idaho, in 1992, and had then destroyed documents in an attempted cover-up. Then, following a seven-week siege in Waco, Texas, in April 1993 the FBI's Hostage Rescue Team used a specially adapted tank to inject tear gas into the compound of an armed Christian sect, the Branch Davidians. The Davidians responded with gunfire, and by lighting several small fires inside their compound. In the ensuing confusion, smoke, fire, and falling debris killed seventy-nine people, including more than twenty children under the age of fifteen. If these incidents were offensive to conservatives, they also suggested a need to have some women on the FBI's over-macho crisis negotiation teams.

Both Ruby Ridge and Waco took place before Freeh assumed the directorship, yet his detractors added them to the litany of complaints against his FBI. There were further botched jobs during his tenancy. One was the FBI investigation of the fatal bomb attack at the Atlanta Olympics in 1996. Another later in the same year was the inadequate FBI investigation of the Hezbollah terrorist bomb outrage in Khobar, eastern Saudi Arabia, where nineteen Americans lost their lives. Freeh tried to blame the Clinton White House for obstructing his inquiries. As for the Wen Ho Lee prosecution, it annoyed both liberals (because it took place) and conservatives (because it failed).

Ronald Kessler, whose exposé of Sessions had opened the way for Freeh to become the FBI boss, now turned his guns on his erstwhile beneficiary. In an article for the *Washington Post* called "Fire Freeh," he roasted the director for having failed to introduce polygraph tests for FBI employees in the aftermath of the Ames case. He reminded his readers of Freeh's other failings, such as his poor handling of the Wen Ho Lee case. This instance of incompetence stemmed partly, in his view, from Freeh's having forced several Chinese computer-intelligence specialists to retire.

Freeh still had two years to run on his ten-year contract, but, on 1 May 2001, he gave one month's notice of his resignation. He had been struggling to make ends meet on his salary of $141,300 and no doubt anticipated greater rewards in the private sector. At the same time, the Hanssen case was demoralizing and contributed to his decision.[4]

Scenting a wounded beast, the press had a field day, listing the various failings of the Freeh era. With Freeh still in office, the story broke that the FBI had incompetently withheld three thousand documents from the McVeigh trial, a discovery that led to a delay in the bomber's execution. Another of the charges brought to bear against the now vulnerable director was that he had charmed Congress into appropriating ever larger sums for the support of his agency, and then delivered too little in return for the dollar. Critics thought he had expanded the FBI indiscriminately. Senator Charles Grassley (R-Iowa) said the bureau was "overburdened with jurisdiction," and there were complaints that, with fifty-six field offices and forty-four legations overseas, it was finding it difficult to control its own data—a problem that had been at the root of the McVeigh case.

Though it sounded impressive when critics said that in 2001 the FBI had 27,000 agents and support workers and cost the taxpayer $3.4 billion, a comparative perspective is needed. In his eight-year tenure, Freeh increased the number of FBI employees at an annual rate of 362, achieving an overall personnel increase of 12 percent. In the corresponding period, appropriations rose by 69 percent. These figures are dwarfed by those for the period 1939–45, when the average annual growth of employees was 1,647 with an overall increase of 517 percent, appropriations rising by 572 percent. As those are wartime statistics, a more telling comparison might be with the Cold War directorship of William Webster, 1978–87. In Webster's nine years in charge, the number of bureau workers rose by an average of 318 per annum, but the increase was from a lower base than under Freeh's aegis, and the summative increase percentage was 14.7 percent, appreciably higher than under Freeh. Webster's nine-year budget growth was 135 percent—at 69 percent over eight years, Freeh's expansion was markedly lower.

Freeh, then, was overly expansionist by reputation, not results. Moreover, at least some of the areas he chose for particular expansion would have been applauded after 9/11. With the globalization of threats to the USA, his international outreach fell into this category. And, between 1984 and 2001, he persuaded Congress to raise the FBI's counterterrorism budget from $79 million to $372 million, an increase of 471 percent.[5]

Yet, it is irrefutable that, even before the Al Qaeda terrorist attacks of September 2001, the FBI had an image problem. In June 2001, the Senate Judiciary Committee held a hearing titled "Oversight: Restoring Confidence in the FBI." The committee chairman, Patrick Leahy, was a Vermont Democrat and long-standing defender of privacy in the computer age. Seeing no reason to hold back with another Republican Bush installed in the White House, he was unstinting in his criticism. Senator Leahy rehearsed the Hanssen, McVeigh, Ruby Ridge, and Wen Ho Lee failures, attacked the FBI for its "insular arrogance," referred to its bad public image, and cited a recent Gallup poll indicating that the FBI had the support of only 23 percent of Americans, compared with 60 percent support for local police forces.

Senator Leahy said that Congress should end its policy of appropriating ever-larger sums of money to the FBI without asking questions. Utah's Orrin G. Hatch, the ranking Republican on the Judiciary Committee, offered no effective rebuttal and supported the principle of tighter oversight. He had supported the FBI in its struggles with the previous Democratic administration, and in his response to Leahy called for a sense of "perspective," pointing out that the bureau had had some successes. However, he still argued that "we should look critically at the culture of the FBI." As the Leahy and Hatch statements suggest, the FBI had an all-round image problem by the summer of 2001.[6]

To depict the FBI as effective and triumphant in the 1980s, but profligate and incompetent in the 1990s, would be to oversimplify history. Under Reagan, the bureau recovered its sense of mission; under Bush Sr. and Clinton it began to deliver on that mission. But there were weaknesses. Foul-ups in Waco and elsewhere contributed to the bureau's unpopularity, but these were actually less important than the recurrence of failings in that vital area of American justice, racial equality. Although the campaign to recruit women maintained its momentum, black enrollment began to fade. Then there was the Wen Ho Lee case against a background of fewer Chinese experts working for the FBI. The recruitment of Arab and Muslim special agents was notable only by its absence. In the past, affected minorities had paid the price for such discrimination. This time, the whole of America would.

14

9/11 and the quest for national unity

Bassem Youssef was an American citizen who had been born in Cairo. He put his grasp of Arabic to good effect when working for the FBI on such counterterrorist investigations as those into the 1993 World Trade Center bombing, and the bombing of the U.S. Embassy in Nairobi, Kenya, in 1998. Serving as legal attaché in Riyadh, he established a useful relationship between the FBI and the Saudi Arabian intelligence agency, the Mabahith. By the time he returned to Washington in 2000, he had won praise in bureau evaluations of his work. As a senior expert on Arab-based terrorism, he now expected a promotion.

Instead, the bureau assigned Youssef to routine translation work. Aggrieved, in 2003 the agent filed suit against his employer, claiming adverse discrimination on account of his ethnicity, and arguing that the national security of America had been impaired because of FBI prejudice that barred a specially qualified agent from doing the work he did best.

Youssef's complaint came two years after the catastrophic attack on New York and Washington known as 9/11. Yet, out of a total of 11,500 agents in the FBI of 2003, there were still only about six Muslims. The 2000 census listed 1.3 million Arab Americans officially present in the United States, and the real number may have been three times as high. Yet a mere 21 agents were able to speak Arabic.

The September tragedy seemed to demonstrate that the whole of America had been affected by the blinkered attitude that had frozen out experts like Youssef and allowed those planes to be hijacked. Poor coordination, the other important intelligence failing that inquirers identified as having been at the back of 9/11, could also be said to have stemmed in good measure from racial causes, those that had precipitated the Gestapo fears and consequent intelligence schism of the 1940s. Deficient hiring practices and disunity in the intelligence community came to be regarded as chief among the avoidable causes of the 9/11 debacle.

The consequences of 9/11 were momentous. From the beginning, the FBI was identified as the main culprit. But, while there was evidence to support this charge, the idea was convenient for the administration of President George W. Bush, as it implied the White House had not been culpable. The Bush administration introduced reforms that confirmed the impression of the FBI being to blame. More money was showered on the FBI to improve it, a reward of failure that had the additional intent of sealing, with a dollar kiss, the lips of knowledgeable critics. There was an accompanying clawback of civil liberties guarantees, with the FBI acting its part on the stated premise that it had previously been too disempowered to do its counterterrorist job.

But there were other consequences, too. Not everyone agreed it was necessary to sacrifice so many liberties in the interest of national security. A few years after 9/11, a CIA veteran with twenty-five years of experience in dealing with the FBI argued "our liberties are a powerful antidote to violent extremism," as they encouraged belief in American values and "local opposition" to any terrorist conspiracies. Like-minded citizens resisted the erosion of civil liberties, and encouraged the administration and the FBI to maintain fair hiring practices and to tolerate foreign people and religions. Further prompted by intelligence failures relating to the 2003 decision to go to war in Iraq, they pushed for a reform of the entire intelligence community, and in particular for its coordination under a single head. This quest of unity became a salient feature of the years following 9/11.[1]

In the aftermath of 9/11, the FBI did not at first come under heavy fire. As the nation reeled from the shock of 2,973 acts of murder, it seemed inappropriate to rush to judgment on the conduct of one of America's iconic institutions. There were other reasons for restraint, too. Director Freeh had seemed to be on the right track. His repeated warnings to congressional appropriation committees about the dangers of terrorism had secured budget increases to combat the menace. Because he resigned in May 2001, a few months before the September attack, immediate blame could not be attached to him for not providing due warning.

Freeh's successor, Robert S. Mueller III, took office on September 4. Potential critics could hardly fault him for failing to anticipate the madness that occurred only seven days later. In any case, Mueller's pedigree in the short term gave him armadillo-like immunity to attack. He was a Princeton graduate, a decorated hero of the Vietnam War, and a successful lawyer who, as boss of the Justice Department's Criminal Division, had overseen the successful prosecutions of Manuel Noriega and John Gotti. When the critics did finally train their guns on the new director, they found him to be a tough customer—as Attorney General John Ashcroft noted, he was a "battle-hardened person."[2]

Although it was in the firing line, the FBI benefited, in the course of the 9/11 post mortem, from the emergence of a multiplicity of theories about what had gone wrong. Some pointed to a widespread inability to connect the dots, that is, to analyze the information at the government's disposal that might have given timely premonition. Others thought there had not been enough dots to connect, as the government had skimped on information gathering. However, national security adviser Condoleeza Rice preferred to emphasize that there had been "a lot of chatter in the system," meaning it was hard to distinguish real danger signals from a vast mass of data that poured into the intelligence community. That was reminiscent of post–Pearl Harbor analysis, as were references to the "brilliance" of the Al Qaeda attack. Another reminder of the 1940s was talk of what the CIA's James Pavitt called "compartmentation." Government officials hoarded their secrets and would not communicate with people outside their own patch. Here, the FBI came under the cosh for not talking to the CIA, but, in a process of dilution, the latter agency took some of the blame.[3]

The vulnerability of the administration to charges of negligence was a further factor that took some of the heat off the FBI. After all, the president had failed to protect America from a known threat. Al Qaeda, the terrorist umbrella organization behind the atrocity, had been in existence since 1987 and its aims were public knowledge. As its Saudi Arabian leader Osama bin Laden stated in 1998, his followers were expected to "comply with God's order to kill the Americans." Also known to the security forces prior to 9/11 were the supposed ringleader of the attack, the devout if pork-chop-eating Egyptian Mohammed Atta, and the Kuwaiti of Pakistani origin to whom Atta reported, Khalid Shaikh Mohammed.

This was not all. Following disturbing reports about terrorist activity in the first half of 2001, Rice and White House chief of staff Andrew H. Card failed to attend a meeting of counterterror officials that they themselves had summoned on July 5. Five days later, CIA director George J. Tenet told Rice in an emergency meeting in the White House that there was an acute threat of an imminent attack by Al Qaeda. On August 6, an intelligence briefing delivered to Bush at his Texas ranch carried the title "Bin Laden Determined to Attack Inside the United States." This warning, like others from the CIA and other sources, was nonspecific. Still, the administration was open to the charge that nobody had had the presence of mind to show this document to acting FBI director Thomas J. Pickard, who might have been able to take preemptive action. With evidence of such apparent complacency lying around, it was not in the interest of the Bush administration to start firing people who might run to the press.[4]

So the presidential response was to refrain from punishing FBI personnel. Instead, the Bush administration and its congressional supporters boosted the FBI's powers and budget. This served several purposes. It implied that the liberal Clinton administration had underresourced the bureau; it suggested that this, not Republican drowsiness, had left the nation vulnerable; it sweetened top officials in the FBI; and it strengthened national security in a manner consistent with neoconservative precepts.

The immediate response to 9/11 by the administration and Congress—strengthing the powers of the FBI—was imposed at a cost to civil liberties. To defend liberty, the argument ran, America had to curtail it. To this end, President Bush on 26 October 2001 signed into law a bill that Congress had passed by huge majorities, the Uniting and Strengthening America by Providing Appropriate Tools Required to Intercept and Obstruct Terrorism (USA PATRIOT) Act.

The Patriot Act reversed previous reforms. It explicitly removed or reduced some of the safeguards codified in the Foreign Intelligence Surveillance Act (FISA), the law passed in 1978 with the goal of preventing any recurrence of Hoover-era surveillance abuses. The monitoring of Internet surfing, e-mail, and voice mail could now take place with reduced court oversight. So could wiretapping, and the bureau could henceforth listen in to a suspect's conversations on a roving or multipoint basis, no matter which phone he was using. In spite of the Fourth Amendment to the Constitution protecting citizens from "unreasonable searches and seizures," the FBI would under its provisions be permitted to undertake secret searches so long as the individuals affected were informed in due course. Non-U.S. citizens suspected of terrorist offenses could be detained for a week without benefit of hearing, and, if deemed a threat to national security, such persons could be detained indefinitely. The Patriot Act was not a permanent abrogation of the liberal tradition. It contained a "sunset" clause whereby its provisions, unless renewed, would run out in October 2005. Nevertheless, Daniel Benjamin and Steven Simon, who had served as counterterrorist officials in the Carter White House, claimed that the law "included the Justice Department's wish list of provisions that legislators perennially rejected before September 11."

The jargon used in the debate presumed that FISA had built a "wall" between criminal investigations, where the highest standards of civil-rights protection were observed, and counterintelligence surveillance, where greater latitude was allowed. Because of a culture of risk aversion, with FBI agents fearful of prosecution if they overstepped the mark, the high-standards FISA conventions had been applied inappropriately to terror investigations. In one much publicized example, investigators had failed, in August 2001, to search a laptop computer disk and other artifacts belonging to a French citizen of Middle Eastern origin, Zacarias Moussaoui. FBI agents in Minneapolis had been suspicious of Moussaoui because he was an extremist, was training to be a passenger airliner pilot, and seemed to be a potential hijacker. In the event, Al Qaeda did not use Moussaoui on September 11, citing his unstable personality. However, even in his subsequent trial (he received a life sentence in 2006), Moussaoui himself insisted he was a dangerous member of the conspiracy to take American lives. In the more immediate aftermath of the attack, it was disturbing to supporters of the Patriot Act that the search of his possessions that might have yielded clues leading to a preemption of the 9/11 attack had not taken take place—because of due process concerns.[5]

Attorney General Ashcroft was one of the leading advocates of the new approach. The son of a preacher, Ashcroft was a devout member of the evangelical Assembly of God Church. A graduate of Yale and the University of Chicago, he had experienced a checkered political career, provoking controversy as governor of Missouri for opposing racial integration in the state's schools, and entering the U.S. Senate only to be defeated for reelection in 2000. His appointment as attorney general dismayed liberals aware of his vehement opposition to abortion, gay rights, and gun control. In contrast to earlier Republican reformers Harlan Fiske Stone and Edward Levi, he was a populist who emphasized threats to public safety and the need for restrictive and punitive measures. He defended the Patriot Act and sought to strengthen its provisions—in 2003, for example, he called for amendments making it an offense to help terrorists, and demanded the death penalty for any terrorist act.[6]

New FBI guidelines in the Ashcroft years gave force to and strengthened the impact of the Patriot Act. On 30 May 2002, the Attorney General's Investigative Guidelines authorized, for example, Internet and commercial database surveillance. Further FBI "National Security Investigations Guidelines" had secret provisions that presumably went further. By the end of 2003, the "wall" having been dismantled, criminal and terrorist investigators were working side-by-side and exchanging information without fear of being charged with invasions of privacy or infringements of citizens' rights.

The way in which Section 215 of the Patriot Act was applied signaled a proactive approach by Ashcroft's Justice Department. Section 215 empowered a secretly convened Foreign Intelligence Surveillance Court to authorize searches and wiretaps in counterterror cases. This was a reiteration of the process that had existed since 1978. However, the manner and extent of actions taken scotched any tendency to believe that the Patriot Act was just a repackaging of old laws. The post–Patriot Act assumption was that the court would be more sympathetic to FBI requests in the future. In practice, some bureau surveillance would be subject only to retrospective review, and in other cases the bureau did not bother to consult the court. The Bush administration wanted more speed and agility. Under Ashcroft's aegis, the philosophy was that surveillance would be tolerated so long as it was potentially in the interest of national security, was of a type likely to be approved if it were to go before a FISA court, and did not blatantly contravene a U.S. citizen's rights.

Under a further Section 215 provision, the FBI developed the practice of sending a "national security letter" to the custodian of information it required, bypassing any other judicial process. The legal vehicle used was that of the administrative subpoena, and again the legislative authority predated the Patriot Act, running back to the Controlled Substance Act of 1970. Once again, though, it was the manner of application that made the difference. Within four years, the FBI was issuing more than thirty thousand national security letters per annum.

Critics of the ever more powerful national security guidelines complained that the lessons of past abuses were being ignored, that there were no compensatory oversight mechanisms, that the FBI was becoming a national police force, and that, in the words of New York lawyer Joshua Dratel, the government's policies were "an end run around the Fourth Amendment." However, the objectors failed to block the money needed for the expanded activities. On the contrary, Congress typically demanded that more money be spent—if it's broken, fix it with dollars. Noting the changes introduced by the Patriot Act and May 2002 FBI guidelines, the terrorism subcommittee of the House Intelligence Committee reported in July 2002 that what had been done was "insufficient."

Democrats acted on the same principle as Republicans. In the 2004 presidential election, they made an issue of the fact that the Republican administration had pared down Ashcroft's immediate post-9/11 demand for an extra $1.5 billion for the FBI, awarding the bureau a mere $531 million. With so many guns pointing in the same direction, the bureau's budget blasted upward, rising from $3.3 billion in 2001 to $4.3 billion in 2003. There was a 68 percent increase from 2000 to 2005, and the president's budget for 2006 envisaged a 76 percent increase over 2001.[7]

But the Bush administration's response to terrorism was not just about extra powers and extra spending. It was also about structural changes that set the security bureaucracy on a new course. Soon after 9/11, the president had asked his old friend Tom Ridge, governor of Pennsylvania, to fill the new post of director of homeland security. Ridge had impeccable credentials that included blue-collar union jobs in Erie, Pennsylvania, a bronze star for valor in Vietnam, and Harvard. Thus far, he had no department of his own, and the need for greater unity seemed imperative. FBI-CIA divisions were still proving troublesome in spite of a catalog of complaints about the problem, including reports by two congressionally sponsored investigations into terrorism in the last year of the Clinton presidency. In a message to Congress on 18 June 2002, President Bush promised what he described as the biggest shakeup of police and intelligence apparatus since the National Security Act of 1947. With "thousands of trained killers spread across the globe plotting attacks against America," it was no longer satisfactory that "homeland security" responsibilities should be "dispersed among more than 100 different entities of the Federal Government."

Bush called on Congress to legislate to create a new Department of Homeland Security (DHS), whose director would have a seat in the president's cabinet. Once the DHS was approved, he nominated Ridge as its director. The outfit was an official entity by 1 March 2003. This initiative was at the heart of a new philosophy of governance in which the FBI would play an integral role. American conservatives, once opposed to strong federal government and policing, were now fiercely committed to the use of executive power, often at the expense of legislative and judicial process. Their critics saw them as engaging in a "power grab." But President Bush and his team saw a need to create the instrument for quick-fire reactions to terrorists who threatened U.S. security. Supporters like John Choon Yoo, a middle-ranking Justice Department official from 2001 to 2003, insisted that the all-action approach was philosophically defensible.

The creation of the DHS was a first, tentative step toward the erasure of the principle of keeping domestic and foreign intelligence separate. Notionally, it was a huge agency, with 180,000 employees and a budget to match. In practice, largely preexisting units made up its numbers. It had to rely for some of its crucial work on the already established Terrorist Threat Integration Center (TTIC), a unit directed by a senior CIA official and composed of both CIA and FBI specialists. For in his message, Bush had fudged on the margins: the DHS would "incorporate" some agencies, would be "responsible" for the Secret Service, but would merely "complement" the FBI and the CIA. On a different level, however, Ridge and his colleagues pressed on with a program of which Hoover would have approved, cooperation with local units. By February 2004, the DHS claimed to have established "connectivity" with all fifty states and with National Guard units, police, local emergency services, and private security operators in major cities. It declared that federal coordination of national security related computer systems was at long last imminent, with the goal of making "real time" communication possible between local and national antiterror units.[8]

The campaign for tighter security was unrelenting. Agitation in favor of extending the Patriot Act began well before the act was scheduled to lapse according to the sunset clause. In April 2003, Senator Orrin G. Hatch, working with the backing of the White House, took the lead. A Republican from Utah whose humble origins included a spell living in a refurbished chicken coop, Hatch was an FBI hardliner—he had been among those who had sided with Director Freeh and accused the Clinton administration of being soft on Chinese espionage. Hatch called not just for repeal of the sunset provision, but also for additional legislation enabling the FBI to move against "lone wolf" terrorist suspects. In the loose-knit world of anti-Western terrorism, it was sometimes difficult to pin a suspect to an alien organization and to produce the evidence to justify a warrant. The Moussaoui incident had been one such case. Hatch and the Judiciary Committee that he chaired succeeded by 2004 in plugging a gap in existing legislation by inserting a clause into the Intelligence Reform and Terrorism Prevention Act that enabled the FBI to move against individuals who threatened American security but were not agents of a foreign state.

The American Civil Liberties Union opposed this "license to fish," and Congress initially dragged its feet. A number of high-profile stories were beginning to influence public opinion. In spite of an initial surge of renewed support inspired by the March 2003 invasion of Iraq, which the administration mistakenly depicted as having been a haven for Al Qaeda terrorists, the FBI was encountering renewed criticism. In part, the attacks were a result of the Bush administration's cavalier approach to civil liberties. However, they were also a delayed reaction to the bureau's alleged shortcomings in not anticipating 9/11. The latter complaint was an objection not to reform, but to its inadequacy. The developing critique therefore prepared the way for a more thoroughgoing shake-up of the U.S. intelligence community.

Naturally, partisan criticism was prominent in the election year of 2004. At the start of the election campaign, the Democrats made an issue of FBI surveillance of their candidate John Kerry in the days when he had been a leader of Vietnam Veterans Against the War. Though the tactic backfired when Bush partisans questioned Kerry's combat record, excessive FBI surveillance was once again on the political agenda. In a move reminiscent of the Vietnam era, the FBI came under further criticism for its alleged suppression of U.S. dissent against the American occupation of Iraq. In August 2004, a group of Democratic legislators called for an investigation into the bureau's "systematic political harassment and intimidation of legitimate antiwar protesters."

Earlier assaults had been less high profile, but were nevertheless significant. Walter Mosley, a campaigner for racial justice through the much-loved medium of his fictional Los Angeles private detective "Easy" Rawlins, complained of being stopped and questioned every time he passed through an airport: "I guess I look vaguely Arabic." Incidents with racial overtones proliferated. There was the story of an inoffensive Buddhist from Nepal, Purna Raj Bajracharya, whose unwitting offense had been filming tourist footage of a building in Queens, New York, that housed an FBI office. The video had been intended for his wife in Katmandu, but, courtesy of a zealous FBI agent, the cameraman was subjected to strip-searches and clapped into solitary confinement in a permanently lighted cell, where he languished for almost three months.

Civil libertarians worried about the targeting of ethnic or religious minorities. The FBI interviewed thousands of men of Arab descent in the wake of 9/11, and a further 11,200 Iraqi Americans shortly after the U.S. invasion of Iraq. What offered greater potential for revolt, though, was a widespread invasion of citizens' privacy that seemed to threaten the rights of all Americans. Over the decades, critics as diverse as U.S. Supreme Court justice Louis Brandeis and sociologist Vance Packard had warned of the creeping phenomenon later dubbed the "soft cage" or the "security-industrial complex." The Privacy Act of 1974 had addressed some of the excesses of FBI surveillance, giving individuals the right to view their files and correct misinformation. But, by the twenty-first century, private digital search engines like

ChoicePoint and LexisNexis collected information on individuals on a massive scale, and the bureau plugged into the unverified data without having to offer the right of redress.

Director Mueller sought to apply to the world of public detection techniques developed by the private-industry marketeers of the 1990s, and to marshal masses of information to answer particular questions or to focus on special groups. The plan was that the dragnet inquiry executed by door-busting G-men would give way to the gentler but more accurate techniques of data mining. The headline-grabbing discovery that the FBI had sequestered CD-ROMs containing airline passenger records (6,000 CD-ROMs from Northwest Airlines alone) confirmed the fears of privacy advocates. Meanwhile the federal government for its part was engaging in a splurge of secrecy, classifying documents at a record rate of 125 a minute. We can watch you, the government message seemed to run, but you can't watch us.[9]

However, civil libertarian and privacy objections came in a poor second to the main gripe about the FBI, that it had been ineffective. Whereas the critical onslaught of the 1970s had focused on civil liberty infractions with effectiveness as a lesser issue, the post–9/11 attack heavily concentrated on the bureau's national security shortcomings. The idea that the intelligence community was doing a bad job received reinforcement from 2003 on, when it emerged that the nation had gone to war in Iraq on the basis of wrong intelligence about that nation's harboring of terrorists and development of weapons of mass destruction. Rightly or wrongly, America lost faith in the basic competence of its government detectives.

Criticism of the bureau came from the press, Congress, private foundations, and government inquiries. One powerful voice exposing the FBI's shortcomings rose within the Justice Department itself. Glenn Fine was a graduate of Harvard and a Rhodes scholar in Oxford, after which he had become a successful prosecutor. He joined the Justice Department and in 2000 became its inspector general. In this position, he directed his penetrating gaze at a number of problems, including the shortcomings of the McVeigh trial. After 9/11, he subjected the FBI to unrelenting scrutiny and, while not all of his findings were disclosed to the public, some of them were, and the media made much of those disclosures. His 131-page audit in 2002 of the FBI's counterterror program was classified "secret," but he released an unclassified summary and testified before the terrorism subcommittee of the Senate Judiciary Committee. His findings were little short of scathing; the bureau had not completed a risk assessment promised back in 1999; it had failed to develop an intelligence capability of its own in relation to possible attacks on the United States by terrorists using weapons of mass destruction; its translation team sometimes gave drug investigations priority over anti-terror work; its training program was unsatisfactory.

But even Fine could not hope to match the critical intensity generated by FBI whistle-blowers who had been unmoved by the administration's largesse toward their agency. These disgruntled employees did not want to stop the bureau doing what it did; they wanted it to do better. The media paid attention because they had something to say, and because the administration tried to stop them saying it. Typically, the government would produce that old chestnut, silence in the name of national security, and then impede the career of anyone who spoke out: in the words of Iowa's Republican senator Charles Grassley, "Most whistle-blowers are not dismissed, most whistle-blowers are herded professionally, put off in the corner, their work taken away from them and they go nuts and they resign." But in spite of its intended subtlety, this herding tactic just made the whistle-blowers angry and their tales more newsworthy.

Two pioneering whistle-blowers, who broke the consensual post–9/11 silence and attracted national attention in early 2002, were both women. Having succeeded in a man's world, perhaps they found it unacceptable that men, having for so long excluded women on the ground of their implicitly assumed incapacities, were in reality failing by their own standards.

On 26 February, Coleen Rowley wrote a letter to Director Mueller stating her concerns. One of the FBI's earliest female recruits, this University of Iowa law graduate had been with the bureau since 1980. She had been angered by what she depicted as the FBI hierarchy's foot-dragging in response to the Minneapolis office's perception that Moussaoui was a terrorist threat in urgent need of investigation. Especially, the blocking of the special warrant to search his possessions upset her. She was also unimpressed by the FBI's professions of post–9/11 reform.

Rowley was prudent in her use of diction, and she cited whistle-blower protection legislation in her letter to Mueller. Reaching the retirement age of fifty in 2005, she would quit the bureau on full pension without having suffered any retribution. But if her critique was measured, it was also determined. Testifying to the Senate Judiciary Committee in June 2002, she advanced a whole litany of complaints about the FBI, winning considerable respect in the process (*Time* magazine rated her one of three "persons of the year" in 2002). In her Senate testimony, Rowley gave the most emphasis to the problem of careerism and risk aversion among employees. She claimed that the "idea that inaction is somehow the key to success" had taken root in the FBI. In the following year, 2003, Rowley alienated some of her supporters by warning that the U.S. invasion of Iraq would increase the risk of terrorism, but her critique of the FBI and 9/11 continued to influence opinion makers in the press and in Congress.[10]

While Rowley's revelations may have been embarrassing to the White House, at least they confirmed its view that the FBI should take bolder action. Sibel Edmonds offered a more disturbing critique, which suggested that the bureau held foreign cultures in such low esteem that it allowed its translation program to degenerate, even after the sharp lesson administered by 9/11.

Edmonds was born in Iran, grew up in Turkey, attended college in the United States, and became an American citizen. Fluent in several languages, she accepted work as a contract linguist with the FBI, starting on 20 September 2001 and working twenty hours a week. Beginning on 8 February 2002, Edmonds filed a series of complaints with the bureau. The bureau's Foreign Language Program was, she maintained, riddled with corruption and incompetence. Sensitive documents were disappearing from her desk; someone was appending her initials to translations she had not made; Farsi speakers were being dispatched to Guantanamo Bay to interrogate Al Qaeda suspects who were in fact Turkish speakers; her supervisor told her to conform to his unit's work-slow ethic, and then was promoted; attempts were made to intimidate her when she complained.

The FBI, for its part, discovered that Edmonds had breached a security procedure by keying in on her home computer some items pertaining to bureau business, namely an inventory of her complaints against it. On 26 March 2002, the bureau terminated her services.

This was the beginning, not the end, of the FBI's troubles over Sibel Edmonds. The whiff of bad news suppressed can very soon become a stench. Pushing on an open media door, Edmonds just kept telling her story, appearing, for example, on the CBS show *60 Minutes*. Inspector General Fine investigated, and senators demanded that the result be made available. The Department of Justice released an unclassified summary, which concluded that the charges Edmonds had made were mostly true, that the FBI's translation division was seriously flawed, that the bureau stubbornly refused to investigate its problems, and that it had dismissed Edmonds in order to silence her. In spite of the inspector general's findings, for years Ashcroft and his congressional allies continued their efforts to suppress the Edmonds story. Her appeals for reinstatement had to go through the courts, Congress allowed her only closed hearings, and the *Village Voice* accused the government of making "endless attempts to shut her up." The campaign to keep her quiet became a story in itself, reminding people of her original message.[11]

The Edmonds affair invested with additional intensity a debate that was taking place anyway about the adequacy of translation provision. Some of the criticism was directed at agencies other than the FBI. For example, it became known that although the eavesdroppers par excellence at the National Security Agency had picked up messages on 10 September 2001 referring to the next day as "zero hour," and although they had been listening in to Mohamed Atta's conversation just before he boarded one of the fated aircraft, the translations from Arabic were not completed until 12 September.

The FBI acknowledged the need for languages expansion and devoted resources to it, giving it a claim to being one of the world's most cosmopolitan police forces. From a small number of linguists in the early 1980s, the bureau's translation personnel expanded to 1,100 by 2002, and, with $48 million extra funding following 9/11, they developed the capacity to handle 60 languages spoken by 95 percent of the population of the globe. In April 2004, the bureau reported that since 9/11 it had processed more than 30,000 applicants for translator posts, hiring 700. However, it remained vulnerable to charges of incompetence due to lack of commitment. According to a report by Fine that inevitably hit the headlines, even three years after the 9/11 attacks 120,000 hours of recordings with possible anti-terror significance remained untranslated.[12]

Underpinning the translator issue were worries over security clearance and alien penetration. Citing the Italian proverb "Traduttore, traditore," the *Los Angeles Times* articulated the fear that he who translates may be a traitor. Whether Arabic or Farsi translators were born outside the United States or came from one of America's language heritage communities, there was always the suspicion that they could be double agents.

Such worries extended also to the hiring of agents and analysts, and, in all cases, some further cautionary principles applied. Talented members of some ethnic groups have been antagonistic to the FBI, or have seen better opportunities elsewhere, and have therefore been reluctant to apply for jobs in the bureau. Again, while prejudiced officials have abused the idea, there is sometimes a genuine question as to whether recruitment should be in proportion to the size of an ethnic group or to the security needs of the nation.

Hiring an "ethnic" can be problematic for reasons to do with the reverse of disloyalty. If you recruit, say, an Arab American analyst, his judgment may be impaired by breakthrough syndrome; in other words, he may be so keen to prove his American patriotism that his perspective becomes conformist instead of challenging and different. There is also the time-warp problem. Immigrants tend to remember their ancestral lands as they were when they left them, and sometimes even as they were when their grandfathers left them. They forget that Poland has flush toilets and that all four nations of the Indian subcontinent have had women leaders.

However, arguments in favor of diversity in hiring outweigh these various concerns. A nation of immigrants has the precious gift of potential expertise about every nation, ethnic group, and religion in the world. Again, the wider the recruitment base, the tougher the selection and the higher the talent of the resultant pool of agents. Finally, the FBI needs to be diverse in its hiring practices to command the support of the public for its investigations and budget.

The post–9/11 FBI did present itself as being in favor of increased diversification. It began a recruitment drive in eight schools with heavy concentrations of black, Hispanic, and Asian American students. An African American, Mark Bullock, became assistant director of the bureau's Recruitment Division. By 2003, 16.5 percent of special agents were from black, Hispanic, Asian American, and Native American backgrounds.

There remained, however, a serious problem over the recruitment of personnel with Arabic and Middle Eastern expertise. In November 2003, Representative Porter J. Goss (R-Fla.) chaired a House Intelligence Committee hearing on diversity, affirming the "pressing need" for outreach to Middle Eastern countries. In her testimony to the committee, Juliette N. Kayyem of Harvard University noted long-term Arab American grievances about unfair treatment by the Immigration and Naturalization Service and the FBI. She said that when she served in the Civil Rights Division of President Clinton's Justice Department, she had been the only Arab American in the whole of the department. Though Attorney General Reno had tried to open a dialog, the federal law enforcement authorities "had almost no ties to the Arab community." A few months after the Goss hearing, Mueller acknowledged the problem by directing FBI field offices to enlist the support of local Muslims, Arab Americans, and Sikhs. The results were poor. By early 2007, FBI agents able to speak Arabic still made up less than 1 percent of the workforce. Many of those listed as having proficiency could muster no more than a few words. Only thirty-three were fluent, and the bureau employed a mere twelve Muslims.[13]

As time passed, however, the nation did acquire a more reflective and better-informed outlook on 9/11. There were numerous studies of the event, and some major inquires began to report their findings, and to make recommendations. Congress, having done the bidding of the commander in chief in a crisis, began to assert itself and to push for more thoroughgoing reform. There was a rising demand for a more effective unification of the federal counterterrorism effort. A chorus of dissent over the CIA's alleged mishandling of intelligence on Iraq affected the context of the FBI debate, and increased still further the pressure for unity. All this culminated in the Intelligence Reform and Terrorism Prevention Act of December 2004, and the appointment of a director of national intelligence.

The first major investigation was a joint congressional inquiry that reported in June 2002, with its findings being made public just over a year later. Its report pointed to specific FBI failures, such as the poor tracking of Al Qaeda operatives and mishandling of the Moussaoui case. It debated the desirability of creating a new intelligence organization, on the lines of Britain's MI5, that would replace the FBI as the agency responsible for handling the intelligence side of counterterrorism. But the main recommendation was that there should be a cabinet-level director of national intelligence, a powerful new tsar who would stamp out bureaucratic rivalries and enforce coordination.

At first, this recommendation met with a hostile reception, running into powerful opposition from Secretary of Defense Donald Rumsfeld, a master of bureaucratic maneuver who wanted to keep control of the military's vast intelligence budget. The congressional inquiry was unable to overcome such resistance. Because it was a joint investigation by the Senate and House intelligence oversight committees—which were supposed to have kept an alert eye on the FBI at the time when the bureau was making the mistakes leading up to 9/11—it was regarded as investigating shortcomings in which its members had been complicit. Critics began to demand an independent commission of inquiry.[14]

Public discussion at the time of the joint inquiry focused on an issue, poor intelligence coordination, and on a solution, the MI5 idea. There were harsh words for the FBI and the CIA over their failure to exchange information in the prelude to 9/11. The *Los Angeles Times* noted the fifty-year FBI-CIA feud stretching back to the bureau's loss of Latin American assets. The feuding was now "relentless" because each agency blamed the other for past communicative failures, the FBI complaining that the CIA had in 2000 withheld the names of terrorists later involved in 9/11, and the CIA retorting that it had, in fact, supplied the information. The *Los Angles Times* thought that public patience was running out on the issue. When President

Bush reacted to the joint investigation by blaming 9/11 on intelligence fail-ings, he singled out poor FBI-CIA cooperation. Things were getting better, he said in June 2002, but the FBI-CIA bickering over who had told whom what was undermining the chances of reform.

One of the problems was that intelligence agencies are necessarily secu-rity conscious, and e-mail, the universally preferred means of communica-tion in the twenty-first century, is notoriously insecure. Better not to com-municate at all, runs the siege mentality argument, than to communicate insecurely. The FBI had made some progress under the provisions of the Regional Information Sharing Systems (RISS) program, a crime-fighting tool that spawned RISSNET, a semi-secure intranet arrangement based on encryption, smart cards, and other measures. In September 2002, the bu-reau's Law Enforcement Online system connected with this network and became available for homeland security work against terrorism. But the system did not address the challenge of exchanges of classified information between the FBI and the CIA. In April 2003, the General Accounting Office found that the FBI and the CIA lacked not just the means to exchange ter-rorist watch lists but also a policy on the matter. In December 2003, the Jus-tice Department's inspector general noted that the bureau lacked the tech-nology to forward e-mails securely to the CIA. Primitively, special agents were printing out e-mails and delivering the paperwork to their CIA coun-terparts. The nation's media reported these matters in stunned, deadpan prose.[15]

MI5 had been established in 1909, at about the same time as the U.S. Bureau of Investigation. Until very recently, and in contrast to its U.S. coun-terpart, MI5 did not have a crime-fighting responsibility. Lacking the power to make arrests, its primary occupation was counterespionage. For decades it operated against the Soviet intelligence services, with mixed success in the detection of communist penetration, as the Kim Philby scandal demon-strated. At the end of the Cold War, MI5 feared underemployment and looked for new jobs. It usurped army and local police intelligence units hitherto responsible for attempting to counter the activities of the Irish Re-publican Army. Because Northern Ireland gradually became more stable from the 1990s on (a political achievement), it was possible to infer that MI5 had contributed to the process and that it was good at anti-terrorist in-telligence work.

MI5 had been the subject of serious American interest for some time. The study that resulted from the Princeton conference on the FBI in the early 1970s had considered the agency and ultimately warned against importing British practices that threatened privacy and civil liberties. In 2003, a Congressional Research Service primer on the applicability of the MI5 model to the United States saw the matter in part as a liberty versus security issue, and also identified as a "core question . . . the possible integration of domestic intelligence and law enforcement functions." Sir Adrian Fortescue, a British diplomat who had recently served as director general for justice and home affairs at the European Commission, suggested that the United States emulate not the United Kingdom but the European Union, which was, after all, a federal entity. A comparative study of policing on behalf of the Rand Corporation pointed to cultural and contextual differences between the USA and the U.K., for example the more highly centralized nature of the British state. These differences suggested a need for caution in revising counterterrorist arrangements, but, Rand concluded, something might nevertheless be learned.

As the foregoing studies suggest, the MI5 emulation proposal inspired mixed reactions. The idea that America should have an MI5 was further undermined by stories of reverse emulation. In 2004, the British press trumpeted Home Secretary David Blunkett's plan for a "British FBI." As terrorism and the fear of it spread, there was also talk of a "European FBI," and the Council of Europe expanded the budget of Europol, a federal police force based in The Hague. British and European talk of emulating the FBI undermined the idea that foreigners had more advanced policing arrangements than America, and in the short term bolstered the positions of America's stand-pat turf-defenders. However, the MI5 debate remained significant. Its common premise was that, while the British model might not be an ideal fit, some kind of new path would have to be taken.[16]

By the fall of 2002, there were already demands for a major new governmental inquiry into 9/11. The White House was reluctant. It wanted closure, feared that there would be revelations of its own incompetence, and seemed to doubt that systemic upheaval was the way to nullify the terrorist threat. But Bush could not ignore the emotional armlock imposed by lobbying relatives of those who had died on 11 September 2001, lobbyists who won the backing of the Senate by a vote of 90 to 8. His administration tried instead to ensure that the inquiry conducted its affairs in a manner that was, from their point of view, fair. Thomas H. Kean became chairman of the National Commission on Terrorist Attacks upon the United States (the 9/11 Commission). A Republican with liberal credentials, Kean seemed to embody the unifying ideal that the nation craved. His commission reported in

July 2004 after one of the biggest government investigations in American history.

Even before that report, Kean delivered his verdict on the FBI: "It failed. . . . This is an agency that does not work. It makes you angry. And I don't know how to fix it." His commission did not, however, opt for an MI5 clone. There were fears that a new agency would take too long to set up, and that it would "stovepipe" key intelligence up to the White House instead of sharing it with the rest of the intelligence community, in effect simply creating another level of bureaucracy. Kean and his colleagues wanted "to establish a strong national intelligence center . . . that will oversee counterterrorism work, foreign and domestic." The 9/11 commissioners recommended the creation of an intelligence tsar who would operate independently of existing agencies. In their July 2004 report, they further urged the creation of "a specialized and integrated national security workforce" within the FBI that would include analysts and linguists. Their concluding chapter was devoted to the theme of "unity of effort."

The 9/11 commissioners made an effort to publicize their report. It came out as a book under the Norton imprint at a low price, and there were further editions of the volume and accompanying staff reports. Moreover, the commissioners reconstituted themselves as the 9/11 Public Discourse Project, a ginger group dedicated to keeping the pressure on the administration to take appropriate action.

Further investigations reinforced the impact of the high-profile 9/11 Commission inquiry. Inspector General Glenn Fine's report on the FBI's performance over 9/11 offered blistering criticisms. Completed as a classified document in July 2004, it was released eleven months later, reminding everyone that the bureau had deficiencies and that something would have to be done about them. Nor was this the end of the story. When a further commission looked into the circumstances that had dragged the nation into war on the basis of faulty intelligence about Iraq's (nonexistent) weapons of mass destruction (WMD), its report devoted a chapter to the FBI. While it adopted a wait-and-see stance on whether an American MI5 should take over some of the FBI's functions, it emphasized the need for a revitalized national security service.[17]

Like the joint congressional inquiry, the 9/11 Commission report attracted criticism. A *New York Times* editorial declared that the real problem had been White House mismanagement of the FBI. The theologian David Ray Griffin saw the FBI as a pawn in a more effective executive game. In a brace of prominent books, he drew an analogy with Pearl Harbor. According to Griffin, FDR had allowed that attack to happen because he wanted to get America into the war with Germany by the back door; Bush similarly wanted America on a military-imperialist footing, and knew that a terrorist attack would give him the mandate he needed, so he deliberately ignored warnings about Al Qaeda. For Griffin, the 9/11 inquiry was a cover-up, run not by Kean, but by White House crony Philip Zelikow, executive director of the commission's staff.

In a review of the book version of the 9/11 report, Chicago judge and law professor Richard A. Posner attacked from a different angle. In his view, the MI5 idea was a good one, would not lead to an American Gestapo, and would assuage FBI-CIA rivalries. Centralization via an intelligence tsar as proposed by the commission would just slow the flow of information. The Bush cabinet had made real mistakes, more Americans should learn Arabic, and it was wrong to believe that "systemic" solutions could be found. Intelligence veteran Art Hulnick also questioned the proposal that wholesale reorganization should be triggered by what, after all, was merely the "threat du jour." Both of these commentators showed awareness of the principle that you cannot prevent future surprise attacks by guarding against previous ones, for, of its nature, surprise is nonsystemic, and cannot reliably be anticipated by means of administrative reshuffling.[18]

However, the 9/11 commissioners insisted there would have to be painful operational and administrative changes. Neither the White House nor the FBI was overjoyed at this prospect, and they resorted to alternative means of winning public support. The administration resorted to scaremongering, episodically on the American political agenda ever since the Jacobin panic of the 1790s, but now resurrected in a modern form. One DHS tactic was to use color codes to indicate the level of probability of terrorist attack, so American citizens would know how scared they should be at any given time. The more frightened people were, the more they would support FBI powers, tolerate FBI transgressions, and oppose attempts to tamper with the iconic bureau. As time went by, reminders had to be issued. There was an "immediate and serious threat" of Al Qaeda attack, Tom Ridge warned in November 2002. When in January 2004 the administration lowered the security threat status to yellow ("elevated"), FBI director Mueller insisted that Al Qaeda still wanted to kill lots of Americans, and might attack at any time.

Meanwhile, the FBI provided a measure of reassurance by arresting people. In March 2003, agents in Rawalpindi, Pakistan, captured the person suspected of having been the operational leader of the 9/11 attack, Khalid Shaikh Mohammed. Attorney General Ashcroft intimated that this was an FBI arrest, that the bureau had sharpened its intelligence, that it was now operating fully in tandem with the CIA, and that America was "winning the war on terrorism."

The bureau also made progress in tracking down cases of hawala, or "Arab handshake," which meant money laundering aimed at financing terrorist operations. An investigation appropriately code-named Black Bear uncovered a plot to ship terrorist money in honey containers. The bureau secured the arrest and conviction in a federal court in Brooklyn of Yemeni-born Mohammed Ali Hassan al-Moayed, who had sent the honeyed funds to the Palestinian terrorist group Hamas.

The FBI presented itself as being able to solve cases, and additionally as being committed to self-reform. Its budget expansion made it possible to pump money into new activities without too drastically cutting back and demoralizing existing personnel. Between 2001 and 2005, the number of analysts rose by 76 percent to 1,800.

The FBI director had announced that reorganization would go beyond enhanced e-mail surveillance and the like, and change the bureau's "operational cultures." The bureau had already established a national Joint Terrorism Task Force to coordinate the work of 103 local networks when, in January 2003, the president in his State of the Union address announced the formation of the Terrorist Threat Integration Center, to be directed by a CIA-appointed person and having as its goal national coordination—it had a staff of 600 by 2005.

With resources pouring into his agency, Mueller felt he had to announce improvements and changes on a regular basis. Thus in April 2003, he hailed the advantages of the FBI's new Trilogy network, which involved placing a billion records securely online and making them available to authorized users. The system was capable of emulating some of the data-handling techniques used in the private sector. Potentially, it could search not only for signature data that might identify an individual, but also for autarkic data spreads suggesting attempts at concealment. In October of that year, the FBI established within each of its fifty-six field offices a Field Intelligence group, consisting of analysts, surveillance personnel, and linguists. In principle, they would be able to benefit from Trilogy instantaneously.

By the end of 2003, Maureen Baginski was operational as executive assistant director for intelligence. Although there were gripes that it had taken too long, post–9/11, for this intelligence initiative to be launched, "Mo" Baginski's appointment was widely hailed. A veteran of the National Security Agency, she convinced the media that she was going to teach the flatfooted G-men how to spy. Referring to Web data retrieval, she declared she wanted to "stop the vacuum cleaner" and "get at the secrets worth knowing." She dazzled with her grasp of the technologies of "geolocation" that could be used to pinpoint the whereabouts of terrorists, so that the CIA could kill them. Zelikow thought Baginski was the personification of FBI reform; her staff gave her a figure of Xena the Warrior Princess to keep on her bookshelf.

In November 2004, the newly reelected President Bush sent the attorney general a memorandum requesting further reform of the FBI, notably the establishment of a national security unit within the bureau on the lines recommended by the 9/11 Commission. In January, the Intelligence Reform and Terrorism Prevention Act required the establishment within the FBI of a "National Intelligence Workforce" and stipulated that every agent hired by the bureau in the future should have intelligence as well as police training. In February 2005, Mueller responded with a "Comprehensive Plan" aimed at securing these goals.

The context in which the bureau operated just kept on changing. On the day after the announcement of the Comprehensive Plan, President Bush named John D. Negroponte as director of national intelligence, ostensibly giving him very high standing. The former ambassador to the United Nations assumed authority over the FBI (he could appoint the director) and also the CIA, whose director had previously served as the director of central intelligence. Yet, just two years later, Negroponte relinquished the post and seemingly diminished its prestige by agreeing to become deputy secretary of state. Tom Ridge had resigned from Homeland Security in February 2005, also after just two years in office. Mueller was a more durable leader at the FBI, but he was required to transform his agency even while he adjusted to revolving senior personnel. In June 2005, for example, Bush directed the FBI to establish a National Security Service, in line with the WMD commission's recommendation.[19]

In the midst of all this change and after it, the FBI was still expected to be the nation's premier police detective agency. As ever, it engaged in a wide variety of cases. Some of the highest profile investigations were into alleged federal malpractices. When U.S. military personnel were accused of abusing prisoners in Iraq, the FBI investigated. When neoconservative government officials were suspected of passing classified information to their Israeli allies, the bureau made inquiries. When there were indications of corruption in the award of Middle Eastern oil contracts, it was once again a job for the

Feds. When administration officials were accused of taking revenge on a critic of the Iraq war by leaking the fact that his wife was an undercover CIA official (the Valerie Wilson/Plame case), special agents launched an inquiry. China did not stop spying just because the Feds were under the cosh, and in November 2005 special agents in Los Angeles arrested Chi Mak and four others on charges of stealing naval secrets. In the following spring, Feds raided the office of Congressman William J. "Dollar Bill" Jefferson (D-La.), who had been accused of being on the take. Some of the foregoing investigations may have seemed palliative, a cynical attempt by the government to run soft inquiries into its own malfeasances, but the FBI did tend to secure results.

In the meantime, the bureau continued to engage in non-federal business. It conducted a three-year probe into the alleged excesses of Los Angeles private investigator Anthony Pellicano, who was thought to have wiretapped some Hollywood celebrities at the request of others; when FBI agents stormed his home they found hand grenades and plastic explosives. In 2005, Joseph C. Massino, said to be "the last don," sang to the Feds. Just afterward, the FBI moved against New Jersey racketeers who fatally underestimated its continuing potency. "I can smell a cop a mile away," politician-on-the-take Raymond O'Grady told the agent who was secretly taping his conversation. The bureau cracked the case, and could still present itself as the great national sheriff.[20]

In spite of the bureau's best endeavors, and in spite of the reform efforts of the Bush administration, it remained open season on the FBI. On one hand, civil libertarians continued to be angry. The use of national security letters provided a focal point for their ire. In the summer of 2005, George Christian, a librarian in Windsor, Connecticut, refused to accede to one letter's request to hand over "all subscriber information, billing information and access logs of any person" who had used a certain computer terminal, and his employers sued for the right to reveal details of the case, a right denied under the terms of the Patriot Act. Expressions of indignation over this issue competed for space in the newspapers with reports about how Attorney General Ashcroft and the FBI had (in the view of a federal judge) ignored the fundamental human rights of restaurant proprietor Ehab Elmaghraby and other Muslim detainees in a Brooklyn Metropolitan Detention Center. The *Washington Post* meanwhile reported that the FBI was conducting clandestine surveillance on U.S. residents for as long as eighteen months at a time with no proper paperwork or judicial oversight. In the following year, there were complaints that the allegedly oversecretive administration was reclassifying already declassified documents, and that the FBI had coerced the aged widow of the columnist Jack Anderson into allowing agents to extract items from his private papers before they were deposited at George Washington University.[21]

On the other hand, the FBI endured barbs not for doing too much, but for doing too little, and badly. In October 2005, the former 9/11 commissioners charged that the FBI in particular had been reluctant to implement their recommendations on the improvement of the nation's anti-terrorism provision. That summer, the promised National Security Service had come into being to oversee the FBI's counterterror, counterespionage, and intelligence activities, apparently meeting one of the commissioners' main demands. However, Mo Baginski had been passed over for the post of director, which went to Gary M. Bald, a veteran bureau agent who had worked on the Whitey Bulger case. Senator Grassley thought that Bald lacked intelligence credentials, and then, in May 2006, with sources in the bureau saying that things had gone downhill since Baginski's departure, Grassley complained that the FBI had failed to assert itself as the leading domestic intelligence agency.

Skepticism about the bureau's performance levels remained widespread. The press had a field day when it was disclosed that special agent James J. Smith, who had been assigned to "handle" the American spy Katrina Leung, had been having an affair with her for eighteen years, and that Leung was a Chinese double agent. In the aftermath of Hurricane Katrina, which struck the Gulf Coast in 2005, the FBI went in to help restore the rule of law in devastated New Orleans, and there were some familiar complaints. The bureau would not cooperate with other agencies, resented having to use the DHS framework, and insisted on secrecy except when hogging the limelight.[22]

Those devoted to America's security did address the FBI's needs in the years after 9/11. Their push for more diversity was in character with the best FBI traditions, even if it did not entirely succeed. They pressed for a change in culture, for more analysis. They tried to provide a new administrative framework that would be conducive to a unified effort. But the FBI had always been a showcase for human frailties and bitter controversies, and no reformer could reasonably expect to change that.

NOTES

ABBREVIATIONS

APP   American Presidency Project (presidential statements posted on the Internet)

BHL   Bentley Historical Library, Ann Arbor, Michigan

BKWF   FBI file on Burton K. Wheeler, FOIA

CIA-CD   Declassified CIA documents on CD-ROM, NA ("CD" followed by a CIA serial number)

CJB   Charles Joseph Bonaparte Papers, MLC

CRS   Congressional Research Service

EC   Ernest Cuneo papers, FDRL

ERF   FBI file on Eleanor Roosevelt, FDRL

FAS   Federation of American Scientists Web site

FBIWF   FOIA documents obtained from the Federal Bureau of Investigation's Web site (abbreviation followed by an FBI report number)

FCP   Ford Congressional Papers, GRF

FDR   Franklin D. Roosevelt Papers, FDRL

FDRL   Franklin D. Roosevelt Library, Hyde Park, New York

FM   Frank Murphy Papers, BHL

FOIA   Files obtained under the Freedom of Information Act

FMS   Ferenc M. Szasz Papers, Center for Southwest Research, General Library, University of New Mexico, Albuquerque

GMWP   G. Mennen Williams Pre-Gubernatorial Papers, BHL

GPNF   FBI file on Gerald P. Nye, FOIA

GR   Group Research collection, RBMC

GRDT   General Records of the Department of the Treasury, NA

GRF   Gerald R. Ford Library, Ann Arbor, Michigan

HSTL   Harry S. Truman Library, Independence, Missouri

JAJ   Department of Justice file on John Arthur Johnson, RG 60, Central Files, Straight Numerical Files 1904–37, Box 1457, File 164211, NA2

JEC   James E. Connor files, GRF

JHR   James H. Rowe, Jr., Papers, FDRL

JL   Joseph Lash Papers, FDRL

JLC   Joseph Labadie Collection, Graduate Library of the University of Michigan, Ann Arbor, Michigan

LAT   *Los Angeles Times*

LBJL   Lyndon B. Johnson Library, Austin, Texas

LL   Loen and Leppert files, Congressional Relations Office, GRF

MLC   Manuscript Collections, Library of Congress

NA   National Archives, Washington, D.C.

NA2	National Archives, College Park, Maryland
NSF	National Security Files (in identified presidential libraries)
NYT	*New York Times*
OC	Records of the office of the counselor, Department of State, NA
OF	Official Files in presidential libraries
PFCR	President Ford Committee Records, GRF
PNDA	Records of the Pinkerton National Detective Agency, MLC
PPF	President's Personal Files in presidential libraries
PSF	President's Secretary's File in presidential libraries
PWB	Philip W. Buchen files, GRF
RAC	Rose A. Conway Files, HSTL
RBMC	Rare Book and Manuscript Library, Columbia University, New York, New York
RDP	Richard D. Parsons files, GRF
RHJ	Robert H. Jackson papers, MLC
RHN	Ronald H. Nessen, Press Secretary to the President Files, GRF
SCFBI	Small Collections, FBI files, FDRL
SCMD	Small Collections, Miscellaneous Documents, FDRL
SN	Secrecy News, the online journal of the Federation of American Scientists' Project on Government Secrecy
TR	Papers of Theodore Roosevelt (Microfilm), MLC
UC	Unidentified clipping
WHT	Papers of William H. Taft (Microfilm), MLC
WP	*Washington Post*
WT	*Washington Times*

CHAPTER 1 Race and the Character of the FBI

1 Opening statistics based on Table No. 13, "Resident Population by Sex, Race, and Hispanic Origin Status: 2000 to 2003," U.S. Census Bureau, "Statistical Abstract of the United States 2004–2005," Census Web site (because Web search engines now do a more effective job for the researcher, Web addresses are not given in this book); Amer, *Black Members,* 59–61; 2003 FBI employee statistics for 30 June 2003, accessed June 2004 on FBI Web site. See also Cummings and McFarland, *Federal Justice,* 373, and Monet, *Polices et Sociétés,* 27; *Christian Science Monitor,* 25 June 2001; Sandusky *Register,* 16 February, quoted in *NYT,* 21 February 1860; 28 U.S.C. 533 (3) quoted in Church 3, 379. The remarks on Europol are based on interviews with members of the European Parliament as part of research for Jeffreys-Jones, "Idea of a European FBI."

2 Foner, *Reconstruction,* xix–xx; Dunning, *Reconstruction,* 122, 203–14; 19-year-old shotgun victim quoted in Zinn, *Southern Mystique,* 147; no references to the Klan appear in Ansley's otherwise competent history "The United States Secret Service."

3 Andrew and Dilks, *Missing Dimension; NYT,* 30 October 1883.

4 Ward, *Unforgivable Blackness,* 311; Du Bois quoted in Lewis, *Du Bois,* 7; Ellis, *Race,* 175.

5 Garrow, *FBI and King,* 221.

6 McFeely, *Grant,* 367.

7 Cooper, "Introduction," viii–xvii; Whitehead, *FBI Story,* 7, 16, 96–98, 103. For context, see Jeffreys-Jones, "The Historiography of the FBI."

8 Waldrep, "American Lynching."

9   Funder, *Stasiland,* 57.

10   Kendall, "The Function of Intelligence," 548.

11   Theoharis, *FBI and American Democracy,* 3; Sibley, *Red Spies,* 225; Powers, *Broken,* 314–15; *NYT,* 9 December 2003.

12   Hodgson, *More Equal than Others,* 117.

13   Aldrich, *Espionage,* 5.

CHAPTER 2 **Secret Reconstruction, 1871–1905**

1   Whitley's instruction paraphrased in his report, January 1872, 100, RG60: General Records of the Department of Justice, Letters Received, Source Chronological Files, 1871–84, Treasury, NA2.

2   Whitley report, 29 September 1871, 5–6, 11, 14–18, 35, 64–69.

3   "Hiram C. Whitley," in Connelley, *Kansas and Kansans,* 5:2217–19. See also Melanson, *Secret Service,* 14, *KKK Report,* 507.

4   Miller, *Revenuers and Moonshiners,* 1, 15; *NYT,* 9 March 1871; Melanson, *Secret Service,* 14–18.

5   *NYT,* 8 April 1872; Foner, *Reconstruction,* 342.

6   Cresswell, *Mormons and Cowboys,* 2; Post, "Carpetbagger," 65; 1871 statute, quoted in Church 3, 379.

7   Akerman to Whitley, 28 June 1871, in NA2, RG60, Letters sent by the Department of Justice: General: Misc., 1818–1904, M699, Roll 13, Vol. H.

8   *KKK Report,* 41; Hall, "Political Power," 924–45; interview with the historian Stephen Budiansky, who is working on a biography of Major Merrill, Washington, D.C., 20 April 2006; Post, "Carpetbagger," 41, 43.

9   Hook, *From Goosecreek to Gandercleugh,* 198; McWhiney, *Cracker Culture,* 149–51; Fischer, *Albion's Seed,* 770–71; *KKK Report,* 514; Lieut. Colonel W. Harry Brown to R. M. Wallace, 13 April 1872, in NA2, RG60, General Records of the Department of Justice, Letters Received from South Carolina, 1871–84, M 947.

10   Swinney, *Suppressing the Klan,* 186.

11   Blain, "Mississippi Secret Service," 119, 121, 128; Foner, *Reconstruction,* 439; Whitley report, 29 September 1871, 2.

12   Akerman to Whitley, 28 June 1871, in NA2, RG60, Letters sent by the Department of Justice: General: Misc., 1818–1904, M699, Roll 13, Vol. H; Swinney, *Suppressing the Klan,* 185. Whitley's pension claim is dated 17 November 1916, classifies him as an invalid, and relates to service in both the Seventh and the Fifth Louisiana Infantry: digital image in Civil War Pension Index, accessed via Ancestry Plus.

13   Whitley report, 29 September 1871, 2–4, 72; Swinney, *Suppressing the Klan,* 185.

14   Whitley report, 29 September 1871, 5, 13, 15, 19, 25, 29, 30.

15   Whitley report, 15 August 1872; Gilmore's oral recollections in Rawick, ed., *South Carolina Narratives,* 120; L. C. Northrop to U.S. attorney general, 21 May 1878, in NA2, RG60, General Records of the Department of Justice, Letters Received from South Carolina, 1871–84, M 947.

16   Merrill to Akerman, 13 November 1871, in NA2, RG60, General Records of the Department of Justice, Letters Received from South Carolina, 1871–84, M 947.

17   Du Bois, *Black Reconstruction,* 30; Dunning, *Reconstruction,* 2; Dunning, *Essays,* 361; Rhodes, *History,* 6:297n1, 312, 318–19. On underresourcing and lack of political will,

see Williams, *South Carolina Klan Trials,* 146–47, and Trelease, *White Terror,* 388–89, 409–12.

18 Whitley reports, 29 September 1871, 72–73, 15 September 1872, 1, 42–50, 62–63, 67.

19 Post, "Carpetbagger," 15, 34.

20 Swinney, *Suppressing the Klan,* 185.

21 Post, "Carpetbagger," 61.

22 Post, "Carpetbagger," 47, 66.

23 Corbin to attorney general, 2 November 1872, 28 March 1874, and 21 August 1876, in NA2, RG60, General Records of the Department of Justice, Letters Received from South Carolina, 1871–84, M 947. Corbin's reports refer to "Dr E. T. Avery"; other documents identify this fugitive from York, S.C., as "Dr William T. Avery," as "James W. Avery," and as the "merchant" J. W. Avery: see Shapiro, "Klan," 51, and Simkins, "Klan," 643, 645.

24 *NYT,* 8 April 1872; Corbin to attorney general, 21 August 1876, in NA2, RG60, General Records of the Department of Justice, Letters Received from South Carolina, 1871–84, M 947.

25 Trelease, *White Terror,* 185, 411, 415; Shapiro, "Klan," 46; Whitley report in *NYT,* 14 August 1872; Corbin to attorney general, 2 November 1872, and Williams to Corbin, 7 December 1872, in NA2, RG60, General Records of the Department of Justice, Letters Received from South Carolina, 1871–84, M 947. Williams refers to Corbin's letter of "the 2nd instant" but this is probably an error or a late transcription, and he is replying to the November letter.

26 Cummings and McFarland, *Federal Justice,* 242, Foner, *Reconstruction,* 437; Lemann, *Redemption,* 4, 5, 16, 18.

27 Swinney, *Suppressing the Klan,* 182–83; McFeely, *Grant,* 391; Smith, *Grant,* 560, 584.

28 Melanson, *Secret Service,* 15; Closing argument of Hon. A. G. Riddle for prosecution, at trial of Hiram C. Whitley, Richard Harrington, and Arthur B. Williams for conspiracy, in Criminal Court of D.C., 23–25 November 1874 (Microfiche: Congressional Information Service, 1993, DC2802–3).

29 Budiansky interview; Cresswell, *Mormons and Cowboys,* 23, 30–34.

30 Beck quoted in Cummings and McFarland, *Federal Justice,* 248; *KKK Report,* 587.

31 Kaiser, "Origins," 104, 121n10; Noakes, "Enforcing Domestic Tranquility," 11–13; Melanson, *Secret Service,* 21–24; Williams, "Without Understanding," 34; Tolnay and Beck, *Southern Lynchings,* 271.

32 Dixon, *Clansman,* 103.

33 Whitley, *In It,* 91; "Hiram C. Whitley," in Connelley, *Kansas and Kansans.*

34 Kaiser, "Origins," 104, 121n10; Noakes, "Enforcing Domestic Tranquility," 11–13.

35 Post, "Carpetbagger"; Davis to attorney general, 30 August 1921, Campbell to Department of Justice, 4 October 1921, "AMERICAN" to Daugherty, 26 September 1921, and other letters in Box 3033, in NA2, RG60, Department of Justice Central Files, Straight Numerical Files, 1904–37.

36 Ned Cobb quoted in Foner, *Reconstruction,* 611.

CHAPTER 3 **Proud Genesis, 1905–1909**

1 Order of Charles J. Bonaparte, Attorney General, 26 July 1908, FBI Web site.

2 Bonaparte to Roosevelt, 14 January 1909, Department of Justice File, 44-3-11-Sub 3, 12/5/08–4/6/09, FBI Web site.

3 Bishop, *Bonaparte*, 162; Bonaparte, "Lynch Law," 342–43; Goldman, *Bonaparte*, 16, 87.

4 Roosevelt quoted in Berman, *Police Administration*, 102. See also Mowry, *Era*, 106–9; Jackson, ed., *New York City*, 449–50; Tyler, *Organized Crime*, 139–49.

5 Roosevelt quoted in Berman, *Police Administration*, 65; 1903 Parry speech to NAM quoted in Jeffreys-Jones, *Violence*, 17.

6 David M. Parry, *The Scarlet Empire* (Indianapolis: Bobbs-Merrill, 1906); Upton Sinclair, *The Jungle* (New York: Grosset and Dunlap, 1906); Jack London, *War of the Classes* (New York: Macmillan, 1905), and *Iron Heel* (New York: Macmillan, 1907), Frank Harris, *The Bomb* (New York: M. Kennerly, 1909); Jeffreys-Jones, *Violence*, 28–29; Monkkonen, *Police*, 7, 85, 156–57, 213.

7 Steffens, *Autobiography*, 285–91.

8 Lamont, *Rise of the Indian Rope Trick*, 80–81, 94.

9 Kaiser, "Origins," 108–9; Willard Mann, "The Chief's First Case," *True Detective* (October 1941), 20–25, 95; letter of appointment, Gage to Wilkie, 28 February 1898 (supplied by the Secret Service and kindly shown to me by Peter Lamont); Wilkie, *Agent*, 7. Graeme Mount suggests Wilkie did not entirely mop up the Spanish spy ring: Mount, *Canada's Enemies*, 9, but see Jeffreys-Jones, *Cloak and Dollar*, Chapter 4.

10 Gatewood, *Art of Controversy*, 238, 246; Kaiser, "Origins," 108, 114.

11 Noakes, "Enforcing Domestic Tranquility," 16, 73; Carper, "Slavery Revisited," 88; Wessel, "Republican Justice," 2.

12 Coates, *In Nature's Defence*, back cover; Noakes, "Enforcing Domestic Tranquility," 75–76; *Annual Report of the Chief of the Secret Service Division for the Fiscal Year ended 1908*, 8.

13 Jeffreys-Jones, *Cloak and Dollar*, 85; Noakes, "Enforcing Domestic Tranquility," 76.

14 Gatewood, *Art of Controversy*, 263; Lowenthal, *FBI*, 185, 292; *New York Sun*, 23 November 1910.

15 *Annual Report of the Attorney General of the United States* (1907, FBI Web site), 9–10. See also Gatewood, *Art of Controversy*, 245.

16 Bonaparte testimony, "Hearings Before the Subcommittee of the House Committee on Appropriations for Deficiency Appropriations for 1908 and Prior Years on Urgent Deficiency Bill," 202–3, FBI Web site.

17 Roosevelt to Cannon, 29 April 1908, *Letters*, 6:1019; Gatewood, *Art of Controversy*, 250–55.

18 Roosevelt quoted in Noakes, "Enforcing Domestic Tranquility," 80.

19 Roosevelt to Secretary of War William H. Taft, 30 April 1908, Roosevelt, *Letters*, 6:1021; Gatewood, *Art of Controversy*, 255–56.

20 Gatewood, *Art of Controversy*, 259–62, 280.

21 *Philadelphia Public Ledger*, 27 December 1908; *Wall Street Journal* of 22 December 1908 quoted in Gatewood, *Art of Controversy*, 259–60.

22 *Philadelphia Record*, 29 December 1908; Roosevelt to Senator Eugene Hale (R-Maine), 19 February 1909, Roosevelt, *Letters*, 6:1530.

23 *North American*, 22 December 1908; Wilkie to H. C. Gauss, secretary to the attorney general, 31 March 1908, in Box 131, CJB.

24 *Leader*, n.d., in Scrapbooks, Vol. 14 (1908), Box 261, CJB.

25 Williams, "Without Understanding," 40–41; Roosevelt to Kermit Roosevelt, 10 Janu-

ary 1909, Roosevelt, *Letters,* 6:1472; note by the editor (Elting Morison) in Roosevelt, *Letters,* 6:1460; Gatewood, *Art of Controversy,* 236–38, 267–73.

26 Wessel, "Republican Justice," 233–36; Foraker quoted in the *Philadelphia Press,* 13 January 1909; Lane, *Brownsville Affair,* 152; Julia Foraker, *Memories,* 269, 286–89.

27 *Extracts from Hearings Before Subcommittee of House Committee on Appropriations,* 6, 8, 13, 15.

28 Noakes, "Enforcing Domestic Tranquility," 84–85; Sherley quoted in Lowenthal, *FBI,* 8, Gatewood, *Art of Controversy,* 270, and in Williams, "Without Understanding," 36; Roosevelt to Senator Eugene Hale (R-Maine), 19 February 1909, Roosevelt, *Letters,* 6:1529.

29 Gatewood, *Art of Controversy,* 283; Theoharis, *FBI Guide,* 325–26; Wessel, "Republican Justice," 339, 341.

30 Noakes, "Enforcing Domestic Tranquility," 93, 99; Gatewood, *Art of Controversy,* 286; Wessel, "Republican Justice," 339.

CHAPTER 4 Loss of Mission, 1909–1924

1 Grand Jury indictment, Northern District Court of Illinois, Eastern Division, 9 November 1912, JAJ.

2 George W. Harris to President, 12 November 1912, copied to Bielaski, JAJ; Roberts, *Papa Jack,* frontispiece; Damon Runyon, "Jack Johnson Could Fight," in Johnson, *In the Ring,* 15.

3 J. Q. Moses to President, telegram, 11 November 1912, JAJ.

4 Roberts, *Papa Jack,* 152; Ward, *Unforgivable Blackness,* 311.

5 Higham, *Strangers in the Land,* 158. One might wonder whether the bully is by definition a person of weak confidence, as implied by Higham. But although Higham's book first appeared in 1963, his interpretation still rides high: Carl J. Guarneri, "In Memoriam: John Higham," *OAH Newsletter* 31 (November 2003): 22–23.

6 Tolnay and Beck, *Festival of Violence,* 29–31, 271; memo, 31 March 1910, on the authority of the U.S. "to Protect Negroes," in bureau files, quoted in O'Reilly, *Racial Matters,* 9; Finch to Pres. Taft's secretary, 10 January 1912, WHT; Finch to Roosevelt, 10 January 1912, TR; Special Agent A. T. Bagley to Finch, 20 December 1909, attorney general to president, 22 December 1909, President Taft to Secretary of the Treasury Franklin MacVeagh, 25 December 1909, all in WHT; Noakes, "Enforcing Domestic Tranquility," 90–93.

7 Smith, "Black Appointed Officials," 371; Anonymous NAACP official (Roy Wilkins?) quoted in Sitkoff, *Struggle,* 213; Addams quoted in Keire, "Vice Trust," 8; Finch, "White Slave Traffic," 570, 572, 580, 585.

8 Finch, "White Slave Traffic," 586–87, 591–92.

9 Finch, "White Slave Traffic," 586–87; Ellis, *Race,* 236n20; James G. Findlay, "Memorandum for the Director: Re: Early History of the Bureau of Investigation, United States Department of Justice," Los Angeles, 19 November 1943, FBI Web site. Findlay had served as a special agent under Finch.

10 Lowenthal, *FBI,* 14; Keire, "Vice Trust," 20; Langum, *Crossing Over the Line,* 49.

11 Noakes, "Enforcing Domestic Tranquility," 109.

12 African American legends quoted in Levine, *Black Culture,* 432; London, *London Reports,* 259, 265; Johnson, *Black Manhattan,* 65–69; Johnson, *Mes Combats,* 12, 75;

Johnson, *In the Ring*, 63; London quoted in Sammons, *Beyond the Ring*, 37; *Observer Sunday Magazine*, December 2002, 66.

13 Report to D. S. Dickerson, President, Board of Parole, Washington, D.C., 20 January 1921, based on bureau files, Bryan to Consul-General, Montreal, 26 June 1913, quoted in reply, 30 June 1913, all in JAJ.

14 Tennyson to Pres. Taft, 3 January 1913, JAJ; Roberts, *Papa Jack*, 159–60.

15 Governor Cole Blease quoted in Roberts, *Papa Jack*, 151.

16 Undated depositions by Johnson's mother and brother, Report to Dickerson, Acting Secretary of State Frank Polk to attorney general, 26 February 1919, all in JAJ; Johnson, *In the Ring*, 83; Roberts, *Papa Jack*, 147.

17 Doerries, *Imperial Challenge*, 141–90.

18 Jensen, *Price of Vigilance*, 13–15; Jeffreys-Jones, *American Espionage*, 57–65.

19 Noakes, "Enforcing Domestic Tranquility," 146–47.

20 Jeffreys-Jones, *American Espionage*, 62; Jensen, *Price of Vigilance*, 14.

21 Memorandum enclosed with letter, Lansing to President, 20 November 1915, Wilson to Navy Secretary Josephus Daniels, 8 December 1915, Gregory to President, 10 December 1915, all in Link, ed., *Wilson Papers*, 35:227–30, 316–17, 336.

22 Noakes, "Enforcing Domestic Tranquility," 155–59; Witcover, *Sabotage at Black Tom*, 24; Doerries, *Imperial Challenge*, 188–89; testimony of Inspector Thomas J. Tunney of the New York Bomb Squad, 21 January 1919, cited in Talbert, *Negative Intelligence*, 16; 28 U.S.C. 533 (3), quoted in Church 3, 379; Jeffreys-Jones, *American Espionage*, 111, 114–16.

23 Lansing to President, 8 April 1917, in Link, ed., *Wilson Papers*, 42:16–17; McAdoo to Wilson, 16 April 1917, enclosed with McAdoo to Gregory, 16 April 1917, cited in Fox, "Bureaucratic Wrangling," text at footnote 19 (the text is unpaginated on the Web). The source for Fox's citation is given as Whitehead Research Materials, FBI Office of Public Affairs.

24 Ellis, *Race*, 27, 31, 38.

25 Noakes, "Enforcing Domestic Tranquility," 134.

26 Noakes, "Enforcing Domestic Tranquility," 169.

27 H. L. Mencken in the *Baltimore Sun*, 18 October 1920, reproduced in *A Carnival of Buncombe*, ed. Malcolm Moos (Westport, Conn.: Greenwood, 1983), 33; O'Reilly, *Racial Matters*, 13; Kornweibel, "Black on Black," 122–27; Preston, Jr., *Aliens and Dissenters*, 242.

28 Noakes, "Enforcing Domestic Tranquility," 171; Burns quoted in Belknap, "Uncooperative Federalism," 27.

29 Belknap, "Uncooperative Federalism," 28, 30, 43.

30 Lewis, *Du Bois*, 68; Williams, "Bureau of Investigation and Its Critics," 569, 573; Goodall, "Emergence of Anti-Communism," 354.

31 *New York Sun*, 8 December 1911; *Philadelphia Press*, 25 April 1911; Caesar, *Incredible Detective*, 18, 31; Fine, *Without Blare*, 117; James B. McNamara quoted (or, more probably, misquoted) in Burns, *Masked War*, 299; Jeffreys-Jones, *Violence and Reform*, 16, 73–76; Oney, *And the Dead Shall Rise*, 387, 397, 420.

32 Oney, *And the Dead Shall Rise*, 103; Edwards, "Introduction," xxx; photograph opposite page 64 in Caesar, *Incredible Detective;* Burns to President Taft's secretary, 22 September 1910 and patronage requests and denials, 10, 14 June and 3, 10 July 1911, all in

WHT; *Brooklyn Eagle,* 14 March 1917; Statement of Meier Steinbrink for complainant in hearing before New York State Comptroller William Boardman, 24 April 1917, 36, 38, Box 65, and Matthew J. Carroll deposition, recorded in Lewis A. Barker memorandum, 9 May 1917, Box 63, both PNDA.

33 Burns to an addressee (name redacted), 10 January 1925, in section on John Wilkes Booth in the FBI's FOIA Web site that runs through to the 1970s; Walsh to Daugherty, 27 November 1922, and Daugherty to Gov. A. J. Allen of Kansas, 13 December 1922, both in Box 3033, in NA2, RG60, Department of Justice Central Files, Straight Numerical Files, 1904–37; Waldrep, "American Lynching," note 41, referring to FBI files 44-21 (KKK in Boston) and 44-16 (KKK in Kansas); Powers, *Secrecy and Power,* 140.

34 Vern Countryman, "The History of the FBI: Democracy's Development of a Secret Police," in Watters and Gillers, eds., *Investigating the FBI,* 69–70; Goodall, "Emergence of Anti-Communism," 39, 41–42, 44; Brookhart quoted in Sinclair, *Available Man,* 262; Noggle, *Teapot Dome,* 185.

CHAPTER 5 The First Age of Reform, 1924–1939

1 It is testimony to the effectiveness of Hoover's public relations machine that there were many accounts of the Karpis and Lepke arrests. The foregoing details are taken from Gentry, *Hoover,* 192–97; Kessler, *Bureau History,* 43–51; Powers, *Secrecy and Power,* 207–9; Summers, *Official and Confidential,* 98, and Toledano, *Hoover,* 124–35.

2 Cooper, "Introduction," viii; Burrough, *Public Enemies,* 9, 543, 545.

3 Church Hearings 6, 553; Mason, *Stone,* 144, 149–53; Stone and Hoover quoted in Schmidt, *Red Scare,* 324–26.

4 Extract from Wickersham commission report (1931) in Waldrep and Bellesisles, *Documenting American Violence,* 293–97.

5 Potter, "Guarding the Crossroads," 118, 126; Hoover address to International Association of Chiefs of Police and International Association for Identification, Chicago, 31 [March?] 1933, OF 10, 10b, Box 10, FDR; Department of Justice, Bureau of Investigation, Manual of Instruction, 1927, *FBI Manuals, 1927–1978,* 7, 13, 35, 45, 154; Department of Justice press release, 7 January 1939, Box 89, folder "FBI Training School," FM.

6 Potter, "Guarding the Crossroads," 123, 131.

7 "The Establishment of a Technical Laboratory in the Division of Investigation," memorandum enclosed with Hoover to attorney general, 29 March 1934, OF 10, 10b, Box 10, FDR; Theoharis, *Comprehensive Guide,* 173–74; Lowenthal, "The Filing System," in *FBI,* 368–87; Potter, "Guarding the Crossroads," 132–33, 141.

8 Mason, *Stone,* 151; "United States Bureau of Investigation," 17 March 1933, OF 10, 10b, Box 10, FDR, 2, 3, 7; Hoover to attorney general, 20 September 1939, enclosing memorandum of the same date, Box 87, folder "Hoover Memos—Immigration and Naturalization Service," FM; FDR telegram to director FBI, 15 January 1942, SCMD; Roger Daniels, "Immigration and Naturalization Service," in Whitnah, ed., *Government Agencies,* 282.

9 Angevine, "Gentlemen," 7; Jeffreys-Jones, *Cloak and Dollar,* 108–9; Badger, *New Deal,* 68; *Washington Herald,* 8 January 1935; FDR to attorney general, 4 April 1939, OF 10, Box 1, folder "Justice Department," FDR.

10 Adamic, *Dynamite,* 350; FDR quoted in O'Reilly, "Roosevelt Administration and Black

America," 13; Cummings, "Predatory Crime," radio address, 12 September 1933, and "The Campaign Against Crime," CBS broadcast, 22 November 1933, OF 10, Box 1, folder "Justice Department," FDR.

11   Cummings and McFarland, *Federal Justice*, vi, 230–49; clippings from *The Law Journal* 83 (26 June 1937) and *The Juridical Review* 49 (June 1939), in PPF, FDR.

12   Cummings, "Modern Tendencies and the Law," address to the American Bar Association, Grand Rapids, Mich., 31 August 1933, and "The Recurring Problem of Crime," NBC radio broadcast, 12 October 1933, both in OF 10, Box 1, folder "Justice Department," FDR; address in Durham, N.C., 27 April 1936, in Cummings, *Selected Addresses*, 6.

13   Pierpont and Cummings quoted in Gentry, *Hoover*, 167, 172.

14   Address in Durham, N.C., 27 April 1936, in Cummings, *Selected Addresses*, 7, 11.

15   FBI Manual of Instruction, 1936, *FBI Manuals, 1927–1978*, section 29; Hoover, "Crime and Your Home," address to General Federation of Women's Clubs, Kansas City, Mo., 17 May 1938, and "Lawlessness—A National Menace," address to the Economic Club, Detroit, Mich., 14 November 1938, both in OF 10, Box 1, folder "Justice Department," FDR.

16   Hoover, "Your Task as a Citizen," address to the U.S. Junior Chamber of Commerce, Tulsa, Oklahoma, 21 June 1939, in OF 10, Box 1, folder "Justice Department," FDR.

17   Department of Justice press release, 7 January 1939, Box 89, folder "FBI Training School," Hoover memo for attorney general, 4 May 1939, Box 88, folder "Hoover Memo K," Hoover to Frank Murphy, 10 August 1939, Box 87, folder "FBI Invitations," all in FM; "The Work and Functions of the United States Bureau of Investigation" (1 June 1933), enclosed with Hoover to FDR's secretary Louis M. Howe, 29 May 1933, in OF 10, Box 1, folder "Justice Department," FDR. Here and in further cases below, names mentioned in the Frank Murphy FBI files are withheld, a condition of use of that section of the Murphy papers.

18   Cummings and McFarland, *Federal Justice*, 230–42; Waldrep, "American Lynching," 20, 22; Mack, "Rethinking Civil Rights Lawyering," 343 and passim.

19   Dudziak, *Cold War Civil Rights*, 7, 12; Borstelmann, *Cold War and Color Line*, 31; Representative John Rankin quoted in McMahon, *Reconsidering Roosevelt*, 149; Waldrep, "American Lynching," 20–25; Jones's Charge to the Grand Jury and opinion in *Ex Parte Riggins* in Waldrep, ed., *Lynching in America*, 219–22.

20   Hoover to attorney general, 20 June 1939, enclosing FBI report dated 16 June 1939 (title with names of victims withheld in conformity with Murphy conditions), Box 88, folder "Hoover memo K," and Hoover to attorney general, 7 August 1939, Box 88, folder "White Slavery," all in FM; *Buffalo Evening News*, 28 July 1939.

21   Murphy quoted in *New York Daily Mirror*, 15 July 1939.

22   Telegram, Lester Hill, City Editor, *Minneapolis Journal*, to Hoover, 14 July, telegram, Hoover to Hill, 15 July, and Hoover, Memo for attorney general, 15 July, all 1939 and in Box 88, folder "WPA Strikes," FM; Weiss, *Farewell to the Party of Lincoln*, 36; Hoover (in October 1919) quoted in O'Reilly, *Racial Matters*, 13.

23   Elliff, "Aspects," 609–29; Hill, *FBI's RACON*, 8.

24   Elliff, "Aspects," 609–29; Hoover quoted in Waldrep, "American Lynching," 17–18.

25   Attorney quoted in Carr, *Federal Protection*, 154.

26   Corwin, "Passing of Dual Federalism," 5, 20; Fairclough, *Better Day Coming*, 168, 208; O'Brien, *Color of the Law*, 251.

CHAPTER 6 **Counterespionage and Control, 1938–1945**

1   Turrou, *Nazi Spy Conspiracy,* 18, 20; *Dundee Courier and Advertiser,* 3, 4, 5, 11, 14 March 1938; Adolf Hitler quoted in Compton, *Swastika and Eagle,* 17, 27; Theoharis, *Spying,* 71. For examples of executive orders and presidential directives, see items, September 1939 to January 1942, in folder "FBI Report on Western Hemisphere Intelligence Work, 12/22/41," in SCMD.

2   Hoover memo for the record, 7 November 1938, Box 1, SCFBI; Theoharis, *Comprehensive Guide,* 16; *New York Herald Tribune,* 2 April 1939.

3   *New York Herald Tribune,* 26 September 1939.

4   FDR memo for secretaries of state, treasury, war, navy, commerce, and for attorney general and postmaster general, 26 June 1939, OF 10, 10b, Box 10, FDR; Hoover to Edwin M. Watson, 3 June 1940, and Biddle memo for pres, 8 October 1941, both in Box 5, folder 9, JL. Major General "Pa" Watson was military aide and appointments secretary to the president.

5   "Memorandum in re: Necessity of military plans under best evidence rule in espionage prosecution," n.d., pp. 1, 7, 15, 18, 21, in Box 4, folder "Ass't, 2 of 6," GMWP; Hoover quoted in Batvinis, "In the Beginning," 40.

6   Hoover recalling World War I "confusion" in letter to attorney general, 29 May, 1 June 1942, Box 36, folder "AAG FBI," JHR; FDR memo for secretaries of state, treasury, war, navy, commerce, and for attorney general and postmaster general, 26 June 1939, OF 10, 10b, Box 10, and Murphy to president and presidential directive, both 6 September 1939 and in OF 10, 10b, Box 10, all in FDR; Berle quoted in Jeffreys-Jones, *American Espionage,* 164–65; Hoover memo for Jackson, 5 June 1940, and Jackson, memo of approval, 22 June 1940, Box 93, folder 5, RHJ.

7   Jeffreys-Jones, *American Espionage,* 166; Hoover to Watson, 29 October 1940, in Box 5, folder 9, JL; Gentry, *Hoover,* 180, 191, 225; Tamm memo for director, 3 December 1940, Box 1, SCFBI.

8   Clegg and Hince telegram to Hoover, 20 January 1941, quoted in Charles, "Before the Colonel Arrived," 231; Batvinis, "In the Beginning," 281–82.

9   Hoover reports to Watson, 5 and 6 March 1941, paraphrased in Charles, "Before the Colonel Arrived," 232.

10 Hoover memo for Jackson, 7 April 1941, Box 93, folder 5, RHJ; Hoover to Watson, 2 June 1941, and Berle to Under Secretary of State Sumner Welles, 27 September 1941, both in Box 5, folder 9, JL; Tamm quoted in Valero, "World War to Cold War," 189.

11 Summers, *Official and Confidential,* 122–27; Bruce-Briggs, "Another Ride," 85.

12 Morimura message quoted in Stinnett, *Day of Deceit,* 85, 116.

13 Stinnett, *Day of Deceit,* 85–103.

14 Corson, *Armies of Ignorance,* 163–65; Valero, "World War to Cold War," 60; Smith, *Shadow Warriors,* 62, 161–63; Hoover memo of 17 December 1941 quoted in Irons, *Justice at War,* 28.

15 Ennis quoted in Irons, *Justice Delayed,* 334; Persico, *Roosevelt's Secret War,* 200–201; Hoover to attorney general, 29 May, 1 June 1942, together with Hoover to James H. Rowe, Jr., 29 May 1942, Box 36, folder "AAG FBI," and Rowe, memo for Attorney General, 16 April 1943, Box 33, folder "Alien Enemy Control Unit," all in JHR.

16 Hoover to Marvin H. McIntyre (assistant sec to the president), 10 March, and FDR memo to Hoover, 13 March 1939, in Box 57, folder "Justice: Hoover, Edgar. 1937–40,"

PSF/FDR; Hoover to Harry L. Hopkins at the White House, 16 November 1944, in Box 5, folder 8, JL; Holt, *Deceivers,* 452–56.

17 Wilkie quoted in *Extracts from Hearings Before Subcommittee of House Committee on Appropriations,* 8; Raat, "Covert Action in Mexico," 621; Bureau of Investigation, Weekly Bulletin of Radical Activities, 26 June and 3 July 1920, in OC; Haines, "Eagle's Wing," 375.

18 "Memorandum prepared by Assistant Secretary of State Berle June 24, 1940, and Approved by the President," in folder "FBI Report on Western Hemisphere Intelligence Work, 12/22/41," in SCMD; Paz, *Strategy,* 192–94; Hoover memos to Jackson, 25 June 1940, Box 14, folder 6, and 15 March 1941, Box 93, folder 5, RHJ.

19 Rout, *Shadow War,* 44–45.

20 Paz, *Strategy,* 155–59, 168, 181, 183–85, 189, 200, 208; Rout, *Shadow War,* 75–76; Raat, "Covert Action in Mexico," 630–32.

21 Mount, *Chile and the Nazis,* xix, 32, 111, 154.

22 Rout, *Shadow War,* 212; Batvinis, "In the Beginning," 321n, 322; Schoonover, "Hitler's Secret Threat," quoting *NYT,* 6 September 1942—see 2, 3, 5, 7, 8; Galvis, *Colombia Nazi,* 48, 146–47, 213; Latin American summaries in Boxes 22, 23, OF 10b, FDR.

23 Hoover, memo for Attorney General Clark, 29 August 1945, *Emergence of the Intelligence Establishment,* 25.

CHAPTER 7 The Alienation of Liberal America, 1924–1943

1 Williams, "They Never Stopped," 10; Theoharis, *Secret Files,* 295–96; Theoharis and Cox, *Boss,* 94.

2 Williams, "They Never Stopped," 11; O'Reilly, "Herbert Hoover," 50–51. On Dreiser: Robins, *Alien Ink,* 81.

3 According to Paul Foster and Glenn Howell, the ONI officers responsible for the New York burglary, President Hoover personally requested the investigation and then personally terminated it: Dorwart, *Conflict of Duty,* 3–4. See also Gentry, *Hoover,* 110; Powers, *Secrecy,* 142.

4 Hoover quoted in Williams, "They Never Stopped," 23; Theoharis, "FBI Wiretapping," 104.

5 Hoover memos for record, 24, 25 August 1936, and Hoover, memo for Tamm, 10 September 1936, Box 1, SCFBI; Church Hearings 6, 561–62; Church 2, 25; Church 3, 393–94.

6 Sibley, *Red Spies,* 8; Church 3, 278–81; FBI manual 1936, section 30, 1–2; Wheeler and Cummings quoted in transcript of Senate report "Prohibiting the Use of Communication Facilities for Criminal Purposes" (20 April 1938), enclosed with Tamm memo for director, 7 May 1940, in BKWF.

7 Hoover memorandum as approved by FDR on 2 November 1938, quoted in Church Hearings 6, 566; FDR memo for secretaries of state, treasury, war, navy, commerce, and for attorney general and postmaster general, 26 June 1939, OF 10, 10b, Box 10, FDR; FDR memo for Attorney General Francis Biddle, 21 May 1940, quoted in Church 3, 279; Jackson and Hoover memoranda quoted in Schmidt, *Red Scare,* 357; Jackson, *That Man,* 68; FDR memo to Hoover, 3 April 1942, in Box 57, folder "Justice: Hoover, Edgar. 1937–40," PSF/FDR.

8 FDR quoted in Cole, *Lindbergh,* 128–29; Charles and Rossi, "FBI and Lindbergh," 843–44; Charles, "Political Surveillance," 217, 222.

9   Charles, "Anti-Interventionist Movement," 162; Hoover to Edwin M. "Pa" Watson, 12 May 1941, in Box 57, folder "Justice: Hoover, Edgar. 1937–40," PSF/FDR; Hoover to Watson, 15 May 1941, Box 5, folder 9, JL.

10   Roosevelt quoted in Charles, "Political Surveillance," 225, 228.

11   Charles, "Political Surveillance," 226; U.S. Attorney B. Howard Caughan to Special Agent in Charge Indianapolis E. J. Wynn, 17 July, Drayton to director FBI, 20 September, and Hoover to SAC Indiana, 22 September, all 1941 and in GPNF; Nye to Haase, 14 January 1942, encl with Hoover, memo to assistant attorney general James H. Rowe, 28 May 1942, JHR; Charles, "Anti-interventionist Movement," 168, 173, 183–85.

12   Doenecke, "Non-Interventionism of the Left," 224, 226, 229; Barnes, *Battling the Crime Wave,* 1, 115; Special Agent in Charge, Albany, 23 January 1941, quoted in Charles, "Anti-Interventionist Movement," 282; Moser, *Twisting the Lion's Tail,* 118.

13   Robins, *Alien Ink,* 77, 80, 85, 87, 91, 96, 99, 413–48; Morgan, *FDR,* 679–83; Summers, *Official and Confidential,* 92; Mann quoted in Weiss, "Perversion," 476.

14   Hoover, *Masters of Deceit,* 53–66; Biddle memo to Hoover, 29 May 1942, Hoover memo to attorney general, 1 June 1942, both in Box 1, SCFBI. On the iconic standing and substantial sales of *Masters of Deceit,* see Warren Hinckle, review of Joseph L. Schott, *No Left Turns* (New York: Praeger, 1975), unidentified clipping in Box 5, folder 8, JL, and Powers, *Secrecy and Power,* 343.

15   O'Reilly, "Roosevelt Administration," 81, 90; Goodman, *The Committee,* 110, 113–14.

16   Black, *Casting Her Own Shadow,* 149; ER to Arthur Grafflin, 3 December 1955, in Black, ed., *Courage,* 269; Morgan, *FDR,* 670–73; Goodwin, *No Ordinary Time,* 420–21; Franklin D. Roosevelt, Jr., foreword in Lash, *Love, Eleanor,* viii.

17   SAC reports from Memphis, 13 November 1942, and Huntington, W.Va., 7 January 1943, ERF 411–12, 422; Howard W. Odum, *Race and Rumors of Race* (Chapel Hill: University of North Carolina Press, 1943), cited in Wynn, *Afro-American,* 110; Hoover quoted in O'Reilly, "Roosevelt Administration and Black America," 22.

18   O'Reilly, *Racial Matters,* 14; O'Reilly, "Herbert Hoover," 51; Du Bois quoted in Lewis, *Du Bois,* 470; Wynn, *Afro-American,* 103.

19   Duberman, *Robeson,* 253; O'Reilly, "Roosevelt Administration and Black America," 21; Reed, "FBI, MOWM, and CORE," 473; Hoover to Pa Watson, 19 June 1941, Box 5, folder 9, JL; Hoover to Pa Watson, 29 September 1943, OF 10, 10b, Box 21, FDR; Hill, *FBI's RACON,* xvii; Banister quoted in Washburn, *A Question of Sedition,* 170.

20   Washburn, "Hoover and Black Press," 32; Rowe memo for attorney general, 16 April 1943, Box 33, and Rowe to FDR, 15 April 1943, Box 34, JHR.

21   Kornweibel, "Black on Black," 129–31; Joint e-mail to author from FBI historian John F. Fox and former FBI historian Susan Rosenfeld, 11 May 2006; John A. Salmond, "The CCC and the Negro," *JAH* 52 (June 1965): 75–88; Sitkoff, *New Deal for Blacks,* 300; *Nation* quoted in Washburn, *A Question of Sedition,* 171.

CHAPTER 8   Gestapo Fears and the Intelligence Schism, 1940–1975

1   Rhodri Jeffreys-Jones, "Why Was the CIA Established in 1947?" *Intelligence and National Security* 12 (January 1997): 23–24, 28; Kendall, "Function of Intelligence," 548; Nash, *Conservative Intellectual Movement,* 230.

2   Crane, "Foreword," Civil Rights Federation, *The Facts Concerning the FBI Raids in Detroit* (pamphlet, 1940), JLC.

3   Williams, "Without Understanding," 366–72; *Nation*, 2 March 1940; *Philadelphia Inquirer*, 4 March 1940; Hoover to attorney general, 4 March 1940, Box 93, folder 6, RHJ; Malvina C. Thompson (ER's secretary) to attorney general, 23 February 1940, Box 93, folder 6, RHJ; Beard and Holtzoff quoted in Lowenthal, *FBI*, 301; Denny in *Columbus (Ohio) Citizen*, 29 February 1940, and in *Washington News*, 11 March 1940.

4   Wheeler quoted in *Philadelphia Inquirer*, 31 May 1940; Breitman, "Allied War Effort and Jews," 137, and *Official Secrets*, 225, 227, 229, 231.

5   Jeffreys-Jones, *Cloak and Dollar*, 157; Truman, *Memoirs*, 1:157; Donovan memo to Roosevelt, 23 February 1945, folder "OSS. Donovan—Intelligence Services," Box 15, RAC. Tom Troy, a former official historian of the CIA, gave an authoritative account of the *Tribune* leak in an article published in 1986: Troy, "Knifing of the OSS," 97–98. Two years later, historian Athan Theoharis offered the undocumented observation that Hoover "saw to it that Donovan's proposal was leaked to a sympathetic news source, *Chicago Tribune* reporter Willard Edwards": Theoharis and Cox, *Boss*, 189.

6   Clark quoted in Rudgers, *Creating the Secret State*, 79; Chiles memo to Hoover, 2 October 1945, *Emergence of the Intelligence Establishment*, 55; Truman and Elsey quoted in Jeffreys-Jones, *CIA and American Democracy*, 29–30; Alsops column in *WP*, 29 April 1946.

7   Theoharis, *Comprehensive Guide*, 4; memos, Sidney W. Souers to President Truman, 17 April, Tamm to Hoover, 10 August, Leahy to Vandenberg, 12 August, and Hoover to Attorney General Tom C. Clark, 12 August, all 1946 and in *Emergence of the Intelligence Establishment*, 276, 296, 298, 300; Ryan, *Barbie*, 57; *Washington News*, 17 April 1948.

8   Dulles, *Craft*, 72; Colby reported in memo by director of CIA Mid-Career Training Course, 23 May 1975, CIA-CD RDP80-00536A000400060001-5; Helms in answer to a question following the director's state of the agency address, 30 June 1972, CIA-CD RDP82M00311R000100210001-8; Hoover, handwritten comments on letter, Helms to Hoover, 26 February 1970, quoted in Riebling, *Wedge*, 254.

9   Statement for Historical Staff, CIA, by William J. Kelly, 10 November 1970, CIA-CD RDP90-00708R000200130001-3; *New York Daily News*, 26 May 1965; *Schenectady (N.Y.) Gazette*, 27 October 1975.

10 Montague, *Smith*, 254–56; Felix Johnson memo to DCI, 26 June 1950, CIA-CD RDP67-00059A000400170013-5; CIA minute: "**** (FBI) Interest in Flying Saucers," 11 December 1952, CIA-CD RDP79-01041A000100010001-3.

11 "1947" (undated draft of history of the CIA Security Division, probably the work of the CIA's history office staff), 13, CIA-CD RDP78-04007A000300010034-1. Also, "History of Field Offices," n.d., 5, CIA-CD RDP78-04007A000900230010-7; Memo, Security Division, CIA, to Col. D. H. Galloway, on conference with FBI officials, 26 September 1946, CIA-CD RDP78-04007A000300050016-7.

12 Hillenkoetter letter of 18 November 1947 quoted in "1947" (above), 15.

13 "History of Field Offices," n.d., 6, CIA-CD RDP78-04007A000900230010-7; "1947" (above), 16 (blank).

14 (CIA) Chief Instructor, CI/OPS to CI Staff and expurgated recipients, 6 January 1965, CIA-CD RDP78-04092A000300030005-7; Theoharis, *Comprehensive Guide*, 373; nomenclatively deleted official of the Office of the General Counsel, CIA, memo for the record, 20 December 1976, CIA-CD RDP79-0049A000700080001-5; CIA Director of Security Charles W. Kane, memo for deputy director for administration, 16 June 1975,

CIA-CD RDP83B00823R000800020005-3; assistant legislative counsel, CIA, memo for the record, 14 June 1971, CIA-CD RDP83B00823R000100120002-2; CIA/RAD Weekly Report, "Retirement Planning—FBI," November–December 1976, CIA-CD RDP79-00498A000500160005-4; Riebling, *Wedge*, 341, 447; Masse, *Domestic Intelligence*, 13.

CHAPTER 9 Anachronism as Myth and Reality, 1945–1972

1 Schlesinger, *Thousand Days*, 113; Turner, *Hoover's FBI*, 3; Flamm, *Law and Order*, 2, 126; *Daily Worker*, n.d., quoted in Powers, *Broken*, 193; Lamphere, *FBI-KGB War*, 10–12, 134–35, 144; Granatstein and Stafford, *Spy Wars*, 63–64; Benson and Warner, eds., *Venona*, xv, xix; Weinstein and Vassiliev, *Haunted Wood*, 172; Hoover quoted in Sibley, *Red Spies*, 192; "Report [to FBI director] of Hugh H. Clegg and Robert J. Lamphere covering interviews with Klaus Fuchs in London, England," 4 June 1950, 4, 10, 43, 44, in FMS; Williams, *Klaus Fuchs*, 1–4, 165; Goodman, "Who," 6; Goodman, "Grandfather," 1, 15, 21; Haynes and Klehr, *Venona*, 48–51.

2 Theoharis, *Chasing Spies*, 56.

3 Whitaker, "Cold War Alchemy," 177–78, 206.

4 Legnitto, *Rosenberg File*; Theoharis, *Chasing Spies*, 81–82.

5 McCarthy quoted in Rovere, *McCarthy*, 11; Weinstein, *Perjury*, 300; Lowenthal, "Venona and Alger Hiss," 115.

6 Schrecker, *Many Are the Crimes*, 203; Heale, "Beyond the 'Age of McCarthy,'" 133–38.

7 Rovere, *McCarthy*, 3, 23.

8 Black, *Casting Her Own Shadow*, 149; O'Reilly, "Adlai," 46, 58; Keller, *Liberals and Hoover*, 72; Theoharis, "How the FBI Gaybaited Stevensen," 617, 635; Schrecker, *Age of McCarthyism*, 22.

9 *Cincinnati Post*, 28 March 1950; [Name redacted] to Hoover, n.d., accompanying Hoover to [name redacted], 5 April 1950, FBIWF 121-23278-134; director's notation on memo, assistant director D. Milton Ladd to director, 25 April 1950, FBIWF 121-23278-[128?].

10 Johnson, *Lavender Scare*, 108–12, 202, 208; Theoharis, ed., *Secret Files*, 77–79, 357–78.

11 Hoover memo to assistant directors FBI, 18 March 1953, in Theoharis, ed., *Secret Files*, 259; *Chicago Tribune*, 23 July 1953; Charles, "FBI and Gay Subversion," 3; Woods, *Fulbright*, 184–85; Goodman, *The Committee*, 416; Gerard, "Program of Cooperation," ii–iii, 57.

12 Church 2, 45–46.

13 Schrecker, *Many Are the Crimes*, 208, 212; Davis, *Assault on the Left*, 3; Hall, *Oxford Companion to Supreme Court*, 799–800, 947; Trohan quoted in O'Reilly, "Origins," 383; Vaughan, "Spies," 354–58, 366, 370; Bayley, *McCarthy and the Press*, 217; Theoharis, "FBI and American Legion," 280, 282.

14 Diamond, *Compromised Campus*, 151ff; Powers, *Not Without Honor*, 225–27; Davis, *Assault on the Left*, 3, 6; author's personal observations and conversations with Herbert Aptheker (1965) and Philip Foner (1964, 1968).

15 Powers, *Secrecy and Power*, 307–8, and "FBI in Popular Culture," 284; Jeffreys-Jones, "Historiography of the FBI."

16 Kennedy, *Enemy Within*, xiv, 318; Schlesinger, *Robert Kennedy*, 269.

17 Clark, *Crime in America*, 81; Gentry, *Hoover*, 328–29; Schlesinger, *Robert Kennedy*,

266n; Theoharis, *Sex, Crime* (for a debunking of some of the wilder theories), 16; Webster quoted in Marx, *Undercover*, 1.

18 Kefauver Committee report quoted in Woodiwiss, *Organized Crime,* 22; Bell, "Crime as an American Way of Life" (*The Antioch Review,* 1953), reprinted in Bell, *End of Ideology,* 127–50, at 139, 141ff; Gentry, *Hoover,* 327, 452–53; Powers, *Secrecy and Power,* 335. The New York anti-communist taskforce engaged in contra-subversion activities, but also had the more serious job of countering Soviet-bloc espionage.

19 Kennedy, *Enemy Within,* 166, 167, 174, 191; Friedman, *Crime and Punishment,* 273; Clark, *Crime in America,* 19.

20 Flamm, *Law and Order,* 10, 162; *FBI's Ten Most Wanted Fugitives Program,* 3, 47.

21 Navasky, *Kennedy Justice,* xv, 9; Cook, "Organized Crime: The Strange Reluctance," 155; *Alleged Assassination Plots,* 74–77; Carter quoted in Hersh, *Camelot,* 311.

22 Theoharis, *Sex, Crime,* 148–49, 158, 162; Friedman, *Crime and Punishment,* 267; Graham, "Contemporary Crime," 499–502.

23 John W. Fain report, 12 May 1960, and James P. Hosty, Jr., report, 10 September 1963, both in Warren Commission File, 1963–76, FCP.

24 Epstein, *Legend,* 48, 253; *Lynchburg (Va.) Advance,* 20 November 1969; Nelson, "Review Board," 212; *WP,* 21 May 1976; Posner, *Case Closed,* 407; Newman, *Oswald and CIA,* 429.

25 Davis, *Assault on the Left,* 6; Sullivan quoted in Davis, *Spying on America,* 32; Church 3, 15.

26 Sullivan report of 8 January 1964 and Hoover quoted in Garrow, *FBI and King,* 105, 107; McKnight, *Last Crusade,* 1–2, 5.

27 FBI memo of 30 July 1964 quoted in Church 3, 18; Davis, *Spying on America,* 82; May, *Informant,* 292–93; Rowe testimony in Church Hearings 6, 118.

28 Drabble, "COINTELPRO," 525–26; Powers, *Secrecy and Power,* 407, 412–15.

29 Church 2, 251; Hoover in *FBI Law Enforcement Bulletin,* 1 February 1966, excerpted in Box 127, folder "FBI Newsclippings, 1966–2006," GR; Church Hearings 6, 434–39.

30 Helms memo to Johnson enclosing CIA report, 15 November 1967, in folder "U.S. Peace groups—International Connections," Intelligence File, NSF/LBJL.

31 White House instruction quoted in Dallek, *Flawed Giant,* 490.

CHAPTER 10 A Crisis of American Democracy, 1972–1975

1 Gentry, *Hoover,* 387n; Cook, *FBI Nobody Knows,* 411, 423, and *The Unfinished Story of Alger Hiss* (New York: Morrow, 1958); Stout, *The Doorbell Rang,* 8; *Ramparts* press release, 27 July 1966, Box 127, GR; Turner, *Hoover's FBI; NYT,* 24 April 1966; *Time,* 15 December 1975; *Newsweek,* 5 January 1976.

2 Feldstein, "Muckraking Model," 111; *Time,* 15 December 1975; *Newsweek,* 5 January 1976; *Los Angeles Herald-Dispatch,* 17 June 1971.

3 Sullivan, *Bureau,* 239, 262; Kelley, *Kelley,* 18–19; Epstein, *Agency of Fear,* 216–17; *Boston Globe,* 20 August 1978.

4 Hoover letter of 7 October 1971 in Watters and Gillers, eds., *Investigating the FBI,* 415–23; *Broken Seals* (pamphlet, Alexandria, Va.: Western Goals, 1980), 12, 69, 101, JLC.

5 Pincus, "Bureau's Budget," 76, 81.

6 Kelley, *Kelley,* 21; Axelrod and Phillips, eds., *Cops,* 146.

7 *LAT,* 2 December 1975; Hoover quoted in Reeves, *Nixon,* 237.

8 Kutler, *Wars of Watergate,* 187–88, 210; Olson, *Watergate,* 9; Woodward, *Secret Man,* 46–47, 105–6; Elliff, *Reform of FBI,* 4.

9 Olmsted, *Challenging,* 17; *Washington Star-News,* 16, 21 November 1974; Elliff, *Reform,* 56; Kelley quoted in *Chicago Tribune,* 19 November 1974.

10 Olmsted, *Challenging,* 37; DeLoach quoted in Kessler, *Bureau,* 188.

11 *Congressional Record,* 94 Cong., 1 sess., 23 January 1975, 16 June 1975, H 278, H 5543, and 11 June 1975, S 10310; Pike Hearings 1, 281–87, 312; *NYT,* 20 February 1975, 26 February, 29 April 1976; Johnson, *Season of Inquiry,* 216; Abzug quoted in Subcommittee on Government Information and Individual Rights press release, 25 February 1976, folder "Intelligence—Interception of Non-Verbal Communications by FBI and NSA: General (1)," Box 15, LL.

12 *NYT,* 20 May 1975. Thomas H. Brennan, Chief of the Freedom of Information–Privacy Act Branch, FBI, told Lash "the only record we have concerning you since your request of January 16, 1978, is correspondence pertaining to your previous FOIPA request. . . . Copies will be made available to you, if you so desire": Brennan to Lash, 9 February 1981. On 2 April 1981, Lash met the Justice Department's Quinlan J. Shea, Jr., who showed him FBI files portraying him as an admirer of the former American presidential candidate and opponent of the Vietnam War George S. McGovern, and of the left-wing British former cabinet minister Anthony Wedgwood Benn. He also showed him five files detailing his relationship with the late Eleanor Roosevelt. Lash's memo of this meeting and the Brennan letter are both in Folder 7, Box 5, JL. Cf Robins, *Alien Ink,* 143.

13 *NYT,* 12 August and 21 December 1975; Levi quoted in *Chicago Sun-Times,* 7 February 1976.

14 *WP,* 24 February 1976; Pike Report, 262–63; Church 2, 297, 315–39.

15 Douglas Charles, one of Theoharis's MA students, identified the following historians of the FBI as having come from the same stable: Susan Dion, Patrick Jung, Francis MacDonnell, Kenneth O'Reilly, and David Williams; Charles, e-mail to author, 15 January 2006.

16 Drabble, "COINTELPRO," 536–37; Church 3, 16; Church Hearings 6, 22; interview with former Church Committee Professional Staff Member Loch Johnson, 22 April 2006, and subsequent e-mail, 12 May 2006; Smist, "Congress Oversees," 41, 439; Garrow, *FBI and King,* 226.

CHAPTER 11 Reform and Its Critics, 1975–1980

1 Transcript, *Face the Nation* (CBS News), 21 December 1975, in Box 63, RHN; *U.S. News and World Report,* 8 March 1976, 12.

2 Elliff, *Reform,* x, 3, 8, 13, 58; "Status of Laws Affecting Provision by International Communications Carriers of Communications to U.S. Government," n.d. but enclosed with correspondence dated 5 April 1976, in folder "Intelligence—Interception of Non-Verbal Communications by FBI and NSA: General (2)," Box 15, LL; *NYT,* 12 December 1975.

3 Church Hearings 6, 314, 317, 332; Transcript, *Face the Nation* (CBS News), 21 December 1975, in Box 63, RHN.

4 Executive Order 11905, 22: CIA-CD RDP81-00896R100100003-4; *WP,* 7, 11 March 1976; *U.S. News and World Report,* 8 March 1976.

5 Memo, Duval to Jack Marsh, 23 October 1975, in folder "Intelligence Community Co-ordinating Group—General," Box 57, JEC; Kutler, *Vietnam War,* 104; *LAT,* 17, 29 February 1976.

6 *Washington News,* 25 October 1966; *Human Events,* 4 November 1978, 8, 15 December 1979, 2 August 1980; Reagan, broadcasts on 15 June and 27 September 1977, in *In His Own Hand,* 125–26; Group Research Report, 29 June 1977, 28 February 1978, Box 126, GR; Philbrick, *I Led Three Lives: Citizen, "Communist," Counterspy* (New York: McGraw-Hill, 1952).

7 *NYT,* 24 June 1976; Buchen, memo for the president, 26 June 1976, in folder "Justice—FBI: General (2)," PWB; Church 2, 110; Wills in *Baltimore Sun,* 11 August 1976; Transcript, *Face the Nation* (CBS News), 8 August 1976, in Box 63, RHN; 2006 correspondence with a confidential source; *WP,* 18 April 1976; *New York Daily News,* 13 May 1976; Felt quoted in *Newsweek,* 30 August 1976; *Human Events,* 2 August 1980.

8 Memo on Anna Mae Aquash, Robert H. Feldkamp to Dick Parsons, 7 June 1976, with enclosed FBI press release, 26 May 1976, in file "Federal Bureau of Investigation in General," Box 7, RDP; Brown quotations from *Washington Star,* 24 May 1976; James Goodman in *Oregon Times Magazine* (September 1976), 15.

9 Michael Raoul-Duval memo for Jack Marsh, 23 October 1975, and agenda/proposals for meeting on the intelligence community attended by Henry Kissinger, Donald Rumsfeld, Levi (but not Kelley), Bush, Jack Marsh, Buchen, and Brent Scowcroft enclosed with Marsh memo, 30 January 1976, both in folder "Intelligence Community Decision Meetings, Jan 1976," Box 57, JEC.

10 Undated and anonymous memo summarizing 30 August 1976 report from the Office of Professional Responsibility, in folder "Justice—FBI: Allegations Against Clarence Kelley—General (1)," Box 22, PWB; *Newsweek,* 30 August 1976; *WP,* 1, 10, 12 September 1976; *Washington Star,* 7, 17 September 1976; *Christian Science Monitor,* 2 September, 15 October 1976; original text of Kelley speech, scheduled for release on 15 October 1976 but subsequently modified, with White House interception notes, and Buchen memo for president via Dick Cheney, 28 September 1976, both in folder "Justice—FBI: General (2)," Box 23, PWB; UPI and AP reports, 13 August 1976, folder "FBI," Box H25, PFCR; *NYT,* 6 September 1976; "Kelley's Perquisites," *New Republic,* 18 September 1976, 5–6.

11 Carter statements 24 March, 17 August 1977, and 10 January, 31 July 1979, APP; Hogue, *Nomination of FBI Director,* 2–3.

12 *Baltimore Sun,* 12 January 1976; *Wall Street Journal,* 4 March 1976; Transcript, *Face the Nation* (CBS News), 8 August 1976, in Box 63, RHN; Elliff, *Reform of FBI,* 10–11; *WP,* 8 May 2003; *Human Events,* 16 February 1980.

13 Wilson, *Investigators,* 29; *U.S. News and World Report,* 26 June 1982; Marx statement, 25 February 1981, in *FBI Undercover Guidelines,* 47.

14 *U.S. News and World Report,* 8 March 1976; *Chicago Tribune,* 15 November 1976; Shull, *American Civil Rights,* 41, 122–23; Smith, "Black Appointed Officials," 375–76; Mitchell quoted in Dumbrell, *Carter Presidency,* 89.

CHAPTER 12 Mission Regained, 1981–1993

1 *Broken Seals* (pamphlet, Alexandria, Va.: Western Goals, 1980), 69, JLC; Theoharis, *Secret Files,* 115–17; Reagan statements, 14 October 1982, 26 and 28 July 1983, 2 November 1987, APP.

2 Reagan quoted in *WP*, 16 April 1981; Friedman and Friedman, *Free to Choose*, 268; remarks of Congressman Leo C. Zeferetti, chairman, Select Committee on Narcotics Abuse and Control, 30 March, 1982, in *DEA/FBI Reorganization*, 5; Mary Anastasia O'Grady, "Drugs Beget Thugs in the Americas," *Wall Street Journal*, 28 April 2006; Webster quoted in Wannall, "Limbo," 453; *FBI and DEA: Merger or Enhanced Cooperation?* 1; Jacobs Panel report, Web site of the National Counterintelligence Center.

3 *San Francisco Chronicle*, 17 November 2002; Gelbspan, *Break-ins*, 3–4; *WT*, 29 January 1988; *Human Events*, 13 February 1988; *CISPES and FBI Counterterrorism Investigations*, 119, 169, Appendix 4; *NYT*, 1 May 1987; Senate report quoted in *St. Louis Post-Dispatch*, 1 August 1989.

4 Fitch, "Library Awareness," 101–6.

5 Freeh, *My FBI*, 127; Blum, *Gangland*, 327, 329; *Independent*, 21 June 2002.

6 Mackenzie on *60 Minutes*, CBS television show, 14 July 2002, transcript, LexisNexis; *Boston Globe*, 7 May 2003; Lehr, *Black Mass*, xv, 211; *NYT*, 6 December 2002, 21 November 2003.

7 Reagan statements, 13 March and 29 June 1981, APP; Dumbrell, *Carter Presidency*, 89; *FBI Affirmative Action*, 226, 228; Shull, *American Civil Rights*, 230; Smith, "Black Appointed Officials," 373.

8 Quotations and figures in *FBI Affirmative Action*, 2, 25, 226. See also Shrestha, *Changing Demographic Profile*, 20–21.

9 FBI Female Special Agent Web site, accessed June 2004; Powers, *Broken*, 299; Wang and Jaquith, *FBI vs. Women*, 13; Greene, *Presidency of Bush*, 74, 156–59; Kessler, *FBI*, 400; William J. Clinton exchange with reporters, 19 July 1993, APP; undated clipping from *WT* in GR.

10 DeLong, *Special Agent*, 9, 28, 226; Anderson, *Reno*, 252; Kessler, *FBI*, 409, 417; Theoharis, *FBI Guide*, 136; FBI Facts and Figures 2003 Web site, accessed June 2004.

11 FBI Civil Rights/Hate Web site, accessed June 2004.

12 Hoover, memorandum for Mr. Edwards, 25 May 1935, FBI Electronic Reading Room; Pike Hearings 1, 285–86; Inspector General report on Sibel Edwards case, January 2004, Department of Justice Web site, 4; Freeh, *My FBI*, 138; *Guardian*, 13 April 2006; Clinton statement, 12 December 1993, APP; *WT*, 27 August 2002; Jentleson, *Foreign Policy*, 7; Freeh, "Message from the Director," *FBI's Ten Most Wanted Fugitives Program*, 1.

CHAPTER 13 Strife and Slippage, 1993–2001

1 Moynihan, *Secrecy*, 9–10, 170; Daniel Franklin, "Freeh's Reign," American Prospect online, 1–14 January 2002, 8; Clinton, *My Life*, 763.

2 Anderson, *Reno*, 243; Giuliani quoted in Walsh, "Last Case," 3; William J. Clinton news conference, 11 February 1993, APP; Clinton, *My Life*, 763–64; Blumenthal, *Clinton Wars*, 286; Freeh, *My FBI*, 18.

3 Reagan statements on 30 November 1985, 2 November 1987, APP; Wise, *Nightmover*, 179–80; Stober and Hoffman, *Convenient Spy*, 42, 70, 168, 269, 329–30; Powers, *Broken*, 418–20; Lee, *My Country*, 1, 224–25, 330; *NYT*, 16, 20 May 1999, 3 June 2006; Bill Mesler, "The Spy Who Wasn't," *Nation*, 9–16 August 1999, 13; Freeh, *My FBI*, 219; *WP*, 3, 5 July 2000.

4 Affidavit sworn on 16 February 2001 by special agent Stefan A. Pluta, U.S. district court, eastern district of Virginia, Alexandria division, in support of arrest and search

warrants in *United States v. Hanssen,* FAS; Vise, *Mole,* 96, 216 (quoting Hanssen), 221, 240; *Independent,* 22 February 2001; *WP,* 27 February 2001; *NYT,* 15 August 2003; *Houston Chronicle,* 15 August 2003; Clarke, *Against All Enemies,* 104, 109, 113–16; Freeh, *My FBI,* 18; Powers, *Broken,* 417, 423.

5 *NYT,* 17 May 2001; Theoharis, *Guide,* 4–5; Grassley quoted in *Christian Science Monitor,* 25 June 2001; Daniel Franklin, "Freeh's Reign," American Prospect online, 1–14 January 2002, 3.

6 Statements of Senators Leahy and Hatch, 20 June 2001, *Oversight of the FBI,* 1–8; *NYT,* 17 May 2001.

CHAPTER 14 9/11 and the Quest for National Unity

1 CNN.com, 20 July 2003; *NYT,* 20 July 2003; *Newsweek,* 20 October 2003; *Economist,* 29 March 2003; Testimony before the Senate Judiciary Committee of John C. Gannon, 2 May 2006, in SN, 8 May 2006.

2 Ashcroft on *This Week,* ABC television show, 2 June 2002, LexisNexis.

3 Rice and Pavitt quoted in Hersh, "Missed Messages," 40, 42.

4 Kennedy's remark to Richard Bissell quoted in Wyden, *Bay of Pigs,* 311; bin Laden quoted in Gunaratna, *Inside Al Qaeda,* 1; Griffin, *Omissions,* 20, 58; Benjamin and Simon, *Sacred Terror,* 40, 142; *9/11 Commission Report,* 160; *NYT,* 4, 9 April 2004, 3 October 2006; *WT,* 15 April 2004.

5 Benjamin, *Sacred Terror,* 393; Bazan, *Foreign Intelligence Surveillance Act,* 1, 87; *9/11 Commission Report,* 273–76; *NYT,* 21, 31 March 2006.

6 Ashcroft address to the House Judiciary Committee paraphrased in AP report on Yahoo, 5 June 2003.

7 SN, 31 May 2002; *USA Today,* 8 October 2003; Doyle, *Administrative Subpoenas,* 3; Dratel quoted in *WP,* 13 December 2003; *Congressional Record* (Senate), 20 November 2003, S15275; Department of Justice fact sheet on NSI Guidelines, 5 November 2003, FAS; *WT,* 9 June 2005; "Counterterrorism Intelligence Capabilities and Performance Prior to 9-11," *Report of the Subcommittee on Terrorism and Homeland Security,* House Permanent Select Committee on Intelligence, July 2002, FindLaw; *WP,* 22 March 2004, 6 November 2005; Office of Management and Budget FY2006 Budget priorities, FAS; Cumming, "Intelligence Reform Implementation," 1.

8 *Independent,* 7 June 2002; Miller, *Cell,* 333; Bush message to Congress, 18 June 2002, WhiteHouse.gov; *NYT,* 25 November 2002; Hulnick, *Keeping Us Safe,* 18, 117, 167; Conley, "Renaissance of Managerial Presidency," 305, 319–22; Drew, "Power Grab"; Norton, *Strauss,* 171; Relyea and Seifert, *Information Sharing for Homeland Security,* 6.

9 Mosley quoted in *Observer Review,* 18 August 2002; *NYT,* 15 May, 22 March, 9 April 2003, 23 March, 1 May, 30 June, 18 August (quoting Democrats) 2004, 27 May, 3 July 2005; *Economist,* 29 March 2003; Robert O'Harrow, Jr., *No Place to Hide* (New York: Free Press, 2005), 40, 131, 204, 248–49.

10 Fine testimony to Subcommittee on Technology, Terrorism, and Government Information, 9 October 2002, LexisNexis; Grassley on *This Week,* ABC television show, 2 June 2002, LexisNexis; Rowley testimony to Senate Judiciary Committee, 6 June 2002, Web site of the committee; *NYT,* 3 July 2003, 2 January 2005; Griffin, *Omissions,* 91.

11 Department of Justice Inspector General's "Review of the FBI's Actions in Connection with Allegations Raised by Contract Linguist Sibel Edmonds" (Unclassified Summary,

citizen.org Web site), 3, 9; transcript of *60 Minutes*, 27 October 2002, LexisNexis; *Village Voice*, 21 April 2005.

12   *WP*, 19 June 2002; Department of Justice Inspector General Edmonds review, 4; *9/11 Commission Report*, 473n25; *NYT*, 28 September 2004.

13   *LAT*, 11 December 2004; Cox News Service, 11 July 2003, and Mark Bullock interviewed on National Public Radio, 19 August 2003, both LexisNexis; 2003 FBI employee statistics for 30 June 2003, accessed June 2004 on FBI Web site; *Building Capabilities*, 203, 63–64; Toronto *Globe and Mail*, 10 July 2004; report by Washington correspondent Barbara Ferguson in Jedda, Saudi Arabia, *Arab News*, 11 February 2007; *NYT*, 10 October 2006; *WP*, 11 October 2006.

14   *Report of the Joint Inquiry into the Terrorist Attacks of September 11, 2001*, 107 Cong., 2 sess. (2002), xi, xiii, xv; *NYT*, 25 July 2003; Hulnick, *Keeping Us Safe*, 189.

15   *LAT*, 28 May 2002; *WP*, 4, 5 June 2002; *NYT*, 30 April 2003; SN, 30 December 2003; Relyea and Seifert, *Information Sharing for Homeland Security*, 7, 9, 11.

16   C. H. Rolph, "The British Analogy," in Watters and Gillers, eds., *Investigating the FBI*, 352–53, 366; Masse, *Domestic Intelligence in the United Kingdom*, summary and 14–15; Fortescue, *European View*, 30; Chalk and Rosenau, *Confronting the "Enemy Within*,*"* 2, 55–56; *NYT*, 3 October 2003; *Gloucestershire Echo*, 1 April 2004; *Independent*, 24 November 2004; Occhipinti, *Toward a European FBI?*

17   Thomas H. Kean, *The Politics of Inclusion* (New York: Free Press, 1988); Kean quoted in *NYT*, 14 April 2004; *NYT*, 29 August, 21 December 2004, 10 June 2005; *9/11 Commission Report*, 423, 425; Cumming, *FBI Intelligence Reform Since September 11, 2001*; *Commission on WMD Report*, Chapter 10, 468.

18   *NYT*, 14 April, 29 August 2004; Griffin, *New Pearl Harbor*, xxi–xxii, and *9/11 Commission Report*, 281, 283; Hulnick, *Keeping Us Safe*, 189.

19   Cumming and Masse, *Intelligence Reform Implementation*, 5, 7, 17–18, 21, 25, 26, 29–30; Mueller testimony to Senate Judiciary Committee, 6 June 2005, LexisNexis; Jean Kumagai, "Mission Impossible?" Institute of Electrical and Electronics Engineers (IEEE) Spectrum Online, 7 April 2003; Baginski quoted in Elsa Walsh, "Learning to Spy," *New Yorker*, 8 November 2004, 97; *NYT*, 17, 18 February 2005.

20   *NYT*, 26 December 2003, 31 August, 1, 6 September, 29 October, 21 December 2004, 28 January, 2 August 2005, 14 April, 29 May 2006; O'Grady quoted in *NYT*, 23 February 2005.

21   National security letter quoted in *WP*, 6 November 2005; *NYT*, 29 September 2005; *WP*, 25 October 2005, 19 April 2006.

22   *NYT*, 19 October 2005; *Baltimore Sun*, 2 May 2006; April 2006 interview with anonymous Department of Justice lawyer.

BIBLIOGRAPHY

Abernathy, David. *And the Walls Came Tumbling Down.* New York: Harper and Row, 1989.

Adamic, Louis. *Dynamite: The Story of Class Violence in America.* New York: Viking, 1931.

Adams, Graham. "Burns, William John (1861–1932)," in *American National Biography.*

Aldrich, Richard J. *Espionage, Security, and Intelligence in Britain, 1945–1970.* Manchester: Manchester University Press, 1998.

Alleged Assassination Plots Involving Foreign Leaders. An Interim Report of the Select Committee to Study Governmental Operations with Respect to Intelligence Activities. 94 Cong., 1 sess., 1975.

Alperovitz, Gar. *The Decision to Use the Atomic Bomb.* New York: Vintage/Random House, 1996.

Amer, Mildred L. *Black Members of the United States Congress, 1870–2005.* Washington, D.C.: Congressional Research Service, 2005.

American National Biography. New York: Oxford University Press, 1999.

Anderson, Paul. *Janet Reno: Doing the Right Thing.* New York: John Wiley, 1994.

Andrew, Christopher, and David Dilks, eds. *The Missing Dimension: Governments and Intelligence Communities in the Twentieth Century.* London: Macmillan, 1984.

Angevine, Robert G. "Gentlemen Do Read Each Other's Mail: American Intelligence in the Interwar Era." *Intelligence and National Security* 7 (April 1992): 1–29.

Ansley, Norman. "The United States Secret Service: An Administrative History." *Journal of Criminal Law, Criminology, and Political Science* 47 (May–June 1956): 93–109.

Attorney General of the United States. *Annual Report.* 1907, 1908. FBI Electronic Reading Room.

Axelrod, Alan, and Charles Phillips, eds. *Cops, Crooks, and Criminologists: An International Dictionary of Law Enforcement.* New York: Facts on File, 1996.

Bacon, Donald C., and others, eds. *The Encyclopedia of the United States Congress.* 4 vols. New York: Simon and Schuster, 1995.

Badger, Anthony J. *The New Deal: The Depression Years, 1933–1940.* New York: Noonday, 1989.

Barkum, Michael. "Millennial Groups and Law Enforcement Agencies: The Lessons of Waco." *Terrorism and Political Violence* 6 (1994): 75–95.

Barnes, Harry Elmer. *Battling the Crime Wave: Applying Sense and Science to the Repression of Crime.* Boston: Stratford, 1931.

Barron, John. *Operation Solo: The FBI's Man in the Kremlin.* London: Robert Hale, 1997.

Batvinis, Raymond J. "'In the Beginning' . . . An Examination of the Development of the Federal Bureau of Investigation's Counterintelligence Program, 1936 to 1941." Ph.D. diss., Catholic University of America, 2001.

———. *The Origins of FBI Counterintelligence.* Lawrence: University Press of Kansas, 2007.

Baughman, Urbanus E. *Secret Service Chief.* New York: Harper and Row, 1962.

Bayley, Edwin R. *Joe McCarthy and the Press.* Madison: University of Wisconsin Press, 1981.

Bazan, Elizabeth B. *The Foreign Intelligence Surveillance Act: An Overview of the Statutory Framework and Recent Judicial Decisions.* Washington, D.C.: Congressional Research Service, 2004.

———. *The U.S. Foreign Intelligence Surveillance Court and the U.S. Foreign Intelligence Surveillance Court of Review: An Overview.* Washington, D.C.: Congressional Research Service, 2007.

Bazan, Elizabeth B., and Brian T. Yeh. *Intelligence Reform and Terrorism Prevention Act of 2004: "Lone Wolf" Amendment to the Foreign Intelligence Surveillance Act.* Washington, D.C.: Congressional Research Service, 2006.

Belknap, Michael. "Uncooperative Federalism: The Failure of the Bureau of Investigation's Intergovernmental Attack on Radicalism." *Publius* 12 (1982): 25–47.

Bell, Daniel. *The End of Ideology.* New York: Free Press, 1962.

Benjamin, Daniel, and Steven Simon. *The Age of Sacred Terror.* New York: Random House, 2002.

Benson, Robert L., and Michael Warner, eds. *Venona: Soviet Espionage and the American Response, 1939–1957.* Washington, D.C.: NSA and CIA, 1996.

Berens, John. "The FBI and Civil Liberties from Franklin Roosevelt to Jimmy Carter: An Overview." *Michigan Academician* 13 (1980): 131–44.

Berman, Jay S. *Police Administration and Progressive Reform: Theodore Roosevelt as Police Commissioner of New York.* New York: Greenwood, 1987.

Bernstein, Barton. "The Road to Watergate and Beyond: The Growth and Abuse of Executive Authority Since 1940." *Law and Contemporary Problems* 40 (1976): 58–86.

Bewley-Taylor, David R. *The United States and International Drug Control, 1909–1997.* London: Pinter, 1999.

Bishop, Joseph B. *Charles Joseph Bonaparte: His Life and Public Services.* New York: Charles Scribner's Sons, 1922.

Black, Allida M. *Casting Her Own Shadow: Eleanor Roosevelt and the Shaping of Postwar Liberalism.* New York: Columbia University Press, 1996.

————, ed. *Courage in a Dangerous World: The Political Writings of Eleanor Roosevelt*. New York: Columbia University Press, 1999.

Blain, William T. "Challenge to the Lawless: The Mississippi Secret Service, 1870–1871." *Journal of Mississippi History* 40 (1978): 119–31.

Blum, Howard. *Gangland: How the FBI Broke the Mob*. London: Hutchinson, 1994.

Blumenthal, Sidney. *The Clinton Wars: An Insider's Account of the White House Years*. London: Viking, 2003.

Bonaparte, Charles J. "Lynch Law and Its Remedy." *Yale Law Journal* 8 (May 1899): 335–43.

Borstelmann, Thomas. *The Cold War and the Color Line: American Race Relations in the Global Arena*. Cambridge, Mass.: Harvard University Press, 2001.

Breitman, Richard. "The Allied War Effort and the Jews, 1942–1943." *Journal of Contemporary History* 20 (January 1985): 135–56.

————. *Official Secrets: What the Nazis Planned, What the British and Americans Knew*. London: Penguin, 1999.

Bruce-Briggs, B. "Another Ride on Tricycle." *Intelligence and National Security* 7 (April 1992): 77–100.

Building Capabilities: The Intelligence Community's National Security Requirements for Diversity of Languages, Skills, and Ethnic and Cultural Understanding. Hearing Before the Permanent Select Committee on Intelligence. 108 Cong., 1 sess., 5 November 2003.

Bunche, Ralph. *The Political Status of the Negro in the Age of FDR*. Edited by Dewey W. Grantham. Chicago: University of Chicago Press, 1973.

Burns, William J. *The Masked War: The Story of a Peril that Threatened the United States by the Man Who Uncovered the Dynamite Conspirators and Sent Them to Jail*. New York: George H. Doran, 1913.

Burrough, Bryan. *Public Enemies: America's Greatest Crime Wave and the Birth of the FBI, 1933–34*. New York: Penguin, 2004.

Caesar, Gene. *Incredible Detective: The Biography of William J. Burns*. Englewood Cliffs, N.J.: Prentice-Hall, 1968.

Candeloro, Dominic. "Louis F. Post and the Red Scare of 1920." *Prologue* 11 (1979): 40–55.

Carper, N. Gordon. "Slavery Revisited: Peonage in the South." *Phylon* 37 (1976): 85–99.

Carr, Robert K. *Federal Protection of Civil Rights: Quest for a Sword*. Ithaca, N.Y.: Cornell University Press, 1947.

————. *The House Committee on Un-American Activities, 1945–1950*. Ithaca, N.Y.: Cornell University Press, 1952.

Carson, Claybourne. *Malcolm X: The FBI File*. New York: Ballantine, 1991.

Cecil, Matthew C. "Seductions of Spin: Public Relations and the FBI Myth." Ph.D. diss., University of Iowa, 2000.

Chafee, Zachariah, Jr. *Free Speech in the United States*. Cambridge, Mass.: Harvard University Press, 1941.

Chalk, Peter, and William Rosenau. *Confronting the "Enemy Within": Security Intelligence, the Police, and Counterterrorism in Four Democracies.* Santa Monica, Calif.: Rand Corporation, 2004.

Charles, Douglas M. "Before the Colonel Arrived: Hoover, Donovan, Roosevelt, and the Origins of American Central Intelligence." *Intelligence and National Security* 20 (June 2005): 225–37.

———. "The FBI, Franklin Roosevelt, and the Anti-Interventionist Movement, 1939–45." Ph.D. diss., University of Edinburgh, 2002.

———. "The FBI and Gay Subversion." Paper, Organization of American Historians annual meeting, 22 April 2006.

———. "Informing FDR: FBI Political Surveillance and the Isolationist-Interventionist Foreign Policy Debates, 1939–1945." *Diplomatic History* 24 (Spring 2000): 211–32.

———. *J. Edgar Hoover and the Anti-Interventionists: FBI Political Surveillance and the Rise of the Domestic Security State, 1939–1945.* Columbus: Ohio State University Press, 2007.

Charles, Douglas M., and John P. Rossi. "FBI Political Surveillance and the Charles Lindbergh Investigation, 1939–1944." *The Historian* 59 (1997): 831–47.

Church 2. Senate. *Intelligence Activities and the Rights of Americans. Book 2, Final Report of the Select Committee to Study Governmental Operations with Respect to Intelligence Activities.* 94 Cong., 2 sess., 1976.

Church 3. Senate. *Supplementary Detailed Staff Reports on Intelligence Activities and the Rights of Americans. Book 3, Final Report of the Select Committee to Study Governmental Operations with Respect to Intelligence Activities.* 94 Cong., 2 sess., 1976.

Church Hearings 6. *Federal Bureau of Investigation. Volume 6, Hearings Before the Select Committee to Study Governmental Operations with Respect to Intelligence Activities of the United States Senate.* 94 Cong., 1 sess., 18, 19 November, and 2, 3, 9, 10, and 11 December 1975.

CISPES and FBI Counterterrorism Investigations. House of Representatives. *Hearings Before the Subcommittee on Civil and Constitutional Rights of the Committee on the Judiciary.* 100 Cong., 2 sess., 13 June and 16 September 1988.

Clark, Ramsey. *Crime in America: Observations on Its Nature, Causes, Prevention, and Control.* New York: Simon and Schuster, 1970.

Clarke, Richard A. *Against All Enemies: Inside America's War on Terror.* London: Free Press, 2004.

Clinton, William J. *My Life.* New York: Alfred A. Knopf, 2004.

Coates, Peter. *In Nature's Defence: Americans and Conservation.* Keele: BAAS, 1993.

Cole, Wayne S. *Charles A. Lindbergh and the Battle Against American Intervention in World War II.* New York: Harcourt Brace Jovanovich, 1974.

Connelley, William E. *A Standard History of Kansas and Kansans,* 5 vols. Chicago: Lewis Publishing, 1918.

Commission on the Intelligence Capabilities of the United States Regarding Weapons of Mass Destruction: Report to the President of the United States. Washington, D.C.: Government Printing Office, 2005.

Compton, James V. *The Swastika and the Eagle: Hitler, the United States, and the Origins of the Second World War.* London: The Bodley Head, 1968.

Conley, Richard S. "Reform, Reorganization, and the Renaissance of the Managerial Presidency: The Impact of 9/11 on the Executive Establishment." *Politics and Policy* 34 (2006): 304–42.

Cook, Fred J. *The FBI Nobody Knows.* London: Jonathan Cape, 1965.

———. "Organized Crime: The Strange Reluctance." In Pat Watters and Stephen Gillers, eds., *Investigating the FBI,* below.

Cooper, Courtney R. "Introduction." In J. Edgar Hoover, *Persons in Hiding,* below.

Corson, William R. *The Armies of Ignorance: The Rise of the American Intelligence Empire.* New York: Dial, 1977.

Corwin, Edward S. "The Passing of Dual Federalism." *Virginia Law Review* 36 (February 1950): 1–24.

Cresswell, Stephen. *Mormons and Cowboys, Moonshiners and Klansmen: Federal Law Enforcement in the South and West, 1870–1893.* Tuscaloosa: University of Alabama Press, 1991.

Cumming, Alfred. *FBI Intelligence Reform Since September 11, 2001: Issues and Options for Congress.* Washington, D.C.: Congressional Research Service, 2004.

Cumming, Alfred, and Todd Masse. *Intelligence Reform Implementation at the Federal Bureau of Investigation: Issues and Options for Congress.* Washington, D.C.: Congressional Research Service, 2005.

Cummings, Homer S. *Selected Addresses of Homer Cummings, Attorney General of the United States, 1933–1939.* Washington, D.C.: Government Printing Office, 1938.

Cummings, Homer S., and Carl McFarland. *Federal Justice: Chapters in the History of Justice and the Federal Executive.* New York: Macmillan, 1937.

Cunningham, David. *There's Something Happening Here: The New Left, the Klan, and FBI Counterintelligence.* Berkeley: University of California Press, 2004.

Dallek, Robert. *Flawed Giant: Lyndon Johnson and His Times.* New York: Oxford University Press, 1998.

Daniel, Pete. "Up From Slavery and Down to Peonage: The Alonso Bailey Case." *Journal of American History* 57 (December 1970): 654–70.

Davis, James K. *Assault on the Left: The FBI and the Sixties Antiwar Movement.* Westport, Conn.: Praeger, 1997.

———. *Spying on America: The FBI's Domestic Counterintelligence Program.* New York: Praeger, 1992.

DEA/FBI Reorganization. House of Representatives. *Hearing Before the Select Committee on Narcotics Abuse and Control.* 97 Cong., 2 sess., 30 March 1982.

DeLoach, Cartha. *Hoover's FBI: The Inside Story by Hoover's Trusted Lieutenant.* Washington, D.C.: Regency, 1995.

DeLong, Candice. *Special Agent: My Life on the Front Line as a Woman in the FBI.* New York: Hyperion, 2001.

Diamond, Sigmund. *Compromised Campus: The Collaboration of Universities with the Intelligence Community, 1945–1955.* New York: Oxford University Press, 1992.

Dion, Susan. "FBI Surveillance of the Woman's International League for Peace and Freedom, 1945–1963." *Journal for Peace and Justice Studies,* 3 (1991): 1–21.

———. "Pacifism Treated as Subversion: The FBI and the War Resisters League." *Peace and Change* 9 (1983): 43–59.

Dixon, Thomas, Jr. *The Clansman: An Historical Romance of the Ku Klux Klan.* Ridgewood, N.J.: Gregg Press, 1967 (1905).

Doenecke, Justus D. "Non-Interventionism of the Left: The Keep America Out of the War Congress, 1938–1941." *Journal of Contemporary History* 12 (April 1977): 121–236.

Doerries, Reinhard R. *Imperial Challenge: Ambassador Count Bernstorff and German-American Relations, 1908–1917.* Chapel Hill: University of North Carolina Press, 1989.

Donner, Frank J. *The Age of Surveillance: The Aims and Methods of America's Political Intelligence System.* New York: Alfred A. Knopf, 1980

Dorwart, Jeffery M. *Conflict of Duty: The U.S. Navy's Intelligence Dilemma, 1919–1945.* Annapolis, Md.: Naval Institute Press, 1983.

Doyle, Charles. *Administrative Subpoenas and National Security Letters in Criminal and Intelligence Investigations: A Sketch.* Washington, D.C.: Congressional Research Service, 2005.

Drabble, John. "COINTELPRO–WHITE HATE, the FBI, and the Cold War Political Consensus." Ph.D. diss., University of California, Berkeley, 1997.

———. "To Ensure Domestic Tranquility: The FBI, COINTELPRO–WHITE HATE, and Political Discourse, 1964–1971." *Journal of American Studies* 38 (August 2004): 297–328.

Drew, Elizabeth. "Power Grab." *New York Review of Books* 53 (22 June 2006).

Duberman, Martin B. *Paul Robeson.* London: Pan, 1991.

Du Bois, W. E. Burghardt. *Black Reconstruction in America.* Cleveland: Meridian, 1964 (1935).

Dudziak, Mary. *Cold War Civil Rights: Race and the Image of American Democracy.* Princeton, N.J.: Princeton University Press, 2000.

———, ed. *September 11 in History: A Watershed Moment?* Durham, N.C.: Duke University Press. 2003.

Dulles, Allen. *The Craft of Intelligence.* London: Weidenfeld and Nicolson, 1963.

Dumbrell, John. *The Carter Presidency: A Re-evaluation.* 2nd ed. Manchester: Manchester University Press, 1995.

Dunning, William A. *Essays on the Civil War and Reconstruction.* Gloucester, Mass.: Peter Smith, 1969 (1897).

———. *Reconstruction, Political and Economic, 1865–1877.* New York: Harper, 1962 (1907).

Edwards, Owen Dudley. "Introduction." In Arthur Conan Doyle, *The Valley of Fear*. Oxford: Oxford University Press, 1993 (1915), xi–xlii.

Elliff, John T. "Aspects of Federal Civil Rights Enforcement: The Justice Department and the FBI, 1939–1964." *Perspectives in American History* 5 (1971): 605–73.

———. "The Attorney General's Guidelines for FBI Investigations." *Cornell Law Review* 69 (April 1984): 785–815.

———. *The Reform of FBI Intelligence Operations*. Princeton, N.J.: Princeton University Press, 1979.

Ellis, Mark. *Race, War, and Surveillance: African Americans and the United States Government During World War I*. Bloomington: Indiana University Press, 2001.

Emergence of the Intelligence Establishment. U.S. Department of State. *Foreign Relations of the United States, 1945–1950*. Washington, D.C.: Government Printing Office, 1996.

Epstein, Edward J. *Agency of Fear: Opiates and Political Power in America*. New York: G. P. Putnam's, 1977.

———. *Legend: The Secret World of Lee Harvey Oswald*. London: Hutchinson, 1978.

Extracts from Hearings Before Subcommittee of House Committee on Appropriations in Charge of Sundry Civil Appropriation Bill for 1910 Relative to Secret Service. 60 Cong., 2 sess., 1909.

Fairclough, Adam. *Better Day Coming: Blacks and Equality, 1890–2000*. New York: Penguin, 2002.

FBI Affirmative Action and Equal Opportunity Efforts. House of Representatives. *Hearings Before the Subcommittee on Civil and Constitutional Rights of the Committee of the Judiciary*. 100 Cong., 2 sess., 31 March and 8 June, 1988.

FBI and DEA: Merger or Enhanced Cooperation? House of Representatives. *Joint Hearings Before the Subcommittee on Civil and Constitutional Rights and the Subcommittee on Crime and Criminal Justice of the Committee on the Judiciary*. 103 Cong., 1 sess., 29 September 1993.

FBI Electronic Reading Room: http://foia.fbi.gov/room.htm.

FBI Files on Eleanor Roosevelt. Microfilm. Wilmington, Del.: Scholarly Resources, 1996.

FBI Manuals, 1927–1978. Microfilm. Wilmington, Del.: Scholarly Resources, 1983.

FBI's Ten Most Wanted Fugitives Program: 50th Anniversary, 1950–2000. Lisbon, Md.: K. & D. Limited, n.d.

FBI Undercover Guidelines. House of Representatives. *Oversight Hearings Before the Subcommittee on Civil and Constitutional Rights and the Subcommittee on Crime and Criminal Justice of the Committee on the Judiciary*. 97 Cong., 1 sess., 19, 25, and 26 February 1981.

Feldstein, Mark. "A Muckraking Model: Investigative Reporting Cycles in American History." *Harvard International Journal of Press/Politics* 11 (Spring 2006): 105–20.

Finch, Stanley W. "The White Slave Traffic." In *Self Knowledge and Guide to Sex Instruction*, edited by Thomas W. Shannon. Marietta, Ohio: S. A. Mullikin, 1913.

Fine, Sidney. *Frank Murphy: The New Deal Years.* Chicago: University of Chicago Press, 1979.

———. *"Without Blare of Trumpets": Walter Drew, the National Erectors' Association, and the Open Shop Movement, 1903–1957.* Ann Arbor: University of Michigan Press, 1995.

Fischer, David Hackett. *Albion's Seed: Four British Folkways in America.* New York: Oxford University Press, 1989.

Fisher, David. "Home Colony: An American Experiment in Anarchism." M.Litt. diss., University of Edinburgh, 1971.

Fitch, Stephen D. "The FBI Library Awareness Program: An Analysis." *Intelligence and National Security* 7 (April 1992): 101–11.

Flamm, Michael W. *Law and Order: Street Crime, Civil Unrest, and the Crisis of Liberalism in the 1960s.* New York: Columbia University Press, 2005.

Foner, Eric. *Reconstruction: America's Unfinished Revolution, 1963–1977.* New York: Harper and Row, 1988.

Foraker, Julia. *I Would Live It Again: Memories of a Vivid Life.* New York: Harper, 1932.

Fortescue, Adrian. *A European View of the U.S. Department of Homeland Security.* Brussels: European Union Directorate General of Justice, Freedom, and Security, n.d.

Fox, John F., Jr. "Bureaucratic Wrangling over Counterintelligence, 1917–1918." *Studies in Intelligence* 49 (2005). https://www.cia.gov/csi/studies.

Freeh, Louis J. *My FBI: Bringing Down the Mafia, Investigating Bill Clinton, and Fighting the War on Terror.* New York: St. Martin's, 2005.

Friedman, Lawrence M. *Crime and Punishment in American History.* New York: Basic, 1993.

Friedman, Milton, and Rose Friedman. *Free to Choose: A Personal Statement.* Harmondsworth: Penguin, 1980.

Funder, Anna. *Stasiland.* London: Granta, 2005.

Galvis, Silvia, and Alberto Donadío. *Colombia Nazi, 1939–1945: Espionaje Alemán la Cacería del FBI: Santos López y los Pactos Secretos.* Bogotá: Planeta, 1986.

Garrow, David J. *The FBI and Martin Luther King, Jr.* New York: Penguin, 1983.

Gatewood, Willard B., Jr. *Theodore Roosevelt and the Art of Controversy: Episodes of the White House Years.* Baton Rouge: Louisiana State University Press, 1970.

Gelbspan, Ross. *Break-ins, Death Threats, and the FBI: The Covert War Against the Central American Movement.* Boston: South End Press, 1991.

Gentry, Curt. *J. Edgar Hoover: The Man and the Secrets.* New York: Norton, 1991.

Gerard, Christopher J. "'A Program of Cooperation': The FBI, the Senate Internal Security Committee, and the Communist Issue, 1950–1956." Ph.D. diss., Marquette University, 1993.

Gertz, Bill. *Breakdown: How America's Intelligence Failure Led to September 11.* Washington, D.C.: Regnery, 2002.

Geyer, Dominic. "Watergate Investigations: Woodstein and the FBI." M.Litt. diss., St. Andrews University, 1996.

Goldman, Eric F. *Charles J. Bonaparte, Patrician Reformer: His Earlier Career.* Baltimore: The John Hopkins Press, 1943.

Goodall, Alex. "Aspects of the Emergence of American Anticommunism, 1917–1944." Ph.D. diss., University of Cambridge, 2006.

Goodman, Michael. "Grandfather of the Hydrogen Bomb? Anglo-American Intelligence and Klaus Fuchs." *Historical Studies in the Physical and Biological Sciences* 34 (2003): 1–22.

———. "Who Is Trying to Keep What Secret from Whom and Why? MI-5–FBI Relations and the Klaus Fuchs Case." *Journal of Cold War Studies* 7 (Summer 2005): 124–46.

Goodman, Walter. *The Committee: The Extraordinary Career of the House Committee on Un-American Activities.* New York: Farrar, Straus and Giroux, 1968.

Goodwin, Doris Kearns. *No Ordinary Time: Franklin and Eleanor Roosevelt: The Home Front in World War II.* New York: Simon and Schuster, 1994.

Graham, Fred P. "A Contemporary History of American Crime." In *Violence in America: Historical and Comparative Perspectives,* edited by Hugh D. Graham and Ted R. Gurr. New York: Bantam, 1969.

Granatstein, Jack L., and David Stafford. *Spy Wars: Espionage and Canada from Gouzenko to Glasnost.* Toronto: McClelland and Stewart, 1992.

Greene, John R. *The Presidency of George Bush.* Lawrence: University of Kansas Press, 2000.

———. *The Presidency of Gerald R. Ford.* Lawrence: University of Kansas Press, 1995.

Griffin, David R. *The New Pearl Harbor: Disturbing Questions About the Bush Administration and 9/11.* Northampton, Mass.: Olive Branch, 2004.

———. *The 9-11 Commission Report: Omissions and Distortions.* Morton-in-Marsh, Gloucs.: Arris, 2005.

Gunaratna, Rohan. *Inside Al Qaeda: Global Network of Terror.* New York: Columbia University Press, 2002.

Haines, Gerald. "Under the Eagle's Wing: The Franklin Roosevelt Administration Forges an American Hemisphere." *Diplomatic History* 1 (1977): 373–88.

Haines, Gerald, and David Langbart. *Unlocking the Files of the FBI: A Guide to Its Record and Classification System.* Wilmington, Del.: Scholarly Resources, 1993.

Hall, Hermit L., ed. *The Oxford Companion to the Supreme Court of the United States.* New York: Oxford University Press, 1992.

————. "Political Power and Constitutional Legitimacy: The South Carolina Ku Klux Klan Trials, 1871–1872." *Emory Law Journal* 33 (1984): 921–51.

Haynes, John E., and Harvey Klehr. *Venona: Decoding Soviet Espionage in America.* New Haven: Yale University Press, 1999.

Heale, Michael J. "Beyond the 'Age of McCarthy': Anticommunism and the Historians." In *The State of U.S. History,* edited by Melvyn Stokes. Oxford: Berg, 2002.

————. *McCarthy's Americans: Red Scare Politics in State and Nation, 1935–1965.* London: Macmillan, 1998.

Hersh, Seymour M. *The Dark Side of Camelot.* Boston: Little, Brown, 1997.

————. "Missed Messages: Why the Government Didn't Know What It Knew." *New Yorker* (3 June 2002): 40–48.

Higham, John. *Strangers in the Land: Patterns of Nativism, 1860–1925.* New York: Atheneum, 1969 (1963).

Hill, Robert A., comp. and ed. *The FBI's RACON: Racial Conditions in the United States During World War II.* Boston: Northeastern University Press, 1995.

Hodgson, Godfrey. *More Equal than Others: America from Nixon to the New Century.* Princeton, N.J.: Princeton University Press, 2004.

Hogue, Henry B. *Nomination and Confirmation of the FBI Director: Process and Recent History.* Washington, D.C.: Congressional Research Service, 2005.

Holt, Thaddeus. *The Deceivers: Allied Military Deception in the Second World War.* New York: Scribner, 2004.

Hook, Andrew. *From Goosecreek to Gandercleugh: Studies in Scottish-American Literary and Cultural History.* East Linton: Tuckwell, 1999.

Hoover, J. Edgar. "The Crime of the Century: The Case of the A-Bomb Spies." *Reader's Digest* (May 1951): 113–48.

————. *Masters of Deceit: The Story of Communism in America and How to Fight It.* New York: Henry Holt, 1958.

————. *Persons in Hiding.* London: J. M. Dent, 1938.

Hulnick, Arthur S. *Keeping Us Safe: Secret Intelligence and Homeland Security.* Westport, Conn.: Praeger, 2004.

Irons, Peter, ed. *Justice Delayed: The Record of the Japanese American Internment Cases.* Middletown, Conn.: Wesleyan University Press, 1989.

————. *Justice at War: The Story of the Japanese Internment Cases.* Berkeley: University of California Press, 1993.

Jackson, Kenneth T., ed. *The Encyclopedia of New York City.* New Haven: Yale University Press, 1995.

Jackson, Robert H. *That Man: An Insider's Portrait of Franklin D. Roosevelt,* edited by John Q. Barrett. New York: Oxford University Press, 2003.

Jeffreys-Jones, Rhodri. *American Espionage: From Secret Service to CIA.* New York: Free Press, 1977.

————. *The CIA and American Democracy.* New Haven: Yale University Press, 1989.

————. *Cloak and Dollar: A History of American Secret Intelligence.* New Haven: Yale University Press, 2002.

————. "The Historiography of the FBI." In *A Handbook of Intelligence Studies,* edited by Loch Johnson. New York: Routledge, 2007.

————. "The Idea of a European FBI." In *Counterintelligence and Counterterrorism,* edited by Loch Johnson. New York: Praeger, 2007.

————. *Violence and Reform in American History.* New York: New Viewpoints, 1978.

Jensen, Joan M. *The Price of Vigilance.* Chicago: Rand McNally, 1968.

Jentleson, Bruce W. *American Foreign Policy: The Dynamics of Choice in the 21st Century.* 2nd ed. New York: Norton, 2004.

Johnson, David K. *The Lavender Scare: The Cold War Persecution of Gays and Lesbians by the Federal Government.* Chicago: University of Chicago Press, 2004.

Johnson, James Weldon. *Black Manhattan.* New York: Knopf, 1930.

Johnson, John A. *Jack Johnson In the Ring and Out.* Chicago: National Sports Publishing, 1927.

————. *Mes Combats.* Paris: P. Lafitte, 1914.

Johnson, Loch K. *A Season of Inquiry: The Senate Intelligence Investigation.* Lexington: University Press of Kentucky, 1985.

Kaiser, Frederick M. "Origins of Secret Service Protection of the President: Personal, Interagency, and Institutional Conflict." *Presidential Studies Quarterly* 18 (Winter 1988): 101–27.

Keire, Mara L. "The Vice Trust: A Reinterpretation of the White Slavery Scare in the United States, 1907–1917." *Journal of Social History* 35 (2001): 5–41.

Keller, William W. *The Liberals and J. Edgar Hoover: Rise and Fall of a Domestic Intelligence State.* Princeton, N.J.: Princeton University Press, 1989.

Kelley, Clarence M. *Kelley: The Story of an FBI Director.* Kansas City: Andrews, McMeel and Parker, 1987.

Kendall, Wilmoore. "The Function of Intelligence." *World Politics* 1 (1948–49): 542–52.

Kennedy, Robert F. *The Enemy Within.* New York: Harper, 1960.

Kessler, Ronald. *The Bureau: The Secret History of the FBI.* New York: St. Martin's, 2002.

————. *The FBI.* New York: Simon and Schuster, 1994.

KKK Report. United States Congress. *Report of the Joint Select Committee to Inquire into the Condition of Affairs in the Late Insurrectionary States.* 42 Cong., 2 sess., 1872.

Kornweibel, Theodore, Jr. "Black on Black: The FBI's First Negro Informants and Agents and the Investigation of Black Radicalism During the Red Scare." *Criminal Justice History* 8 (1987): 121–36.

Kutler, Stanley I., ed. *Encyclopedia of the Vietnam War.* New York: Charles Scribner's Sons, 1996.

————. *The Wars of Watergate: The Last Crisis of Richard Nixon.* New York: Norton, 1992.

Lamont, Peter. *The Rise of the Indian Rope Trick: How a Spectacular Hoax Became History.* London: Abacus, 2004.

Lamphere, Robert J. *The FBI-KGB War: A Special Agent's Story.* New York: Random House, 1986.

Lane, Ann J. *The Brownsville Affair: National Crisis and Black Reaction.* Port Washington, N.Y.: Kennikat, 1971.

Langum, David J. *Crossing Over the Line: Legislating Morality and the Mann Act.* Chicago: University of Chicago Press, 1994.

Lash, Joseph P. *Love, Eleanor: Eleanor Roosevelt and Her Friends.* Garden City, N.Y.: Doubleday, 1982.

Lee, Wen Ho. *My Country Versus Me.* New York: Hyperion, 2001.

Legnitto, Jan, producer. *The Rosenberg File: Case Closed.* Princeton, N.J.: Discovery/Films for the Humanities and Sciences, 2002.

Lehr, Dick, and Gerard O'Neill. *Black Mass: The True Story of an Unholy Alliance Between the FBI and the Irish Mob.* New York: HarperCollins, 2001.

Lemann, Nicholas. *Redemption: The Last Battle of the Civil War.* New York: Farrar, Straus and Giroux, 2006.

Levine, Lawrence W. *Black Culture and Black Consciousness: Afro-American Folk Thought from Slavery to Freedom.* Oxford: Oxford University Press, 1977.

Lewis, David L. *W. E. B. Du Bois: The Fight for Equality and the American Century, 1919–1963.* New York: Henry Holt, 2000.

Link, Arthur S., ed. *The Papers of Woodrow Wilson.* 69 vols. Princeton, N.J.: Princeton University Press, 1966–94.

London, Jack. *Jack London Reports: War Correspondence, Sports Activities, and Miscellaneous Writings.* Edited by King Hendricks and Irving Shepard. Garden City, N.Y.: Doubleday, 1970.

Lowenthal, John. "Venona and Alger Hiss." *Intelligence and National Security* 15 (Autumn 2000): 98–130.

Lowenthal, Max. *The Federal Bureau of Investigation.* New York: Harcourt Brace Jovanovich, 1950.

McFeely, William S. *William S. Grant: A Biography.* New York: Norton, 1982.

Mack, Kenneth W. "Rethinking Civil Rights Lawyering and Politics in the Era Before *Brown*." *Yale Law Journal* 115 (November 2005): 256–354.

McKnight, Gerald D. *The Last Crusade: Martin Luther King, Jr., the FBI, and the Poor People's Campaign.* Boulder, Colo.: Westview, 1998.

McMahon, Kevin J. *Reconsidering Roosevelt on Race: How the Presidency Paved the Road to Brown.* Chicago: University of Chicago Press, 2004.

McWhiney, Grady. *Cracker Culture: Celtic Ways in the Old South.* Tuscaloosa: University of Alabama Press, 1988.

Marx, Gary T. *Undercover: Police Surveillance in America.* Berkeley: University of California Press, 1988.

Mason, Alpheus T. *Harlan Fiske Stone: Pillar of the Law*. New York: Viking, 1956.

Mason, Robert. *Richard Nixon and the Quest for a New Majority*. Chapel Hill: University of North Carolina Press, 2004.

Masse, Todd. *Domestic Intelligence in the United Kingdom: Applicability of the MI-5 Model to the United States*. Washington, D.C.: Congressional Research Service, 2003.

May, Gary. *The Informant: The FBI, the Ku Klux Klan, and the Murder of Viola Liuzzo*. New Haven: Yale University Press, 2005.

Melanson, Philip H. *The Secret Service: The Hidden History of an Enigmatic Agency*. New York: Carroll and Graf, 2002.

Miller, John, and Michael Stone and Chris Mitchell. *The Cell: The 9/11 Plot and Why the FBI and CIA Failed to Stop It*. New York: Hyperion, 2002.

Miller, Wilbur R. *Revenuers and Moonshiners: Enforcing Federal Liquor Law in the Mountain South, 1865–1900*. Chapel Hill: University of North Carolina Press, 1991.

Monet, Jean-Claude. *Polices et Sociétés en Europe*. Paris: La documentation Française, 1993.

Monkkonen, Eric H. *Police in Urban America, 1860–1920*. Cambridge: Cambridge University Press, 1981.

Montague, Ludwell L. *General Walter Bedell Smith as Director of Central Intelligence, October 1950–February 1953*. University Park: Pennsylvania State University Press, 1992.

Morgan, Ted. *FDR: A Biography*. New York: Simon and Schuster, 1985.

Moser, John E. *Twisting the Lion's Tail: Anglophobia in the United States, 1921–1948*. London: Macmillan, 1999.

Mount, Graeme S. *Canada's Enemies: Spies and Spying in the Peaceable Kingdom*. Toronto: Dundurn, 1993.

———. *Chile and the Nazis: From Hitler to Pinochet*. Montréal: Black Rose, 2002.

Mowry, George E. *The Era of Theodore Roosevelt and the Birth of Modern America, 1900–1912*. New York: Harper, 1958.

Moynihan, Daniel P. *Secrecy: The American Experience*. New Haven: Yale University Press, 1998.

Naftali, Timothy. *Blind Spot: The Secret History of American Counterterrorism*. New York: Basic, 2005.

Nash, George H. *The Conservative Intellectual Movement in America Since 1945*. New York: Basic, 1976.

Navasky, Victor S. *Kennedy Justice*. New York: Atheneum, 1971.

Nelson, Anna K. "The John F. Kennedy Assassination Records Review Board." In Athan G. Theoharis, ed., *A Culture of Secrecy*, below.

Newman, John. *Oswald and the CIA*. New York: Carroll and Graf, 1995.

The 9/11 Commission Report: Final Report of the National Commission on Terrorist Attacks upon the United States. New York: Norton, 2004.

Nixon, Richard M. *Nixon and the FBI: The White House Tapes.* National Security Archive Electronic Briefing Book No. 156 (2005).

Noakes, John Allen. "Enforcing Domestic Tranquility: State Building and the Origins of the (Federal) Bureau of Investigation, 1908–1920." Ph.D. diss., University of Pennsylvania, 1993.

Noggle, Burl. *Teapot Dome: Oil and Politics in the 1920s.* New York: Norton, 1965.

Norton, Anne. *Leo Strauss and the Politics of American Empire.* New Haven; Yale University Press, 2004.

O'Brien, Gail Williams. *The Color of the Law: Race, Violence, and Justice in the Post–World War II South.* Chapel Hill: University of North Carolina Press, 1999.

Occhipinti, John D. *The Politics of EU Police Cooperation: Toward a European FBI?* Boulder, Colo.: Lynne Rienner, 2003.

Odom, William E. *Fixing Intelligence for a More Secure America.* New Haven: Yale University Press, 2003.

O'Harrow, Robert. *No Place to Hide.* New York: Free Press, 2005.

Olmsted, Kathryn S. *Challenging the Secret Government: The Post-Watergate Investigations of the CIA and FBI.* Chapel Hill: University of North Carolina Press, 1996.

———. *Red Spy Queen: A Biography of Elizabeth Bentley.* Chapel Hill: University of North Carolina Press, 2002.

Olson, Keith W. *Watergate: The Presidential Scandal that Shook America.* Lawrence: University Press of Kansas, 2003.

Oney, Steve. *And the Dead Shall Rise: The Murder of Mary Phagan and the Lynching of Leo Frank.* New York: Pantheon, 2003.

O'Reilly, Kenneth. "Adlai E. Stevenson, McCarthyism, and the FBI." *Illinois Historical Journal* 81 (Spring 1988): 45–60.

———. "The FBI and the Origins of McCarthyism." *Historian* 45 (1983): 372–93.

———. "Herbert Hoover and the FBI." *Annals of Iowa* 47 (1983): 46–63.

———. *"Racial Matters": The FBI's Secret File on Black America, 1960–1972.* New York: Free Press, 1989.

———. "The Roosevelt Administration and Black America: Federal Surveillance Policy and Civil Rights During the New Deal and World War II Years." *Phylon* 48 (1987): 12–45.

Oversight of the FBI. Senate. *Hearings Before the Committee on the Judiciary.* 107 Cong., 1 sess., 20 June, 18 July 2001.

Palermo, Joseph A. *In His Own Right: The Political Odyssey of Senator Robert F. Kennedy.* New York: Columbia University Press, 2001.

Paz, Maria E. *Strategy, Security, and Spies: Mexico and the U.S. as Allies in World War II.* University Park: Penn State University Press, 1997.

Persico, Joseph E. *Roosevelt's Secret War: FDR and World War II Espionage.* New York: Random House, 2001.

Pike Hearings 1. *U.S. Intelligence Agencies and Activities: Intelligence Costs and Fis-*

cal Procedures. Part 1 of 2 parts. House of Representatives. *Hearings Before the Select Committee on Intelligence*. 94 Cong., 1 sess., 31 July, and 1, 4, 5, 6, 7, and 8 August 1975.

Pike Report. *CIA: The Pike Report*. Nottingham: Spokesman, 1977.

Pincus, Walter. "The Bureau's Budget: A Source of Power." In Pat Watters and Stephen Gillers, eds., *Investigating the FBI*, below.

Posner, Gerald. *Case Closed: Lee Harvey Oswald and the Assassination of JFK*. New York: Random House, 1993.

Posner, Richard A. *Preventing Surprise Attacks: Intelligence Reform in the Wake of 9/11*. Lanham, Md.: Rowman and Littlefield, 2005.

Post, Louis F. "A 'Carpetbagger' in South Carolina." *Journal of Negro History* 19 (January 1925): 10–79.

Potter, Claire B. "Guarding the Crossroads: The FBI's War on Crime in the 1930s." Ph.D. diss., New York University, 1990.

Powers, Richard G. *Broken: The Troubled Past and Uncertain Future of the FBI*. New York: Free Press, 2004.

———. "The FBI in American Popular Culture." In *The FBI: A Comprehensive Reference Guide*, ed. Athan G. Theoharis, below.

———. *Not Without Honor: The History of American Anticommunism*. New Haven: Yale University Press, 1995.

———. *Secrecy and Power: The Life of J. Edgar Hoover*. New York: Free Press, 1987.

Preston, William, Jr. *Aliens and Dissenters: Federal Suppression of Radicals, 1903–1933*. New York: Harper, 1966.

Raat, W. Dirk. "U.S. Intelligence Operations and Covert Action in Mexico, 1900–1947." *Journal of Contemporary History* 22 (October 1987): 615–38.

Rawick, George P., ed. *The American Slave: A Composite Autobiography. Vol. 2: South Carolina Narratives*. Westport, Conn.: Greenwood, 1972.

Reagan, Ronald. *Reagan, In His Own Hand*. Edited by Kiron K. Skinner, Annelise Anderson, and Martin Anderson. New York: Free Press, 2001.

Reed, Merl E. "The FBI, MOWM, and CORE, 1941–1946." *Journal of Black Studies* 21 (June 1991): 465–79.

Reeves, Richard. *President Nixon: Alone in the White House*. New York: Simon and Schuster, 2001.

Relyea, Harold C., and Jeffrey W. Seifert. *Information Sharing for Homeland Security: A Brief Overview*. Washington, D.C.: Congressional Research Service, 2004.

Report of the Joint Select Committee to Inquire into the Condition of Affairs in the Late Insurrectionary States. Washington, D.C.: Government Printing Office, 1872.

Rhodes, James F. *History of the United States from the Compromise of 1850 to the Final Restoration of Home Rule in the South in 1877*. 9 vols. New York: Macmillan, Vol. 6: *1866–1872*, 1906.

Riebling, Mark. *Wedge: From Pearl Harbor to 9/11: How the Secret War Between the FBI and CIA Has Endangered National Security*. New York: Touchstone, 2002.

Roberts, Randy. *Papa Jack: Jack Johnson and the Era of White Hopes.* New York: Free Press, 1983.

Robins, Natalie. *Alien Ink: The FBI's War on Freedom of Expression.* New York: William Morrow, 1992.

Roosevelt, Theodore. *The Letters of Theodore Roosevelt.* 8 vols. Edited by Elting E. Morison. Cambridge, Mass.: Harvard University Press, 1951–54.

Rout, Leslie B., Jr., and John B. Bratzell. *The Shadow War: German Espionage and United States Counterespionage in Latin America During World War II.* Frederick, Md.: University Publications of America, 1986.

Rovere, Richard H. *Senator Joe McCarthy.* Berkeley: University of California Press, 1996 (1959).

Rudgers, David F. *Creating the Secret State: The Origins of the Central Intelligence Agency, 1943–1947.* Lawrence: University Press of Kansas, 2000.

Ryan, Allan A., Jr. *Klaus Barbie and the United States Government: The Report, with Documentary Appendix, to the Attorney General of the United States.* Frederick, Md.: University Publications of America, 1984.

Sammons, Jeffrey T. *Beyond the Ring: The Role of Boxing in American Society.* Urbana: University of Illinois Press, 1988.

Schlesinger, Arthur M., Jr. *Robert Kennedy and His Times.* London: André Deutsch, 1978.

———. *A Thousand Days: John F. Kennedy in the White House.* London: André Deutsch, 1965.

Schmidt, Regin. *Red Scare: FBI and the Origins of Anticommunism in the United States, 1919–1943.* Copenhagen: Museum Tusculanum Press, 2000.

Schoonover, Thomas. "Hitler's Threat to North America, Nazi Spy Heinz Lüning in Havana." Paper delivered at annual meeting of the Society for Historians of Foreign Relations, 23–25 June 2006.

Schrecker, Ellen. *The Age of McCarthyism: A Brief History with Documents.* Boston: St. Martin's, 1994.

———. *Many Are the Crimes: McCarthyism in America.* Boston: Little, Brown, 1998.

Shapiro, Herbert. "The Ku Klux Klan During Reconstruction: The South Carolina Episode." *Journal of Negro History* 49 (January 1964): 34–55.

Shrestha, Laura B. *The Changing Demographic Profile of the United States.* Washington, D.C.: Congressional Research Service, 2006.

Shull, Steven A. *American Civil Rights Policy from Truman to Clinton: The Role of Presidential Leadership.* Armonk, N.Y.: M. E. Sharpe, 1999.

Sibley, Katherine A. S. *Red Spies in America: Stolen Secrets and the Dawn of the Cold War.* Lawrence: University Press of Kansas, 2004.

Simkins, Francis B. "The Ku Klux Klan in South Carolina, 1868–1871." *Journal of Negro History* 12 (October 1927): 606–47.

Sinclair, Andrew. *The Available Man: The Life Behind the Masks of Warren G. Harding.* Chicago: Quadrangle, 1969.

Sitkoff, Harvard. *A New Deal for Blacks: The Emergence of Civil Rights as a National Issue.* New York: Oxford University Press, 1978.

———. *The Struggle for Black Equality, 1954–1992.* Rev. ed. Cambridge, Mass.: Harvard University Press, 1993.

Smist, Frank J., Jr. "Congress Oversees the United States Intelligence Community, 1947–1984." Ph.D. diss., University of Oklahoma, 1988.

Smith, Bradley F. *The Shadow Warriors: OSS and the Origins of the CIA.* New York: Basic, 1983.

Smith, Jean E. *Grant.* New York: Simon and Schuster, 2001.

Smith, Robert C. "Black Appointed Officials: A Neglected Area of Research in Black Political Participation." *Journal of Black Studies* 14 (March 1984): 369–88.

Steffens, Lincoln. *The Autobiography of Lincoln Steffens.* New York: Harcourt, Brace, 1931.

Stinnett, Robert B. *Day of Deceit: The Truth About FDR and Pearl Harbor.* New York: Free Press, 2000.

Stober, Dan, and Ian Hoffman. *A Convenient Spy: Wen Ho Lee and the Politics of Nuclear Espionage.* New York: Simon and Schuster, 2001.

Stout, Rex. *The Doorbell Rang* (1965). In *The First Rex Stout Omnibus.* Harmondsworth: Penguin, 1975.

Sullivan, William C. *The Bureau: My Thirty Years in Hoover's FBI.* New York: Norton, 1979.

Summers, Anthony. *Official and Confidential: The Secret Life of J. Edgar Hoover.* New York: G. P. Putnam's Sons, 1993.

Swinney, Everette. *Suppressing the Ku Klux Klan: The Enforcement of the Reconstruction Amendments, 1870–1877.* New York: Garland, 1987.

Talbert, Roy, Jr. *Negative Intelligence: The Army and the American Left, 1917–1941.* Jackson: University Press of Mississippi, 1991.

Theoharis, Athan G. *Chasing Spies: How the FBI Failed in Counterintelligence but Promoted the Politics of McCarthyism in the Cold War Years.* Chicago: Ivan R. Dee, 2002.

———, ed. *A Culture of Secrecy: The Government Versus the People's Right to Know.* Lawrence: University Press of Kansas, 1998.

———. *The FBI and American Democracy: A Brief Critical History.* Lawrence: University Press of Kansas, 2004.

———. "The FBI and the American Legion Contact Program, 1940–1966." *Political Science Quarterly* 100 (Summer 1985): 271–86.

———, ed. *The FBI: A Comprehensive Reference Guide.* New York: Facts on File, 2000.

———. "FBI Wiretapping: A Case Study of Bureaucratic Autonomy." *Political Science Quarterly* 107 (1992): 101–22.

———, ed. *From the Secret Files of J. Edgar Hoover.* Chicago: Ivan R. Dee, 1993.

———. "How the FBI Gaybaited Stevenson." *The Nation* 250 (7 May 1990): 617, 635–36.

————. *J. Edgar Hoover, Sex, and Crime: An Historical Antidote.* Chicago: Ivan R. Dee, 1995.

————. *Spying on Americans: Political Surveillance from Hoover to the Huston Plan.* Philadelphia: Temple University Press, 1978.

Theoharis, Athan G., and John S. Cox. *The Boss: J. Edgar Hoover and the Great American Inquisition.* London: Harrap, 1988.

Tinsley, James A. "Roosevelt, Foraker, and the Brownsville Affray." *Journal of Negro History* 41 (January 1956): 43–65.

Toledano, Ralph de. *J. Edgar Hoover: The Man and His Time.* New Rochelle, N.Y.: Arlington House, 1973.

Tolnay, Stewart E., and E. M. Beck. *A Festival of Violence: An Analysis of Southern Lynchings, 1882–1930.* Urbana: University of Illinois Press, 1995.

Trelease, Allen W. *White Terror: The Ku Klux Klan Conspiracy and Southern Reconstruction.* Baton Rouge: Louisiana State University Press, 1971.

Troy, Thomas F. *Donovan and the CIA: A History of the Establishment of the Central Intelligence Agency.* Frederick, Md.: University Publications of America, 1981.

————. "Knifing of the OSS." *International Journal of Intelligence and Counterintelligence* 1 (1986): 95–106.

Truman, Harry S. *Memoirs,* 2 vols. Garden City, N.Y.: Doubleday. Vol. 1: *Year of Decisions,* 1955.

Turner, William W. *Hoover's FBI: The Men and the Myth.* New York: Dell, 1971.

Turrou, Leon G. *The Nazi Spy Conspiracy in America.* London: Harrap, 1939.

Tyler, Gus. *Organized Crime in America.* Ann Arbor: University of Michigan Press, 1962.

Valero, Larry A. "From World War to Cold War: Aspects of the Management and Coordination of American Intelligence, 1941–1953." Ph.D. diss., University of Cambridge, 2002.

Vaughan, Stephen. "Spies, National Security, and the 'Inertia Projector': The Secret Service Files of Ronald Reagan." *American Quarterly* 39 (Fall 1987): 355–80.

Vise, David A. *The Bureau and the Mole: The Unmasking of Robert Philip Hanssen, the Most Dangerous Double Agent in FBI History.* New York: Atlantic Monthly Press, 2002.

Waldrep, Christopher. "American Lynching, Civil Rights, and the Meaning of Community, 1865–1965." Paper delivered at the University of Edinburgh, 11 January 2006.

————, ed. *Lynching in America: A History in Documents.* New York: New York University Press, 2006.

Waldrep, Christopher, and Michael Bellesisles, eds. *Documenting American Violence: A Sourcebook.* Oxford: Oxford University Press, 2006.

Walsh, Elsa. "Learning to Spy." *New Yorker* (8 November 2004): 96–103.

————. "Louis Freeh's Last Case." *New Yorker* (14 May 2001): 68–79.

Wang, Diane, and Cindy Jaquith. *FBI vs. Women.* New York: Pathfinder, 1977.

Wannall, W. Raymond. "The FBI's Domestic Intelligence Operations: Domestic Security in Limbo." *International Journal of Intelligence and Counter-Intelligence* 4 (Winter 1990): 443–73.

Ward, Geoffrey C. *Unforgivable Blackness: The Rise and Fall of Jack Johnson.* New York: Alfred A. Knopf, 2004.

Washburn, Patrick S. "J. Edgar Hoover and the Black Press in World War II." *Journalism History* 13 (1986): 26–33.

———. *A Question of Sedition: The Federal Government's Investigation of the Black Press During World War II.* New York: Oxford University Press, 1986.

Watters, Pat, and Stephen Gillers, eds. *Investigating the FBI.* New York: Ballantine, 1974.

Weinstein, Allen. *Perjury: The Hiss-Chambers Case.* London: Hutchinson, 1978.

Weinstein, Allen, and Alexander Vassiliev. *The Haunted Wood: Soviet Espionage in America—the Stalin Era.* New York: Random House, 1999.

Weiss, Andrea. "Communism, Perversion, and Other Crimes Against the State: The FBI Files of Klaus and Erika Mann." *GLQ: A Journal of Lesbian and Gay Studies* 7 (2001): 459–81.

Weiss, Nancy J. *Farewell to the Party of Lincoln: Black Politics in the Age of FDR.* Princeton, N.J.: Princeton University Press, 1983.

Wessel, Thomas R. "Republican Justice: The Department of Justice Under Roosevelt and Taft, 1901–1913." Ph.D. diss., University of Maryland, 1972.

Whitaker, Reg. "Cold War Alchemy: How America, Britain, and Canada Transformed Espionage into Subversion." In David Stafford and Rhodri Jeffreys-Jones, eds., *American-British-Canadian Intelligence Relations, 1939–2000.* London: Frank Cass, 2000.

Whitehead, Don. *The FBI Story.* London: Frederick Muller, 1957.

Whitley, Hiram C. *In It.* Cambridge, Mass.: Riverside, 1894.

Whitnah, Donald R., ed. *Government Agencies.* Westport, Conn.: Greenwood, 1983.

Wilkie, Donald W. *American Secret Service Agent.* New York: Frederick A. Stokes, 1934.

Williams, David. "The Bureau of Investigation and Its Critics, 1919–1921: The Origins of Federal Political Surveillance." *Journal of American History* 68 (1981): 568–79.

———. "'They Never Stopped Watching Us': FBI Political Surveillance, 1924–1936." *UCLA Historical Journal* 2 (1981): 5–28.

———. "'Without Understanding': The FBI and Political Surveillance, 1908–1941." Ph.D. diss., University of New Hampshire, 1981.

Williams, Lou F. *The Great South Carolina Ku Klux Klan Trials, 1871–1872.* Athens: University of Georgia Press, 1996.

Williams, Robert C. *Klaus Fuchs, Atom Spy.* Cambridge, Mass.: Harvard University Press, 1987.

Wilson, James Q. *The Investigators: Managing FBI and Narcotics Agents.* New York: Basic, 1978.

Wise, David. *Nightmover: How Aldrich Ames Sold the CIA to the KGB for $4.6 Million.* New York: HarperCollins, 1995.

Witcover, Tom. *Sabotage at Black Tom: Imperial Germany's Secret War in America, 1914–1917.* Chapel Hill, N.C.: Algonquin, 1989.

Woodiwiss, Michael. *Organized Crime, USA: Changing Perceptions from Prohibition to the Present Day.* Brighton: British Association for American Studies, 1990.

Woods, Randall B. *Fulbright: A Biography.* Cambridge: Cambridge University Press, 1995.

Woodward, Bob. *The Secret Man: The Story of Watergate's Deep Throat.* New York: Simon and Schuster, 2005.

Wyden, Peter. *Bay of Pigs: The Untold Story.* London: Jonathan Cape, 1979.

Wynn, Neil A. *The Afro-American and the Second World War.* London: Paul Elek, 1976.

Zinn, Howard. *The Southern Mystique.* New York: Alfred A. Knopf, 1970.

INDEX

General Intelligence Division/Section
(GID), 73–74, 106, 138
Germany
genocide (Holocaust), 140, 147
Gestapo-citizen ratio, 11
intelligence operations, 65–70, 100–
102, 104–6, 114, 115–18, 129
Lusitania sunk, 67
See also Gestapo parallel; World War II
Gestapo parallel, 10–11, 94, 132, 138–
42, 145, 147, 207, 231, 248
Giancana, Sam, 166–67, 186
GID. *See* General Intelligence Division/
Section
Gilmer, Sallie and Stump, 18
Gilmore, Brawley, 26
Gingrich, Newt, 221, 224
Giuliani, Rudolph, 222
G-Men (film), 91
"G-men," origin of term, 89
Godfrey, Mary, 18
Goldman, Emma, 73
Goldschmidt, Helmut, 113
Gompers, Samuel, 76
Good, John, 26
Goodman, James, 200
Goss, Porter J., 243
Gotti, John, 212, 232
Gouzenko, Igor, 151
Grant, Ulysses S., 9, 22, 32, 33, 36
Grassley, Charles, 240, 250
Gravano, Sammy, 212
Gray, L. Patrick, 179, 182
Greenglass, David, 154
Gregory, Thomas W., 66, 67, 68
Griebl, Ignatz T., 102
Griffin, David Ray, 247–48
Group Research, Inc., 197
growth of the FBI
1908–29, 51, 55, 62–63, 72, 87
1930–69, 87, 103, 104, 160 (*see also*
Latin America, FBI and)

1970–present, 204, 228, 242, 249
See also budget of the FBI; hiring practices of the FBI
guns
agents and, 56, 85, 91, 196
the Barkers and, 81–82
gun control, 85–86, 149, 196, 234
Sessions and, 222

Haldeman, H. R., 159
Hanssen, Robert, 225–26, 227
Harrington, Richard, 33–34
Hatch, Orrin G., 229, 237
hate crimes, 218–19. *See also* Ku Klux
Klan; white terrorism
Hauptmann, Bruno Richard, 88
Hayes, Michael, 26
Hazen, William P., 45–46
headquarters of the FBI, 180
Hearst, Patty, 192
Hellman, Lillian, 178
Helms, Richard, 143, 173
Hersh, Seymour, 183
Hester, J. G., 18, 26
Higham, John, 58–59
Hillenkoetter, Roscoe, 145, 158
Hince, Lawrence, 108
hiring practices of the FBI
1919–69, 8, 86, 135–36, 215–16
1970–2001, 14–15, 204–5, 213–15,
216, 218, 229
after September 11, *2001*, 230, 242–43
September 11 intelligence failure and,
230–31
See also diversity in the FBI; racial bias
in the FBI
Hispanics (Latinos), 1, 135, 204, 214,
215–16, 217, 243. *See also* diversity
in the FBI
Hiss, Alger, 154–55, 157, 176
Hoar, George Frisbie, 46
Hobart, Sarah, 86